MONEY AND POLITICS
TOWARDS A LEGAL FRAMEWORK

LEON HOSANG

minna
PRESS

ISBN 978-976-95896-0-5

A catalogue record of this book is available from the National Library of Jamaica.

Ordering Information
Quantity (Bulk) Sales: Special discounts are available on quantity purchases by corporations, associations, and others. For details, contact the publisher:
sales@minnapress.com

Executive Editor: Lena Joy Rose
Book and Cover Design: Mark Steven Weinberger
Proofreader: Amelia Jenkins

Published in Kingston Jamaica by Minna Press
204 Mountain View Avenue, Kingston 6, Jamaica

www.minnapress.com

DEDICATION

To all those who despise politicians and, if they had a choice,
would rather live in a world free from politics.

CONTENTS

CONTENTS (CONTINUED)

TABLE OF ABBREVIATIONS

BQ	Bloc Québécois
CAFFE	Citizens Association for Free and Fair Election
CDU	Christian Democratic Union
CPS	Crown Prosecution Service
DPP	Director of Public Prosecutions
ECJ	Electoral Commission of Jamaica
FATCA	Foreign Account Tax Compliance Act (USA)
IMF	International Monetary Fund
IRS	Internal Revenue Service
JCC	Jamaica Council of Churches
JLP	Jamaica Labour Party
MCFA	Michigan Campaign Finance Act
MP	Member of Parliaments
NDM	National Democratic Movement
NGO	Non-governmental organisations
NNC	New Nation Coalition
OAS	Organisation of American States
OBA	One Bermuda Alliance
PAC	Political Action Committees
PNP	People National Party
PPERA	Political Parties Elections and Referendums Act
PSOJ	Private Sector Organisation of Jamaica
ROPA	Representation of the People Act
RPI	Retail Price Index
SDP	Social Democratic Party
SGP	Staatkundig Gereformeerde Partij

PREFACE

The attempt to control the influence of money in politics is fraught with difficulty, philosophical/ideological and practical. This is compounded by the almost universally negative lens used to view the practice of politics and the behaviour of members of the political class. In such a dispensation the role of the citizen/voter is minimised, if not entirely discarded. Apathy and alienation on the individual level translate into the malaise which characterises political relations in society.

In its reform project, the Electoral Commission of Jamaica (ECJ) has seemingly managed to obtain the Senate's approval (December, 2014) for its two-pronged approach: firstly, the registration and funding of parties and secondly, state funding of their campaigns also, tied to donation and expenditure limits. At stake in this approval was traditional adherence to a parliamentary 'convention' of non-interference with the ECJ recommendations. Procedurally, this affront to reason left unanswered a host of issues of fundamental social/political principle: the right of the state to dictate the citizens' rights to spend their money to support causes not criminal in themselves; using state revenue to subsidise parties with whose policies and programs a particular taxpayer may strongly disagree; the use of state funds to seek to distort the essentially voluntary nature of political organisations.

It may not be surprising that the convention now seems to have been departed from with regard to the public financing aspects of the proposals.

If the defining structural feature of politics is competition/rivalry on the levels of ideas, marketing and organisation, on which pegs might it be appropriate to hang political finance reform proposals?

The "level playing field" and "who pays the piper" notions are less than useful tools for the design of an efficacious electoral system: the first seeks to change the nature of politics, as against its *modus operandi*, while the second, deterministic as it is, would have us elevate rumour, allegation and belief over evidence, charge and verdict, in accordance with the rule of law.

It is not only the non-politician who deserves a fair hearing, in keeping with the legal system's provisions as to the burden and standard of proof. That being so, the legitimacy of the traditional approach to the assessment of the nature of the relationship between those interacting in different ways in national governance may warrant more rigorous determination.

Indeed, it may be worth considering whether the widespread presumed inevitability of the corrupting influence of money in politics can rationally co-exist with an acknowledegment of the need for state financing. The challenges posed for countries' effective enforcement capability are equally well established. What is Jamaica's rating in this regard? Questions of this nature might best be confronted before the launch of a legislative reform project.

Money and Politics critically examines philosophical/ideological, theoretical, and practical approaches to the study of the issues involved in the financing of political activity, comparatively, including the problems of implementation and enforcement.

It is expected that such a perspective will allow for more accurate predictability as to the new regulatory regime's likely effectiveness in significantly changing the behaviour of the actors, and the perceptions and reactions of the audience in the Jamaican political arena.

INTRODUCTION

Political finance represents one of the more 'troublesome' regulatory areas. Control initiatives tend to seek, firstly, to achieve some minimal 'political equality', when, in fact, wealth is unequally distributed, and face, secondly, as Scarrow notes, the issue of whether "… elected officials can be trusted to regulate in an area that so fundamentally touches on their own interests".[1]

Often unacknowledged is the fact that it is several competing principles and values, all legitimate in the abstract, which inform and compete for predominance,[2] in the debate about political party finance reform.

Because the cause in favour of state subsidy has been championed virtually without prominently sustained challenge, it is here conceded that even when those arguments have been pontificatory in style, if unconvincing intellectually, they have quantitatively, far exceeded those against. The rallying cry having been overwhelmingly in support, with 'tongue in cheek', it could be said that this imbalance may be regarded as an attempt to 'level the playing field', in the interest of the fuller and freer flow of ideas and the expansion of political dialogue. Such a situation obviates the rigorous demands of the scientific method in problem-solving and caters instead to the aversion to empiricism which challenges and subverts objective enquiry. The danger to be avoided is that what amounts really to catering to current popular sentiment is camouflaged as 'necessary' reform.

This certainly does not mean that one must "look at the world without passion and interest" and approach an area under consideration as the scientist who has traditionally been expected to "approach facts with sterile hands as a surgeon approaches his patient". As Fromm reminds us,

The result of this relativism, which often presents itself by its concern for

---

1 Scarrow, Susan E., 'Explaining Political Finance Reforms, Competition and Contest, in Party Politics', *Sage Publication*, Vol. 10, No. 6, p. 653. The Chairman of Trinidad and Tobago's Integrity Commission, Ken Gordon, recently called for amendment of the 'Integrity in Public Life Act' which would allow the Commission to take action rather than be "almost entirely dependent upon the co-operation of those being investigated", *The Gleaner*, (18 December 2013), p. D11.

2 The point was one of the major issues for resolution in the Netherlands case to which extensive reference is made below.

the correct usage of words, is that thinking loses its essential stimulus—the wishes and interests of the person who thinks ... the quest for truth is rooted in the interests and needs of individuals and social groups. Without such interest the stimulus for seeking the truth would be lacking.[3]

It is not denied that "money greases the wheels—good, bad or indifferent".[4] While this is hardly confined to the political system, the problem here is seen to be two-fold: dirty money and big money. The corrupting influence of 'dirty' or 'big' money may not seem difficult to trace once donations of amounts above a reasonable threshold are reported. Dissenting views on both aspects of regulating the role of money in politics will be reported: the issues of transparency and donation caps. It is arguable, putting it at the lowest, that the traditional definition of 'dirty money' is limited by the pervasive self-serving interest of big 'clean money' seeking to make itself respectable. Paradoxically, as it may understandably appear, the view is nevertheless canvassed here that big money, in a substantially, rather than merely procedurally democratic society, is entitled to the political influence it can 'earn'. In this respect, 'dancing around the truth', which the denial of the 'legitimate' pursuit of conflicting vested interests represents, is one of the primary obstacles to accurate analysis.

As should be known,

> Interlocking membership [Commission/party membership and 'contacts', in the Jamaican contexts, 'networking', in the current jargon] formal conferences, and informal talks have become the means by which policy comes to mature. The government ... has to modify its course to rally support and counter opposition ... consultation cannot be analysed as being simply the natural end-product of a long chain of representation. Power is disseminated in relation to a certain economic structure as well as according to the representative character, real or supposed, of many bodies: the two are juxtaposed, indeed amalgamated.[5]

Any assessment of the functioning of governments and institutions to

---

3 Fromm, Erich, *The Fear of Freedom*, Routledge and Kegan Paul Ltd., (UK, 1763), p. 214.

4 Recorded in a conversation taped by the US FBI in circumstances leading to the arrest of some five New York Public officials on charges of corruption, including, a Democratic Senator for attempting to bribe his way to getting the Republican mayoral nomination: reported on 'The Rachel Maddow Show', *MSNBC, a* U.S. TV channel, Tues April 4, 2013. The observation quoted should not, however, be taken to justify the inference that politics is accurately defined as a 'poisonous fantasy of limitless corruption and ethical decadence'.

5 Blondel, Jean, Voters, Parties and Leaders: The Social Fabric of British Politics, Penguin Books Ltd, (London, 1963). pp. 232, 233.

which the making of policy may be delegated would best be made bearing in mind that, "The rule by elite is anonymous, the government is diffused ... and apparent authors of plans and decisions are not their real authors".[6]

In this regard, criticism ought not to be diluted, and certainly not deflected by virtue of any high level status and reputation ascribed to either independent Electoral Commission of Jamaica (ECJ) members, or leading representatives of so-called 'civil society' groups of whatever category.

If the argument is that the quantum of available funds for political party organisation and campaigning is the ultimate determinant of electoral results, then, it could be said that that is what the electorate would deserve. Suffering would be their vote's penalty, and apathy and alienation the chosen antidote for their misery. Some people, we imply, will always use money better than others. An obvious example is vastly different levels of effectiveness in advertising campaigns, with little regard for budget size,

The nation was told, at the time of writing of the first draft of this piece (September, 2011), that Part II of the ECJ's Draft Report on Campaign Finance, promised for December 2010, had been made available to the two major political parties. After the parties made their comments, the Legal Committee would begin to work on the Final Report, which would then be subject to debate in Parliament, so that, "... it is now up to Parliament to decide if proposed legislation ... will be passed into law before the next election".[7] Suffice it to say that the Jamaican Parliament's predisposition for postponement and thus the delay[8] of debate on issues is unhealthy for society's adaptation to change, even in a less than dynamic environment.

Not surprisingly, there was no passage of legislation before the election.

The allergy to truth, in these matters, with respect to motive—whether directly self-serving, politically, or in terms of one's preferred version of the social and economic relations appropriate in the resolution of societal

---

6 Ibid, p. 232.

7 The *Jamaica Observer*: Saturday, Sept 17, 2011, p.7

8 The explanation, in more recent times, for legislative paralysis in the enactment of campaign finance regulations, is obvious yet largely unacknowledged. The disjuncture between 'professionalism', political preferences and a belated, more negative, backlash from prominent spokespersons. At another level, the incompatibility takes the form of party political interests, as against national economics, vying for predominance in the decision-making process. As it has been put, many of the voices raised in concern at specific proposals, have submitted arguments 'enveloped in unease', Pinsky, Robert. *The Figured Wheel*, Farrar Straux and Giround, (New York, 1997), p. 217

conflicts—is manifested in Herbert Alexander's peroration that:

> Whether the motive for change was financial stringency, the reduction of the burden of rising election costs, or the desire to escape the taint of corruption, or a mixture of these, the effort is always made to justify electoral reforms in terms of liberal democratic ideology.[9]

Greater citizen engagement with the democratic system is a widely shared objective. This should mean increasing the number of members of the public that are involved in politics and with political parties, and using politics as a means for people to more actively participate in determining the quality of their lives. Any proposed state funding regime should, therefore, be guided accordingly, and thus be submitted to rigorous and unapologetic scrutiny and criticism from such a vantage point.

While it may be good for political stability, assuming always that the *status quo* is worth preserving in the interest of the majority,[10] 'party system institutionalization' and its alleged benefit for democracy[11] must be balanced against the dynamics of public funding's effect on the essential, in contrast to a pseudo-ideal, conception of the nature of politics.

It is interesting to note that Scarrow begins her article with a general discussion of, "… how perceived interests and circumstances may affect the course of reform".[12] More explicitly, both Leonard[13] and Paltiel[14] suggest that

---

9 Alexander, Herbert, ed., 'Money and Politics: Rethinking a Conceptual Framework', *Comparative Political Finance in the 1980s*, Cambridge University Press, (London, 1989), p.16.

10 Prudence requires that the silence of the 'lambs' should be taken for consent, for as we are reminded by Pinsky, 'The clock of the cancer ticks', and 'Local Politics', in *The Figured Wheel New and Collected Poems*, Farrar, Straus & Ginoux, (NY, 1997), p. 204

11 Dix, Robert, 'Democratization and the Institutionalization of Latin American Political Parties' in *Comparative Political Studies*, pp. 24: 488 - 511 and in Mainwaring, Scott P., *Rethinking Party Systems in the Third Wave of Democratization: The Case of Brazil*, Stanford University Press, (California, 1999).

12 Scarrow, supra, p. 654, One needs to be particularly alert to the danger inherent in the presumption of correctness of their views, as often related by the tone and content of so-called civil society leaders in the debate on campaign finance reform; one has witnessed the attempt to justify and legitimize the contemptuous exclusion of opposed vested interest-inspired responses; some members of this 'coalition' see, in their mirror of society what they wish to see, one-dimensionally: a conspiracy in retreat from reality.

13 Leonard, Dick, 'Contrasts in Selected Western Democracies: Germany, Sweden, Britain', in Alexander, Herbert (ed*) Political Finance*, Sage Publications, (California, 1979), pp. 41 - 73.

14 Paltiel, Khayyam, Zev, 'Public Financing Abroad: Contrasts and Effects', in Michael Malbin (ed), *Parties, Interest Groups and Campaign Finance Laws*, American Enterprise Institute, (Washington, DC, 1980), pp. 354 – 370. It is observed that the type of laws passed will depend, for example, on whether they were prompted by a scandal or from the dire financial state of the major parties, as related to possibly sharply rising election costs; further, hostile public opinion, as prevails in Jamaica, is likely to make parties more inclined to countenance disclosure and capping legal regulation (Paltiel p. 355).

---

under arrangements, unlike with the cartel model, to which we will later refer, a party will react to financing proposals according to its assessment of how much money it needs relative to its judgment about the other contending parties' actual and potential funding situation. 'Ideological heritage' can be, and has, for example, been dislodged as a prohibitive factor in the acceptance of state funds in the case of the Social Democratic Party (SDP) and later the Green Party in Germany. Both parties initially refused—on the basis of stated principle, despite 'organisational imperatives'—to rely for funding on the state. They even took their objections to the Constitutional Court, with some success, only to find it possible—especially if included in a coalition government, as was the case in 1998—to reverse their positions.[15]

It is agreeable as Booth and Robbins argue,[16] that the social value of avoiding drastic, possibly disruptive change is not always self-evident, and that the factors which ameliorate this institutionalization process need scholarly examination. This involves not only the identification of those factors, but also the underlying conditions, which 'catalyse' the institutionalization process. Some argue that,

> there is a disjunction between the very public role of the political party, and its very closed and private legal internal organisation. Their legal status is

---

15 See Scarrow, supra, pp. 660 – 664. After the Constitutional Court decided on the SPD's initiative that tax deductible donations were unconstitutional as this favoured parties with wealthier supporters and, later, that state subsidies could not be confined to Parliamentary parties, nevertheless (1957-67) . "Under this newly discovered alignment of interest, in 1967 all the parliamentary parties worked together to produce a constitutionally acceptable parties Law". The revision of this Law in 1983 "was negotiated by the treasurers of all four of the 'established' parties in the Bundestag".

16 See Booth, Eric, and Robbins, Joseph, 'Assessing the Impact of Campaign Finance on Party System Institutionalization', in *Party Politics*, Vol. 16, No. 5, (2010), p. 630. One of their hypotheses, unsurprisingly, perhaps, is that electoral systems with limitations on both public funds and campaign finance [as is proposed by the ECJ] exhibit lower levels of volatility and party replacement. Given the popular very negative image of the two major Jamaican parties and the vociferous calls for change, one is left to wonder if the possible consequences of state funding have been fully contemplated. The availability of funds in any amount is likely to have the same effect. With respect, we find the ECJ's analysis of the political context, for anticipated evasive tactics and enforcement sanctions, to be "plagued by limitations". Jamaica has certainly not reached the stage, by any assessment, where by a "process of social learning the party actors have realised that there are common interests among the 'political class' which form the basis for collective action".
Additionally, party electoral-vulnerability, evidenced by closeness of election results with low voter turnout, reflecting declining loyalty and a more volatile electorate, rather than promoting greater attention to representative activities has, instead, led to an increase in aspirations to govern, without the benefit of the 'necessary' preparation. This can only further erode the links between an increasingly professionalised politician and party organisation and the average citizen, as the trend to an urbanization of political style manifests itself in an essentially rural environment.

not appropriate to their actual role and their public status.[17]

Are observations of this nature sufficient to justify registration and external oversight and management, in exchange for state financing?

Rather than attempting to answer such a question, some have instead sought to broaden the compass of registration and disclosure of sources of funding and their agendas to include civil society groups, special interest groups, and lobby groups[18] and even churches[19]. The question could now, *ex post facto*, be perverted to become: if even such groups *have to register* and make disclosure, why not political parties?

Contrary to this *quid pro quo* departure, it is not difficult to agree with Canadian analysts that the debate about electoral reform must be grounded in the *values* that are most important to a society.[20] That should be the starting point. Societies being dynamic, to a greater or lesser degree, the values regarded as pre-eminent for the purposes of electoral system design would be expected to be reflective of the priority problem areas identified in the political system as being in most urgent need of reform.

But deciding on an electoral system, given the complexity of modern society, whether in developed or developing states, inevitably involves choosing between *competing* values.

Those considered to be definitive of Canadian political democracy are enumerated as fairness, representation, equality and accountability. 'Fairness' "refers to whether the voting system has any built-in or systemic biases"; 'representation': the system's "ability … to broadly [through Parliament] reflect

---

17 Cass, Deborah Z., and Burrows, Sonia., 'Commonwealth [Australian] Regulation of Campaign Finance - Public Funding Disclosure and Expenditure Limits', *Sydney Law Review*, Vol. 22, p. 483. As will be indicated below, this is a position with which, the more philosophically inclined, People's National Party, now (2014) the Government in Jamaica, has stated its agreement, formally, in its submission to the ECJ and the press.

18 The Public Notice, from the Clerk of the Houses of Parliament, carried in the *Jamaica Observer*, Friday, February 20, 2015, p.6, invited written submissions of views and comments on Private Member's Motion 22/2013. One MP, Mikhail Phillips' justification was that 'like charity organisations [they] benefit from government tax exemptions". Presumably in order to qualify for any such exemption, especially given the island's ever-present fiscal challenges, appropriate investigation would have preceded approval.

19 See also the *Jamaica Observer*, Friday, February 20, 2015, p. 18, where the associate editor reports in, 'Call for Churches to open books to scrutiny', that a group of 'influential Christian Businessmen who are aiming to address corruption in all spheres of the society, say churches should allow for the same level of scrutiny of their financial affairs as *other public entities* [Italics added], At least political parties are getting state financing in exchange for regulation; in an implementation-deficient political/legal environment, the increased bureaucracy implied will be a matter of concern to anyone not carried away by this particular reform frenzy. Why should anyone other than church members have the right of scrutiny contemplated?

20 'Law Commission of Canada, Renewing Democracy: Debating Electoral Reform in Canada', (2002), p.29.

the diversity of ideas, interests and perspectives that characterizes society";
'equality', being the commonly held notion that 'every vote counts'; and
'accountability', meaning the electorate's ability to identify "those responsible
for decision-making and hold them responsible for their performance."[21]

It is our intention to take a multi-jurisdictional approach in critically
discussing the issue of Party Registration and Campaign Financing, an area of
national life of great current interest meriting priority academic attention, yet
to be received. The subject matter is discussed with regard to arguments for
and against state funding; regulatory/legislative options; limits on donations
and expenditure; position papers from civil society and political parties in
Jamaica, the local watchdog body, Citizens Association for Free and Fair
Election (CAFFE); Reports by the ECJ; the proposed model law advanced by
the Organisation of American States' (OAS) Secretariat of Political Affairs;
as well as the Jamaican Representation of The People Act, 1944 (ROPA), as
amended.

A consideration of ROPA is given its place of prominence, in the context
of the subject matter under purview, following the ECJ's observation that:

> Currently, there is no legislation on the subject of political party registration
> or financing. However, Sections 53 to 61 of the Representation of the People
> Act (ROPA) addresses the issue of Campaign Financing. While registration
> and financing of political parties involves fresh legislation, campaign
> financing requires the amendment of existing legislation.[22]

THE REPRESENTATION OF THE PEOPLE ACT (ROPA)*

It has been stated that "the first effort to address Jamaica's electoral issues
was conducted in 1979 when the Government created the Electoral Advisory
Committee ... focused on improving transparency and reducing fraud
charges and did not address party finances. ..."[23] The point has also been
made that "... the *Representation of the People Act* ... provides the framework

---

21 Ibid, p. 4; see also, Blaise, Andre. 'Criteria for Assessing Electoral Systems', Paper presented to the Advisory
Committee of Registered Political Parties, Elections Canada, Apr. 23, 1999.
22 Electoral Commission of Jamaica (ECJ), Report to Parliament on Political Party Registration and
Financing, July 2010, p. 2.
*Sections referred to are set forth in Appendix IV
23 FRIDE Comment May 2007, Angélica Durán Martinez, Monograph titled 'Jamaica', p.4.

for campaign funding."[24] There has certainly, then, been enough time for useful experience to have been accumulated in this area.

Jamaica having attained universal adult suffrage in 1944, with its British colonial status and tutelage, it should perhaps be unsurprising that machinery and mechanisms would have been put in place for some degree of regulation of behaviour in the arena of political contestation.[25] Whatever their policy omissions/neglect, colonizers do tend, for obvious reasons, to make provisions for the maintenance of law and order.

The earlier widespread late 1930's labour disturbances, consequent on the collision of post-war economic conditions with emergent socio-political ambitions, had led to the beginning of the institutionalization of industrial conflict by the establishment of a limited legal framework with the passage of the trade union and other industrial conflict-related laws.[26] But since much of the thrust of nascent trade union consciousness and objectives makes for ready kinship with the striving for political power, certainly in the colonial context, the *Representation of the People Act* must be seen for what it was: a part of that framework for the control of political conflict within a system of multi-party parliamentary democracy in keeping with the British tradition.

The provisions of the *Act* may be divided, for present purposes, into operational and moral/ethical features. We limit our perusal to the issues which are here especially deserving of note.

Under section 6(1), which, dated as it is, is somewhat obscure and unreasonably restrictive, it is provided that:

> Subject to the provisions of subsection (2) every person *employed* by *any* person for pay or reward in *reference* to an election in *the* constituency in which such person would *otherwise* be entitled to vote shall be disqualified from voting and incompetent to vote in such constituency at such an election. [Italics added in each instance].

It would seem that no objection is raised against a person being so employed in one constituency as long as his vote is to be polled in another

---

24 Ibid.

25 *The Representation of the People Act (ROPA)* (20th November 1944) in Laws of Jamaica Vol. XVI

26 The list includes *The Arbitration Act, 1909, The Protection of Property Act 1905, The Trade Union Act 1919, The Emergency Powers Act 1938,*

constituency. Since, whatever the purposes of any such employment, this could so easily be evaded, in the absence of an apartheid-like "Pass" system, restricting freedom of movement across geographical boundaries, the Section's objective is not obvious. Persons who may be legally employed, so as not to suffer the disqualification imposed by section 6(1), are listed in (3) (a) – (d). One does not have to be a fervent exponent of free enterprise economic principles to declare such specific limitations to be another instance of unwarranted "over-regulation". Apart from election officials, messengers and candidates' agents and subagents, subsections (c) and (d) permit the employment of:

> persons engaged in printing election material … [and] … in advertising of any kind or as clerks or stenographers or as managers … so, however, that the total number of persons so employed does not exceed one for each three hundred electors in the constituency and that the name, address and occupation of every person so employed is communicated, in writing, to the returning officer.

Widespread breach, no doubt partly through ignorance of the existence of such provisions, set the stage for the theatrics which define the major ingredient of the troubling political culture which has emerged. It is generally agreed that convenient, self-interested, selective enforcement of laws brings the entire legal system and all the legislative enactments processed by it into disrepute.[27] Having laws on the statute book which do not 'justify' enforcement has the same effect, which deserves to be noted by those responsible for the review of legislation.

Section 54(2) encourages dishonourable conduct, it seems, by virtue of its provision that any contract, whereby expenses are incurred "… on account of or in respect of the conduct or management of an election", is not enforceable unless made by the candidate or agent. Under the proviso ending the section, it is stated that it, (the section), does not apply to "… any sum disbursed by *any* [Italics added] person out of his own money for any *small* [Italics added]

---

27 See, 'FEC Can't Curb 2016 Election Abuse', by Kendrick Brinson. *The New York Times*, May 5, 2015. The report quoted the Chairman of the United States Federal Election Commission, Ann M. Ravel, as advising that given the Commission's composition, which includes six political appointees, it was unlikely that the four votes necessary for effective enforcement of existing legal regulations would be obtained. As a result, it was said that, "The likelihood of laws being enforced is slim". Action might better be expected, it was claimed, from the Justice Department. But see also, 'FEC: Ex-Sen. Craig misused campaign funds', *Miami Herald*, Apr. 12, 2005, p.5A., where the FEC stated that the now charged ex-senator, "appears to have gambled that he would not be pursued for his violation".

expense legally incurred by *himself*" [Italics added]. There can not only be an unlimited number of small expenses, but what is 'small' is, of course, a relative matter depending on wealth, as well as, *inter alia*, the worth, the nature and the context of the transaction.

The playing field is levelled, some might argue, by the insertion by way of amendment of the Act in 1989, in relation to its constituency expenditure limit, now set out in section 55(1) of the provisions prevailing prior to the 2011 general election, in declaratory language: "subject to the provisions in subsection (2), no expenditure shall be incurred in relation to the candidature of any person at *any* [Italics added] election, in excess of three million dollars".[28]

If the playing field analogy usually invoked in political party funding is to be useful, there may be the need for discrimination between general elections as against by-elections, and, certainly, local government as against Parliamentary. Astonishingly, the limit does not apply to, "… any expenditure incurred before the issue of the writ for the election in respect of services rendered or materials supplied before the issue of such writ."[29]

The reality is of course, that political parties, candidates, and their agents are in most cases put in "election mode" well before the formal calling of an election, barring the isolated instances of a real "snap" election. Without fixed election dates, the *Act* clearly puts the governing party at a considerable advantage.

The tendency to evade reality persists in section 56(1), which seems to criminalize the voluntary expenditure of a private individual's funds in support of a candidate of his choice, since it is declared that, "… [no] expenditure shall be incurred in respect of the candidature of any person … except by the candidate, or his agent, *or some person authorized in writing* [Italics added] by the agent."[30]

Given the dynamics of local electioneering, one wonders if the legislators did indeed expect compliance with such a provision. Many totally "innocent" persons could easily be guilty of an offence, and become liable on conviction to a fine of one hundred dollars or a term of imprisonment not exceeding six

---

28 This figure was increased to ten million dollars in time for the 2011 general election. The more than 300 % increase suggests that the limit was either grossly inadequate before or over-generous after, or, was of little consequence, being, perhaps, largely ignored.

29 ROPA, s. 55(2)(b)

30 Ibid, s. 56(1) See the strongly opposed sentiments of Ronald Mason in 'Damn dictatorship on campaign financing', *The Gleaner*, (Oct. 6, 2013), p. A9.

months.[31] A criminal record, for even the most minor offence, can be a source of great inconvenience, if not real hardship in relation to employment and certainly international travel involving obtaining of visas.

The restriction on payments by candidates to *any* person other than his agent, excepting amounts under the unrealistically low maximum of ten thousand dollars for his personal living expense and "petty expenditure" of two thousand dollars simply continues the farce. And while, under the accompanying proviso, the section does not apply to a candidate who is his own official agent, does this mean that in such a situation there is no limit on the amount that may be spent for "personal living expenses"? Further, can this item of expenditure have been omitted in arriving at the three million dollar limit imposed by section 55(1)? Can it now be properly omitted from the new maximum of ten million dollars? (an amount increased by 50% for the 2016 general election).

Under section 57, campaign expense payments by a candidate can only be made to his agent. This is provided, however, that under (b) of the section, that is obviously not the case where the candidate is "his own official agent". The rationale for the distinction is not readily discernable. Why shouldn't the candidate be also able to make payments to third parties where he has an agent. Since regulations such as this involve the commission of offences, they should not be taken lightly.

Apparent ignorance of the unstructured nature of the conduct of election campaigning is further manifested by section 58(1), where expenditure by any person above the limit authorized *in writing* by a candidate's agent incurs a fine similar to that under section 56 (2); this in a country where the mass of the population tend to engage in informal undocumented transactions in a sector of the economy of considerable significance.

The opportunity to craft more common-sense based provisions has not, it would seem, been grasped over a period of several decades.

Section 59(1) creates the special offence of an "illegal practice" for contravention of sections 53 to 58, from which a candidate will be excused, with the exception of section 57 matters, "... if the candidate proves *affirmatively* [Italics added] that such expenditure was incurred without his

---

31 ROPA,, s. 56(2)

knowledge or consent *and* [Italics added] that he took all reasonable steps to prevent the incurrence of such expenditure."[32]

Proving the absence of consent is difficult enough in such a context, proving lack of knowledge is even more problematic.

These matters being of a criminal nature, as against situations arising under the Law of Agency, is there justification for the departure from the fundamental requirement of *mens rea,* as disclosed by evidence adduced, or reasonable inference, and the traditional imposition of the burden of proof on the prosecutor?[33]

Lack of knowledge and consent is obviously not enough here to establish 'innocence', if 'all reasonable' preventative steps have also not been taken in the eyes of an adjudicator. If the purpose of the *Act* is to promote honesty and integrity in the political system and, in particular, electoral processes, shouldn't the provisions be dictated by, and find congruence with, basic notions of morality and ethical conduct in arriving at decisions on questions of guilt/innocence?

Could it be that it is the failure of the application of a sense of 'reasonableness' in *debate,* and hence legislative drafting, which accounts for provisions such as this in statutes being largely ignored? Is the situation "redeemed" by the apparently superfluous inclusion of the word "affirmatively"

---

32 Ibid, s. 59 (2)

33 Anyone posing a critique of the functioning of the political system, even if limited to the behaviour of those perceived to the principal actors, must, if their views are to pass muster, face the issue of 'the benefit of the doubt'. In any society governed by the principles of the rule of law, whoever, in terms of occupational category, the alleged delinquent, it ought not to be a matter of, 'if enough people say it often enough it becomes accepted as the truth'. See also, 'Party treasurer held in Brazil kick back case', by Jenny Barchfield, *Miami Herald,* (Thu. April 16, 2015), p. 5A, where the Workers' Party President (the Party involved), is reported as stating, "We reaffirm our confidence in Joao Vaccaris innocence, not only because of his conduct as treasurer, but also in a democracy *everyone* [Italics added] is innocent (sic) until proven guilty. The allegations were that Brazil's largest company Petrobas paid out over $800 million in bribes to secure inflated contracts, with the money going to the Workers' and other parties for campaign purposes.

On the issue of proof, see also, 'Law makers defend freebies loophole', *Miami Herald,* Sunday, April 19, 2015, p. 66. Some politicians, it was reported, "… routinely used their committees for reimbursements that could not easily be explained". One lobbyist, we are told, who provided the use of his private airplane explained, "It's perfectly legitimate because it is fundraising related, or at least, that's what they tell me the trips are for. … I'm providing transportation. That's all I'm doing." But as the Research Director for Integrity Florida, a non-partisan political watchdog explained, as a result of the broad nature of the committees, "… it's difficult to distinguish between campaign and personal expenses. … Nothing has changed [since the 2005 ban on gifts]. These committees, (Political Action Committees, PAC), are just a way to get around the gift ban". See also, *Miami Herald,* (Sunday April 19, 2015), pp. 3B, 6B, 'Gifts part of doing businesses'. Exploiting a loophole - according to the State Division of Elections - Sen. Tom Lee, who had been the chief advocate of the 2005 ban of gifts from special interests, "… now … indirectly … has received more in personal reimbursements from his political committee than any other state senator since 2013", having earlier vowed that his ban would change the behaviour of legislators.

---

in the subsection? Would affidavit evidence of lack of knowledge or consent be acceptable?

Consistent with the above is the very low spending limits stipulated and the approved limited items of expenditure listed, resulting in the absurdity of what is actually normally reported by candidates, as is required by section 60(1), of every election agent within six weeks after Election Day.[34]

What this calls for is:

> a full statement under the appropriate head specified in the return of *all* [Italics added] expenditure incurred in connection with the election by or on behalf of the candidate ... and shall be supported by *vouchers* [Italics added] for *all* [Italics added] payments in excess of *four dollars* [Italics added].[35]

Section 60(5) continues:

> Every return under this section shall be supported by a declaration sworn to before a Justice by the candidate stating:
>
> (a)   that the return fully and accurately sets out *all* [Italics added] payments made by the candidate himself; and
>
> (b)   that to the best of his knowledge, information and belief the return is a full and accurate return of *all* [Italics added] expenditure incurred by *any* [Italics added] person and of all moneys, securities or the equivalent of money received by the election agent from any source in connection with the election. ..."[36]

The items of expenditure then (1973) considered legitimate include, the candidates' personal living expenses; rental of premises; lighting in connection with hired premises; printing, newspaper advertising and the distribution of such material; payments made to canvassers and speakers, with names and amounts paid to each to be recorded; remuneration paid to clerks and messengers; postage, stationery and other miscellaneous expenses. Can anyone really have contemplated compliance with the requirement for recording of payments to speakers on a campaign platform, or, indeed, in

---

34   As an example, see 'Return Of Election Expenses Parliamentary General Elections', *Jamaica Observer*, (Mon. Apr. 2, 2012), p.15

35   ROPA, s. 60(2)

36   Ibid

any election forum? Whatever the negative state of the practice of intra-party politics, it should certainly be well known that this is a form of contribution which is hardly ever made for payment.

Every candidate/official agent is required to make a declaration in confirmation of (a) and (b) above, under section 60(5). The punishment[37] provided for these Section 60 offences is specified in Section 101, under the old law, as follows:

1. for an agent contravening or failing to comply with section 60, a fine of one thousand dollars or maximum imprisonment of twelve months;

2. for an agent knowingly making a false return or one he does not believe to be true, imprisonment, *without the option of a fine*, for a maximum of two years, after conviction in the circuit court;

3. a candidate breaching subsection 60 (5), is subject to similar punishment as the agent at (1) above;

4. a candidate guilty of the behaviour indulged in by an agent at (2) above, suffers the same fate.

Amendments[38] in 1996 resulted in a change where the absence of the option of a fine in (2) above was "corrected" and both agent and candidate were given the opportunity of paying a fine of between twenty and eighty thousand dollars or, in the alternative, imprisonment for not less than three years. Additionally, a court *may* [Italics added] order either guilty party to be disqualified from holding "any *post* of election *officer* [Italics added] for a period of not less than seven years from the date of conviction."[39]

All election expenses are required by section 61(2) to be paid within six weeks after election day. Any financial obligations paid at a later date causes the agent to be "guilty of an illegal practice", regardless, it seems, of questions of honour and morality.

Although everyone with knowledge of the reality in these matters knows that almost all election returns are grossly false, no one has ever been

---

37 Despite the distance from reality/reasonableness of many of these regulations, Government Senator, Lambert Brown and others named herein, call for effort to be directed to the enforcement of the *Act*. See, 'Government Senator says there's no evidence for 'BIG MONEY FEARS', *The Gleaner*, Sat. Nov. 2 2013, pp.A13. Nor apparently, does the ECJ see the need for substantial repeal of the many ignored aspects

38 ROPA, as amended, s. 40

39 Ibid, s.101(3)

prosecuted to the writer's knowledge; a serious blow to respect for law, *per se*.

The notorious backlog of cases for trial in the courts, given the absence of a 'special' court, as in some larger jurisdictions, warrants consideration. What is to be the status of the agent or candidate pending trial, in the event an election is held in the interim, in which the person awaiting trial as against an appeal seeks to participate, in either capacity, bearing in mind the fundamental principle of the criminal law of the presumption of innocence until conviction. If such an individual had participated in an elective capacity and be sometime later found guilty of having committed an offence at a date before the election, he/she would face retroactive disqualification with all its several implications, it seems, under section103(b) referred to below.

It can scarcely be seriously doubted that virtually every candidate and agent has been in breach of section 70 of the *Act*, which states, *inter alia*:

> Where a person knowingly provides money for any payment which is contrary to the provisions of this *Act*, or for any expenses incurred in excess of any maximum amount allowed by this Act … such person shall be guilty of illegal payment.

A candidate or an election agent who is personally guilty of "illegal hiring" or "illegal payment" shall be guilty of an "illegal practice" under section 85(2). Peculiarly, section 85(1) provides that "any person" engaging in similar activity would be guilty of the offences of "illegal hiring and illegal payment".

What, on paper at least, appears to be a serious sanction for breach of this provision is to be found in section 103: "[a]ny person who is convicted of any offence declared to be an illegal practice under this *Act* shall, in addition to any other penalty for such offence be incapable during a period of five years from the date of his conviction …", under (a) of being registered as an elector or voting in an election at either the local government or Parliamentary level, and (b) of being elected as a Councillor or Member of Parliament, respectively, or of retaining his seat, if elected before conviction. The period of disqualification, under the present law[40], has been increased to ten years.

The penalty for a guilty *candidate* in the above, by virtue of a proviso, is set at fifteen years in both instances, at (a) and (b). Since some may argue that these mandatory periods of disqualification could be reasonably regarded as lengthy,

---

40 Ibid, s. 103(b)

taking all the possible mitigating circumstances into account, would a lifetime ban, as we shall see has recently been imposed in China, ever be considered, with justification to be found within the context of the island's alleged pervasively corrupt political culture?

The phenomenon[41] of "Vote Buying" in Jamaica, which represents somewhat of a reversal of the roles of parties in the "Cash for Peerages" scandal in the United Kingdom, is addressed by section 91(1)(a) and (b). The first, 91(1) (a), deals with inducing any voter to vote or refrain from voting by giving, lending or "[agreeing] to give or lend, or [offering, promising or promising to procure or endeavouring to procure] any money or valuable consideration", while (b) addresses the prospect of "… any office, place or employment" being offered in exchange for a person voting or refraining from voting".[42] Of course, anyone engaging in any act of inducement would want to do more than ensuring that the voter simply voted or refrained; he/she would expect that the voter would vote for a particular candidate. One would hardly be paying in cash or kind to induce a voter to just do what may be considered "the duty of a responsible citizen". [43]

---

41 See with respect to this issue in the last (2011) general election, 'votes for sale' by Arthur Hall, Senior Staff Reporter, The Gleaner, Fri. Nov. 25, 2011, p.A.1; 'Buy out the bar? No way, says Crawford', The Jamaica Observer, (Nov. 27, 2011), p.9; 'Vote – buying intensifies, survey finds'; The Jamaica Observer, (Dec. 4, 2011), pp. 8, 9. 'Not every voter willing to sell vote'. The Jamaica Observer, Dec. 11, 2011, pp.1, 10; 'Teacher files election petition against Mair', The Gleaner, (Fri. Mar. 9, 2012), p.2; and 'CAFFE shift focus on campaign funding, vote-buying; The Gleaner, (Fri. Dec. 6, 2012), p.6.

42 Both the former ECJ Chairman Professor Errol Miller and current Government Senator Lambert Brown question the extent and effect of the phenomenon, which undoubtedly exists, see 'Government Senator says there's no evidence for 'BIG MONEY FEARS' , The Gleaner, (Sat. Nov. 2, 2013), pp. A 1, 3 and Miller's observation, noted elsewhere herein, of the cultural tendency to use a broad corruption brush to paint virtually all public figures, noting further that with secret voting in Jamaica 'vote buying' is unlikely to have the intended effect on an elector's choice, see 'ECJ chairman weighs in on vote-buying debate', The Jamaica Observer, Fri. Dec, 9, 2011, p.4. Of interest is the fact that one successful JLP candidate in the last general election, Gregory Mair, had legal proceedings instituted against him based on allegations of bribing voters to vote for him.

43 The 'controversial' MP Everald Warmington has again raised an issue of public interest: should voting be made compulsory, as in Australia, with applicable sanctions, given the fact that only some 52% of registered electors voted at the last general election, coupled with the fact that all employers are by law required to allow time off with pay for all workers to vote, not to mention the cost of the entire electoral system. For mixed response, see 'Warmy's burning comment worth serious debate', editorial, The Gleaner, Thur. Jan. 16, 2014, p. A6; Mario Boothe, "Warmington wrong … again!, the Jamaica Observer, Thur. Jan. 16, 2014, p. 12; Patrick A., Gallimore, Warmington's 'bootoo' and/or dictatorial kind of mentality', The Gleaner, Thur. Jan. 16, 2014, p. A. 6. Mark Wignall, 'Andrew Holness can't touch Warmington!', the Jamaica Observer, Thur. Jan. 16, 2014, p. 15; Maurice Saunders, 'Let's vote for nobody!', Carlton C. Daye, 'Too many just don't care, and C. Anthony, ' Warmy right this time', in Letters to the Editor, The Gleaner, Fri. Jan. 17, 2014, p. A.10; Errol W. A. Townsend, 'What benefits can Warmington really withhold?', The Gleaner, Mon. Jan. 20, 2014, p. 13; Michael A. Dingwall, ' Can Warmington really check votes?'. The Jamaica Observer, Wed. Jan. 29, 2014, p. 12; Michael Burke, 'Diversions', the Jamaica Observer, Thur. Jan. 3, 2014, p. 14; Webster W. McPherson, 'The vote repay', The Gleaner, Fri. Apr. 11, 2014, p. A.8; Daraine Luton, Gleaner Writer, 'Registered non-voters should be fired – Warmington', The Gleaner, Fri. Apr. 11, 2014, p. A. 10; ' I don't joke about the poor',/'PM: In my constituency I don't ask people whether they vote for me [Italics added] [MP Warmington definitely was not insisting that to 'qualify' for benefits the person should have voted for him.]

Under an electoral system dedicated to the principle of the 'secret ballot', the heretical question becomes: is it really necessary, or, indeed, meaningful to deal with these issues at the legislative level?[44]

Whereas (e) of the subsection deals directly with "bribery", there being no definition of bribery, in addition to the circumstances already specified at (a) to (d), the words "... with the intent that such money ... shall be expended in bribery at any election ...",[45] if not the entire paragraph, would seem to be redundant.

Perhaps less expectedly, (f) and (g) of the section deal with the *receiver* of the inducements, whatever their nature, and whether before, during or after an election, in the identical manner as the preceding paragraphs, that is, they "... shall be deemed guilty of bribery within the meaning of this *Act*". Again, perhaps needless to say, we know of no instance of a voter being charged much less convicted under these 'legally binding' provisions. Existing legislation has certainly not, in this respect, had any practical effect in "levelling the playing field".

Section 91 (2) deals with the peculiarly, if appropriately, named offence of "treating". This involves inducing a person to vote for a particular candidate, with the use of "food, drink, entertainment or provision." Suffice it to say that many, if not most conferences, but more particularly mass rallies, constitute seemingly classic examples of breaches of the law, regardless of what is technically arguable. Interestingly, it is not only those doing the 'treating', but also "every elector who corruptly accepts or takes any such food, drink, entertainments or provision" is guilty of the offence.

With a fine not exceeding $400 or, in the alternative, imprisonment for a term not exceeding one year, the amount of the fine may be taken as indicative of the seriousness attached to such matters by the politicians in the legislative chamber. Amendments to the *Act, in 1980* and 1996, eventually increased

---

44   See, 'Campaign against vote buying coming soon', *The Gleaner*, Sat. May 30, 2015, p. A3.

45   One of the very familiar cases to reach the courts is the current one where an elector Donnel Mariott alleged in his petition to the Supreme Court seeking to have Member of Parliament Gregory Mair ousted, based on allegations of illegality in the giving of food items to persons on the voters' list for the Constituency; it was further alleged that the MP, through several of his agents, corruptly paid monies to persons on the voters' list for them to vote for him. see *The Gleaner*, Fri, Mar. 9, 2012, p.2; see also Supreme Court Case ' Donnel Mariott vs Gregory Mair', Suit No. 2012HCV638; see also 'Teacher files election petition against Mair' – jamaica-**gleaner**.com/ **gleaner**/20120309/lead/lead2.html. It has been reported, however, that the Petitioner intends to withdraw the Petition,

the penalties for breach from a minimum fine of twenty thousand dollars to a maximum of eighty thousand. The alternative sanction of imprisonment, "… with or without hard labour …", is likely to have little impact, given the usual circumstances in which there will be many willing and able pockets for the 'dutiful' payment of fines within this modest range. A dissimilar situation but which, nevertheless, is of relevance, is that of a senior police officer who, having been charged and convicted with attempting to prevent the course of justice, had his fine of (J) $800,000.00 paid within minutes,[46] his co-accused being a prominent Member of Parliament and a business magnate. He was also strongly supported by a large contingent of members of the Police Force in attendance at his sentencing.

With respect to candidates, the more meaningful sanction appears in the form of the incapacity to hold elected political office for a period of seven years. All guilty persons are also barred from being on the voters list or voting for the same period.

Generally speaking, *The Representation of the People Act* seeks to define the roles and establish procedures and control mechanisms for the financial activities of agents, subagents and election candidates themselves during elections. Further, it stipulates the making of election expenditure returns, thereafter. It is ironic, indeed, that the 'Financial Provisions' contained in Part VI of the Act, characterized by the use of trenchant prohibitory language, have been very largely ignored.[47] But, then, the sentence of hanging, for murder, is still on the statute books and Jamaica has one of the highest, if not the highest, murder rate in the world. If statutorily provided sanctions are to have any preventative effect, the lesson is still to be learnt that vigilant, efficient investigation, prosecution and offence adjudication are essential prerequisites.

Any consideration by the ECJ of a collision of law, and the regulations which may be derived from them, with social and political reality seems

---

46 See, 'Sighs of Relief as Forbes gets non-custodial sentence', by Karyl Walker, Editor – Crime/Court Desk, The *Jamaica Observer*, Fri. May 16, 2014, p. P4.

47 Citizens Action for Free and Fair Elections (CAFFE) undertook the task of "monitoring the financing and spending by candidates in the campaign for the then imminent election … which it is hoping will prevent tainted money from influencing the outcome of the elections …", with the aid of a handbook. See, the *Jamaica Observer*, Tue. Oct. 11, 2011, p.3. Given the alleged level of corruption, in its various forms, which plague the political process and most evidently, during elections, one would have expected an informative, perhaps critical, if not damning post-election CAFFE Report. That does not, for whatever reason, seem to have been the case.

to have been submerged by the orthodoxy that to bring about change in behaviour in society all that one needs to do is to pass a law.

One suspects that in the 'serious business' of electioneering in Jamaica, reference to the details of these sections of the *Act* would provide little more than comic relief. The ECJ might usefully have studied the degree of ignorance existing and the reasons for widespread non-compliance in relation to these legal regulations. Amendment of ROPA, without a meaningful assessment of the existing law's effectiveness would therefore seem to be ill-advised. Otherwise, this can amount to nothing more than rationality being overwhelmed by the presumed wisdom of popular sentiment.

For sound policy formulation, the establishment of causal relationships is mandatory: this requires more than the conduct of unsophisticated opinion surveys. Prescriptions based on data so derived, or worse, anecdotal evidence is, at best, likely to treat symptoms only.

With these observations as our backdrop, we now begin to treat the key related issues of funding and transparency by examining how the ECJ's proposals discriminate between parties and candidates.

Chapter 1
The Electoral Commission
of Jamaica (ECJ) Report

Party Registration & Funding

The rationale for the public funding of political parties, including their election campaign expenses, has been seen by van Biezen[48] as having three bases:

1. Strictly financial: the rising cost of the democratic process, coupled with a decrease in revenues to its principal protagonists.

2. Concerns for equal opportunities, fairness and the equality of political competition.[49] The argument here is that since all parties are not equally resourceful in raising private funding, the less able, in this respect, should not be 'disadvantaged' because they were at an incipient stage of formation, their small size or lack of broad mass appeal. If political party programs do not appeal to the wealthy or other established sectional interests, such as trade unions, or if because they now have no linkages with sympathetic groups capable of providing significant financial support, this variation on the 'democratic' theme apparently dictates that the same alienated public has an obligation to ensure their existence and survival. We argue, to the contrary, that their small size or lack of traction may be 'deserved' and, consequently, should not merit public funding.

---

48 van Biezen, Ingrid 'Political Parties as Public Utilities in Party Politics', *Sage Publications*, Vol. 10, No. 6, (2004), p. 706

49 Gunlicks, Arthur B., ed., *Campaign and Party Finance in North America and Western Europe*, Westview Press, (Boulder, CO, 1993); The Law Commissions of Canada, supra, pp.3, 29; Since there is scope for formula variety in the disbursement of state funds, how parties fare will obviously depend on the formula: in Hungary, for example, 25% of public money is divided equally among the parties with at least one seat, and the balance shared in keeping with votes obtained. Whereas the ECJ proposes a maximum of 40% state funding, in Spain and Portugal the state contribution is an average of 75 – 85% of the parties' total income. [van Biezen, 2000]. State support is about 20% in Denmark and as much as 85% in Finland, despite which range, state dependence is nonetheless assessed (Katz, 2002, p.114) as "non-trivial"; Switzerland is an exception in Europe there is not only no state subsidies on the federal level, but also no regulation of parties' financial affairs (Nassmacher, 2001, b, pp. 103, 105); van Biezen in her review concludes that whereas most European jurisdictions, except Belgium and France, permit corporate donations, "only a small minority of countries (unlike the ECJ's recommendations) have capped the amount of private donations or have put a ceiling on the total amount of donations parties and candidates may receive per year or per election cycle", (van Biezen, 2004, p, 713)

---

3. The desire to restrict the use of 'tainted', and the influence of private funds, so as to limit its "... potential for distortion of the democratic political process ... (for) since public funding relieves parties from having to satisfy their financial supporters, it is anticipated that [this will] have a diminishing effect on corruption."[50]

The premise used by the ECJ to justify public financing of political parties is equally applicable to *independent* candidates: "... the performance of important public services in representing general and specific interests of people".[51] Despite this, there are two instances only in which those candidates are mentioned in its Report. Firstly, their nomination will be permitted if they are "described as such on his nomination paper".[52] The other reference is of an exclusionary/punitive nature: "State funding shall not apply to any five or more members of Parliament who contested as independent candidates at a general election but subsequently formed a political party".[53] Neither the futuristic application of the exclusion nor the arbitrary number to whom the provision relates invests it with any particular appeal, certainly not on the basis of rationality or democratic principle.

There does not seem to be any intention to provide funding to 'first time' independent candidates. Success at the polls, or obtaining any specified share of the vote could obviously be of funding consequence in relation to a later election, or for reimbursement of expenditure purposes. For first time independents, neither alternative is likely to be particularly attractive, given the traditional two-party electoral dominance. If the ECJ's proposals were conceived as situation-specific and problem-solving prescriptions for broadening the democratic political representational process, the funding approach might have been more inclusive.

It is accepted that the ECJ is neutral in a *partisan* political sense. One cannot therefore fathom the justification for this apparently anti-democratic exclusion of funding to independents who may later, to better serve the public's interests they seek to advance, decide to merge. The presence of

---

50 Alexander, Herbert E, and Shiratori, Rei (eds) *Comparative Political Finance among the Democracies*, (Boulder, Co, 1994), Westview

51 ECJ Report p. 9

52 Ibid p. 3.

53 Ibid p. 6,See the contrary position taken by The Gleaner's Parliamentary reporter in, 'Behind the veil of that UNCONSCIONABLE ECJ campaign financing proposal', *The Gleaner*, Mon. Nov. 4 2013, pp. A6,7.

two representatives of both main parties on the ECJ could be the possible explanation, to the substantial discredit of the Commission.[54]

Indeed, this provision might impinge, to the extent of it being an "unlawful discrimination", on the right to freedom of association, guaranteed by the Jamaican Constitution.[55] Peripheral as the issue may seem to be, with the greatest of respect to the members of the Commission, it may be regarded as significant in exposing the absence of depth and breadth of thought—and/or, the self-serving political influence which resulted in such recommendations. Again, this may be put down to a failure to adequately identify its "mission/vision", among which elements ought properly to have been the deepening and broadening of participation in the processes of democratic governance.

Institutional administrative control, in exchange for cash, is a far too limited socio-political transformational formula.

Assuming that any five or more independent candidates/Member of Parliaments (MPs) "subsequently formed a political party", we urge that so long as it satisfied all the criteria for public funding, any law, or the exercise of any discretionary authority under any law, seeking compliance with the proposal as set out would invite serious constitutional challenge. The law being proposed, if passed as is, in this regard, would be promulgated for precisely the purpose of conferring benefits on *others* acting in combination to further their collective, institutional and, thereby, segmentally, the national interest.

The contents of the first paragraph of the Commission's Report to Parliament seems to be indicative of the perspective taken by the authors of the submission: "... Given the vital and important role that political parties play in the life of the country this (*sic*) [lack of] oversight is no longer

---

54 See, "The Gavel", 'Remove politicians from ECJ', *The Gleaner*, Mon. June 13, 2011, p.B.12, where the Parliamentary reporter expressed the following sentiments: "We do not share (MP) Warmington's view that Parliament should be the body that determines how the ECJ functions. Indeed, it is our view that the ECJ is wrongly constituted and the time has come to remove the politicians from the centre of the commission's operations. ... The general secretaries of both political parties ... are joined by political strategists ... "The Gavel" believes it is unhealthy for democracy for the PNP and the JLP which have monopolized the political process to be given such free rein ... serves only to reinforce the two-party system and undermine the stated objectives of the ECJ. The responsibility of the Commission is to protect the electoral process from the immediate direction, influence and control of the Government ... to the detriment of persons with opposing views who may wish to participate in the process. ..."
55 Constitution of Jamaica, s. 23

tenable".[56] Any sense of urgency conveyed is, however, immediately negated by the statement that the report comes, "... after extensive consultation over the last six years. ..."[57]

Being distinguished by the vital and important nature of their role in society is hardly exclusive to political parties. Yet there does not seem to be any plans currently, or in contemplation, requiring the registration and the regulation of the financial affairs of other "vital and important" organisations, which are in essence characterized, as most are, by the voluntary nature of the bond between them and their members/supporters.

There is, and has been, the trumpet call for "... civil society [as against political parties] ... to lead Jamaica's rescue."[58] Of note is the fact that of the "civil society groups" referred to, the only one specified is the private sector, which would wish to operate, traditionally, in a facilitative environment, being, of necessity, as they see it, one largely unregulated?[59]

It is not impossible that the civil society sector might well do a better job at leading the *political* rescue mission than its performance over the last forty years, as the proverbial "engine of growth", with respect to the national economy. This prospect is left open because it needs to be recognised, if not emphasized, that a more positive performance in the area of job creation, in particular, would not have eliminated, but would certainly have substantially reduced, the scope for the emergence of the negative features which define the island's politics, on the level of the supporter, the party and governments.

Corruption tends to feed most voraciously on serious shortages of resources and 'betterment opportunities', and the better the jobs that people have the less likely they are to look to parties or the state for succour of a personal-benefit kind.

---

56 ECJ, 'Report to Parliament on Political Party Registration and Financing' (July 2010) p. 1; Andrew Holness, Opposition Leader is quoted as saying "I think it [the approval of state political financing] needs to happen as quickly as possible ... the political party is not a private club and for the enhancement of democracy they should be regulated", the *Jamaica Observer*, 'Holness for campaign financing but ... ', May 5, 2013, p. 26.

57 After the six years of extensive consultation what was produced was the first part of a two stage process, with that on Campaign Finance to follow at a later date. This is despite the fact that the ECJ was in "the final stages of seeking agreement on ... limits to campaign financing and disclosure of contributions ..." in *2007*: ECJ Report (n. 12) p.2, above.

58 Editorial, 'Civil Society Has To Lead Jamaica's Rescue' *The Gleaner*, Apr. 6, 2011, p. A8

59 The Private Sector Organisation of Jamaica (PSOJ) and the Jamaica Chamber of Commerce have both been strong in their call and support for political party and campaign finance regulation, See, *The Gleaner* Tue. June 22, 2010, p.A2; the *Jamaica Observer*, Fri. Nov. 26, 2010 pp. 14.

The position taken by this writer on the subject matter of the ECJ's Report warrants, without adoption, a quotation from an editorial in one of Jamaica's leading newspapers:

> This model of discreet intervention [by civil-society groups] which would individually pay attention to those matters that had specific areas of interest might have been good for another era when the world, and the issues that confront leadership, were less complex. Its application is even less efficacious in the Jamaican context of a crisis of leadership: where political parties often operate like crude gangs,[60] assembled *merely* for the cause of power and partisan control; where parties will resort to muscled roughnecks to keep whole communities in check and to rustle votes; and where party leaders lack the moral authority, and certainly the will, to lead transformation of their organisations and the broader society."[61]

To the extent that the above portrayal is accurate, one would certainly have expected more than a mere allusion to the nature and scale of the party-political problems to be confronted by the ECJ's proposals for reform.

Absent from the introductory comments of the Report is any reference to a pressing public-need motive[62]. What we are told is that, "... currently there is no requirement for political parties in Jamaica to be registered or for their financial arrangements to be regulated."[63] It is as if the absence of regulations is, *per se*, a sufficient reason for the introduction of regulation in an environment where legal rule enforcement is decidedly problematic.[64]

Elections Canada was among the organisations invited to present papers

---

60 The newspaper in a series of editorial headlines referred to the two parties represented in Parliament as "the Gangs of Gordon House", Gordon House being the name of the parliament building. See *The Gleaner*, April 5, 8 and 19, 2011, pp. A8, A6 and A6, respectively; somewhat more politely, Peter Osborne uses the term "political class" whose, members are not beyond "crossing the floor" where this furthers otherwise opposed parties mutual interests; by calling, in this context, "for even more money from public coffers ..."; Michael Pinto-Duschinsky, 'Political Funding in Britain: what can we learn from history?', (*BBC History Magazine*,), <http://www. historyextra.com/feature/political-funding-britain-what-can-we-learn-history>

61 Editorial, 'Civil Society Has To Lead Jamaica's Rescue' *The Gleaner*, (May 15, 2011), p. A8

62 This is in stark contrast to the explicit statement of the public's concern, which was to be confronted by reform consideration in Canada and Britain.

63 ECJ Report, p.1

64 *The Noise Abatement Act* and *The Anti-Litter Act* are just two notorious examples of unsanctioned statutory non-compliance, evidenced by the frequent complaint in the press. In respect of the former Act, see *Jamaica Observer*, (Tuesday May 3, 2011), p.1, with the front page headline "Nastiness! NSWMA boss laments lack of respect for litter law"

at the ECJ's two-day Conference in July, 2006.[65] Given that country's emphasis on, and approach to the felt need[66] for legal regulation and reform, one wonders if the maximum benefit has been derived from their participation.

The early development of Canadian electoral legislation has been traced as having its origin when:

> In 1873, then Prime Minister, Sir John A. MacDonald was accused of demanding large campaign contributions from promoters of the Canadian Pacific Railway— behaviour which eventually led to the toppling of his Conservative government. The subsequent Liberal government enacted the *Dominion Elections Act* which required election candidates to disclose how and where campaign funds were spent.[67]

In Jamaica's case, the ECJ's Report seems to engage two areas of concern. Firstly, it is recognised that individuals and organisations will support political parties on the basis of ideology, policy, or candidate personality and quality. However, it argues that,

> the danger to be avoided is that no single individual or organisation contributing to the funding of a political party should be able to contribute a sum that gives that individual or organisation sufficient voice and influence to disproportionately influence the decision-making of the party by virtue of the size of that contribution.[68]

In the Commission's view, the propriety of the regulation of the role of money in elections is apparently beyond contestation, which, if true, would make its seemingly blinkered approach in the treatment of such a complex issue appropriate and adequate. However, in an age of the virtual omnipresence of the free market ideology this is surely not indisputable.

---

65 ECJ Report, p. 1. For the Law Commission of Canada's discussion paper, 'Renewing Democracy: Debating Electoral Reform in Canada, 2002, see, www.lee.gc.ca, Catalogue Number: JL2-20/2002.

66 The Article, 'Federal Campaign Laws in Canada', admits in its very first sentence that "concerns regarding the role of money in elections are not a modern issue in Canadian politics.": J. Makarenko, 'Federal Campaign Laws in Canada' (Mapleleafweb, 21 July 2009) < http://mapleleafweb.com/featu`res/federal-campaign-finance-laws-canada> p. 2

67 Ibid.

68 ECJ Report, pp. 8-9; Vernon Daley in 'Avoiding error in campaign reform' hopes that, "… they do not suggest any upper limits on the contributions that may be made to political parties and their candidates from private sources". The emphasis, he argues, should "not be on the limits but rather on disclosure": V. Daley, *The Gleaner*, Apr. 29, 2008, p.A7. It should not be surprising that as late as September, 2014, after the Bill to amend ROPA was tabled in the House of Representatives, serious divisions and uncertainty persisted, see Debbie-Ann Wright, 'Senate approves state funding of political parties', *The Gleaner*, Sat. Dec. 6, 2014, p. A1. See also, Balford Henry, 'That Bill which seeks to register and fund political parties', the *Jamaica Observer*, Dec. 7, 2014, p. 32.

But it also calls into question the comprehensiveness of the Commission's members' purview which yielded the published proposals.

It has been argued, for example:

> Politics, in many ways, is no different from business. Political parties are about marketing ideas in the same way that firms market foods and services. In that fierce marketplace, sometimes a party has to do a great deal of spending on its marketing campaign to get people to buy into its vision. Having good ideas is not good enough.[69]

This contributor to the reform debate argues that, as is the case with long-sitting members in the United States political arena, there is a considerable advantage enjoyed by those already in office. In the Jamaican context, this would have meant that,

> [had] there been contribution and spending limits the JLP [Jamaica Labour Party] would not have been able to compete with an entrenched Government fortified by a popular leader who had built up great admiration across the country over many years.[70]

One controversial Jamaican MP, Everald Warrington, surprisingly for a politician, and therefore a prospective beneficiary of the intended reforms, has, it is reported, "… vehemently objected to the proposal … for taxpayers to help finance political parties"[71]. Promising in any parliamentary debate to vote against the Report, the MP based his objection on the lack of means of the "poor man of this country" who should not be further burdened. In elaborating on his position on both party and campaign state financing, the MP continued:

> We cannot expect a poor person in Jamaica, who is unable to get assistance … to send his or her child to high school or college, to finance the campaign of members to come to this House. … It is wrong.[72]

Assuming that the proposals were accepted, he, "… would want a clause to allow individuals to decide against accepting the money".[73]

---

69 V. Daley, supra.

70 Ibid.

71 Luton, Darain, 'Taxpayers shouldn't foot election bill ' *The Gleaner*, (Wednesday, November 3, 2010), p.A3

72 Ibid.

73 Ibid.

Does the fact that the ECJ-surveyed members of the public were not in favour of an additional/special tax for party funding lend any support to this Parliamentarian's stance? Is support of the majority of respondents for state funding, nevertheless, more a reflection of a lack of sophistication about the realities of public finance, combined with what could be perceived to be a warped manifestation of the "freeness mentality"?

Legislation to provide candidate, party, and campaign financial state support, with the implications properly understood, would, one suspects, be rife with the potential for negative public response and noisy condemnation, in a worsening economic environment. This legislation would be similar to the situation where MPs grant themselves large salary increases while asking for sacrifice from workers, in the form of wage freezes, grounded in appeals to patriotism and the welfare of *future* generations. However, neither the political nor private sector 'lead singers', nor those joining in the chorus seem to make these sacrifices themselves, not even symbolically.[74]

Apart from the "danger" referred to above, as seen by the ECJ, the other area of concern, as gleaned from the Report, seems to be the perceived need for oversight of the conduct of the internal affairs of a registered political party. Qualification regulations for the right to apply for state funding go well beyond matters of finance, however.

The calling of the tune by the Commission, on behalf of the state, which will be 'paying the piper', is clearly exposed, beginning with the section dealing with the Procedure for Registration.

The first requirement of note is that it is not just the names and addresses, but the "telephone numbers of at least five hundred members in good financial standing" which must be disclosed on the prescribed form.[75] On a small island, this is the first over-sized step on the road to the heavy work

---

74   See 'Big bucks, big cars', *The Gleaner*, (Thur. Nov. 22, 2012), p.1; 'Holness: Government must take paycuts', *The Gleaner* (Mon. Feb. 11, 2013), p. A3; 'Let's be realistic, Phillips pleads with Jamaican to understand economic dilemma ', *The Gleaner*, (Fri. Feb. 15, 2013), p.1; 'Bunting: This is the bitter medicine, Cabinet Minister defends new tax package', the *Jamaica Observer*, (Fri. Feb. 15, 2013), p.4 and the editorial of the same date, 'Sacrifice demands that Government lead by example'; 'Symbolic sacrifice lost on Dr. Davies ... perhaps', *The Gleaner*, (Wed. Mar. 13, 2013), p. A9, 'Politicians must sacrifice too', the *Jamaica Observer*, (Thur. Mar. 14, 2013), p. 14.
75   ECJ (n. 12), 'Procedure for Registration', 'a', p.4

load of record keeping, accounting, and auditing activity envisioned.[76] The daunting level of administrative detail contemplated, seems to ignore the context of a semi-literate society where emerging parties are likely to be quite small. Even more importantly, should the details of ordinary members of what, despite registration, is by its very nature a pre-eminent example of a voluntary organisation be thus made public? This we suggest is an issue deserving of review, even if one chooses to discount the personal security implications arising from the traditional tribalistic and violence-prone nature of the island's politics.

Under the heading 'Application for State Funding', one finds that the signatures of at least five hundred party members, in good financial standing, must support the application. Significantly, the ECJ's oversight function is linked to the requirement for a written constitution.[77]

In the context of a document that has been so long in gestation, it would perhaps have been expected that "contesting elections" would have been perceived as a *means* towards the achievement of the party's policy aims and objectives. Instead, contesting elections must be a "principal objective".[78] Despite this, the party needs to provide a declaration that it *intends* to contest one election, only, in applying for state funds. No time period over which this intention must be given effect is stated.[79]

---

76 The name of the auditor has to be provided along with written confirmation of acceptance of the appointment, p4; names, addresses and signatures of at least 500 members, p.4; the arrangements for regulating the financial affairs of the party, p.5.; Current annual lists of political representatives of differing status, including candidates, caretakers, chairpersons and electoral liaison officers for <u>all</u> constituencies (the reality is that some of the persons in these positions are always yet to be selected, especially so in the case of small/new parties), with the Commission being informed of all changes with the dates, pp.7-8; the names of all party affiliates (undefined) and the rights and privileges enjoyed by such affiliates and their officers, p.8; submissions of an annual budget and audited financial accounts to the Annual General Meeting and submission of a consolidated statement of income and expenditure of the party <u>and all affiliate bodies</u> that the party funds, to the Commission, p.8; stipulation of the specific items of expenditure for which state funding may be used in the case of party Headquarters–presumably funds cannot be mixed with excess, if any, to be refunded? p.9; in the case of constituency operations, the contrast is stark: state funds may only be used for the very general purposes of Administration and Organisation, p. 10; apart from the party's own auditor, the Commission's independent approved auditor must also audit the financial records, p.10; expenditures on administration are to be recorded separately from those for campaigning, p. 11; <u>all</u> receipts for expenditures must be supplied to the Commission, p.11;

77 ECJ , 'Procedure for Registration', 'a) on, p.5

78 Ibid; The combination of cynicism and naiveté which is not untypical of the attitude of the 'modern individual' is exemplified by the view of Howard Hamilton, Q.C., that, "Unless and until we get a government which doesn't give a second thought to winning the next election, we shall continue to wander aimlessly through the deserts of time". This is, of course, only possibly the case in a one-party state, by law, or *de facto*, due to the supreme dominance of one party over others. See Hamilton's comments in *The Gleaner*, (Mon. Aug. 15, 2011), p. A7.

79 Supra, ECJ '(f)' p. 5

Other matters to be provided for in a party's constitution include, qualification for membership; *annual* election of officers (although, later on, the Commission is given the power to suspend state funding where the election of officers has not been held *in accordance with its constitution*).[80] The objection can certainly be reasonably made that it is for the membership to decide on the length of the term of office for different office holders. As if in agreement with this suggestion, the very next constitutional stipulation is for the inclusion of "the titles of all officers and delegates, qualifications of officers, and the *length* [Italics added] of their terms of office".[81]

It is easy enough to insist on what is likely to be a forbidding level of formality, far removed from the fluidity and dynamism of informal relations and procedures 'on the ground', where anonymity in interpersonal party relationships is likely to be somewhat rare. It should be known that office holders at various levels, in an activity which, to date has not been marked by bureaucratisation to any significant degree, very often emerge, unofficially and spontaneously to fill a vacuum.[82]

If the essential distinguishing feature of politics, as against other pursuits, is the unapologetic seeking and use of power, often in situations of fierce competition, then the worth of dispute resolution constitutional provisions must be seen in precisely those terms. Those bent on mischief can have their designs facilitated by over-elaborate administrative and finance procedures allowing scope for technical legalistic trivializing challenges.

These comments may gain significance from the fact that under the Commission's recommendations,

> A political party that qualifies for state funding shall be entitled to receive the same provided that the party:
>
> a.   adheres to the provisions of its constitution.[83]

Parties that intend to seek state funding therefore need to exercise care in the constitution rule-making exercise. Otherwise, what may appear to

---

80   Ibid, p. 7
81   Ibid
82   Under the ECJ Report, e (vii) on p.5, "The procedures for selection of caretakers /chairpersons of constituencies and electoral divisions, candidates for constituencies and electoral divisions, and electoral liaison office holders representing all constituencies" must be set out in the party's constitution.
83   Ibid. p. 7

be "model" rules could in fact prove dysfunctional, rather than facilitative, with respect to operational dynamics and organisational goal achievement in different situations and times. Put differently, the "best practice" is often situationally determined, according to the weight assigned to factors which may well be in conflict on levels both "factual" and judgmental.

Monitoring compliance with the details of a party's constitution is, practically, a difficult knowledge-gathering task, perhaps best left to the vigilance of members, but, then, the ECJ, not unreasonably, expects something in exchange for 'its money'. The Companies Office of Jamaica, the agency responsible for a similar registration function with respect to incorporated organisations, except for the limited role of seeing to companies being in good standing (the filing of returns etc.), certainly does not seek to monitor the affairs of companies in any substantial way, not even in terms of procedures. With respect to what is relevant here, the distinctions between these two 'regulatory' bodies would seem to be that since governments do not give taxpayers' moneys to companies (except in the not unfamiliar cases of 'bail outs'), little attempt is made to monitor their operational activities in any detail, in keeping with their Articles of Association, or otherwise.

ECJ's Funding Proposals

It is only towards the latter part of its Report that the ECJ engages in discourse that might have more appropriately, prefaced its substantive proposals. In a welcomed declaratory tone, it is said that, "Persons who come together to form a political party must accept responsibility for the financial operations of that party."[84]

Although some would shout 'Amen' and others, in the current colloquialism, 'Argument done' to that acknowledgement, the ECJ's position on funding principles does not end there.

Three of the four financing sources it identifies would fall within the ambit of its statement: "1. Dues charged to their members; 2. Contributions from individuals and organisations and fundraising events, and, possibly, 4. Income earned from legal sources."[85]

---

84 Ibid, p.8
85 Ibid

No limit on the size of party membership fees or the structure of dues is contemplated. This could, therefore, in theory, between classes of members, for example, be highly differentiated, thus providing a route by which to evade contribution caps and loans regulations.

Be that as it may, the obvious question becomes, given the trenchant tone in which the party members' financial obligation was stated, why the necessity for the inclusion of number 3. "Funds from the State".[86]

Is it possible that regulation in exchange for state funding might reach the point where a cap is placed on membership fees/dues? A negative answer would mean that parties could legitimately, from private sources, raise funds well over the campaign's spending limits. Would such a development then invite further calls for more regulation, perhaps even seeking to stipulate the items on which such 'excess funds' could, under ECJ recommended legislation, be properly spent? Or, alarmingly, would such funds be required to be paid over to some general political fund?

It is troubling for anyone who does not accept that state funding is beyond objection, to also accept that the presentation, or even recognition of views based on *laissez-faire*[87] and free market[88] principles, do not legitimately factor into the 'debate'.

Adherents of the first approach hold the view, not surprisingly, that minimum state regulation of the activities of the parties involved in the electoral system and political process is to be preferred. There should, consequently, be no limits placed on contributions or expenditure whether by citizens, organisations, interest/lobby groups or indeed, candidates or parties.

Harper v. Canada (Attorney General)[89] is a leading decision of the Supreme Court of Canada. The central question was whether specific sections of the *Canada Elections Act* relating to election advertising spending limits infringed individuals' right to vote, freedom of expression or freedom of association, all of which are guaranteed under the Canadian *Charter of Rights and Freedoms*. A majority of the Court concluded that the new spending thresholds imposed by the federal government were constitutional under the

---

86 Ibid
87 *BBC History Magazine*, Supra
88 Ibid
89 [2004] 1 S.C.R. 827

Charter. Two of the judges dissented, finding that the provisions of the *Canada Elections Act* are unconstitutional. These two judges were of the opinion that the spending limits reduce a person's freedom of *expression* and are therefore invalid. They also found that there is no connection between spending limits and "unfairness" in the electoral process.

In the important American case, **Buckley v. Valeo,**[90] which will be referred to at some length later, the issue before the court was whether various provisions of the 1974 amendments to the *Federal Election Campaign Act* of 1971 regulating campaign contributions were unconstitutional. It was held that expenditure limits in political campaigns violated the free speech clause of the First Amendment which provides that Congress shall not abridge the right to freedom of speech. It was also decided that provisions limiting contributions are not unconstitutional. The Court held, *inter alia*, that the Government's asserted interest in preventing "corruption and the appearance of corruption,"[91] provided sufficient justification for contribution limits. In coming to its decision, it drew a distinction between limits on contributions and expenditure limits. It was explained that the difference between the two is that expenditure limits "impose significantly more severe restrictions on protected freedoms of political expression and association"[92] than do contribution limits.

In **Randall v. Sorrell**[93], a decision by the Supreme Court of the United States, the issue involved a State of Vermont law which placed a cap on financial donations made to politicians. The court ruled that the law, the strictest in the nation, unconstitutionally hindered the citizens' First Amendment right to free speech.

In Canada, justification for the *laissez-faire* position may be found in the low level of trust existing that action in these matters is likely to be taken in a less than self-serving manner, the expectation being that "politicians will

---

90   424 U.S. 1 (1976)

91   Ibid, 25

92   Ibid, 23

93   548 U.S. 230 (2006)

use this power to manipulate the electoral system for their own gains."[94] Recent confirmation of the legitimacy of this concern has come from various quarters.[95] Several cases of MP expense scandals have surfaced in England, resulting in the recent imposition of prison sentences on two, one then current, and one former member of the House of Commons.[96] This is against a background where, "… state aid to party politics is now huge because of the growth of indirect forms of public funding, such as allowances to MP's … which are growing … and to councillors".[97]

Associated with free market dogma is the position that:

> … optimum political outcomes and decisions occur when citizens are left in a state of liberty … Just as free markets bring equilibrium to supply and demand … free competition in the political sphere ensures optimum political outcomes.[98]

---

94 J. Makarenko, 'Federal Campaign Laws in Canada' Mapleleafweb, (21 July 2009), p.11 < http://mapleleafweb. com/featu`res/federal-campaign-finance-laws-canada>. So pervasive is the lack of trust in politicians that the Law Commission of Canada in its Discussion Paper, 'Renewing democracy: Debating Electoral Reform in Canada', asks whether in considering systemic electoral changes politicians should take the lead or "might there be the need for a more formal process (for example, a referendum)?"; See Law Commission of Canada, (2002), p. 40. It should be noted that the Paper sought to examine alternative voting systems with a view to remedying "the democratic malaise that has come that has come to characterize the Canadian political landscape", apparently much broader Terms of Reference than those of the ECJ.

95 BBC History Magazine, for example; [in a newspaper report headed "Ecuador President linked to slain rebel", it is alleged that Columbian officials had confirmed that documents from a slain rebel's computer revealed that "leftist guerrillas" had discussed the making of financial contributions to the President's 2006 election campaign, in The Gleaner Mon, March 10, 2008, p. C8.

96 The MP David Chayton was, in January 2011, sentenced to 18 months imprisonment for making false expense claims. MP Eric Illsley pleaded guilty, and resigned a week later, to similar charges; Former United States House majority leader, Tom Daley, was also, in January, 2011, sentenced to serve three years imprisonment for "his role in a scheme to illegally funnel money to Texas candidates in 2002, The Gleaner, Jan 16, 2011, p.7. See also, 'Scandals plague democratics in California', The Gleaner, Fri. Mar. 28, 2014, p.B7, and 'Mayor arrested on corruption charge' on the same page; 'Political parties, courts seem as most corrupt'. The Gleaner, Mon. Mar, 31, 2014, p. A6; 'Israeli court convicts ex-PM Olmert of 'bribery', Jamaica Observer, Tue. Apr. 1, 2014, p.25; In fact he was sentenced to six (6) years imprisonment, see, 'Former PM Olmert sentenced to six years', The Gleaner, Wed. May 14, 2014, p. B.9; 'Energy group chair charged with bribing former (Croatian) PM, The Gleaner, Thur. Apr. 2, 2014, p. A11; and 'Congress (Mexico) hit by major corruption scandal', The Gleaner, Fri. Apr. 11, 2014, p.B6. In 'Country's ex-top judge gets life for corruption', there is the report of an antigraft court in Indonesia sentencing that country's former Chief Judge of the Constitutional Court to life imprisonment for corruption and money laundering. The report states, that' the Corruption Eradication Commission captured him red-handed, accepting bribes to fix the results of two local elections', The Gleaner, Wed, Jul. 2, 2014, p.B7. See also, 'Sarkozy [ex-President of France] detained in French corruption probe, the allegations were that he took $50,000,000.00 in illegal campaign funds from Libya's ex-ruler Muammar Gaddafi. In the following day's press report, 'Sarkozy fights back in face of corruption charges', Sarkozy is reported to have accused France's Justice System of trying to humiliate and destroy him in what was said by a political historian to be, 'yet another thing to erode the image of the political class because it gives the image of an all-powerful group that believes itself to be above the law'. Sarkozy is accused of tapping political allies to gain intelligence on a flurry of probes linked to campaign finance. The Jamaica Observer, Thu. Jul. 3, 2014, p. 23. While we would not hold Jamaica up as a model of political purity, we do believe that the alleged extent of corrupt political behaviour is significantly overstated, in the absence of cases, in the juridical sense and data,

97 BBC History Magazine, Supra, p. 19

98 Jay Makarenko, Supra, p.11

From this perspective, the notion of some "third party" providing a "level playing field" is fundamentally wrong as those competitors with disabilities need to adopt strategies to compensate for them. The expectation would be for the state to refrain from any but a minimum operational role in the electoral process.

LEVEL PLAYING FIELD

The state of the 'playing field' should be determined by consenting to the possibility of positive, although quite un-contemplated, member/public party-donation attitude changes, yet to be experienced elsewhere. Substantial state subsidy will continue to seem like a solution, rather than the mirage that it actually is. The preferred view might be that voter support, mobilised into partisan commitment sufficient to elicit contributions in accordance with personal or corporate means, and the parties' needs should be the answer to the question of funding/state of the playing field in a multi-party democracy. On this view, parties would, to that extent, be compelled, one would expect, for mere survival, to more actively, strategically and effectively market their vision, policies, programs and projects.

The Commission's proposed method of sharing available state funding fails to accommodate the likely discriminatory effects on the beneficiaries, resulting from party size (however measured), organisational structure or any empirically derived relationship between administrative 'ongoing', as against electioneering/campaign expenses. Disproportionalities in allocation are therefore inevitable, were the recommendations to be accorded legislative approval. This will particularly be the case in the absence of any agreed framework of clearly defined reform objectives against which apparent disparities can be evaluated.

But it can be argued that the 'playing field' will never be level.[99] Politics and the social, economic and cultural environment in which it is practised, is much too complex to be the subject of serious discussion with the use of that popular figurative sports-related term. Money by itself, regulated or

---

99 It is not certain where the recent situation of the UK Independence Party would fit into the 'level playing field' conceptual scheme. In that case, due to the imposed limits on election expenditure, particularly restrictions on party political advertising it was found that this Party could not lawfully spend the full amount of the state funds it had received; see Stephen Castle, 'Britain's Campaign Finance Laws Leaves Parties with Idle Money' , *The New York Times*, May 4, 2015.

unregulated, from the income or expenditure side is never likely to fully determine an election's results:[100] there are just too many other factors in the victory equation.

An excessive focus on the effect of money, important as it undoubtedly is, discounts the possibly overarching effect of candidate selection, policy postures and the effectiveness of the parties' communication and campaign strategy in all aspects and at all levels. The creativity and perceived relevance of all forms of advertising, to the extent that this will determine the electorate's image of the party and its leader, and the quality of party organisational machinery and personnel, among other things, are too important to be ignored as determining factors. The effect of fully mobilised grassroots activism should, of course, not be accorded insignificant weight.

Some states in the United States have taken the state funding option to the point where, under so-called "Clean Election" laws, in Arizona and Maine, for example, candidates for state offices are provided with full public funding for their campaigns. The presumption that this provides citizens with an equal "political voice" is clearly open to challenge. The policy lobby and organisational impact which special interest groups may have on election outcomes can, most definitely, not be limited to the effect of the size of their monetary contributions.

It has, indeed, been observed that "… unless the stream of social life continuously flows from below upwards",[101] the pursuit of career and economic interests will tend in the direction of group and institutional member estrangement/manipulation/confrontation, rather than cooperation.

Under the Arizona and Maine regimes, qualification guidelines require that,

> … a candidate would have to agree not to raise private funds, to limit the spending of public funds and to prove he is not a fringe candidate by raising

---

100 See 'Organisation, the key to winning elections', Michael Burke, *Jamaica Observer*, June 2, 2011, p. 11. According to Ronald Mason, "Those persons who live and have a non-transferable interest in an election will be under pressure to nyam (eat) them [rival party candidates] out and vote for the best candidate, as judged by the elector's criteria", *The Gleaner* Oct. 6, 2013, p. A9. See also 'Government Senator says 'There's no evidence for 'BIG MONEY FEARS', *The Gleaner*, Sat. Nov. 2, 2013, pp. A1, 3, where it is argued that incumbent Ministers and parties in government, with greater access to funding often lose their seat and elections, sometimes by 'landslides'. See also 'Issues should motivate voters', Jean Lowrie-Chin, *Jamaica Observer*, Mon. June 20, 2011, p.11.

101 Fromm, op. cit. p. 237.

a number of very small (often $5) donations. If outspent by a privately funded opponent, a "clean" candidate would then receive matching funds.[102]

Issues in dispute immediately come to mind including: (i) The bases on which the limit on public funds expenditure is determined[103]; and (ii) the irony of requiring one to do precisely what is being discouraged, in order to prove he is not a fringe candidate.

Why shouldn't "fringe" candidates be publicly funded?

Presumably, they do represent some citizens, however small the number, who would also, thereby, be given a political voice. Perhaps even more problematic, at precisely what point of being surpassed in spending would matching funds be made available? The timing of campaign activity, with associated costs, is often critical in an extremely time-sensitive situation, involving planned responses, sometimes to anticipated competitive action/ strategy.

For the latter aspect of this approach to have meaning, it would be necessary that there is, in fact, full disclosure of the actual amount of private funding received which could be a major problem in itself.

In advancing the cause of "Clean Election" laws and regulations in the hope that the approach will transcend state boundaries and gain national appeal, Nick Nyhart, Executive Director of 'Public Campaign', a campaign finance reform organisation, is quoted as follows, in reference to the case of former Governor Gray Davis:

> If you wanted to have the Governor's backing", Nyhart stated, "you needed to make campaign contributions in a big way. I think that's part of the reason he was recalled: not standing for anything but the need to raise money.[104]

The important point is the fact that he was recalled; those with the role of arbiters of the appropriateness of his methods and conduct acted as they saw fit.

---

102 Hoover Institution, 'Public Policy Inquiry: Campaign Finance, Reform Proposals', Oct 11, 2004, p.1
103 See Castle, Stephen, 'Britain's Campaign, Finance Laws Leaves Parties with Idle Money', *The New York Times*, May 4, 2015.
104 Ibid p.2

Also worthy of note, in this regard, is that supporters of the *laissez-faire* and free market perspectives, in their desire to maximize citizen electoral choice, on both the personal and institutional levels, are not inherently opposed to a limited state role. Legally required disclosure requirements would, for example, it is postulated, greatly enhance the citizens' ability to make more and better informed decisions as electors. Access to this information would be "highly relevant" to voter behaviour as "consumers in the political market".[105]

It is not easy to find evidence[106] to establish that, while the crucial role of "big money" in politics, as in almost everything else, cannot be denied, and as the ECJ asserts, the decision to seek office and the quality of one's campaign and post-election conduct are thereby necessarily determined.[107]

Financial regulations seeking to provide a "level playing field", a major concern of the Commission,[108] are advocated by those using phrases such as "ensuring fair and equitable participation" of citizens, candidates and parties in the electoral process.

Some go further and expect regulatory regimes to ensure fair and equitable outcomes.[109] The notion of the 'equality of the importance of each vote' has led to experiments with modified forms of proportional representation. The result has often been the relative instability of minority and coalition governments.[110] This is not to deny that where regional and ethnic minority representation issues arise, as in Canada and New Zealand, respectively,

---

105 Jay Makarenko, Supra, p. 2

106 Many examples of "perception" "appearance", and "suspicion", etc. appear in the arguments critical of the *status quo* with respect to political financing.

107 This has led one Jamaican observer to note that "Barack Obama has largely been able to compete with Hillary Clinton because of the huge amount of funding which he has been able to raise on-line. She is almost an institution while he is an unknown. He has been able to erase that deficit not just by his message but by his money", *The Gleaner*, April 29, 2008, p. A.7. The same argument would no doubt hold true for the subsequent Presidential Campaign.

108 See, for example, The *Jamaica Observer*, June 1, 2008, Sec. 3, p.7

109 The Law Commission of Canada in the Preface to its Discussion Paper, in referring to the "democratic malaise" in that country asked whether, "... our voting system continues to respond to our needs and values ... still meet Canadians' democratic aspirations". The democratic values enumerated were Fairness, Representation, Equality and Accountability. One of the very un-circumscribed discussion points mooted is: "Is the current electoral system fair?"; further, "Does it penalize small, nationally based parties?", at p. 32

110 This is a well-known feature of governments in Western Europe. For Example, at the time of writing the first draft, (2011) Canada was having its fourth election in seven years: The *Jamaica Observer*, Mon. May 2, 2011 p.16. Unlike Jamaica, Canada can no doubt afford this. Currently Jamaica is a borrower from the IMF with all the consequences of that relationship.

there may not be benefits to be gained from the adoption of variations of that system in such geographical and demographic contexts.[111]

The ECJ seeks to provide a rationale for an already impoverished state, masochistically, it may appear to some, subsidising parties and their campaign endeavours, in the statement that,

> State funding for political parties is premised on the thesis that political parties in a small growing democracy perform important public services in representing general and specific interest of people. These demands extend beyond the resources available from membership dues and contributions from like-minded individuals and organisations.[112]

Contrary to these sentiments, one would expect that, firstly, in a small island it would be much easier for parties to establish closer direct contact and relations with their supporters/members which would elicit the level of commitment that would translate into dues income. This should be so since, unsurprisingly, there is no intention to place a limit on membership or level of fees and dues.[113] Secondly, under the proposed party registration arrangement, membership by organisations should be possible, with dues being set at any level deemed appropriate.

It can also be argued that, in a society that is said to suffer from the scourge of the "freeness mentality", state funding can be seen as an opportunity missed for the beginning of a much needed campaign of political education[114]. If members, individuals and organisations, as supporters, reasonably expect

---

111 Law Commission of Canada, op. cit. pp. 30-34: After the introduction of Mixed-Member proportional representation in New Zealand in 1996, 15 Maori representatives were elected to the House, proportional to their representation in the population and the percentage of women increased from 21 to 29 per cent. In Canada the Royal Commission has recommended the establishment of an Aboriginal parliament as a preliminary step towards a "House of First Peoples"

112 See 'Little support for State Campaign Financing' reporting poll results showing 72.42% of respondents saying 'No, it'll be too much of a burden on the country', in the *Jamaica Observer* (Sunday Finance), Nov. 27, 2011, p. 3.

113 ECJ Report, p. 8

114 Louis A. Moyston in a letter to the editor in the *Jamaica Observer*, Monday April 18, 2011, p. 9, limits the need for political education to "… make people understand what they [parties] stand for." Equally important, given the traditional clientelistic nature of politician-electorate relationship, is education as to the proper role of all the parties and their relationship in the political system. Political education took on an alien doctrinaire partisan garb under the failed Democratic Socialism experiment of the early 1970s. Somewhat late in the day, we find the anti-corruption watchdog, National Integrity Action, announcing that it would be engaging in an educational campaign fundamental to the integrity of the electoral process and political system: the matter of the buying of votes; see 'Campaign against vote buying coming soon', The Gleaner, Sat. May 30, 2015, p. A3. Such an effort might be viewed as a necessary *precursor* to the ECJ's legal regulatory regime in the interest of the greater likelihood of implementation success, as against the NIA's former emphasis on sanctions.

their views and interests to be effectively promoted they should expect to pay the institutional costs[115] involved. In a very real sense, with active critical participation in their party's affairs, rather than simply voting in elections, they would be getting the representation they deserve.

Implicit in the ECJ's categorization of the island as a "young democracy", are socio-political issues relevant to the subject under discussion.

To begin with, the maturity and political intelligence of the electorate is called into question. Secondly, has the political system ossified to the point where the main differentiating factor between major "electable" parties is their name?[116] Thirdly, what precisely are the national values to be enhanced and advanced by the reform measures contemplated?

If 'democracy' is about freedom to choose interest-specific representation, why shouldn't "big money" support, without restriction, a "big man's party"?[117] To those who are motivated by majoritarian democratic ideals, all that this would mean is that the wealthy minority's party—assuming a mature and, particularly, an intelligent electorate, with partisan-neutral electoral machinery in place—would always lose.

But the immanence of the corruption taint is evident even in balanced commentary, with Barbara Gloudon, noting:

> The drive for full disclosure is based on the *assumption* [Italics added] that, donations can be and will be used to purchase influence. ... It is the democratic right of anyone, individual or group, to donate to any political party of their choice ... to minimize the problem, providers of campaign financing have been known to divide donations equally ... to get out of the

---

115 This remains our preferred view, although in the case of Arizona, with its clean elections laws, it must be noted that attempts to get by the No Taxpayer Money for Politicians groups to inviting the State Supreme Court to strike down those laws and another lobbying to get the Courts to bar the payment of matching funds on the basis of unconstitutionality, both failed.

116 With regard to the usual "political civility, politeness and, well, predictability" of the Canadian scenario, see John Rapley, in *The Gleaner*, May 2, 2011, p. A7, where the telling point is made that, "...that was about it. No major ideological struggles, no mad conspiracy theorists." See also "PNP Far Worse." John Richards in The Gleaner, Thur. April 7, 2011, p. A8, where the attitude that "I do not vote because they are all the same" is one that "folks ... will proudly declare in public"

117 Vernon Daley in The Gleaner Apr. 29, 2008, p. A7 in giving apparent support to this position argues that "What we should be concerned about is who is offering the money so we can apply the appropriate security".

tribal trap. Where is the democracy we like to speak about?[118]

The problems experienced by Jamaica and other countries giving rise to a focus on electoral issues, it is here contended, will not be remedied by reforms of the nature proposed. Rather, it is the maturation process, with self-perpetuation tendencies on the level of the individual politician as a member of the 'political class' and that of political parties, as institutions, which needs serious in-depth investigation.

DISENGAGEMENT: PARTIES/MEMBERS/CITIZENS

Put differently, the disengagement of citizens from the political process, witnessed in many countries for several years now, is reflective of the increasing omnipresence of the phenomenon of multi-class alliances possessing little fundamental ideological differentiation, whether politically, economically, or in terms of an embracing societal vision. A sense of "mission" around which to mobilise strong bonding has been, with a few exceptions, conspicuous by its absence from national mainstream politics in recent times.[119] There no longer seems to be a universally acknowledged ideological schism, as we witness the globalization of politics. The manifestation of compelling associational urges in the workplace or in political relations are exceptional.

The Commission provides no empirical, or, indeed, any evidence for its conclusion that the financial demands of political party representation extend beyond the quantum of traditionally available legitimate resources. How then

---

118 Gloudon, Barbara, 'A time of questions unanswered', The *Jamaica Observer*, (Mon. Sept. 8, 2014), p. 15. For the editor of the Gleaner, the spending of one's money is not, it seems, an "individual freedom" since "political parties and their leaders *become* [Italics added] beholden to those who finance their route to power, see *The Gleaner*, editorial, Sept. 14, 2014, p. A8. The corruption syndrome again prevails over presentation of proof. Traditionally, under normal circumstances, big private sector money lines up behind not any party but the major ones only, "in an effort to pursue their *narrow* [Italics added] interests". According to the editorial, a Contractor General or Integrity Commission which is effective in achieving their appropriately drafted mandate, should minimize the abuse of power, "not least through siphoning of taxpayers' resources to *shadowy* [Italics added] political backers".

119 In the latest Canadian General Election, May 2011, despite the eclipse of the traditional main contender, the Liberals, the victorious Prime Minister, Stephen Harper, "sought to allay fears he would implement a hidden right-wing agenda," reported in the *Jamaica Observer* Wed. May 4, 2011, p. 21. This after his Conservative party had won a "long-sought majority"; "The effect of globalization in diminishing the space allowed for ideologically different initiatives did have a part to play in Harper's victory hinged, in his vow, on the perceived need to "stay the course" in pursuit of the reduction of a record deficit, etc.: The *Jamaica Observer*, Wed April 13, 2011 p.31, "Canada PM face [*sic*] challenges in TV debate"; Despite "The increasingly acrimonious political discourse of recent months" what this meant was trading "barbs ... over character and core values" with the "prosaic" possibility that "each leader's performance during the debates could hugely affect the election outcome"; see also *The Gleaner*, editorial, Tue April 5, 2011, p.A8, sub-heading "No Energy for Revolution".

have the parties managed to survive since 1944, the year of the first election under universal adult suffrage in Jamaica? Be that as it may, as responsibly managed institutions, shouldn't the planned and actual expenditure of parties and, by extension, candidates, be in accordance with their income-generating capability?[120]

The boundaries of the thinking reflected in the ECJ Report, given an apparent disinclination to empiricism and the spirit of detached, investigation and analysis, seem set by little more than conventional wisdom. To the extent that the resulting reform would inevitably become disfigured, one expects that the system designed will be impotent to achieve desired paradigmatic changes in attitudes and values at the individual or organisational level.

According to Gloudon, "The Court of public opinion stages the trial and passes its own judgment and 'green' (JLP) or 'orange' (PNP) will manipulate if they wish". 'Palm tree justice' is no more obnoxious than justice according to the 'court of public opinion', especially in a highly tribalised society.

The question then becomes: Will "… an inattentive citizenry cede their right of choice not only to leaders bundled in political parties",[121] but also their willingness to accept that decisions of any such bodies, including Parliament itself and the ECJ and other national institutional arbiters, are grounded in the application of impartial notions of fairness based on evidence adduced? Governance based on the universalistic concept of the rule of law, and, more specifically, enacted legal rules can scarcely be more critically important in determining the efficacy of the design and administration of dispute mechanisms for resolving the various social/political issues in conflict at all levels in the society. Regrettably, almost all the indicators seem to be in a negative direction.

In a polity in which it is claimed that what ought to be aberrations are in fact the norm, there is nothing in its Report which is addressed didactically to the multitude: the elector/the citizen has managed to escape completely

---

120 March 15, 2007 in 'Public Choice'/Permalink http://www.typepad.com/services/ trackback/6a00d83451cbef69e200d835225d3568e2

121 Gloudon Barbara, 'A Time of Questions Unanswered'. The *Jamaica Observer*, Mon. Sept. 8, 2014, p. 15. See also, *The Gleaner*, editorial, 'A better logic against corruption', Thu. Dec. 18, 2014, p. A8, for possible new initiatives, some imported, for consideration. The editorial was in direct response to a Government Senator's stance that "… lack of evidence means corruption' label unfair to politicians", in, 'Prove it', *The Gleaner*, Wed. Dec. 17, 2014, pp. A1, 3.

the gaze of the Commission. It is as if 'all the fault' lies with the parties, the politicians and the motives of wealthy donors.

Since even a mechanistic solution-outlook can be modified according to other countries' experience, in the absence of reliable evidence on party expenses and election spending in Jamaica, it may be useful to make inquiry as to history elsewhere.

With respect to the British situation, it has been concluded that, "The political spending 'arms race' is a myth".[122] Under the heading, 'Political Funding in Britain, what can we learn from history?' it is reported that:

> In fact the Conservatives, the highest spender of the three main parties, spent about 10 per cent less in the electoral cycle 2001-05 than 1966-70 when measuring inflation by the Retail Price Index. ... Meanwhile in the same 37-year period, combined Labour and Conservative spending increased by less than one per cent per year ... spending by constituency organisations has declined ... In 2003, spending by Constituency Labour parties was 40 per cent lower than 34 years earlier ... and over 60 per cent lower if inflation is measured by the AEI"[123] [Average Earnings Index].

The approach to problems in the political system which seeks their cause and proffers prescriptions largely by attention to the "possible" and "potential" deleterious influence of money, must confront the fact that, at least in Britain:

> The costs of politics were as high in the 19th century as they are today, when measured by RPI (Retail Price Index). ... As a result the problems caused by money in politics are less severe now than in the past".[124]

A British historian, given the information available, chronologically, against a legislative background going back to the *Corrupt Practices Act of 1883*, would go no further than to say "... money influences election results (though it can be hard to disentangle the effects of high spending from other factors)".[125]

Must one conclude that with the lack of empirical evidence and statistical confirmation, the ECJ reform platform is based solely on "perception",

---

122 This in contrast to the view of the then British Minister of Justice, Jack Straw, who regarded the "arms race" in political spending as "the central driver of the other problems that we face."
123 Michael Pinto-Duschinsky in *The BBC History Magazine*, Pamphlet May 2008 p. 2
124 Ibid p.3
125 Ibid

important as that can be, in a rumour-mongering, gossip addicted cultural context? Is this the best way forward?

On one view, to be returned to at a later stage, the problems to be addressed stem not so much from the role of money in politics but rather the very state of politics itself. Should this diagnosis be correct, the position in the island could very well be the replication of that in Britain where although the financing of parties and their campaigns "... should be a matter of importance ... drawing clear conclusions from history for future policy is a far harder task".[126] It is to be anticipated that the task would be even more challenging in Jamaica, given the relative paucity of historical data with any degree of reliability, as against impressionistic conclusions drawn from untested evidence, in a forensic sense.

The assessment of Michael Pinto-Duschinsky, the President of the International Political Science Association's Research Committee on Political Finance and Political Corruption, is instructive in that, in his opinion, "The root problem of British party politics is the precipitous fall in party membership. Further State aid will simply exacerbate this problem."[127]

What then has been the trend in active political party dues-paying membership in Jamaica, especially since the influence on social policy implementation and the consequential severely lessened scope for "pork barrel" type politics[128] due to the budgetary expenditure strictures of the International Financial Institutions after the mid-1970s?

---

126 Ibid. In this regard, see, 'Election director says educate voters to decrease apathy', The Gleaner, Sat. May 30, 2015, p. A4. Such a prescription unsupported by empirical research seeks to treat the symptom. The cause of voter disaffection is not to be gleaned from the popular wisdom of commentators nor the pronouncement of civil society representatives. Historical instances of high voter turn-out need to be identified and analysed, internationally. It is doubtful if the Director's proposed solution, admirably as it is, that. "... voter education and a strong emphasis on civics in schools could help to reduce apathy ... ensure that citizens are aware of their rights and responsibilities towards (sic) the system", would cure the malady.
   It is common knowledge that in countries not lacking an 'educated' electorate, the problem persists. That the Chairman of the ECJ expressed similar sentiments to the press at the same function , the 10th International Electoral Affairs Symposium, held in Jamaica in May 2015, continues to ignore one of the major weaknesses of the ECJ's approach to reform.
   The issue of voter/citizen disengagement from the political process is, we contend, where the focus should properly have been, prior to the attempted design of the reform template. The input of experienced social science researchers, as has been noted elsewhere herein, might well have proved highly beneficial in this respect.

127 Ibid p. 19

128 See 'No more pork barrels? Political parties claim an end to political hand outs', The Jamaica Observer, August 14, 2011, p. 10. See also 'Issues should motivate voters', Jean Lowrie-Chin, The Jamaica Observer, Mon. June 20, 2011, p. 11.

It is common knowledge that the units in the organisational structures which formerly existed for regular "group" (PNP) and "branch" (JLP) membership dues payment have virtually disappeared. Party members who are no longer paying the piper, if they ever did, significantly, are definitely not calling the tune. That privilege now (2013/14) rests with the International Monetary Fund (IMF).

From observation, it is also apparent that, except for special occasions, fundraising activity, especially at the lower levels of the party's structures, is virtually non-existent between, and rare even during elections. This has become more noticeable as the colour and class composition of the membership and voter supporter has taken on an increasingly heterogeneous character and as any real or alleged ideologically-based policy differences have disappeared.

The result of these developments is the metropolitanisation of political relations and activity in which information and communication technology sophistication has been a very significant facilitator.[129] This has no doubt been dysfunctional for fostering or maintaining any semblance of an umbilical relationship between party and member, even in a small island state with a tradition of the personalization of relations, certainly on the political level, including in relatively urban, inner city/ghetto constituencies.

One is entitled to ask, of what use to us is the British scenario as depicted above? If the six year study by the ECJ of the issues involved had been broader and deeper it would have been reasonable to expect some focus on what is clearly a parallel situation in Jamaica. Seeking answers to the reasons for emerging similarities would be likely to yield, one would expect, more efficacious recommendations.

We set out at some length, one specialist observer's experience which might be of some relevance to the Jamaican situation:

> My personal conclusions are that legal reforms may sometimes work ... but frequently prove to be problem-laden. The 2000 Act [the British *Political Parties, Elections and Referendums Act*] certainly appears to fall into the latter category. Its rules about disclosure of donations and spending

---

129 The consequence of these combined developments is the increasing incidence of the constituent's complaint of "not seeing" his/her MP.

limits have forced central party organs to tighten their control over local associations—thus affecting parties' internal structures. Meanwhile the increasing allowances to MPs and councillors have merely served to benefit those already in power ... [130] both in Britain and abroad ... new legislation is, more often than not, beset by pitfalls. For example, unexpected difficulties often arise through the wording of obscure parts of a new Act; when one channel of funding is banned, money flows into political life through other channels[131]; and restrictions on party funding lead to the growth of lobby groups as offshore islands of parties. ...

Yet, above all, laws are of little value if they are not enforced and the enforcement of many of Britain's electoral laws has been minimal. ... The financing crisis ... reflects the public's rapidly diminishing confidence in and support of those who hold political office[132] ... increasing public funding will simply exacerbate the problem, causing greater disillusionment and, in doing so, making parties even less relevant and effective. The gravy train of payments to ... the "political class" is unpopular and rightly so. ... It is expedient for politicians to blame their parties' financial woes[133] on rising costs and then use these to justify more public money for themselves, yet the actual root cause of the problem comes from a very different source.[134]

The authors of such views tend to ignore the fact that a part of the explanation is that free market capitalism in the context of a so-called global economy has exacerbated the process of individualism, as against collectivism, with an accompanying "... increasing sense of aloneness and isolation and [has] imbued him with a feeling of insignificance and powerlessness".[135]

Needless to say, this is reflective of, and a formula for, the alienation and

---

130 This situation is not dissimilar to that in the USA where it has been claimed that "More than two decades of research have established that a major effect of the campaign finance reform of 1974 was to help incumbents ward off challenges": James C. Miller III, 'How Not to Reform Campaign Finance' in the *Hoover Digest*, Winter, 2000. In Jamaica, apart from the usual perquisites of office enjoyed by political office-holders, in the case of MPs there is the Constituency Development Fund available to them for the funding of projects which clearly represent a very considerable promotional advantage over an opposition's "caretaker"/prospective candidate. Money from the public purse given to the opposition party in Parliament in the UK ("Short Money") is relatively small in amount.

131 Thomas E. Mann, in the *Brookings Review*, Winter 1998, pp. 18-21, in relation to the 1996 elections refers to abuses in the United States, such as "the use of conduits to mask impermissible contributions ... improper use of public property ... and issue advocacy to circumvent spending limits ... on publicly funded presidential candidates ..."

132 The Law Commission of Canada reported that "Several commentators have noted a decrease in voter turnout and a general disengagement of the citizenry from traditional political institutions ..." Preface iii.

133 See 'JLP donations dwarf funds collected by PNP', *The Gleaner*, Tue, Nov. 23, 2010, p A3.

134 Pinto-Duschinsky, Michael, in *The BBC History Magazine*, May 2008.

135 Fromm, op. cit., p. 93.

disconnection from national politics and, concomitantly, political parties and indeed trade unions at the institutional level.

Economic crises can only feed the feelings of bewilderment and insecurity, the antidote for which in the more fortunate national populations is acquisitiveness/consumerism, as Fromm, and Tawney before him, recognised.[136]

Fromm notes that:

> Modern man's feeling of isolation and powerlessness is increased still further by the character which all his human relationships have assumed. The concrete relationship between one individual to another has lost its direct and human character and has assumed a spirit of manipulation and instrumentality. In all social and personal relations the laws of the market are the rule.[137]

In essence, what this means is that 'mutual usefulness' rather than cooperation towards mutually beneficial common goal achievement is the order of the day, and a long day it is likely to be.

It is at this point appropriate to focus our attention on what seems to us to be the "actual root cause of the problem", adopting a comparative approach.

Notable for his isolation, among the several commentators on the state of the island's politics, by his seeking to 'benefit from history', is the letter writer, Louis E. A. Moyston,[138] his reference point being the by-election in South West St. Catherine in 2011. This was a by-election that the Opposition PNP party decided against contesting. It is, of course, in this rare case of limited engagement that the party in power and its candidates enjoy the considerable benefit of being able to distribute the "spoils of office,"[139] including the creation of special employment projects in the particular constituency, without the possibility of being, nevertheless, outspent. The overriding desire in such un-rivalled circumstances is to put on a morale boosting, large voter turnout show.

---

136 Tawney, R. H., 'The Acquisitive Society', (London, 1922), G. Bell & Sons Ltd,

137 Fromm, supra. p. 102.

138 Moyston, Louis E. A., 'Learn from political history" The *Jamaica Observer*, Mon. Apr.18, 2011, p. 9.

139 This at the by-election level, is, of course, the same situation multiplied and widened so as to apply more comprehensively at the national level at general elections, giving rise to the term "election budget;" James C. Miller III, supra, argues further through use of the perquisites of office, free media coverage [especially in the case of MPs and party leaders in Jamaica] ... personal contacts ... Thus any measure that makes it more difficult for candidates to raise money or spend their own actually hurts challengers more than incumbents [who] amass enormous war chests from vested interests [and whose party colleagues] ... also make sure a full menu of pork is available".

Moyston, having followed the post-by-election analyses, suggests that some of the lessons from history include the fact that,

> in 1944 the PNP did not contest all the seats … organisational capacity is important in contesting elections … [to] ensure the generation of votes … there must be extensive work in relation to public/political education to make people understand what they stand for. … But political activity is work, very hard work … you have to be prepared to work for those votes.[140]

THROWING MONEY (AND LEGISLATION) AWAY

To some, the view of those who endorse state funding reflect, whatever their intentions and expectations, little more than the hope that throwing not only money but legislation at this kind of problem will prove a cure for what are really mere symptoms.[141]

There has, as far as can be discerned, been no indication of the extent of the public funds, in total, that is contemplated over any particular period. It is not just the administrative and party-building and development expenses of the parties which register that are to be partly funded, but also their campaign costs.

In what appears to be completely arbitrary, given the absence of explanatory computations, the ECJ's Report states that, "State funding for political parties should not exceed 40% of the total income of a political party in any single year".[142] It could well be, however, that it is the party raising the least funds which 'deserves' the most public funding, if the 'level playing field' notion is to be meaningful. In the legislation proposed, there is no attempt to justify what will surely be a heavy additional burden on the taxpayer,[143] (who is already among the most highly taxed in the world), except, reference to "… the danger to be avoided," which is the exercise of influence on party decisions by individuals or organisations in relation to the size of their financial contribution. The "remedy" of any perceived 'mischief' here, can

---

140 Louis E. A Moyston, supra

141 See James C. Miller III supra

142 See, *The Gleaner*, Oct 3, 2010, p. F5, 'Independent Commissioners Did Not Cave In'

143 The reason given by the JLP (the governing party at the time) for being initially against public funding was said to be the "current situation of the Government," as explained by the Chairman of the ECJ. Opponents of the "Clean Elections" movement in the United States have similarly based their arguments on the context of states' struggles with budget deficits: see Hoover Institution, Public Policy Inquiry, Campaign Finance, Reform Proposals <http://www.campaignfinancesetc.org/proposals/clean7.html>

clearly not entirely be the need for transparency, with or without donation caps.

Knowing the identity of large donors can, by itself, obviously not prevent the exercise of 'undue' influence. If the case is a genuine consensus of view as to the appropriate decision to be made or policy option to be chosen as between the substantial contributor and the party, what conclusion is to be drawn? The irony is that it is almost as if one should expect a large financial supporter in respect to any other area of need, to provide that support to an individual or entity whose decisions or policies the contributing individual or organisation opposes.[144]

Has any attempt been made to study if, and to what extent, the improper influence of money has been a determining factor in "questionable" decisions, or policies adopted, in this context?[145] If not, isn't the ECJ merely pandering to gossip, rumour and suspicion? Has a 'before' and 'after' exercise been planned, so as to assess the extent of change resulting from the passage and implementation of the contemplated political finance legislation? What is likely to be the design of the change measurement instrument?

Without the benefit of formal study, however rudimentary or inconclusive the findings, it is stated by the Commission that, "*Accordingly*, the limit of the contribution of any individual or organisation to a political party should not exceed one fortieth of the total income of that party in any single year."[146] Again, there is no explanation whatever as to how this formula is arrived at. One trusts that this is not due to any strong irrationally felt need for consistency, reflecting a fixation on the number 'forty', as seems evident from our reference to another similarly quantitatively limited proposal below.

---

144 The ECJ itself expects private financial support to reflect agreement on ideological principles, policies, personality and quality of proposed office holders, at p. 8 of its Report.

145 Two situations which seem to fall in this category are: 1. The alleged 'sweetheart deal' involving a financial institution, Dehring Bunting & Golding (DB & G), in which two of its Directors currently the General Secretary and Senator of the Opposition PNP (See *the Gleaner* Fri May 13, 2011, p. 1, 'Golding Blasts Show for Sweetheart Deal' claim, and 2. The sale of the Whitehouse hotel to Gordon Stewart's Company in which it was intimated that it was not only being sold substantially below value, and certainly the cost to build (being virtually of new construction) but, further, the present government was allegedly to lend the purchasers U$32.5 million to facilitate the transaction. Subject to the findings of any objective investigation, it would also be interesting to know if either of these two companies or shareholders are or were at relevant times substantial financial contributors to either party or indeed both. It is well known that some individuals or organisations do indeed contribute to both parties. (See *the Gleaner* Jan 16, 2011, pp. C 1 and 3 and C6). Stewart responded through the medium of the editorial of 'his' newspaper, The *Jamaica Observer*, Tue Jan 18, 2011, p. 8, 'Stop the pettifogging over the Whitehouse Hotel.' The Trafigura scandal was of the dimension to deserve more than casual reference.

146 ECJ Report, p. 9

Assuming that the established two main parties, which have alternated as government since 1944, will raise more funds and obtain larger contributions than any third party, at least initially, one is entitled to inquire how such an apparently arbitrary non-discriminating ratio can possibly help to 'level the playing field'. One may assess the merit of the proposal against the Commission's other proposal that state funding be limited to *forty per cent* of a party's annual income. The Commission, at the same time, says that through its budget it will recommend to Parliament, "The *total* [Italics added] amount to be allotted for the support of political parties".[147] It would seem that the parties will be paid state funding 'in arrears', one year, at least, after computing income *achieved*, as against *projected* income,

To make matters even less comprehensible, we are told that "The amount approved by Parliament shall be divided *equally* [Italics added] …"[148] among approved parties, which appears to assume that the incomes earned will be of an identical amount.

This 'even-handed' approach does not seem to be designed to produce equality at the candidate expenditure level[149], and certainly not to achieve one of the six objectives of Canadian electoral reform, that of "… promoting the equality and efficacy of the vote,"[150] by way of laws ensuring "… fair or equitable electoral participation or outcomes".[151] The ECJ's approach seems certain to achieve a maintenance of whatever financing differentials exist between the parties, as against the goal, even if utopian, of "… ensuring that all citizens have their views equally heard and considered in political institutions[152], through the mechanisms of campaign finance regulations which result in ensuring equal political influence for all".[153]

---

147 Ibid

148 Ibid. For example, see Stephen Castle, 'Britain's Campaign Finance Laws Leaves Parties with Idle Money', *The New York Times*, May 4, 2015.

149 Jay Makarenko, supra, p. 8; It is to be noted that under the Canadian approach, which has sought to control expenditure by the imposition of limits, these are based on factors such as constituency population densities, and number of electors, with election spending limits for parties being calculated by multiplying $0.70 (adjusted for inflation) by the number of voters on the voter's list, where a party has a candidate in a constituency. A further feature is that the party's candidate must receive at least 2% of valid votes cast in an election in a constituency. A candidate must get 5% of the votes if the party is to secure a reimbursement.

150 Ibid p. 3

151 Ibid p. 12

152 Ibid

153 Ibid

Good intentions prompting the introduction of laws, even with timely and seemingly appropriate amendments, do not, on the basis of the Canadian experience, necessarily guarantee the objective of a level playing field. Under the *Canadian Election Amendments Act of 2003*, it was found, for example:

> With respect to revenues, the new campaign finance regime has been challenging for some political parties, while highly beneficial for others. The Liberal and New Democratic parties, for example, were traditionally dependent on corporate and labour contributions, respectively. With the tighter restrictions on, and eventual ban of, these sources of revenue both parties have lost significant portions of their customary income. Moreover, neither has been able to make up the shortfall through increases in individual contributions. ... The Conservative Party which benefited greatly from the campaign finance regime ... traditionally enjoyed a large individual contribution base, which has not been restricted by campaign finance laws. The Conservatives have been so successful at collecting individual contributions, that public financial support represents a relatively small portion of their overall revenues.[154]

Against the background of such an experience, one can seriously ask whether the end result of this kind of interference with the forces in the political marketplace is not to purge parties of their truly democratic function: representing class and interest-differentiated demographic segments of the population.

The conversion to the idea of substantial state funded politics is likely to result in institutional transformation in which parties increasingly display oligarchic features. This will be facilitated by a system where the political pioneering spirit has atrophied and where charisma in leadership is, save for the odd exception, not sought nor likely to emerge. The tendency to managerialism, and the consequences for countries at different stages of development, at the ideological level, politically and economically, and the implications for the legal system, warrant critical assessment.

Another significant consequence of the Canadian public funding regime has been the impact on smaller parties, such as the regional party, Bloc Québécois (BQ), which puts up candidates in Quebec only, and the special interest Green Party. In BQ's case, prior to the introduction of changes in the spending limits, not much income was obtained from corporate or union

---

154 Ibid p. 13

sources. Receipt of public money has meant that there is virtually no need for the party to raise funds privately to cover operational or campaign costs. This seems to amount to stripping politics of one of its core defining features: the payment of membership dues and making of donations by those who believe in and share a party's vision, policies and programmes.

Immediately, the seemingly legitimate question arises: if a citizen is not a supporter of either BQ's platform or a sympathizer of the Green Party's agenda, why should his/her tax dollar be used to support them? A particular taxpayer/elector may, in fact, hold very strongly opposed views to either or, indeed, both.

In contrast to the BQ situation, the effect of the changes on the Green Party has been that, having met the qualification criteria for state funding in time for the 2004 election, "… it has been able to expand and professionalize its operations, and raise its national profile".[155] Such results, it has been said, "… suggests greater competitiveness between political parties … [and] a closing of the gap … in terms of what they spend on election activities".[156]

The danger of basing 'one-size-fits-all' type legislative policy proposals on simplistic populist phrases such as "level playing field" becomes apparent.[157] Achievement of such "objectives," without regard for meaningful elaboration, and contextual justification, makes the use here of words such as "competitiveness" highly questionable, if not altogether inappropriate in a discussion of democratic political issues.

James C. Miller III, in emphasizing what not to do in reforming the way the United States finances political campaigns, makes the point that:

---

155 Ibid

156 Ibid

157 In the daily newspaper, *USA Today* of Tue. May 24, 2011, at p. 2A in comparing the fundraising capabilities of two of the possible Republican Presidential Candidates for the 2012 election, it was reported that Texan Ron Paul had "tapped his e-mail list of 700,000 people to raise $1.1 million in one day, earlier this month". Paul's spokesman put it this way: "We don't have the access to Wall Street bankers and big corporate money that Mitt Romney has, but as far as contributions from regular grassroots Americans … Ron [Paul] is unmatched."

The excesses that have given rise to the current public controversy[158] over campaign practices are mere symptoms of the anticompetitive and deceptive features of the political marketplace ... a major effect of the campaign finance reforms of 1974 was to help incumbents ward off challenges ... Thus any measure that makes it more difficult for the candidate to raise money or spend their own hurts challengers more than incumbents.[159]

As is the case with commercial markets, in the political arena it is not surprising that parties, candidates and other participants "circumvent competitive restraints" and find ways over, through and around financial restraints by,

The illegal use and misreporting of campaign contribution ... bundling contributions through Political Action Committees (PACs) and the use of so-called 'soft money' contributions",[160] ['soft money' being funds purportedly designated for 'party-building' as against campaigning activities.]

Miller argues that the then *McCain-Feingold/Shays-Meehan Campaign Finance Bill* was a "misguided attack on the symptoms", since,

by banning soft money, by treating any ad that uses a candidate's name or likeness as a political expenditure (and therefore subject to more stringent regulation) and by strengthening reporting requirements, giving the Federal Election Commission more enforcement tools, and increasing

---

158 *The New York Times* of Thur. May 2011, at p. A16 in an article headed "Edwards Faces Likely Charges of Misusing Election Funds", reported: "The Justice Department is planning to charge Mr. Edwards [former senator who twice ran for U.S president] with violating campaign finance laws; Prosecutors say he used money that should have been reported as campaign donations to cover up the affair, which produced a child, wrecked his marriage and ended his political career. On the same page, the carried a report of the trial of former US Governor, Rod R. Blagojevich, of Illinois, who was charged and 'being tried for the second time, after a hung jury trial previously, based on the allegation of "trying to sell the Senate seat for campaign donations or job offers".

159   A political scientist at Carleton College in Northfield Minnesota, U.S.A., is reported as saying, "at this point, the president (Barack Obama) just has to have a steady flow that approximates what he had four years ago, whereas all the Republicans need money now," in USA TODAY, Tue. May 24, 2011, p.2A. The Report further stated that "The early front runner in the Republican [Presidential Candidate] cash race is former Massachusetts Governor Mitt Romney ... a multimillionaire who pumped more than $40 million of his own money into the last presidential election" [Romney was not on the Republican ticket in 2008]. "Romney announced raising over $10.25 million during a single day last week through a call-in fundraising marathon," the newspaper article further reported. It is worth emphasis that the eventual Republican Presidential Candidate in 2008 raised less than contender Romney and New York-Mayor Giuliani; Hillary Clinton "who tapped a vast donor network built during her husband's presidential campaign, also outraised Obama in the early months of 2007."

160   James C. Miller III, supra, p.2. , The reasons given for these developments are two-fold: firstly the absence of built-in automatic limit adjustment to reflect the effect of inflation, and, secondly, "as incumbents have found more ways to insulate themselves from competition, it takes more money to mount a credible challenge".

penalties, the bill would further strengthen incumbents over challengers[161] ... by barring party expenditures on behalf of candidates who do not limit expenditures from their own pockets to $50, 000, the bill would cut down on what recently has been one of the few avenues for successful challenges – the self-financed candidate.[162]

The partisan politicizing of funding issues became apparent in Canada in 2008. The Conservative minority Government proposed to significantly reduce state subsidies to political parties under the *Canadian Elections Act*, the justification being a saving to the taxpayer of some $30 million dollars per year. In order to prevent the fall of his government, Stephen Harper, the then Prime Minister, was, however, forced to withdraw the controversial measure in the face of fierce resistance by the Opposition parties.

The self-serving purpose of Harper's Conservative proposal becomes clear when one examines the figures representing public funding as a percentage of total income for the parties in 2007 which shows:

Bloc Québécois 86%, Green Party 65%, Liberal Party 63%, New Democratic Party 57% and Conservative Party 37%.[163]

If one accepts that the creation of a 'level playing field' is a legitimate electoral policy objective, which we do not, then the different levels of state subsidy, by way of *reimbursement* under the Canadian system, is, on the face of it, understandable. On the other hand, the ECJ's proposed subsidy of forty per cent of a party's annual income defies rationality and the realities of 'on the ground' political financing in the island.

Since the Commission's Report makes no reference to 'estimated' income, this implies a refund of money, based, presumably, on the acceptance of audited annual financial statements.

---

161 For a contrary theoretical position, based on empirical research findings, however, see Thomas Stratmann and Francisco J. Aparico-Castillo, 'Campaign finance reform and electoral competition : Comment in Public Choice (2007) 133 pp. 107 -110, where the authors point out that "In these regressions the endogeneity problem occurs in part because legislators may change the law in order to increase their election chances ... when a party has a large advantage [size of the state assembly majority] the current campaign finance regime presumably works in favour of that party, and that in this case the party is less likely to implement a change in campaign finance laws." See also James C. Miller III, supra, where Miller writes that "Analysis of the series of votes leading up to the 1974 reform indicates that the votes of individual Members of Congress were driven by cold calculations regarding which version [of campaign finance reform proposals] would help them most in their efforts to be re-elected".

162 James C. Miller III, supra, p.3

163 Jay Makarenko, supra pp. 8-9

This brings into question the inevitable lag involved between the time of any strategic political need for funding and the processing of accounting data to actual disbursement. But if public funding is so critically required by the parties, how can they be expected to spend what it is being posited that they do not have and cannot obtain, without issues being raised about 'tainted money' and the 'buying of favours and influence'.

The answer would seem to be that state funding would, given the reality of the operational mechanics of 'on the ground' political financing, have to be paid in advance. This could mean the use of the previous years' party's income for the purpose of applying the subsidy ratio.

For election year expenditure, to put it mildly, that might clearly be disastrous, politically. This is quite apart from the fact that any year may have just happened to have been particularly good or bad in fundraising terms.

Taking into account the implications of the electoral cycle for party expenditure, for any number of reasons hinged on gaining a competitive advantage, a party may wish, at short notice, to significantly alter its public relations campaign strategy. This may have considerable consequences for its current fundraising and expenditure plans, whereas public funding, as proposed, would only be available sometime later. This could easily result in an instance of "opportunity missed", which could prove tactically decisive.

If state subsidy is not paid in advance, are the parties which qualify to obtain a loan, perhaps to meet pre-subsidy disbursement needs, assuming that all the parties can get one, to meet the "shortfall", between the statutory expenditure limit and income, to be repaid, with or without interest, from the state subsidy when subsequently received? The question raised is by no means intended to be facetious. For any new party, the problem anticipated is likely to be very real. Getting money from governments has never been easy and is likely to get even more difficult in the prevailing national economic circumstances constrained as they are within the grip of the IMF's vice.

CHAPTER 2
REGISTRATION TO QUALIFY
FOR PUBLIC MONEY

Registration as a prerequisite for state funding involves the "finding" of at least five hundred members[164] in good standing. In Canada, with a population of thirty-four million compared to Jamaica's two million plus, the requirement is for parties to regularly show that they have at least two hundred and fifty members in order to maintain registered status and thus be eligible for state funding.[165] As against the ECJ's five hundred threshold, the head of the then ten month old New Nation Coalition, (NNC), is reported by one of the island's daily newspapers to have been "getting ready for 50,000[166] signature drive". The party's leader is quoted as saying, "We are going to undertake this big drive *because it is necessary for us to get state funding* [Italics added] so that we can be recognised as a political movement."[167]

A leading Canadian case is of some interest here. *Figueroa v Canada (Attorney General)*[168] is a Supreme Court of Canada decision on the right to participate in a federal election under section 3 of the *Canadian Charter of Rights and Freedoms*. The nomination threshold laid down by sections 24 and 28 of the *Canada Elections Act* was challenged on the grounds that it violated the Charter-established right to vote. The Court struck down the provision which required a political party to nominate at least fifty candidates before it could receive certain benefits, some of which were financial. It was held that withholding the right to issue tax-deductible receipts and to retain unspent election funds from candidates of parties that have not met the required nomination threshold, undermines the right of citizens to meaningful participation in the electoral process; the offending provision was thus deemed unconstitutional.

---

164 ECJ Report, p. 4

165 'Political Financing and Enforcement Under the *Canada Elections Act*, Elections Canada, July 2006 p.5

166 This reported figure is against that of 500 contained in the ECJ Report, at p. 4

167 Mark Cummings reporting in the **Jamaica Observer**, Tue. May 17, 2011, p. 6, 'Blaine's NNC getting ready for 50,000 signature drive.'

168 [2003] 1 S.C.R. 912

The possible operational effect of the ECJ's registration scheme is disclosed by the subsequent comments of the NNC party leader:

> Originally we were told that the persons signing would have to be on the voters list but that was clarified so anybody under [*sic*] 18 who has a national ID, whether it's a passport, driver's licence or electoral ID can sign and so we expect to get along very, very well with the process.[169]

A sublime element is then introduced, "I expect to get a lot of signatures from the churches. I am a Christian".[170]

In promoting the new political entity, the NNC, the task of mobilizing support is made to appear as an adjunct to the 'necessary' quest for public funding, since, as is reported, "... she argued that the process of obtaining the signatures would allow members of the coalition to face off with people and to encourage people to support us and to get them to know us".[171]

Some might regard this as a clear case of 'abuse of process'.

The ECJ Report does not make it clear whether parties seeking to be registered, so as to be able to have the opportunity to access state funds, must provide in their constitutions the officer and political representative selection procedures for all constituencies or all constituencies to be contested by the party.[172] In this regard, we are further informed that "... the party [NNC] intends to contest *all* [Italics added] the parliamentary seats, whenever the next national polls are held."[173] This, intention must be set, for disclosure of the reasoning behind it, against the party's then very recent performance in a single by-election contested by the *party leader* herself who, the report further informs us, "... fail[ed] miserably in her bid to represent the constituency. ..." Again, in a search for motive, it is worth reminding that this new party's level of electoral participation is contemplated in a political system where there is no fixed election date, nor even a pre-determined mandatory maximum period between elections, the calling of an election

---

169 Mark Cummings, supra.
170 Ibid
171 Ibid
172 ECJ Report (vii), p. 5
173 Mark Cummings, supra.

being entirely at the discretion of the Prime Minister.[174]

We have spent some time on this particular matter because it is not readily conceivable that the average citizen would agree for his/her taxes to be used to support this kind of political enterprise. This is especially so, when the ECJ requires only a qualifying "... declaration that the party *intends* [Italics added] to contest at least *one* [Italics added] election".[175] So what if the election that is in contemplation is the one *after* the next one due? In fact good sense could well justify funding in the interim, so as to enable the party to be properly ready to face the electorate, then, particularly, of course, in the case of a new party.[176]

It may be worth repeating that political parties—despite their importance as vehicles of governance, and their unchallenged role in national policy formulation and implementation—are by their very nature and essence, private voluntary organisations. This, we are well aware, does not accord with the current 'enlightened' view among opinion leaders.[177] The problems allegedly associated with their funding in Jamaica do not justify the claim that there is any persistent or inevitable "... deficit between available resources and the demands and needs of representation".[178] No data is presented, whether obtained from the parties or even by an educated guess, to substantiate this bold, seemingly fact-based, statement.

Even if one were to accept, for the purpose of argument, that the existence

---

174 This also affects the soundness of the ECJ provision, somewhat misplaced under the heading disclosure by political parties and their contributors, on p. 11, to the effect that statutory bodies are prohibited from "covertly using its resources in the year prior to a General Election" in advancing the political interests of the governing party..

175 ECJ Report, (f), p. 5

176 This at present is a mandatory requirement for new parties, since the alternative requirement for registration and state funding is receiving "five per cent of the votes cast at the previous General Election"; See Gary Spaulding, 'ECJ rolls out plans to address campaign financing', *The Gleaner*, Thur. Sept. 2, 2010, p. A4. ... See also Linton P. Gordon, 'Protecting the trough', where Linton likens the parties not so much to 'gangs', a description he does not find unacceptable, but to 'Political pigs, JLP and PNP, in bed together', *The Gleaner*, Fri. June 3, 2011, at p. A9, in which it is argued that, "It is good to the extent that it is an insurance against dictatorship ... on the other hand, it is a hindrance to the development of third parties and the emergence and survival of independent thinkers, in particular those not aligned to either of the tribes". The point is made that even in landslide election victories each of these two established major parties receive no less than 40% of votes cast. In their mutually self-serving interest, the allegation is that "The tribes are united against Greg Christie [the Contractor General] because of the threat he poses to their access to the trough ..." The relevance of such observations to the ECJ task is obvious.

177 See, 'Holness for campaign financing but ... ' *The Jamaica Observer*, May 5, 2013, p. 26; also PNP Policy Commission Document on 'Regulation of Political Party and Finance in Jamaica', mimeo, August 22, 2005, p1

178 ECJ Report p.9

of this "deficit" is a persistent feature of the financing of political parties, what is, in principle, wrong with this gap being filled by loans,[179] whether from supporters or financial institutions, graduated dues or from more creative/ aggressive fundraising activity, including different forms of investment? As an example of the extent to which benefit may be derived from institutional commitment, as is well known, some religious denominations require their members to pay, as a "tithe", a certain percentage of their income, usually ten per cent, towards the maintenance of their organisation. Perhaps, though, the prospect of benefits coming from church support is seen to be greater in the future, if not the present.

Widespread negative public portrayal of the nature of the Island's political culture, which place hurdles in the way of successful fundraising activity, was confirmed by a joint University opinion survey,[180] which revealed that: (a) only approximately 42% of those surveyed had confidence in/regard for the institution of Government, a drop of some 80% from two years before (b) trust in Parliament was down seven percentage points to 40% (c) and, perhaps of more direct relevance, "faith [sic] in the credibility of political parties" was down from 41.4 % to 33.5% and (d) the credibility of the office of Prime Minister had fallen fourteen points to 39%, as against 66% for the army, with a rather surprisingly high one-third of the sample not being overly disturbed by the very unlikely prospect of a military coup.[181] With the possibility of a coup being extremely remote, it would be foolish to be too concerned about it occurring: evidence of the latent intelligence of the electorate, perhaps?

Despite this, to the extent that politicians and their parties are "forced" to raise funds to finance housekeeping expenses and planned campaign activity, advisedly within budgeted limits, to that extent would they be "forced" to increase their appeal to prospective sources of funding, including dues-paying members. The presumption is, of course, that a variant of the

---

179 See the eventual ECJ recommendations at p.70 below.

180 See The Gleaner, Editorial, Fri. Apr. 8, 2011, p. A6

181 Results of the joint University of the West Indies, Mona, Jamaica and Vanderbilt University, USA, study on attitudes towards democracy in Jamaica, reported in 'How the gangs of Gordon House might rescue themselves', The Gleaner, editorial, Fri. Apr. 8, 2011, p. A6

"cash for honours"[182] scandal in England would not be replicated, given the extensive reporting on that matter. It may not be too much to expect that the very negative publicity attending such political behaviour will have some inhibiting effect on others who might otherwise have adopted a similar income earning method.

Even at quite a late stage of the discussion of its Report, the ECJ was accused, and, in particular its independent members, of having "… caved in to the regulatory preferences of the politicians. …"[183] The reason suggested for this alleged contemptible conduct was that the ECJ was "under pressure to reach some sort of compromise agreement rather than no agreement at all", and, further, that,

> Failure to have an agreement because of the unwillingness of the politicians to agree to a [full] transparency measure necessary (if not sufficient) to substantially reduce corruption would have surely resulted in public shame

---

182 'Cash for Peerages' , or 'Loans for Honours or Peerages', were the names given by some in the media to a political scandal in the United Kingdom in 2006 and 2007 concerning the connection between political donations [same as, or ostensibly in the form of loans] and the award of life peerages: See, George Jones, 'Cronyism inquiry holds up new peers', *Daily Telegraph*, Dec. 27, 2005; Phillipe Haughton, 'Criminal probe into cash for peerages controversy', *The Times* Mar. 21, 2006; Marie Wolf 'Labour 'bankrupted' by secret loans'. The Independent, Feb. 4,2007; Greg Hurst, 'Sleaze now as election donors get peerages', The Times, Nov. 8, 2005; 'Money Talks: Twelve Angry Men and one Shame-Faced Prime Minister', *The Independent*, Mar. 26, 2006; Rajeev Syal; 'Your secret loan can stay secret, labour party donors were told', *The Times* (London) Mar. 24, 2006; Colin Brown, 'Developers tower block approved after £200,000 donation to Labour', *The Independent*, Mar. 25, 2006; Webster Philip, 'Backers repaid to stay secret will be named by Tories'; *The Times*, Apr. 3, 2006; 'Email mole' led to aide's [PM Tony Blair's aide] arrest', *The Guardian*, Jan. 21, 2007; 'Honours Police arrest Lord Levy', BBC, Jan 31, 2007; Patrick Wintour, 'Detective reveals how Downing Street hindered honours inquiry', *The Guardian*, Oct. 24, 2007; Gaby Hissliff, 'No. 10 admits link between schools donors and peerages', The Jamaica Observer, Apr. 16, 2006; 'Secret party loans to be banned', *BBC* Mar. 20, 2006; 'Tories' will not name key backers', *BBC*, Mar 20, 2006.

183 For one outspoken politician's views on the ECJ and its work, see Daraine Linton, 'Warmington takes swing at electoral body', *The Gleaner*, Thur. Nov. 4, 2010, p.A10. The senior staff reporter quotes the MP as saying in Parliament, in reference to the ECJ. "There is an organisation, a commission that behaves like they are crown princes and emperors. They believe that whatever they say is law … if you find errors in their reports or recommendations and you bring it to their attention, what you get from the commission is that you must amend the law of Jamaica to take in their recommendation. Parliament is the supreme body and there should not be any organisations or groups that dictate to this House". On reporting the negative responses to the ECJ recommendations, "'The Gavel", being a leading Parliamentary reporter and commentator, details several areas of concerns as follows: the convention that Parliament adopts ECJ recommendations without amendment means that, the hands of legislations are tied … irrespective of how unsound proposals are; in seeking to take on a judicial function, it recommends that in addition to any penalty imposed by a court, the person in breach "shall be liable to pay a monetary penalty to the Electoral Commission", whose emphasis at the initial stages of reform we argue should be one of providing guidance. This purported judicial function relates to infringements concerning impermissible donation; in the latter case the ECJ might order forfeiture (in addition to a court order) "The Gavel" ends the piece, "However, it would be a dark day for democracy if Jamaica travels along some of the routes the ECJ is proposing to take us as the 'don't criticize us' attitude of Tavares-Finson is a worrying sign, we have no choice but to accept the commission's dictates", *The Gleaner*, Mon. April 16, 2012, p. A 6. It is to be noted that even at this very late stage, the leader of the Opposition feels that "more consultation and public sensitization may be necessary", The *Jamaica Observer*, May 5, 2013, p.26

being cried on the politicians ... [184]

Even if one agrees with Espeut's argumentation,[185] —the role played by 'techniques of neutralization', which can effectively free the delinquent from any sense of guilt and shame is under-emphasized. This is but a testament to the usually underestimated inherent complexity of this particular reform issue: 'yet unusually hard criteria are applied quite precipitately in what might best be regarded as social reform *experiments*' [Italics added].[186]

Of some significance here is the fact that Parliament has so far failed to entrench the Commission in the Jamaican Constitution, despite the fact that it (the Commission) "... had been unrelenting in its effort"[187] to have this done.

This seemingly ambivalent politician's stance on the ECJ has not escaped the attention of Professor Trevor Munroe, Executive Director of the National Integrity Action. In addressing the Chairman's club meeting of the Private Sector Organisation of Jamaica (PSOJ) he alerted his audience to the fact that there would be a "push back" by corrupt elements in both politics and the business sector against advances made, and contemplated, to put an end to corrupt activities. Munroe is reported as stating that,

> Also under pressure is Chairman of the Electoral Commission of Jamaica, Professor Errol Miller, as there are two motions on the order paper of Parliament attacking him and 'seeking to discredit the ECJ as a whole'.[188]

This, allegedly, because of the ECJ's recommendations on political finance disclosure. As it would later emerge, it would be 'attacked' on aspects of its framework even more fundamental to the *quid pro quo* 'logic' of its scheme. As will become apparent, law, *per se,* should not be expected to surmount hurdles which would have better been confronted, if not removed,

---

184 Espeut, Peter, 'The Shame Remains' [on the independent members of the ECJ, for allegedly having 'caved in to the wishes of the politicians]', *The Gleaner*, Fri. Sept. 24, 2010, p.A9

185 Espeut 'Shame PSOJ', *The Gleaner*, Fri. June 25, 2010, p. A, 9. And 'Ethically Challenged', *The Gleaner*, Fri. Sept. 27, 2013, p. A. 9.

186 Downes, David,, and Rock, Paul, 'Understanding Deviance', Oxford University Press, 6 ed., (UK, 2011), p. 350

187 The Senior Staff Reporter, Gary Spaulding, noted that this omission "had not escaped [sic] members of the Commission" whose Chairman had produced documentary evidence of their effort in this respect, *The Gleaner,* Thur. Sept. 2, 2012, p.A4

188 Luke Douglas, 'Expect resistance to anti-corruption measures, says Munroe', The *Jamaica Observer*, Wed. June 1, 2011, p.5, The ECJ's Chairperson, Dr. Herbert Thompson, after his 'forced' recent resignation (August 2013) to the consternation of those interested in these matters accused persons, in what was clearly intended as a reference to the JLP, of attempting to 'destroy the ECJ', The *Jamaica Observer*, Wed. Oct 2, 2013, pp. 1, 4.

in the prior process of consultation. When this is not the case, the whole reform initiative and process is likely to be little more than a charade, and the regulatory edifice constructed, more of a facade than providing the impulse to positive behaviour/action change it ought, at best, to represent.

Chapter 3
ECJ Recommendations
on Campaign Financing[189]
Sources of Contributions
and Donations

Legal entities, natural persons, State Funds and a National Election Campaign Fund to be established and operated by the Electoral Commission are the sources from which contributions and donations may be made to candidates and/or political parties.

This National Election Campaign Fund may be replenished by individuals, legal entities and Jamaican Diaspora groups wishing to support the democratic process in Jamaica but not desiring to contribute directly to a particular candidate or named political party. Impermissible donors include:

(a) Foreign or Commonwealth Governments or their Agents or Agencies, whether directly or indirectly.

    i.   No political party, member of a political party, or candidate, shall accept any donation from Foreign or Commonwealth states whether directly from the donor, or, indirectly, through a third person (natural or legal).

    ii.   Any donation accepted by a member of a political party shall be deemed to be accepted by the political party, unless the member wilfully fails to disclose to the political party, in which case the member shall be liable for prosecution.

    iii.   A political party, or member of a political party, or candidate, shall be deemed not to have accepted a donation if within thirty days of

---

189 Source: *The Gleaner*, Wed. May 9, 2012, p. A4 and Thu. May 10, 2012, p. A11.
The more important of these proposals, from the point of view of any principle involved, have been addressed throughout by the writer, as well as of those drawn from a survey of the literature. Additional comments as appear necessary, are set out at p. 79 below.

receiving the donation, the party, or member, or candidate, returns the donation to the donor.

(b) Public institutions, statutory bodies, government and quasi-government organisations or any company with government capital shares regardless of the size of such shares.

(c) Private companies performing a public service pursuant to a contract with a Government body or public office, whether as principals or subcontractors, in circumstances where such contracts came into force within a period of one year prior to, or within a period of one year subsequent to, the making of a donation unless such donation is made subject to full disclosure.

(d) Enterprises and other organisations exercising public authority.

(e) Legal entities with due but unsettled payments to public revenue (i.e. companies and other entities that are not tax compliant).

(f) Donations passed through an intermediary or falsely reported in the name of another person or entity.

(g) Unregulated Financial Institutions.

A legal or natural person providing services or selling a product to a candidate or political party shall make out an invoice, showing the market value of the services or product, to that candidate or that political party, regardless of who is liable for payment for the services or product or whether the services were provided or the product given free of charge.

ECJ PROPOSED LIMITS ON CONTRIBUTIONS/DONATIONS TO CANDIDATES AND POLITICAL PARTIES

1. The total amount of contribution/donation given by a donor shall not exceed in a single campaign period an amount of $1 million to a single candidate, or an amount of $1 million multiplied by the number of constituencies being contested by a political party, provided that the total amount given to all candidates and all political parties does not exceed $10,000,000.

2. Any contribution/donation that is made by a permissible donor shall be regarded as a tax-deductible expense.

3. Any contribution/donation made by a donor must be accompanied by a declaration to the candidate or political party stating the full name, address, occupation or nature of business and that the donor qualifies to make a donation under the regulations. A person, whether legal or natural, who knowingly, or recklessly, makes a false declaration commits an offence.

4. A political party, or a candidate, shall not accept any contribution/donation from an impermissible donor.

5. A person who knowingly makes a contribution/donation to a candidate or political party which includes a contribution from an impermissible donor shall commit an offence.

6. A contribution/donation is accepted by a candidate if it is received and retained by the candidate for the purposes of his or her campaign activities and cannot be used for personal, family or business expenses.

7. A contribution/donation is accepted by a political party if it is received and retained by the political party for campaign expenses and cannot be used for the regular operations of the party.

8. Where a contribution/donation is accepted, the political party, or the candidate, shall issue a receipt for the donation to the donor in the form prescribed by the Electoral Commission.

9. Where in relation to a political party or a candidate:

> (a) money is lent otherwise than on commercial terms; or

> (b) any property, services or facilities are provided otherwise than on commercial terms, the value of the donation shall be taken to be the amount representing the difference between the actual cost and the cost that would have been incurred by the political party, or the candidate, as the case may be, had the loan been made, or the property, services or facilities been provided on commercial terms.

10. Where a contribution/donation is received by a political party, or a candidate, and it is not immediately clear that the political party should refuse the contribution/donation, all reasonable steps shall be taken without delay by, or on behalf of, the political party or candidate to verify or ascertain:

> (a) the identity of the donor

(b) whether the donor is a permissible donor; and

(c) if the donor is a permissible donor, all such details in respect of the donor as may be required by the Electoral Commission to be received and given in respect of the donor in the donation report.

11. Where a political party or a candidate receives a contribution/donation from an impermissible donor, the donation or an equivalent amount must be returned within 30 days.

12. Any contribution/donation received whose donor is anonymous or unidentifiable shall:

(a) if the donor has used a facility provided by an identifiable financial institution, be returned to that financial institution; or, otherwise,

(b) be sent to the Accountant General for lodgement to the Consolidated Fund.

13. Where a contribution/donation which is disallowed has been knowingly accepted by a political party or candidate and not timely [*sic*] returned in accordance with Paragraph 10 above, the Electoral Commission may, in addition to any other penalty that may be imposed by a Court of law, order the forfeiture of such contribution/donation.

14. Every political party and each candidate shall submit separately, to the Electoral Commission during a campaign period, monthly reports of contributions/donations received giving all such details in respect of each donor as may be required by the Electoral Commission.

15. A candidate contesting an election shall, within six weeks of Election Day, submit to the Electoral Commission a consolidated report, in the prescribed form, detailing all contributions/donations received within the campaign period. In addition, every candidate shall submit to the Electoral Commission a declaration in the prescribed form stating that, to the best of his or her knowledge and belief:

(a) No contribution/donation from a person who is not a permissible donor has been accepted by him or her during the campaign period.

(b) No anonymous contributions/donations have been accepted by him or her during the campaign period.

16. Upon receipt of a contribution/donation report and declaration the Electoral Commission, shall no later than 21 days issue the candidate concerned with a certificate stating that the person has complied.

17. The interpretation of the word "donor" as used in the context of these provisions is intended to accord with the definition of the term "connected persons" as used in the *Banking Act* and also with the definition of the word "affiliated" as used in the *Companies Act*.

18. Submission of this report does not relieve a candidate of the responsibility to submit an election expense report within eight weeks after Election Day.

ECJ Proposed Limits on Expenditure by Candidates & Political Parties

1. Where a registered political party contests one or more constituencies in a parliamentary general election, local government election or national referendum, the limit applying to campaign expenditure which is incurred by, or on behalf of, a party during the campaign period shall be $10 million multiplied by the number of constituencies contested by that party, at least one-half of which shall be spent in constituencies in which it has candidates.

2. Where at an election a candidate stands for election in any constituency on behalf of a registered party, or as an independent candidate, the limit applied to campaign expenditure shall not exceed $10 million. This amount is inclusive of any amount received from any political party, or the National Election Campaign Fund, or the State.

3. During a campaign period, each candidate and each political party shall submit to the Electoral Commission, Interim and Final Campaign Expenditure Reports.

The Interim Report shall cover the period from the commencement of the campaign period to the day on which the election is announced and shall be submitted to the Electoral Commission not later than eight days after nomination day.

The Final Report shall cover the entire campaign period and shall be submitted by a candidate not later than eight weeks after election day and by a political party not later than twelve (12) weeks after election day. Both the Interim and Final reports should be submitted to the Electoral Commission in the prescribed form and must show every donation received, whether in cash or kind, and detail all expenditure, loans, advances, goods and services received and debts and liabilities incurred during the campaign period.

4. Where a report is not submitted to the Electoral Commission within the time specified, the candidate, or in the case of a political party, every member of that Executive of the political party, each commits an offence and shall be liable to a fine not exceeding $5,000 for every day beyond the prescribed deadline.

In the case of a continuing offence, a further fine not exceeding $100,000 for every day, or part thereof, during which the offence continues after conviction shall be payable by such a person in default.

5. Any candidate or party official who makes a false declaration shall commit an offence and shall be liable on conviction therefor to a fine not exceeding $5 million, or in default of payment to a term of imprisonment not exceeding three years.

6. The Electoral Commission shall have the power to require disclosure. This power shall apply to the following organisations and individuals:

a. A registered party, i.e., the accounting unit or responsible accounting officer

b. A regulated donor, that is, organisation, group or individual

c. A candidate at an election

d. The election agent of such a candidate.

The Electoral Commission may give a disclosure notice to a person who is, or has been at any time during the period of five years immediately preceding the day on which the notice is given, the treasurer or any other officer of a political party, or group, to which the above paragraph applies.

A disclosure notice is a notice requiring the person to whom it is given to produce for inspection by the Electoral Commission or its agents, any document which:

> (i) relates to the income and expenditure of the organisation or the individual in question and is reasonably required by the Electoral Commission for the purpose of carrying out its auditing functions; or

> (ii) may provide the Electoral Commission, or its agents, with any information or explanation which relates to income and expenditure and is reasonably required by the Electoral Commission for purposes of identifying sources of political finance.

A person to whom a disclosure notice is given shall comply with such notice within the time specified in the said notice.

7. The Commission is further recommending that the nomination deposit paid by candidates on nomination day be increased to $10,000, and Section 23 Subsection 4 Paragraph (b) of the ROPA be amended to reflect the said increase.

8. All the limits and fees prescribed above shall be subject to review and adjustment by the Electoral Commission from time to time.

Further amendments have been added (late 2013) and are set out below:

2013 ECJ AMENDMENTS TO ITS ORIGINAL PROPOSALS

On the occasion of the postponement of the debate on campaign financing in the House of Representatives in the latter part of September 2013, the press reported areas in which there had been significant changes in the ECJ proposals.[190]

It was disclosed that in response to objections/reservations which had surfaced, significant amendments had been introduced which were reported in the press[191] on the occasion of, yet another postponement of the debate on state political party financing in the House of Representatives. The more important of these changes are set out below:

---

190 The *Jamaica Observer*, Fri. Sept.20, 2013, p. 23
191 Ibid.

1. If a Government contract valued at over J$500,000.00 is received within two years before or after a political donation is made, presumably to the governing party, that contract must be reported to the ECJ. No mention was made of the size of donation which would make the report obligatory, neither did the report give any idea as to what use would be made of such information. It is again suggested that vigilant monitoring of agreed guidelines for the award of contracts is to be preferred to this notion of the gathering of more and more information. An interesting situation could arise where the contract is obtained with a certain party forming the Government whereas the donation is made to the party which came to power after winning an election.[192]

2. It is now proposed, it appears, that a single donor cannot contribute more than five percent of the permitted aggregate campaign expenditure. As is the norm, there appears to be no felt need to justify the formula.[193]

3. Campaign expenditure, we are now informed, is to be computed on the basis of the number of seats being contested by the party. Depending on the relation between that factor and disbursement of state subsidy, such an arrangement could clearly be an incentive for fringe parties to put up paper candidates in almost every constituency, so as to maximize the funding received, as intimated above with reference to the NNC.

AUTHOR'S COMMENTS ON THE
ECJ PROPOSALS - DONATION/EXPENDITURE LIMITS

Limited commentary is in order since many observations already made throughout are of direct relevance, in a general way, to these proposals.

Under 'Impermissible Donors', one wonders if under (e) instead of

---

192 Conversely, the donation could of course be made to the party in Opposition whereas the contract was obtained within two years before from another party in Government. What possible significance will the ECJ attach to such situations? And how will they be resolved under the regulations, as they stand?

193 The recent JLP leadership election can certainly be viewed from this angle of vision, bearing in mind the contrasting campaign utterances by the contending comps. See Derrick Smith, 'Big money seeking to influence JLP elections', *The Gleaner*, Sept. 22, 2013, p. A3 and "I'm not for sale", *Jamaica Observer*, Tuesday Sept.24, 2013, pp. 1, 5.

prohibiting entities which are not tax-compliant from making donations, it may not be more appropriate to allow their contribution, but that the tax-deductibility concession be withheld. Apart from any principle involved, the tax liability could well, with merit, be in dispute. As the recommendation stands, it betrays the shortcomings of an approach that oversimplifies issues treated.

The requirement for invoices to be made out "to that candidate or ... party, regardless of who is liable for payment whether given free of charge" is understandable. However, this importantly reveals, as does the comprehensive nature of the transaction details required to be included in different Reports, a surprising unfamiliarity with the more than occasional chaos of the unpredictability and informality which is the reality of decentralized election campaigning. Normative ideals will inevitably be challenged, despite sometimes the best of intentions, and vitiated by factors both institutionally and culturally significant.

This applies with even greater force to reports under "Limits on Contributions/Donations to Candidates and Political Parties" at 14 and 15 requiring details of "all", and "each" transaction respectively, without reference to any applicable thresholds. The virtue of discretion/ reasonableness seems to have been overlooked. It is difficult to fathom how this very burdensome recording/accounting obligation could have eluded the notice and objection of the political party members of the Commission.

Number 4. Under 'Limits' stipulates that "A political party, or a candidate, shall not accept ... from an impermissible donor". Is the omission of "knowingly", since it appears elsewhere in similar contexts, to be put down to inadvertence?

A matter casting serious doubt as to whether fulsome consideration/ consultation was given to, or took place, with respect to specific quantified proposals is the very, recent press report[194] that, even before the recommendations have been passed into law, there is a move to have the suggested donation limit *doubled*. The absence of genuine consensus after the

---

194 'ECJ To Decide If Campaign Funds Soar – Commission To Review Proposal To Double Contribution Limits', in *The Gleaner*, Tue. July 30, 2013, pp. A1, A3 and see under "ECJ Proposed Limits on Contributions/Donations to Candidates and Political Parties". p. 72 above.

considerable period of consultation gives cause for serious concern as to the likely efficacy of such fundamental aspects of the regime.

With respect to Numbers 6 and 7, one wonders how the distinction will be established as to whether the contribution/donation is or is *not* "received and retained for campaign activities (expenses)". The case of former United States Presidential contender, John Edwards, is of some interest in this respect.[195]

The provision of contribution receipts is reasonable enough, if for amounts above some minimum, which is not prescribed under Number 8. This, together with the need to submit campaign period *monthly* donation reports, a *consolidated* report under Number 15, an election expense report under Number 18 and Interim and Final Campaign Expenditure reports as prescribed at Number 3, of "Limits on Expenditure", provide sufficient reasons for anxiety as to the bureaucratic weight of these cost-incurring requirements.

It is unclear as to the proper interpretation to be given to Contribution Limit, Number 9, which deals with loans or property, services or facilities provided "otherwise than on commercial terms". It would appear that the difference between the market rate/value of the 'assistance' given shall be regarded as a donation. In the case of a loan, what is the position if that difference exceeds the permitted donation limit? Such, so far unchallenged aspects of the regulatory regime, raises questions impinging on broad principles of democracy and economic ideology.

It would appear that why there is so much 'whistling in the dark [which] does not bring light' in the identification of weaknesses in the political/electoral processes is the failure to define the concept of 'democracy', in a more than one-dimensional manner. It is suggested that the following approach may be useful:

> Democracy is a system that creates the *economic*, [Italics added] political and cultural conditions for the full development of the individual.[196]

"Limits on Expenditure" proposals now require a response. The constituency campaign spending limit of $10 million continues to seem conspicuously arbitrary, in the absence of any attempt to explain how it is

---

195 Edwards was charged for converting campaign contributions to his personal use. See Note 408 for details. As it transpired, he was acquitted, partly, one suspects, because the donor was not very 'forthcoming'.

196 Fromm, op. cit. p. 236.

arrived at. Concerns in the literature about state management and control of parties' internal affairs, under state funding, is very clearly emphasized by the ECJ 'direction' that of the figure of $10 million multiplied by the number of constituencies the party contests, "at least one-half *shall* [Italics added] be spent in constituencies in which it has candidates". Of note is the fact that the same limit applies regardless of the nature of the election. A seemingly compulsive attachment to certain 'round numbers' is evident: 40%, 5%, $10 million and one-half are ready examples.[197]

Whereas under Number 1, the limit of $10 million applies to the 'campaign period' for *parties*, under Number 2, there is no such reference to 'period' but rather 'campaign expenditure' in relation to *candidates* contesting "on behalf of a registered party, or as an independent *candidate* ..." Is the position such that the party can spend up to $10 million *and* also so can its candidate? If this is not the case, the least that can be said is that there might be need for clarification.

It is stated that the party's Interim Report to the ECJ shall cover "the period from the commencement of the campaign period". How is this 'commencement' to be determined, since there is also reference to the time between then "to the day on which the election is announced".

The Final Report is due in 12 weeks after Election Day, well before some obligations for payment are normally formally brought to attention. To make matters significantly more problematic, it is *every* donation and *all* expenditure that is to be detailed. This we believe strongly promotes and tends to perpetuate misreporting, just as other burdensome procedural regulations promote venality.

Those who hanker for heavy-handed sanctions might find satisfaction with that aspect of the recommendations: for late submission of a report, "the candidate or in the case of a political party, every member of that Executive ... shall be liable to a fine not exceeding $5,000 for every day ...". With respect to

---

197 The application of some of these innocuous seeming ratios will lead to the very opposite of the level playing field ideal. In settling for simplicity, the complexity of real life party financing, both at the party organisation and campaign levels is thus avoided. Dividing money, the amount of which is to be "... *determined* [Italics added]. by Parliament ... *equally* [Italics added] among the parties that qualify", so however that, "this funding cannot be more than *40%* [Italics added] of party's income ..." must rank as one of the ECJ's proposals most in need of reconsideration. It is difficult to think of any good reason(s) that could justify such a basic feature of the financing scheme, which is now actually in place; see, The *Jamaica Observer*, Fri. Sept. 12, 2014, p. 7.

a continuing offence, "a *further* fine of $100,000 for every day or part thereof ... after conviction". The levels of these fines do not support the argument that political parties are short of cash or that there is any gap between 'clean' funds from private sources and the needs of proper representation. The emphasis should, perhaps, as in the British case, be one of guiding, encouraging and assisting compliance. Have the consequences been contemplated where the entire executive of a party is imprisoned for unwillingness or inability to pay such inordinately heavy fines?

The penalty at Number 5, for a candidate or party official who makes a false declaration, presumably 'knowingly', is a fine of up to $5 million or in the alternative up to three years imprisonment. One can understand why it is said to be proving difficult in Britain to get people to *volunteer* for certain political party posts. It would be interesting to search for similar provisions in the Companies Act. In companies, the situation is often one involving full-time, reasonably well paid senior staff, supported by layers of personnel beneath them. One should not expect this to be the case with institutions known to operate traditionally with a large volunteer cadre and which are said to be in need of state subsidy.

A disclosure notice under Number 6, possibly covering a period of five years, given the largely unpaid nature of most positions in political parties, seems unduly lengthy to expect "the treasurer or any other officer of a political party, or group ..." to remain accountable. Nor does the period stipulated reflect positively on the manner and time in which it is anticipated that possible breaches will be investigated and processed. This may be normal in the case of the administration of the justice system: one expected better from the ECJ, starting out on this new role; but then, "Incompetence, recklessness, irresponsibility, decadence – these are all faults found in others, never in you nor your cronies", as pointed out by Melanie Phillips.[198]

Having looked at some of the implications of 'throwing money' at the 'mischief', it is appropriate to consider issues related to legal intervention.

---

198   Phillips, Melanie, 'An icon of our time, The Paul Flowers scandal says much about social and political priorities of modern Britain'. *The Spectator*, Nov, 23, 2013, p.15.

CHAPTER 4
THE ROLE OF LAW

Financing regulation will prove difficult to successfully implement because of cultural issues related to compliance with the law and, importantly, its spirit.

Further,

> although those manning legislative and administrative agencies are themselves motivated by utility [the Benthamite cost-benefit principle] the rules they produce are inefficient. They are the result of pressures brought to bear by competing interest groups and the resulting compromises do not maximize total satisfaction. In particular, the substitution of administrative or adjudicatory processes for low-cost market transactions is inefficient.[199]

But even under a so-called global economy based hegemonically on self-serving free market principles of the leading industrialized countries, it is legitimate to ask, "Does it [law] not have to balance competing claims to power and influence by people who are bound to lose out in any competition based on market competence?"[200] Under the prevailing dominant politico-economic philosophy, the answer would seem to be: "only to the extent that it reflects those principles." We know that there is a certain orientation, which, derives from those principles which indulges in 'the questionable invocation of notional markets', not only in the area of politics, but across the whole spectrum of problems, without limitation, resulting from human interaction. At the same time, some do not find it difficult to argue that even real markets are inappropriate for analytical application to some aspects of social life.

Our subject matter may well be one such area.

---

199 J. W. Harris, op. cit. p. 49.

200 Ibid. pp. 50 & 251. . Ibid. p. 251. See also Roscoe Pound, 'The Scope and Purpose of Sociological Jurisprudence', 1972, 25, *Harvard Law Review*, 489, pp. 514 – 516; Harris, p. 253, concluded that 'where the legal technician cannot accommodate [vested] interests, there is no effective way of resolving conflicts. But it is interests, as perceived, which determine attitudes, which if ingrained, may frustrate an enterprise of law reform, even where law may have an 'educative' role. In view of the overwhelming prospect of the former, being the actual Jamaican frustration fatigue, experience, we would have preferred to see a reform mould configured to accord with the law's latter role. For Dworkin law is not contained in any system of rules, whether in a general or specific sense, however legitimate its source, but consists of 'the best politics which will fit such prescriptions'. Such an orientation allows an important space, we feel, for the consideration of principles and policies in judicial decision-making: see R. M. Dworkin, 'Taking Rights Seriously', Harvard University Press, 1978, chs. 2, 3, 4, 13

There are also difficulties inherent in the process of constructing an efficacious legislative framework, the design of which will ultimately depend, not on civil society's prescriptions, but on some minimum level of bipartisan agreement in the Jamaican parliamentary political context.[201] Given that reality–as reflected in a press report,[202] despite all the clamour for immediate statutory political finance reform –that issue will not be on the national agenda for the remainder of the year.[203] The statement thus becomes somewhat platitudinous that, "… good governance is often the consequence of an informed and courageous civil society, establishing agendas and insisting that political leaders do what is right."[204] The ideologue might quite properly respond: 'right for whom?'

This becomes important in the context of Harris' observation that,

> The mere word 'law' has an honorific ring. How is that to be squared with the positivist contention that law is one thing, good law another? Positivists like Hart, Kelsen and Austin tell us that a legal system exists if rules (norms, general commands) are effectively enforced. By that reckoning there seems to be, 'law' and legality in racist and tyrannical regimes.[205]

From such a viewpoint, "Legal rules are devices for compromising conflicts in society and are to be compared with other *political* [Italics added]

---

201   See, 'No campaign financing bill this year', *The Gleaner*, Mon. Jan. 14, 2013, p.A.8. The PNP's Party Financing Policy Document of August 22nd, 2005, at p. 4, anticipated consensus such that the Law on Political Parties would "be passed before the end of the parliamentary year of *2006*." See also Roscoe Pound, 'The Scope and Purpose of Sociological Jurisprudence', 1972, 25, *Harvard Law Review*, 489, pp. 514 – 516; J.W. Harris, op. cit. p. 253, has concluded that ' where the legal technician cannot accommodate [vested] interests, there is no effective way of resolving conflicts. But it is interests, as perceived, which determine attitudes, which if ingrained, may frustrate an enterprise of law reform, even where law may have an 'educative' role. In view of the overwhelming prospect of the former, being the actual Jamaican frustration fatigue, experience, we would have preferred to see a reform mould configured to accord with the law's latter role. For Dworkin law is not contained in any system of rules, whether in a general or specific sense, however legitimate its source, but consists of 'the best politics which will fit such prescriptions'. Such an orientation allows an important space, we feel, for the consideration of principles and policies in judicial decision-making: See R. M. Dworkin, 'Taking Rights Seriously', Harvard University Press, 1978, chs. 2, 3, 4, 13

202   *The Gleaner*, ibid. There has been what can only be described as an embarrassing divergence of projections of and expectations in legislative action between the ECJ, Parliament, the media, civil society so-called and commentators from the citizenry.

203   *The Jamaica Observer's* Parliamentary reporter, Balford Henry, concludes in the issue of Sunday Nov. 3, 2013, p.30 that "The indication ns are that the House leaders in procrastinating, are hoping to find a solution in the meantime, but it is evident that something will have to give before this debate ends … those with reservations in both Houses have agreed to await the Joint Select Committee's review of the Bill [not yet drafted] and vote on that Committee's report … It is quite unlikely that Parliament will complete its work on the Bill before the end of the calendar year. It is even possible that the contentious issue could be prolonged into 2014/2015".

204   Editorial "Civil society has to lead Jamaica's rescue", *The Gleaner*, Wed. Apr 6, 2011, p. A8.

205   J. W. Harris, op. cit. p. 144

devices used in problem-solving".[206]

If this is accepted, it becomes obvious that, contrary to Don Fuller's[207] criteria for the existence of a legal system/rule of law, it is to be noted that although law works best when it rests on a moral foundation, 'no amount of compliance guarantees that the system has moral worth'.

Indeed, van Biezen goes so far as to argue that,

> the widespread availability of state support and the extensive public control of party activity themselves may have contributed to the persistence of illicit party financing. This is so because, first of all, an abundance of rules may create perverse incentives. Legislation has, at best, only limited potential to diminish corrupt practices or to enhance public accountability. … Indeed, in a context in which political actors often prove reluctant to abide by the rule of law and may even be more inclined to bear a relatively small administrative sanction, solutions to the problem of illicit financing, fraud and corruption should arguably not primarily be sought in tougher legislation.[208]

Whatever the shortcomings of Pound's 'mixture of rather vague methodological and normative precepts', the area being treated here might, with benefit, have been approached by the Commission along some of the lines of sociological jurisprudence outlined by him. This involved, according to Harris,[209] studying the operations and effects of legal institutions and doctrines; carrying out sociological studies in preparation for legislation—particularly the effects of comparative legislation; studying the means of making legal rules effective: 'the life of the law is in its enforcement', a consideration of what effects legal doctrines [of like kind), had had in the past—in this respect, Jamaica's Representation of the People's Act, [ROPA]; individualized application of the principles of reasonableness[210] and justice at the expense of certainty, if appropriate [a dangerous departure, for adoption, perhaps, given the Jamaican political culture, where the exercise of

---

206 Ibid, p. 152.

207 See, *Harvard Law Review* 1958, 630, p. 666, 'The Morality of Law, *Yale University Press*, 1969, pp. 53, 74, 91, 106.

208 van Biezen, in 'Party Politics', 2004, p. 717

209 See the 'Scope and Purpose of Sociological Jurisprudence', *Harvard Law Review*, 1972. 25, 489, pp. 514 – 516.

210 Some support for this approach, in the realm of legal theory, may be found in the natural law school as re-stated by John Fennis: what ought to be expected and done by human beings in their innumerable mix of transactions/interactions may be simply put as, 'What is reasonable'. Accordingly, ideally, laws should bind in conscience, see Fennis, John, 'Natural Law and Natural Rights, *Stanford Encyclopedia of Philosophy*, Dec. 20, 2001, p. 183.

discretion, is almost always likely to be seen as 'prejudice', 'bias', 'favouritism', 'victimization', however sound the basis for differential treatment]; and 'making effort more effective' in achieving the *purpose* [Italics added] of law. Despite the challenges to be hurdled in evaluating and applying propositions contained in Pound's work, this aspect of his work seems potentially useful as a legislative reform project.

For whereas concept formation by the ECJ may be justified, on its part, by appeal to normative arguments, the primary targets of regulations, the political parties, are motivated largely by expediency considerations.

With *shared* values, doubtful cases argued from *principles*, often competing/conflicting, derived/derivable from them, at least reduce the risk of allegations of bias.

Those who would have 'laws with teeth' or 'tough' sanctions, like Hobbes,[211] presume that fear of the consequences of breaking the law will result in conformity. Jamaica's crime statistics effectively negates this view. More relevant, therefore, may be the approach of the Benthamite utilitarians, in constructing social and legal controls on the principle of rational-calculation: breaches will be committed if the utility of non-compliance, is greater than the projected cost.

When there are strong 'situational inducements' in favour of non-compliance, 'the stake in conformity' with the regulation can become minimal: the less a person believes he should obey the rules, the more likely he is to violate them.[212]

The civil society groups like the National Integrity Action and the Coalition of Civil Society Groups have been calling unceasingly for the immediate drafting and passage of legislation. In the words of the latter's Carol Narcisse,

> We were not willing to accept any more excuses [for delay] from Parliament. Our expectation is that the *drafting* [Italics added] process will be expeditiously handled in short order [*sic*] and by the first quarter of next year [2014], the House and the public should be seeing a bill.[213]

---

211 Hobbes, John, 'Elements of Law, Natural and Politic' (1650); Of Liberty and Necessity' (1654); 'Leviathan or the Matter Forme and Power of a Commonwealth, Ecclesiastical and Civil' (1651).

212 T. Hirshi, 'Causes of Delinquency', Berkley, California, 1969, p.26

213 *The Gleaner*, Wed. Sept. 25, 2013, p.1

This is reported in the same article of the issue of the newspaper which advised that:

> Members of the parliamentary opposition ripped into aspects of the report of the Electoral Commission of Jamaica (ECJ) on campaign financing, forcing Leader of Government Business, Phillip Paulwell to promise that a joint select committee would be established to *examine* [Italics added] the proposed campaign financing legislation.[214]

Within days following this press report, without explanation of any interim development, the public was informed that, after distancing themselves from former Chairman Herbert Thompson's comments and 'severely reprimanding' him for accepting the PNP's award, they[215] [the ECJ's Commissioners] noted and welcomed the fact that Parliament had *approved* the Report on Campaign Financing and, had referred the matter to Cabinet for *drafting* [Italics added] and instructions to be issued to the Chief Parliamentary Council and then back to Parliament for passage.[216]

At the level of the legal subsystem with which we are concerned, the electoral, it is contended that the observation above, with respect to the conflict-proneness ameliorative effect of common values and principles, is of no less applicability, hence the critical need for a specification of and agreement on the *supra* legal framework by which regulatory *details* may be screened.

The ECJ's proposals, as they now stand, will almost certainly fail the positivist efficacy definition[217] of law, in its external aspect, which is, "... The regularity of compliance with the norm and/or the imposition of a

---

214 Ibid; see also, 'House postpones debate on campaign financing', The *Jamaica Observer*, Fri. Sept. 20. 2013, p.23 for details of 2013 changes to the ECJ's Report.

215 Dr. Herbert Thompson, the then ECJ Chairman was ultimately 'forced' to resign from all-round pressure, resulting from his attendance and acceptance of an award at a PNP Awards Banquet. Together with politically flavoured statements subsequently made, this seemed to compromise his position as an independent member of the Commission, see press reports, 'PNP says it awarded the ECJ, not Herbert Thompson', The *Gleaner*, Thur. Sept. 19, 2013, p.A3; 'JLP wants Thompson out as ECJ head', The *Jamaica Observer*, Mon. Sept. 23, 2013, p. 8; 'Thompson blasts parliamentarians' action on campaign finance report', 'Attempt to destroy ECJ', The *Jamaica Observer*, Wed. Sept. 2, 2013, pp. 1, 4; 'NDM adds voice to call for Thompson to quit ECJ', The *Gleaner*, Sat. Oct. 5, 2013, p. A2.

216 This refers, one must assume, to the same report in respect of which a joint select Parliamentary Committee was to be established, See The *Gleaner*, Thur. Oct. 3, 2013, p.3 'ECJ selects Pine-McLarty for new Chairman'.

217 For examples of 'pragmatic instrumentalism' and 'legal realism', See Weber, Max, 'Law in Economy and Society' *University Press*, 1978,p.34; Holmes, Oliver Wendell, 'The Path of the Law', *Harvard Law Review*, 10. (1896-7) p.461; Robert S. Summers, 'Instrumentalism and American Legal Theory', *Cornell University Press*, 1982, pp. 116 – 135.

sanction for non-compliance. What counts is observable behaviour, even that requiring interpretation. ..."[218] And also, "... The internal aspect ... [which] consists in the motivation—however generated—for compliance ... and/or for application of the norm. What counts are psychic dispositions."[219]

At the broad societal level it has been propounded that,

> It is an empirical thesis that a legal system that protects neither the life nor the liberty nor the property of any legal subject has no prospect of long-term validity ... Thus it can be said that the satisfaction of certain minimum moral requirements is factually necessary for the long-term validity of a legal system.[220]

Issues of validity may *practically* be seen as being related, not only to morality, but, functionally to some minimum level of conformity. However, it is only within the boundaries of a social order characterized by a culture of instinctive conformity to law, sufficiently embedded in the national psyche to transcend inevitable technical legalistic drafting imperfections, so-called loopholes, that more than nominal/occasional compliance can be reasonably anticipated. Conspicuously, the Jamaican rule of law/law and order environment does not fall into that category. When the legal context contains within it forceful compliance 'distractions' attributable to self-interest, conformity impulses are likely to be further weakened.

Given the island's social and cultural history, it may not be surprising that to some,

> law may be seen as the enemy of freedom, as a set of prescriptions which necessarily detract from natural liberty. From this stance, any restraint on liberty to do what one likes is seen as something requiring justification ... Political rhetoric appealing to 'freedom' [and democracy] in many contexts and the *rhetorical* [Italics added] may become embedded in legal principle.[221]

The potential for friction between principles thus derived, and reality, 'on the ground', is evident.

---

218 Alexy, Robert, 'The Argument from Injustice, a Reply to Legal Positivism', *Oxford University Press*, 2002, pp. 14, 15
219 See for example, Lohmann, Niklas, 'A Sociological Theory of Law', Routledge and Kegan Paul, London, 1985): , p.82
220 Alexy, supra, pp. 20, 21
221 Harris, op cit. p. 129

This is without taking account of the fact that "… two contradictory trends inherent in the evolution of 'freedom from' to 'freedom to' run parallel—or rather, are continuously interwoven".[222]

Conflict with philosophical orientations, such as that of John Stuart Mill's 'harm principle',[223] is altogether of a more intractable nature. Infringement of the unfettered liberty of any member of a social group, from this perspective, is only justifiable on the individual or institutional level, in the interest of self-protection.

However interests are defined and represented, it has been said, not without disagreement, that:

> The constitutional and legal machinery might clearly fix [infringement] responsibility on some Ministers: political practice is a complex network of influences, counter-influences, compromises, arrangements. …With consultation, the growth of interests groups, the development of parties, the political system *seems* [Italics added] to have become open to all and those who have no say seem to have only themselves to blame for their inactivity.[224]

The moral here is that 'apathy', like everything else, has a price, which may be quite exorbitant.

That may suggest that resource emphasis might better be, at least initially, on a supportive behaviour-change education and guidance provision project. This is, however, a most unlikely reform departure. In times of crisis, even the more mature societies' response tends to be of the 'knee-jerk' kind.

This problem-solving approach has been amply exemplified by roundly criticized post-resignation behaviour of the former ECJ Chairman, Dr. Herbert Thompson, triggered by discussion and processing delays resulting from MPs' ECJ proposal concerns. If nothing else, this brings into question the criteria and procedure for appointment of 'independent' Commission

---

222 Fromm, op. cit., p. 105.

223 Mill, John Stuart., 'Essay on Liberty, 1859, while not lacking in qualifying criticism from, among others, Sir James Stephen, 'Liberty, Equality, Fraternity, Holt & Williams, 1873, and H. L. A. Hart, Law Liberty and Morality, Stanford University Press, 1963. We think it useful to assess the propriety of vested interest-inspired legal relations from such a position.

224 Blondel, op. cit., p. 232; see also Nathaniel Thompson, 'Youths must step up to politics', The Gleaner, Sat. Mar. 22, 2014, p. A7, where the statement is made, that 'Change does not roll in on the wheels of inevitability, but comes through continuous struggle'.

members. Academic or other professional qualification is clearly not, *per se*, a sufficiently sound basis for membership: the role/status of the ECJ is too critically important and sensitive for less than discreet, retrained conduct[225] on the part of its members.

If the Commission loses credibility in the eyes of the citizens in any aspect of its role, it is unlikely that it will have the ground support of the 'final arbiters' of the system's worth, which it will need to effectively carry out its control functions.

If law and regulations, in themselves, cannot guarantee a problem-free political process, this, one would think, would make the final design of the draft statutory intervention even more deserving of comprehensive consideration.[226] Impatience, in such a context and any consequential sense of debilitating frustration, ought perhaps to give way to the search for soundness.

Having just resigned in such controversial circumstances, Thompson, while still retaining his position as an independent member of the ECJ, saw it fit to " ... blast parliamentarians" action on campaign finance report', seeing the latest reservations voiced, resulting in intended referral to a joint Select Committee of Parliament, as an "attempt to destroy the ECJ".[227]

Thompson's main points of objection appeared to be, firstly, the departure from the convention whereby Parliament accepted the Commission's recommendations without amendment, a convention that has little to commend it either from the standpoint of legislative efficacy or constitutional

---

225 Unfortunately, Senator Tom Tavares-Finson recently provided another example of the lack of the restraint which is necessary for establishing and promoting the appropriate image of such a delicately positioned national institution: See his response to the position of MP Everald Warmington (then apparently a lone voice in the wilderness , only to be now gaining protest support from weighty sources) in 'All campaign donations should be made public – A. J. Nicholson', in, ' Inside Parliament', by Alicia Dunkley, the *Jamaica Observer*, April 15, 2012, p. 22. See also 'Behind the veil of that unconscionable ECJ campaign-financing proposal', by "The Gavel", The Gleaner's Parliamentary Reporter, *The Gleaner*, Mon. Nov. 4, 2013, pp. A6, 7.

226 At a function she organized at the British Parliament, for the purpose of enabling Professor Trevor Munroe, of the National Integrity Action, to meet with Jamaicans, Diane Abbott, a member of the House of Commons, is reported as stating that 'Where you have politicians and money, inevitably you have corruption ... The British and American experience shows that legislation alone does not ensure integrity. When politicians are desperate for money they always find a way around the rules. But this legislation would be a start.'

227 'Thompson blasts parliamentarians' action on campaign finance report attempt to destroy ECJ', the *Jamaica Observer*, Wed. Oct. 2, 2013, pp. 1, 4.

principle.[228] Secondly, the past conformity to the convention appears to have quite irrationally led him and others, among them Minister Peter Phillips, Senator Tom Tavares-Finson, a politically appointed member, and Leader of Government Business, Phillip Paulwell, from their reported statements, to which reference will be made, to regard the Commission's proposals as, properly, being beyond criticism.

To look at another context in which law and the issue of 'legality' may be relevant, we refer to the press report that "Jamaican political figures reacted swiftly last night to either clarify or distance themselves from fresh claims outlined in a court document [in the Turks and Caicos Islands] that they received millions of dollars in donations from convicted Olint [Ponzi scheme] boss David Smith".[229]

For our purposes, the main point of interest in the report is the response of one of the admitted recipients that "at the time it (the donation) was made, Olint was a legal entity in both Jamaica and the Turks and Caicos Islands".[230] Does this deal adequately with the major concern as to "... where they (contributions) should come from ..." raised by Din Duggan?[231] To put the issue differently, to what extent should one expect, or statutory provisions require, donees to look beyond the status of apparent institutional legality before accepting contributions? That would seem to be a function properly part of the role of regulators.

A confiscation Order by the Supreme Court of the Turks and Caicos Islands for Jamaica's two main political parties to 'return large monetary

---

228 See ' Senate approves campaign financing recommendations', the *Jamaica Observer*, Nov. 3, 2013, p.30, where Balford Henry in 'Inside Parliament' notes: "There are concerns about the various limits on financing , but what is immediately at stake is the convention which has held in the House for years, that the Parliament will not amend or refuse approval of the ECJ's recommendations".

229 *The Gleaner*, Tue. May 8, 2012, pp. A1, A3, under the headline, 'Big Olint handouts'

230 Ibid. In 'Politicians react to being named on Olint's gift list'. it is reported that Vaz (Daryl), "Former JLP Information Minister ... also defended the decision to accept the donation, (he admitted receiving a constituency contribution from Olint/Smith of (US)$50,000.00), pointing out that at the time it was made ..."; see also 'No moral obligation to refund Olint money', The Gleaner, Fri. June 15, 2012, p. ; See also Ralston Nembhard, in, 'Wrong jungle, Mr. Pickersgill', accused the PNP Chairman of being "oblivious of the legal sensibilities demanded by the situation ... , left to those jurisdictions to convict Smith and not Jamaica, where the scheme operated for a considerable period ... as representatives of the people they have a sacred responsibility to behave decently in government or in Opposition at all times". For a similar conclusion, based on a certain reading of the applicable law, see 'David Smith's tainted gifts', The Gleaner, July 11, 2012, p.A.9. It is argued here that under the Turks and Caicos' *Proceeds of Crime Ordinance*, the recipient of a tainted gift has not a moral, but a legal obligation to return it.

231 See 'Public election funding', *The Gleaner*, Wed. Apr. 18, 2012, p. A9

gifts'[232] from David Smith's Olint, has, as did Trafigura,[233] heightened the already frenzied calls for statutory campaign finance reform.[234]

With respect to the 'Order', those in support have apparently failed to consider its problematic jurisdictional and, consequently, possible far-reaching geo-political implications. Perceived threats, other than military, could, under the force of such a precedent, quite conceivably result in a different version of the Cuban embargo, not to mention the much more recent extra territorial implications of the United States' Foreign Account Tax Compliance Act (FATCA), whatever its intended *internal* merit and legitimacy.

In one editorial of *The Gleaner,* titled 'Olint saga makes case for campaign-finance law' one finds repeated use of such words as 'may not have', 'if', 'uncertain', 'may', 'don't know', 'harbour doubt' and 'might have'. The editorial ends: 'David Smith may not have had the [piper's] tune played for him, but we don't know who might have'.[235] This seems to be taking speculation beyond permissible journalistic and, in particular, editorial limits.[236] In such a rumour-prone society, the yearning is for aggressive thorough unrelentingly persistent fact-finding investigative journalists.

What is certain is that the collapsed Olint (Ponzi) Scheme was no secret. Its operations continued for as long as they did under the eyes of

---

232 See, however, 'Parties see no reason to return Olint funds', *The Gleaner*, Thurs. July 18, 2013, p. A3

233 For the latest development in the saga, see "Trafigura blow", court rules PM, other Government members must testify in open court, *Jamaica Observer* on Saturday, Sept. 21, 2013, p.3.

234 See 'After Olint campaign-finance claims … sector groups warn Government of … Urgent need for reform', The Gleaner, Wed. May 9, 2012, pp. A1, A3. See also 'Campaign-financing legislation a priority', *The Gleaner*, Wed. May 9, 2012, p. A4. This is according to the Minister with portfolio responsibility for such matters. For an opposed view, see 'Warmington: We can't impose any more burdens on the poor', *The Gleaner*, Wed. Sept. 25, 2013, p. 1: some support for this approach in the history of legal theory, may be found in the natural law school as re-stated by John Finnes: what ought to be expected and done by human beings in their innumerable mix of transactions/interactions is, simply put, 'what is reasonable'. Accordingly, ideally, laws should "bind in conscience; see Finnes, John., 'Natural Law and Natural Rights', *Oxford University (Clarendon) Press*, 1980, pp.45 et seq, also "Letter of the Day", 'Raise own funds for election campaigns', by Les Francis, *The Gleaner*, Fri, Sept. 27, 2013, p.A8, where the letter writer states that "state financial support for candidates would not only be wrong but immoral".

235 *The Gleaner*, Fri. May 11, 2012, p. A8. See also Din Duggan, 'Public election funding', *The Gleaner*, Wed. Apr. 18, 2012, p.A9. Duggan assumes that public funding of campaigns would make elected officials indebted and accountable to the general public (thus) empowering ordinary taxpayers'. As it is the taxpayer who pays all the costs and expenditures of government, including elected officials' salaries, that has had little or no impact on the quality of governance.

236 It was something of a surprise to see regular columnist Gordon Robinson, not altogether guiltless himself, in, 'Why rumour instead of reason?' write, "If only we could find a way to package our rumour industry for export, we could kiss the IMF goodbye". To us the answer is simple: circulating/rumour, as fact, is the route of least resistance for the lazy and, with respect, the unprofessional in the media and society.

the regulatory agency, the Financial Services Commission. Blame needs to be placed precisely where it belongs for, despite muffled arguments to the contrary, political parties and their officers, are, by law, neither regulators nor prosecutors in matters of this kind.

Peter Espeut, an ardent advocate of transparency, implies that by contributing to both political parties in Jamaica, Smith's scheme and others bought immunity from prosecution. "What did Olint hope to gain from either PNP or JLP victory in 2009? The chance to reopen shop here was next to zero. Is there some other use that this influence would have been put to"?[237]

By his actions, did Smith expect/hope to influence the police and the Director of Public Prosecutions (DPP)? What 'influence', one might ask, has been established and over whom? Would the large private sector firms which gave millions to the two major parties, equally, be seen to have also been buying 'protection', through 'influence peddling', of some sort? Why not also pass a law to prevent the recurrence of such occurrences? Or is it that only 'tainted' money can buy influence? And, importantly, to an aware public, what of the 'taint' of record profits earned from financially stressed customers by higher than 'necessary' prices and transaction charges and fees, even taking into account the possible effect on the bottom line of organisational efficiency initiatives.

The 'tainted' money argument, despite its obvious merit and appeal, taken into this direction, suggests that political contributions from profits so 'earned' are equally open to principled objection.

Choice of government policy, in terms of political, social and economic ideology certainly has the potential, at least, to fundamentally, by legal enactment, affect such private sector financial interests, if not their very existence. Espeut does not, however, seem to be troubled by this latter prospect,[238] although such companies, and their shareholders of substance, certainly do not constitute the majority, in whose interest one version of 'democracy' dictates that governments should govern.

---

237 Espeut, Peter, 'Tainted gifts and political donations', *The Gleaner*, Fri. May 11, 2012, p. A9

238 See Espeut 'Tainted gifts and political donations', supra, p. A9. See also Wayne Campbell, 'Time to deal with party financing', *Jamaica Observer*, Mon. May 14, 2012, p. 9: "Financiers of political parties are not doing so out of the kindness of their hearts … (they) expect favours … or they expect to influence specific policies that may or may not be beneficial to the wider society …"

If the claimed justification for public financing is furtherance of democratic ideals, it is fitting that this presumed complementarity be examined.

CHAPTER 5
ARGUMENTS FOR STATE FUNDING

The Director of Elections in "… urging Jamaicans to support the funding of political parties", did so on the basis that citizens "… should be more comfortable knowing that they have paid for their elections rather than having them funded by tainted money".[239] Taxpayers already fund the cost of all aspects of the country's electoral machinery and government.[240] Many of them, for far too long, have been stretched to breaking point by the burdensome cost of utilities, education, healthcare, and food, even, not to mention the effect of high taxes and comparatively high interest rates. The cost of living will certainly increase significantly with a depreciating dollar and under IMF budgetary targets, with no imminent prospect of any substantial increase in production/productivity, employment or nominal or real wages.

Trevor Munroe in his article, 'Balancing money-power with public-power', uses the term 'public-power' without qualification, thereby perpetuating populist rhetoric over rationality. Of overriding significance, however, is Munroe's observation:

> At the same time, on the other hand, with wealth concentrated at the top in Jamaica, a country which now has the highest income gap in the Western Hemisphere—second only to Suriname—is it a surprise that party operations and electioneering are funded by the wealthy minority and that public policy outcomes disproportionately favour this segment of society.[241]

Since it was conceded that involvement by the masses is 'not through

---

239 The *Jamaica Observer* 'EOJ boss bats for Jamaicans to finance political parties', Wed. Mar. 18, 2009, p.6. For a contrary position, see 'Damn dictatorship on campaign financing' by Ronald Mason. The *Gleaner*, Oct 6, 2013, p. A9.

240 "The Gavel", The Gleaner's Parliamentary reporter notes in The Gleaner, Mon. Nov. 4, 2013, pp.A6,7 that the ECJ Commissioners who remain a drag on the taxpayers' "… posts paying $8 million want … to pay additional staff at the ECJ … in addition to the billions spent on conducting elections and registering and re-verifying the electorate … and the amount lost through the provision of motor vehicle, import [duty] waivers for election campaigning … Seemingly without conscience … divorced from the economic realities … The ECJ is proposing to move the campaign spending limit from $3 million to $15 million", which will have a direct bearing on the amount of state subsidy 'entitlement'.

241 The *Jamaica Observer*, Oct. 12, 2014, 'The Agenda', p.9.

personal disposal income', which they do not have[242], it follows that the rich will always be able to contribute more. Or is it that these reforms will be expected to significantly close the gap, despite the often documented ease with which donation limiting regulations can be circumvented. There was a time when it would have been recognised that it was the *purpose* of politics which mattered, not its funding:[243] the defining nature of the party would determine the direction and strength of its magnetic pull, depending, historically, on the breadth of the franchise. But politics is no longer, it seems, a war of ideas: it is now, quite frequently, and perhaps more appropriately referred to as the 'game'. 'Games' tend to have an enduring interest for the spectators usually only when the contest on the field is intense, in more than one sense and for longer than a 'nine-day wonder' period.

When the mechanic does not diagnose the problem accurately, a lot of 'things' get 'fixed', as Espeut implies.[244]

Why should one accept, in any event, that short of public funding, presumed 'tainted money' is an unavoidable feature of party and campaign financing? On the contrary, in keeping with guidelines relating to forfeiture of contributions from illegal/questionable sources the very opposite is likely to be the case. Effective reform implementation will mean that any such

---

242 Involvement may indeed take the form of demanding to be paid to vote, as reported in *The Gleaner*, Dec. 7, 2014, p. A4, under the heading, 'JLP reviews Central Westmoreland Whipping'. The contrasting view is that taken by Sandra M. Taylor Wiggan in, 'Political hypocrisy ', calling for a better crop of politicians and a better crop of citizens …", the *Jamaica Observer*, Mon, Dec. 8, 2014, p. 12. See also, E. Gager, 'Non-voters cast weighty protest ballot', The Gleaner, Wed, Dec. 3, 2014, p. A8, and 'Opposition senator raises concern about vote-buying', which he says, "undermines our democracy", as reported by Balford Henry, *Jamaica Observer Wed. Dec. 10, 2014, p. 20. It is noteworthy that Minister Mark Golding does not think that state subsidy, which* could be used directly, or otherwise to buy votes, as "an argument against limited state funding for political parties". This is in direct contrast with the view of Wayne Campbell, 'Parliamentarians are selfish', the *Jamaica Observer*, Wed. Dec. 10, 2014, p. 13. The funding of parties, he sees, as of no importance compared to the state of the education system, road and health care, which makes it "truly shameful that our parliamentarians could have passed such a Bill". It would seem obvious that should the economic situation become worse, the greater the demand will be, other factors remaining unchanged, for cash/kind for a secret vote.

243 For an opposed view of these contending issues at the micro/mechanistic level, see 'NIA's stance on campaign financing bill, a 'sell out', Peter Espeut, *The Gleaner*, Dec. 28, 2014, p. A4 Most of these arguments have already been assessed; see also Peter Espeut, 'Sham campaign finance reform', *The Gleaner*, Fri. Oct. 17, 2014, p. A7, where he argues that the approach ought to be to 'fund and fix the loopholes'. See, 'Damaging tribalism', PNP mayor calls for multi- party democracy. Says the two-party system has deeply divided Jamaica; the *Jamaica Observer*, Thu. Dec. 11, 2014; see, 'Needed: Better crop of parliamentarians', where the Letter of the Day writer also proposes the need for "a new non-aligned group of fairly intelligent people to start canvassing for a third party". Clarity of thinking does not seem to have inspired such a proposal. See Mark Trought, The Gleaner, Thu. Dec, 11, 2014, p. A8;, Mark Clarke, ' No need for more parties', *The Gleaner*, Wed. Dec. 17, 2014, p. A8, since, in his view, this might mean more bribes for more voters for more parties.

244 Ibid, Espeut.

funds will find their way into the Consolidated Fund which will be mixed with the 'clean' revenue from taxpayers from which party and campaign subsidies will be disbursed. Moral purists ought instead to insist that all such money, should, like illicit drugs, be destroyed whether in the form of cash, or otherwise, to the extent possible.

In the absence of evidence, tested according to the standards required by our judicial system, what may appear to be the 'low road', as apparently taken by the former ECJ Chairman, Professor Errol Miller,[245] and, more recently, Senator Lambert Brown[246] and columnist Ronald Mason,[247] may merit contemplation. Their position, simply put, is that money does not necessarily buy influence, and allegations of corruption may be little more than rumour-mongering.

In contrast to this national trait for 'judgment' to be arrived at, without evidence being adduced and tested, are the more than rare cases involving United States politicians who have been charged, pleaded guilty or been convicted of taking bribes of one form or another in return for the promise or actual granting of politically influenced financial benefits.[248]

Perceptual distortion is one of the dangers of evangelistic reform overzealousness. So as to avoid falling into the same 'trap', conversely, while it is acknowledged that all adjudicatory mechanisms are imperfect, having matters being put to evidentiary proof may 'exorcise demons,' dispel rumours, cause 'mirages' to vanish and find 'truth'. If perception is reality[249] and is distorted, then so is that 'reality' which it mirrors. One should expect that in

---

245 Not only does he think the actual extent of corruption in the society exaggerated but links that fact to the society's penchant for viewing public figures in a negative light and thus 'painting everybody with the same brush, unsupported by interview responses requesting actual instances of corrupt behaviour experienced, as referred to elsewhere in more detail herein.

246 See 'Government Senator says there's no evidence for ... Big Money Fears,' The Gleaner, Sat Nov. 2, 2013, pp. A1, 3.

247 Ronald Mason, supra

248 In 'Ex-New Orleans Mayor convicted of taking bribes'; The Gleaner, Thur. Feb. 13, 2014, p. C9, the report states that Ray Nagin had been charged with 'accepting pay-offs in exchange for promoting the interests of local businessman Frank Fradella ... from another businessman Rodney Williams for his help in securing city contracts ... each testified that they bribed him ... accepted free trips and other gratuities from contractors in exchange for helping them secure millions of dollars in city work. Nagin's former technology chief Greg Meffert, who is awaiting sentencing after a plea deal, told jurors he helped another businessman, Mark St. Pierre, bribe Nagin with lavish vacation trip ... to Jamaica and Hawaii ...." The striking difference between Jamaica and the United States in this respect is evident: the effort put into ferreting out the 'facts' and the 'willingness' of witnesses to come forward, even if induced by the offer of a plea-bargain, as against trial and conviction by 'anmour', 'suspicion' and 'belief'

249 Claude Robinson, 'In politics perception is reality', The Agenda, the Jamaica Observer, Sept. 29, 2013, p.4

a healthy political system, citizens, whatever their status and role, would not be' charged', tried and convicted on the basis of perception.

It is no exaggeration, nevertheless, to say that the most notable achievement of political leadership since the 1970's, with a short-lived respite in the early part of the nineteen eighties, has been the creation of a pervasive sense of hopelessness and despair. The result, as is portrayed *ad nauseam,* is disillusionment with and disengagement from the parties, caused by their chosen style and the *negative bottom line,* the *outcomes,* of their practise of politics. Therein lies the rub.

But being from a 'democratic' society, with the understandable tendency to defer to popular sentiment, the Director of Elections has, nevertheless, observed:[250]

> These are institutions [the JLP and PNP] that have been in place for a very, very long time … [with political Independence being achieved in 1962, to most Jamaicans, being from a country with a brief history as a nation, the emergence of the parties in the early 1940's no doubt makes them seem ancient, if not exactly venerable in certain respects] … we cannot afford for them to be hijacked by powerful tainted or whatever kind of funds you want to classify it [*sic*]. We don't want the powerful to be able to hold the government of the day to ransom … if there are persons powerful enough to contribute enough money to influence the outcome of elections, to influence the holders of these offices, what that means is that the things

250   See Janice Budd, 'No truth, no trust', The *Jamaica Observer,* Jun. 2, 2011, p. 13, subtitled 'Study suggests most Jamaicans want politicians to appear before a truth commission' where the report states: "Institutions, that people do not trust are not supported by them … we are not prophesying the demise of democracy as a form but it is certainly foreseeable that high levels of dissatisfaction with political leadership may lead to an abandonment of the "politics as usual". The study entitled "No Truth, No Trust: Democracy Governance and the Prospects for Truth-Telling Mechanisms in Jamaica Report " is reportedly the initiative of the Truth and Justice Action Group- comprising members of academia, the Jamaican Council of Churches and the UNDP which provided funding; See also Bishop Howard Gregory 'A nation in search of direction', The *Jamaica Observer,* June. 5, 2011, p. 2: "The message should be clear to all of us that corruption is as strong as ever and is well reposed within the culture of both our political parties"; The Editorial, The *Gleaner,* Wed. Apr. 6, 2011, p.A6 states: "… the rescue of Jamaica demands a new paradigm, starting with the recognition of a fact that Jamaica has missed (sic) with its too-heavy investment in politics as a narrowly partisan process. That is, politicians and political leaders also require leadership", [from informed and courageous civil society, it is claimed]. In the Gleaner, May 15, 2011, p. D8 "Time to renew JLP, PNP, Winnie Anderson-Brown emphasizes what she sees as 'the urgent need for the transformation of our political system'; Franklyn Johnston in 'Your MP, public servant or recycled rogue?', in the *Jamaica Observer,* Fri. May 6, 2011, p. 11, declares: 'Politicians bring politics into disrepute!"; John Richards, in 'PNP far worse', The *Gleaner* Thu. April 7, 2011, p.A8, recounts the frequent frustrated public response: I [will] do not vote because they are all the same".

that we are trying to preserve will be in jeopardy.[251]

What then are we seeking to preserve, or avoid, according to whether we view our objectives positively or negatively? We think it appropriate to take the ECJ Report as our point of departure.

State funding on a substantial scale would, some, including the United Kingdom's Neill Committee, suggest, purify the political process: parties would be immune from the temptation to grant donors privileged access to top politicians or unwarranted influence over policy, or the award of contracts and honours.[252] This is clearly reflective of the ECJ's position.

Further, it is claimed that this would have the virtue of signalling to the public that political parties are valuable, indeed essential institutions in a democratic country. If *matching* funding does form a part of the financing package provided, as in Germany and parts of the United States, this could provide the incentive to raise money from the public, whether in small or relatively large sums, even if subject to a maximum contribution limit.[253] Since whatever is raised by a party would be matched by the state, successful and active forms of engagement with the electorate would clearly be encouraged.

Despite the observation in 2004—which is, no doubt, even more correct today given the worsened economic situation almost universally since then— that there is "… no public appetite for large-scale state funding,"[254] Allan Whitehead, a British MP, still claimed, in making a case for increasing public

---

251 The *Jamaica Observer*, Wed. Mar. 18, 2009, p.6, 'EOJ boss bats for Jamaicans to finance political parties'; See also letter of the Day 'An audit that tells little': "The Opposition Peoples National Party (PNP) has been receiving kudos for producing an audited financial report. … I suspect that this is intended to show a measure of transparency and leadership in the matter of campaign financing … predicated on the promise that clean money translates into clean elections … [but] soft money … increases the power that a clique of power brokers have and weakens the mass membership power," in *The Gleaner*, Thur. Sept. 23, 2010, p.A6.; Again, we find in this a manifestation of the pervasive universalistic syndrome that political parties are for sale, an unfortunate, almost always, unproven consequence of adages – the soundness of which are not self-evident – that "money can buy anything or anybody", "money talks", "who pays the piper …"; See also the Editorial in *The Gleaner*, June 27, 2010, p.A8: "Except that in today's Jamaica the big contributors to parties and politicians are less likely to be legitimate firms than individuals who are awash with cash from other than legitimate enterprises". Such an unenlightened conclusion may easily be labeled 'the libel of the anonymous': little wonder that the newspapers are clamouring for a reform of the libel laws.

252 House of Commons, 'State Funding of Political Parties' by Ruth Winstone of Parliament and Constitution Centre, 30 Oct., 2002, SN/PC/1766, p. 3

253 See Ronald Mason, supra. He argues, "My money is to do with as I please. It is amazing that lobbyists in this country where allegations of long ago had political parties robbing the bank to finance political activities,(sic) can now be so sanctimonious that they dare to tell the citizens what to do with their money". The irony is here exposed: On the one hand the parties are said to be cash strapped, and on the other, wallowing (potentially) in a swamp of 'dirty money'.

254 (UK) Electoral Commission Report Dec. 2004, Hayden Phillips, p. 34.

funding,[255] that such funds would "combat" the rise of what he calls 'anti-politics'. This, he defined as, "… the widespread disinterest and in some cases hostility to politics."[256] The causal relationship of the elements in the 'solution' is not immediately apparent; a lot will obviously depend not only on the purposes for which funds are used, but on how effectively a party's strategies are implemented.

Douglas Alexander, another member of the British House of Commons, and Stella Creasy, jointly published a paper[257] urging parties to re-evaluate how they relate to the communities that they serve, by opening up themselves for engagement with social activists. Quite interestingly, also, a paper by the Young Foundation of the United Kingdom supports the idea of state funding for party activities which could be regarded as being in the public interest, such as policy formulation and leadership development. Activities of that nature, it is argued, should be "legally separate" from strictly traditional political engagements, such as campaigning, with only the former being eligible for public funding through matched funding of donations.[258] This group, the source of these suggestions, quite interestingly describes itself as one whose *raison d'etre* is to, "harness the power of disruptive innovation to address structural inequality in all forms". Suffice it to say that achievements of such an ambitious transformational objective, transmitted transnationally, to Jamaica, would cause the disappearance of the underlying conditions making state financing of politics a matter deserving of *priority* focus.

The effect of the deliberate attempt in the ECJ state funding proposals to stymie the emergence of what could be electorally significant third parties provides evidence of that predatory order, the less open to juridical challenge, precisely because it proceeds according to a rule-driven practice. And as Radbruch reminds us, 'Every legal system [and subsystem] lays claim to correctness'.[259]

---

255 Allan Whitehead, MP., 'Anti-Politics and Political Parties', pamphlet, April, 2006.

256 Hayden Phillips, supra, p. 35; See also Poguntke, Thomas (1996), 'Anti-Party Sentiment – Conceptual Thoughts and Empirical Evidence: Exploration into a Minefield', *European Journal of Political Research* 29, pp. 319 – 344 and Schedler, Andreas (1996) 'Anti-Political Establishment Parties', Party Politics 2: 291 – 312 referred to in Yael Yishai, "Bringing Society Back In", Party Politics, *Sage Publications*, 2001, Vol. 7, No. 6, p. 668.

257 '*Serving a Cause, Serving a Community: The Role of Political Parties in Today's Britain*', Demos, (U.K., 2006)

258 MacTaggart, F., Mulgan. G & Afi, R., (2006) 'Parties for the Public Good', Available: http: //youngfoundation. org/wp.

259 Radbruch, Gustav, 'Legal Philosophy', in *The Legal Philosophies of Lask, Radbruch and Dabin*, Harvard University Press, (Cambridge, Mass., 1950), p. 73.

What this invites is the unfettered discussion of the issues of statutory injustice, 'unveiled as what they are, namely, questions of ethics'.[260]

Philosophically, then, in this respect at least, the separation of legal from moral obligations ought instinctively to prompt a healthy critical orientation to any and every law, with assessment resting on justifiability, since:

> Practically speaking, relevant problems first turn up where the claim to correctness is indeed made but not satisfied ... Clarity in terms of simplicity is not the only goal of concept formation. Simplicity must not prevail at the expense of adequacy.[261]

---

260 Alexy, op cit, p.44.
261 Ibid, p. 35.

Chapter 6
Arguments Against
State Funding

Daniel Hannan, Conservative Party Member of the European Parliament, after a perusal of several European countries' negative political experiences, concludes that the countries 'keenest on state funding, being those in Europe, are generally the ones with the "rankest scandals", which usually involve party funding.[262] He sees the "real scandal" as being "our equation of state funding with honest politics"[263] and the belief that what is achieved is a "trade-off between subvention and corruption."[264] State subsidy of politics is thus, for Hannan, little more than a "conspiracy against the public"[265] by parties alternating in opposition or in control of the state apparatus to their mutual benefit.[266] Taxpayer subsidy in this regard, it is argued, thus facilitates the emergence and maintenance of a separate, insulated political class, with strong and not necessarily healthy *status quo* preservation tendencies.[267]

In 'Behind the veil of that UNCONSCIONABLE ECJ campaign financing proposal', "The Gavel", *The Gleaner's* Parliamentary reporter writes:

> But we are not surprised by the outrageous proposal. The ECJ because of its model is subject to political manipulation ... the two leading political parties here—which admittedly played a role in cleaning up the system they corrupted—have entrenched themselves in the Commission (by each having two of their representatives as members at $8 million per year) in order to maintain the status quo of a two-party system" ... We have little doubt that the offensive and unpalatable aspects of the report are the doing of the political parties".[268]

---

262 Hannan, D., 'State funding for parties will guarantee sleaze: look at Europe', *The Daily Telegraph* (UK), April 3, 2006

263 Ibid

264 Ibid

265 Ibid

266 See, also, 'Independent Commissioners DID NOT 'CAVE IN', by Professor Errol Miller, then Chairman of the ECJ, *The Gleaner*, Oct. 8, 2010, p.F5.

267 Ibid. See also 'Remove politicians from ECJ', "The Gavel", *The Gleaner* Mon. June 13, 2011, p.B12. The problem of enforcement, with politicians on Electoral Commissions, also appears in the United States' system; see, Kendrick Brinson, 'FEC Can't Curb 2016 Election Abuse', *The New York Times*, May 5, 2015.

268 "The Gavel", *The Gleaner*, Mon. Nov. 4, 2013, pp. 6, 7.

With respect to Britain, Daniel Hannan makes the observation:

Politics has been professionalized, and MPs have no career structure other than through their parties. Almost every back-bencher wants to be a front-bencher, making the House of Commons supine on all but exceptional occasions".[269]

As long ago as 1963, Jean Blondel pondered the question:

Is the House of Commons, far from being a representative image of the nation (which socially speaking, at any rate, it never was) in the process of falling into the hands of career politicians anxious to move up the ladder as would professional men, businessmen, or civil servants?[270]

Hannan, sees, as part of the answer, the present British Government's initiative of "… introducing mechanisms … , enormously to its credit … for motions to be put before the Commons by popular petition".[271] We have, perhaps too obliquely, suggested such a possibility with respect to bringing electoral breaches to the attention of the ECJ by members of the Jamaican public.

He further notes, with obvious approval, that,

Possibly the most significant change of all, though, is one that the Conservatives have made unilaterally and quietly, without legislation … in constituency after constituency they are transferring candidate selection from party activists to open meetings … MPs chosen by primaries will, I suspect be commensurably readier to defy their whips.[272]

In a variation on the theme of the undue influence of the parties, The Gavel cites as an example of the pursuit of self-preservation, under the auspices of the Commission,

the ECJ's grand idea of state funding (which) would shut out most independent persons since they would not meet the criteria of having received at least five percent of votes cast in the previous election …

---

269   Daniel Hannan, 'How we [England] invented freedom. It's time to discover the original Bill of Rights' *The Spectator*, Nov. 23, 2013, p. 22

270   Blondel, op. cit. p. 153.

271   Ibid, p. 23. Along these lines, Peter Espeut, *The Gleaner* columnist, inquires, "Will there be some mechanism where the public can provide evidence to expose breaches and so block garrison politicians and flag-flying territorialists' access to public campaign funds"?, The ECJ recommendations are silent about this, *The Gleaner*, Fri. Dec. 6, 2013, p. A.9.

272   Hannan, supra.

similarly, it would lock out third parties as they too need to have secured at least five percent of the votes cast the last time around ... state funding would ensure change does not occur. ... But this is the basis on which the ECJ board is currently constituted ... to fashion the political system they (the two major parties) want. The fact is that self-interest is at the heart of many of the proposals.[273]

Hannan, in making his case, against state subsidy, cites the following examples:[274]

Germany: Helmut Kohl, for former Chancellor, was brought down by sleaze.

France: 7700 politicians were charged with corruption in the past decade.

Italy: "a party membership card, jingling with ribbons and medals was seen as an IOU to be cashed when your capo took power".

Austria: is cited as the classic case of the binary/cartel (Katz & Mair, 1995) political system, in which "the socialists or the Peoples' Party propped each other up like two exhausted boxers".[275]

Belgium: here, parties are seen as not only being supported by taxpayers' money, but by the legal apparatus of the state: "they run newspapers, appoint their supporters to government posts, and even administer part of the state's insurance system. When the Vlaams Blok, the Flemish Nationalist party, started to do too well for the comfort of the cartel parties, they challenged its right to public funding, saying it was a threat to the

---

273   "The Gavel", supra.
274   Hannan, supra.
275   Ibid.

unity of the state".[276]

Netherlands: a Court recently ruled that a Calvinist party, the Staatkundig Gereformeerde Partij (SGP), should have its grants discontinued because it did not champion sex equality;[277] this, "who pays the piper" relationship prevails, Hannan notes in the European Parliament, even, where parties must accept "the values of the European Union" to qualify for subsidy.

In this Netherlands case, ***Staatkundig Gereformeerde Partij (SGP) v the Government of the Netherlands,*** which involved the issue of the 'proper' roles of the sexes, ultimately on appeal to the European Court of Human Rights[278] (Third Section), sitting on July 10, 2012, the decision against the SGP was upheld. The following aspects of the case make it of particular interest, given the political party/state financing implications:

1. The SGP party had consistently held one to three seats in the Dutch Lower House.

2. Both the party's Statement of Principles and Articles of Association state that the party is based directly on its interpretation, according to specific pronouncements of scriptures, on the infallible word of God as revealed in the Bible. Religion thus provides the inspiration for the nature of its politics, with Parliament being the arena for the national expression of its principles.

3. Central to the case is the SGP religious position that men and women

---

276 The most recent example of this 'calling of the tune' is that in Greece where it is reported that the PM, after the arrest of the ultra-right wing leadership of the Golden Dawn Party," was in the process of submitting legislation to Parliament yesterday aimed at cutting state funding … charges [Italics added] of acting as a criminal organisation … state funding could be suspended if any member of its leadership or lawmakers [member of the Party in Parliament] are being prosecuted [Italics added] for felonies. See The Gleaner, Tue, Oct. 1, 2013, p.C6, for further details, see also, The Gleaner, Tue Oct 1, 2013, p. 25, where the Party's anti-Semitic, fierce anti-immigrant stance and its strongly denied suspected connection with the fatal stabbing of a left-wing Greek activist rapper are reported. The lesson for those who believe in state financing as promoting democratic principle is clear: the shoe can, at some point, obviously be on the other foot. More recently, the police were reported to have raided the homes of three Parliamentary members of the Party and confiscated mobile phones, hard discs, SIM cards and data storage sticks, causing the Party to call for a protest rally outside the parliament. The three Parliamentarians are charged with "participating in a criminal organisation". See 'The third most popular party in Greece, according to the report'. The Gleaner, Fri. Dec. 6, 2013, p. B11. A later press report was to the effect that "Greek judicial authorities has ordered the jailing of a lawmaker with the extreme right Golden Dawn party on charges of being a prominent member of a criminal organisation. There, (in jail), they will join Golden Dawn legislators. …the leader, deputy leader … jailed since late September, days after a left wing rapper was murdered by a Golden Dawn member. A third of Golden Dawn's parliamentary group is now behind bars. …" See 'Greece jails lawmakers', The Gleaner, Mon. Jan. 13, 2014, p. D5.

277 The European Court of the Human Rights Application No. 58369/10 Staatkundig Gereformeerde Partij (SGP) v the Government of the Netherlands, 10th July, 2012.

278 Ibid.

---

have, by ordination, different roles in society and family, by virtue of which women should not be eligible for public [political] office.

4. In order to continue to have access to state funding amounting to approximately one-third of its income, and in keeping with the views of the courts, women were admitted to membership.

5. The suits before the different courts which adjudicated on the matter were filed by human and women's equal rights groups.

6. The grounds advanced in support of the claims before the different courts were SGP's alleged violation of the fundamental rights of equal treatment and thereby the general interest of society in the elimination of discriminatory treatment whether gender-based or otherwise, in keeping with the Dutch Constitution.

7. A breach by the Dutch Government of Articles of the 'Convention on the Elimination of all Forms of Discrimination Against Women' was alleged by its grant of a subsidy to SGP and also, thereby, a breach of the 1966 'International Covenant on Civil and Political Rights'.

8. In addition to SGP, the Dutch Government was also a defendant in the proceedings, since the suits were instituted with the primary political aim of stopping the payment of the political subsidy to the party, thus forcing it to change its by-laws provision on women, or cease functioning through lack of funds, membership dues being insufficient to meet its operational requirements.

9. In an earlier judgment given by a Dutch Regional Court, it was held that the State had been in violation of the Convention and was ordered to refrain from granting a subsidy to SGP for as long as the party continued to deny women membership on an equal footing as men. The appeal lodged by SGP was dismissed.

10. Further, the Dutch Minister of the Interior and Kingdom Relations, feeling bound by the court's decision rejected SGP's subsidy application.

11. In opposition to the above views/decisions, it was argued that such a position not only encroached on the "freedom rights of political parties, but also on the public interest of sufficient representation of the full electorate ... [which] included the representation in the elected bodies of small minorities with views divergent from those held by the majority, as long as any such views did not violate criminal law".

12. The Netherlands: *Political Parties Subsidies Act* provides that all parties represented in parliament be granted subsidies on the same conditions except when their conduct led to a criminal conviction of illegal discrimination under article 16 of *the Act*.

13. The Administrative Jurisdiction Division had endorsed 12 above by holding that 'political parties', even those with opinions deviating from the majority should not be excluded from participation in the public debate. Otherwise, the legitimacy of the public debate would be compromised. Further, it was argued that the "Division also noted– that women were not precluded from joining other political parties and standing for public office. In any event, States should show restraint in limiting the freedom of political parties since there were essential for the proper functioning of a pluralistic and democratic society. Intervention in the functioning of political parties could only be justified in cases where a domestic court had found that a political party constituted a danger to the democratic legal order".

14. The Dutch state then appealed to the Court of Appeal, which granted SGP leave to join in the proceedings as a party to the action.

15. The arguments of the Court of Appeal in deciding against the State and SGP are, in our view, specious in the extreme: there was nothing, it was said, preventing the party from organizing itself otherwise and, except for this particular element, wholly in accordance with its basic principles. There can hardly be a more 'classic' example of an inherently self-contradictory statement.

16. The Court of Appeal further held that "if and when the SGP was forced to allow women to stand for election, nothing precluded it from freely deciding on such issues as composition of lists of candidates … and what political opinions such candidates should express". Such opinions "could also include those not shared by the majority of the Netherlands namely that women were by definition not suited for any Government office". This we find, with respect, to be absurdity of the highest order.

17. The Appeal Court concluded that it was for the Government *to take measures effectively leading the SGP* [Italics added] to grant women the right to stand for election, while at the same time not impinging on the fundamental rights of the party's members 'any more than was necessary'. This was although, in its view, it could not competently order a cessation of subsidy by the state.

18. Apart from other considerations, the case which was decided eventually, as one might expect, against SGP, highlights one crucial aspect of the difficulties inherent in regulatory framework design in this contentious area of national life: the conflict of fundamental rights/freedoms/values which surface for weighing and balancing against each other, namely, religion, expression, association, political opinion, gender equality.

The European Court, not unnaturally, came to its decision based primarily on international Conventions. In finding against the SGP, emphasis was placed on the promotion of the ideals and values of a democratic society "as democracy was the only political model contemplated in the Convention under which a *political party may pursue its policies on two conditions. ...*"[279] [Italics added].

The politics involved in the Courts' reasoning was then exposed when it said: "Turning to the present matter, the Court reiterates that the advancement of the equality of the sexes is today a major goal of the member states of the Council of Europe."

In essence, in a conflict between the views of the Council of Europe and those of a political party on the roles of men and women in society, however deeply grounded in religious belief the latter may be, it is the former that should prevail in the adjudication of any resulting dispute.

It is perhaps ironic, therefore, that while seeming to dictate matters of religious belief and internal non-criminal organisation principle and practice, the Court held that in respect of the State itself, the signatory to the Convention, it (the Court) *"must refrain from stating any view as to what, if any, the respondent Government should do to put a stop to the present situation".* [Italics added].

In the interest of contextual relevance, the purview of The Netherland's *Political Parties Subsidies Act*, [280] is limited to the sections set out in Appendix III.

---

279   The numerical specification of conditions here, we find frightening: for the state to circumscribe the boundaries of private institutions' operational freedom so precisely is a precedent we would be reluctant to recommend. The provision, 'The Convention on the Elimination of all Forms of Discrimination against Women', is referred to in the Court's judgment at paragraph 71, where the case of Refah Partise [The Welfare Party] and others v Turkey, reported at 14BHRC1, (2003) 37 EHRR1, (2003) ECHR87 was cited in support at paragraph 98, 100.

280   Go to http://stumblingandmumbling.typepad.com/stumbling_and_mumbling/2007/03/against_state_f.html

The *Act*, in addition to the Dutch Constitution, were the pieces of national legislative enactments against which regional/international treaty/convention obligations contended, juridically, for interpretation.

The Gavel's graphic analogy rivalling Hannan's portrayal, above, of Italy's inter-party relations is 'painful' and eloquent in almost equal measure,

> The politicians ... are like the motorist who believes he should get national honours after carrying an injured pedal cyclist to the hospital, despite the fact that that motorist was responsible for carelessly running over the victim in the first place.[281]

One possible comment, though, is that a vigilant and militant, if necessary, electorate has more effective arsenal in its armoury, in confrontation with a dysfunctional political system of which they are the most essential part, than a cyclist confronted by a reckless motorist.

Hayden Phillips acknowledges that some opposition to state funding is as a matter of principle, "although the principle has been breached in practice for some time."[282] There is likely to be less engagement with voters, if it resulted in greater party administrative centralization, which is likely, due to the concomitant requirement for a more detailed and formally structured recording of activities and transactions. A head office's accounting officer usually has, for easier reporting control purposes, responsibility under law/regulations for compliance with financial regulations.

Whether the proposed reform will weaken the entirety of the parties' internal hierarchical order—a possible consequence of resulting centralization and increased bureaucratisation – and, ultimately, their capacity for institutional integration—important even in a small island polity, is a potential development worth tracking. Comprehensiveness in the study of the reform subject matter would require informed projections that would enable the parties to better weigh the proposals from a broader cost/benefit standpoint. Such data is more likely to reside in, and be more accessible from, party head office.

The growing trend of dependence on the state, as the principal financier of party activity, may thus result in a corresponding increase of power

---

281 "The Gavel", *The Gleaner*, Mon. Nov. 4, 2013, pp. 6, 7.
282 Hayden Phillips, op. cit., p.6.

concentration and administrative responsibility within the party[283], and strengthen the orientation of parties towards the state, at the same time that there is an opposed "shifting away" from their traditional role as instruments representing different, and often overlapping, sections of civil society, as Katz and Mair conclude in their seminal study of the cartel party phenomenon.[284]

The more advanced this development becomes, the less able one would expect parties to be to determine and establish the norms to best cope with adaptation, substantially and procedurally, with revealed weaknesses and changes in a constituency-differentiated political environment. The political class is, understandably perhaps, less adept at displaying the degree of market sensitivity manifested by the business class.

Conflicting claims and interests reflecting and conditioned by the dynamic 'mix of social structures and changes in the dialectic relation between the ambiguities which inhere in collective life', in modern society will tend to be mediated, politically, in the Jamaican case, as dictated by a high-risk-averse orientation. In such an environment, few, if indeed anyone, feel satisfied: one of the less easily paid prices of the phenomenon of stable multi-party parliamentary democracy, particularly in areas where the party contenders for control of state power and resources are of roughly equal electoral strength.

The parlous state of the island's finances,[285] with or without an IMF Agreement in place[286], could, of course, derail political state funding plans.

---

283 See Nassmacher, Karl–Heinz, 'Structure and impact of Public Subsidies to Political Parties in Europe: The Examples of Austria, Italy, Sweden and West Germany' in Herbert Alexander (ed) *Comparative Political Finance in the 1980s*, Cambridge University Press. And, Panebianco, Angelo, *Political Parties; Organisation and Power*, 1988, Cambridge University Press, 1989, pp. 236 – 267.

284 Katz and Mair, 1995; Yael Yishai, proceeds from the Katz & Mair conceptualization to contemplate the response of parties in post-individualistic society by the dual strategy of penetrating civil society by aligning with voluntary organisations [as proposed by *The Gleaner* and others] and by stimulating a politics of identity in which the post-cartel party combines the organisational benefits of the cartel, while at the same time returning to grassroots social forces.' Party Politics', *Sage Publications* 2001, Vol. 7, No. 6, p. 667

285 Even at the intra-party level of a JLP leadership election, the point has been made that "The palpably lavish spend (sic) by persons campaigning ... demonstrates in no uncertain terms that they are completely out of touch with the plight and current struggles of ordinary Jamaicans. ... I have no hesitation in saying that the vast majority of JLP delegates are in dire financial straits at this time". This observation led to the suggestion that instead the better thing to have done with the "extravagant campaign expenditure" was to distribute it "among" the delegates (within the context of widespread poverty, a chronic inability ... to afford the most basic social amenities". The problem with the oft encountered failure to think through propositions is evident here: instant charges of vote-buying corruption would have been leveled and could, as a result, have caused even further internal tension/friction, leading possibly to the questioning of the legitimacy of the election results. ...

286 See 'Jamaica has worst debt-to-revenue ratio in Moody's rating universe' in *The Gleaner*, Wed. July 27, 2011, p. C6.

In such an event, the more corruption there is in the distribution of scarce benefits, the more will 'the power of doing nothing' be in favour of the governing party. That having been said, the concern about influence peddling, by incumbents, as a factor in the funding equation, has not, to date, resulted in any Jamaican politician being labelled as "a special interest slot machine" nor described in the following comparatively specific terms, "one of the most salient distinguishing characteristics of ... tenure as a US Senator has been his crafting, supporting and persuading the Senate to adopt large number of obscure laws that benefited many of his prime campaign contributions".[287]

Such a portrayal of U.S. Senator Bob Dole is appropriately accompanied by evidence, provided in the chapter, "Case studies in Corporate Welfare",[288] with a supporting list of 'made to order laws,'[289] seeming to establish a causal relationship between money and the consequential advancement of public policy / program / project. The Jamaican legislative system is relatively uncomplicated and certainly easier to be monitored for any similar breaches of 'public trust'. In a healthy multi-party system, with both major parties being of roughly equal strength one would expect that that should clearly be one of any Opposition's central functions. [290]

Using public funds to support and enhance 'democracy' overlooks the fact that good intentions for all usually become overwhelmed by the particular constellation of social forces, often mute, yet clamouring for discriminating attention at different points in time. Resulting tensions might, therefore,

---

287 Hilton, Stanley G. 'Senator for Sale, an Unauthorized Biography of Senator Bob Dole', St. Martins Press, (New York, 1995), p.166.

288 Ibid 166 – 177, See also the 'evidence' referred to in 'supporting' allegations that Democratic mayoral candidate, William Thompson, while he was city comptroller, often gave work and business to donors "... sometimes within days of when the donors made their contributions to his campaign." Although it was denied that anyone received favours based on a contribution, "interviews and a review of thousands of pages of records, schedules, e-mails, pension statements and campaign finance reports suggest frequent overlap of Mr. Thompson's political ambitions and the comptroller's operation", The New York Times, Sat. Aug, 31, 2013, pp. A1, 15. In stark contrast in Jamaica, allegations, suspicions and beliefs are almost always bereft of any attempt at preferring supporting details. For our purposes, one of Thompson's donor's response is not only interesting, but indeed instructive: "But Mr. Maitland [a donor and Pension Fund Manager] said "that a mutual beneficial relationship is not necessarily bad, we've done well by the city and the city's done well by us. ... That's how it's supposed to work." See also Ronald Mason, supra, where the columnist declares: "However, do not tell 'us' not to influence the election outcome by the free use of our own resources. We have a right to exercise our options while being aware of the convergence of inappropriate behaviour".

289 Hilton, Stanley, G., supra, pp. 178 – 197

290 Ronald Mason, supra, argues that "This process of securing the return on investment [donation in return for benefit] is subject to the checks and balances from the Parliament, the party, the bureaucracy, and the people. Expose and evidence sufficient to convict will result in appropriate sanctions".

mean that the appearance of systemic stability represents, in fact, a quite precarious equilibrium.[291]

For the political class, a state funding regime is a very reliable guarantor for survival with a governing approach of incrementalism and the maintenance of the *status quo*.[292] This makes, normally, for a 'comfortable' professional political career.

But, those who subscribe to traditional liberal political principles seem unaware of the contradiction inherent in state funding of political parties, coupled inevitably with regulation which "... exercises a degree of control on party activity unprecedented in the context of liberal democracy [and] provide the most unequivocal testimony of such a *new conception* [Italics added]."[293]

It is acknowledged that politics now requires more money because of increasing cost-intensive campaign techniques together with the internal bureaucratisation/professionalization of parties, which means the acquisition of more and higher paid staff, with a decreasing number of volunteers. This disengagement from conventional politics, represented by the significant fall off in unpaid activity by the committed, a weakening of party identification, increasing partisan dealignment and a dramatic fall in membership, are developments noted by Dalton *et al*[294] and Mair and van Biezen et al.[295]

Part of the explanation for this process has been seen by Blondel as resulting from the fact that:

> In becoming larger, the middle class [party members] cease to be an appendage of the manual and white-collar groups. It becomes a group *in itself* [Italics added].[296]

---

291 The present upheaval in Ukraine is a worthwhile example of this.

292 See, "The Gavel", 'Behind the veil of that UNCONSCIONABLE ECJ campaign-financing proposal, *The Gleaner*, Mon. Nov. 4, 2013, pp. A6, 7.

293 van Biezen, Ingrid., 'Political Parties as Public Utilities', in Party Politics, *Sage Publications*, Vol. 10, (2004), No. 6, p. 702. See also Ronald Mason, supra, who concludes his piece: God help us, libertarians, the ECJ seeks to regulate the freedom out of the electoral process": this after observing that, "The Electoral Commission of Jamaica continues to peddle the idea that voters have to be protected from their inability to choose, a notion that I find demeaning ... It is not an infallible process, but democracy is not without blemishes. ..."

294 Russell, Dalton. and Waltenberg, Martin (eds), *Parties without Partisans: Political Change in Advanced Industrial Democracies*, Oxford University Press, (Oxford, UK, 2000).

295 van Biezen, Ingrid and Peter Kopecky', 'On the Predominance of State Money: Reassessing Party Financing in the New Democracies of Southern and Eastern Europe, *Perspectives on European Politics and Societies* 2(3): 401-29.

296 Blondel, op. cit.., p. 144.

Almost inevitably, this has meant a greater measure of intra, and indeed inter party, 'doctrinal unity' where, … "disagreement is more likely to be on issues of administration than policy … divisions which may occur are unlikely to turn themselves into battles of social as well as political or economic interests".[297]

The view has further been advanced that detailed state regulation,

> may curtail the organisational autonomy of parties to such an extent that parties become the annexed institutions of the state. Ultimately, this may lead European parties to converge to the American view in which parties are conceived of as 'part of the machinery' of elections, rather than organisations that themselves *contest* elections.[298]

van Biezen has observed, on the effectiveness of some reform attempts, that,

> Indeed while state regulation of party finance has often been enacted to curtail corrupt practices and to enhance public accountability, illicit party financing in the newer democracies continues to persist perhaps paradoxically, in spite of the relatively stringent legal frameworks.[299]

Gambetta in fact contends[300] that further reliance on state funding may not just contribute to its persistence, as van Biezen posited, but could even increase, rather than diminish the incidence of corruption. Additionally, Katz and Mair argue that, periodically, reliance on the state for substantial funding may create a culture of dependency in which other state resources are expected and sought, such as the unauthorized use of public assets along with attempts to "extract state resources through office-holding positions by resorting to patronage and clientelism"[301] which are core features, according to the late distinguished Jamaican political sociologist Carl Stone, of Jamaica's political culture. Accusations relating to the improper use of state resources by the incumbent party and its representatives during campaigns, in particular,

---

297 Ibid. p. 146

298 Katz, Richard, 'The Internal Life of Parties', in Kurt Richard Luther and Ferdinand Müller Rommel, (eds), *Political Challenges in the New Europe: Political and Analytical Challenges*, Oxford University Press, (Oxford UK, 2002), pp. 87 – 118.

299 van Biezen, in *Party Politics*, supra, p. 716

300 Gambetta, Diego 'Corruption: An Analytical Map', in Stephen Kottin and Andre' M. Bajorat, (eds), *Political Corruption in Transition: A Skeptic's Handbook*, Central European University Press, 2002.

301 Katz, Richard and Peter Mair, "Changing Models of Party Organisation and Party Democracy: the Emergence of the Cartel Party, in Party Politics", 1995, 1(1) pp. 5-28, 1995

are like the 'recurring decimal'.

Against the background of the work of scholars such as Pasquino[302], van Biezen concludes:

> Systems of generous public funding may in fact supplement rather than have substitutory effects on clientelistic and corrupt forms of financing ... the consequences of public funding often therefore appear to have been ill-considered ... has discouraged parties from looking for additional sources of income ... and has removed a key incentive to establish a more structural relationship with civic society ... the potential of public subsidies to curtail improper private financing appears to be limited and may even be counterproductive.[303]

One suspects that however "robust" the ECJ system might be, it would, nevertheless, prove largely inconsequential for achieving significant political behavioural change, beyond what 'good form' dictates, in keeping with the 'logic of appropriateness'.

If voter support, translated into partisan commitment, sufficient to elicit financial contributions in accordance with one's means and one's party's needs, is seen as the primary determinant of the state of the 'playing field', then to the extent that the paradigm prevails, the parties would, to that extent, be compelled, for survival, to more effectively engage in potential marketing activities.

INCUMBENTS' ADVANTAGE

Since state subventions tend to be disbursed on the basis of electoral success or parliamentary numerical strength, they freeze the *status quo* of the party system and make it difficult for outsiders to enter, individually and

---

302   Pasquino quoted by Blanco, Valdes, Roberto, 'La Problematica de la Financoncion de los Partidos Politicas en España: Regulacion Juridica y Propuestas de Reforma: Revista de Estudios Politicos', 87: 165 (trans) 'The Problem of Political Parties in Spain; Legal Regulation and Proposals for Reform'; *Journal of Political Studies.*

303   van Biezen, in *Party Politics*, p. 717; It is always worth stating the incidence of political abuse/corruption in perspective: the relatively high profile of the occupation coupled with media sensationalism makes it easy to forget that "Examples of abuse are the notable exception to the rule": Hayden Phillips, 2006, p. 13.

as organisations.[304] At the same time, the ECJ's proposal for new parties to be registered and therefore qualify for state funding, on the basis of a prescribed minimum number of members' signatures, could easily be the opening of the door to all manner of 'antics' by those with high political ambitions, however ostensibly noble, but no 'traction' in the eyes of the electorate. The history of third parties in Jamaica is not one distinguished by longevity with a citizenry hungry for tangible benefits, not necessarily on/in the personal/clientelistic sense, from a political system that has substantially failed to improve the quality of life of the majority for some forty years. That tradition is not likely to be overturned in the near future.

At the same time, the reality of a virtually empty Treasury—whatever the policy prompting of the relevant prevailing variant of the democratic sentiment—may mean that parties without cash or prospects need to be made meaningfully aware that aspirations are best related to opportunities, objectively identified.

Even where public funding has been viewed as a solution to some of the problems exhibited by multi-party political systems, it is worth noting that it may possess its own pitfalls. Usually, it promotes a clientelistic relationship between *governments* and *parties*, quite apart from the negative implications for internal party democracy, due to resulting tendencies to seek ever increasing state support, normally approved by the very members of the parties who happen to be in Parliament and who form the Government from time to time. One can anticipate 'generosity' even in times of scarcity of national resources, where the donor/legislator is also the current or prospective legatee.

It can also be expected that current beneficiaries will seek to increase the extent of their benefits, subject to the assessment by the governing party, in particular, of rival parties' cash raising prospects, as their total income might thereby be determined. As we are often reminded, money is unlikely to be used, in whatever context, with equal degrees of skill, even in strictly business organisations which, from the perspective of operational efficiency, usually

---

304 See, "The Gavel", 'Behind the veil of that UNCONSCIONABLE ECJ campaign-financing proposal', supra, where the view is expressed: "But never mind the quest to create equality, the ECJ's grand idea of state – funding would shut out most independent persons … so notwithstanding voter apathy indicating that Jamaicans are tired of the People's National Party and the Jamaica Labour Party, state funding would ensure change does not come".

benefit from the specialized training of their financial functionaries. The same certainly cannot be said of political parties.

What this means, as a practical matter, is that whatever the intention, there is thus no guarantee that any amount of state funding can ever 'level the playing field', a concept superficial in its idealistic appeal, which its many distinguished champions consistently fail to excogitate. The notion has no 'supra-partisan truth inherent in it, as the result of sheer logical necessity'. Since people will always use money to very different effects, they will consequently generate very different performance results.

Whatever funds may be provided from taxes in Jamaica for election campaigns, which will include rallies, among other promotional activities, will partly be used to pay for what has been described by an experienced and knowledgeable practitioner in these matters, as "... hype-ocrisy [sic], exaggeration, white lies and twisted truth for the sole purpose of vote-catching."[305]

With respect to the financing of party *organisation* activities, perhaps less prone to abuse, such as a statement of policy to be presented by way of a manifesto, it has been said that, "Saying bluntly what a party really stands for can often be a sure way to lose an election. So election manifestos are often shallow generalities."[306]

Another commentator makes the claim that:

> The sum of money in the ... accounts that was spent on the conference could only pay for transportation. It is the 'pocket-money' and the orgy of food and 'likka' (liquor) before, during and after these events that cost many millions of dollars. Financing political parties with our taxes will only increase the number of Hennessy bottles we have to pick up after each event.[307]

---

305 Jones, Jon, 'Media should do better', *The Gleaner*, Wed. Sep.14, 2011, p. A8. James C. Miller III, supra, notes that "... the competitiveness of political markets is further restrained by the incentives and opportunities candidates have to deceive voters": The Jamaican political culture is notorious for unfulfilled election promises; but parties and politicians are 'rescued' by the short term memory of the electorate: See Kevin O'Brien Chung, *The Gleaner*, May 15, 2011, pp. F3, 6. Even at the level of internal leadership election, as in the case with the JLP (November, 2013) the point has been made that 'all that money could have been put to better use'. The *Jamaica Observer*, Fri. Oct. 4, 2013, p.13. The letter writer, Harold Blake claims that, ' It is no wonder then that so many Jamaicans are ... to question the motives and ultimate agenda of the heavy-spending Shaw backers ... harbouring fears as to whether there is an active plot to buy out the leadership of one of the leading political parties ...'.

306 Levy, Horace., 'A failure of democracy: the hijacking of a country', *The Gleaner*, May 15, 2011 pp. 10, 14

307 Tucker, Glenn, 'An audit that tells little', *The Gleaner*, Thursday September 23, 2010, p. A6. A poll with a sample of 1338 by the Centre for Leadership Governance found only 8% trusting political parties and 10% trusting politicians. Without more, it would seem difficult to use public funds to support entities viewed so negatively: Henley Morgan, 'The evil garrison system', *The Jamaica Observer*, Wed. May 14, 2011, p. 11

Rather than promoting greater engagement with the electorate, state funding, with the existing lack of meaningful regard for non-established parties, is more likely, it has been said, to translate into a greater boycott of elections by the people who will do so, "… rather than vote knowing that they will be conniving in this corrupt tax-theft."[308]

With respect to parties' promotional activity, the charge has also been made that,

> Well-funded parties [as a result of state financing] … use their money to degrade and cheapen political discourse, for example by running misleading advertising campaigns based on subrational arguments.[309]

Yet another commentator concludes, "The parties are struggling to attract funding because people increasingly despise them and rightly so."[310] Astonishingly to some observers, civil society representatives, 'rich in rhetoric and indignation' nevertheless vociferously advocate their subsidy by the people, in an environment decidedly 'lacking in communal rhythm'. Any agreement among party leaders in favour of state funding, is thus regarded as, "… a demonstration of how distant the political class has become from the public. Their problem is a lack of public support, so they choose a solution that is guaranteed to alienate the public ever further."[311]

So, if the press headline, "Campaign finance reform [is] vital to free,

---

308 Tucker, Glenn, supra.

309 See 'Against State Funding' (n. 3); See also 'Let's carefully examine that JEEP,' where one Randolph Ledgister warned of "campaign rhetoric being baptized as authentic undertakings" … , adding, in reference to the Governments' Jamaica Emergency Employment Program (JEEP), that the program should be debated in Parliament and "not left reservedly for the campaign trails where anything can be said and left to the susceptibility of a trustful people". Low-grade advertising is one thing for which state funds may also, of course, be used, as allegedly happened in Mexico's 2012 Presidential elections when, "Pigs, sheep, chickens bought votes", to dramatize the outrageousness of which, "Mexico's leftist presidential candidate [who lost] brought a pig, a sheep and chickens to a news conference yesterday": The *Jamaica Observer*, Wed. Aug. 15, 2012, p. 18. The report further advised: "the pig was the most vocal of the group. The sheep quietly munched on the grass placed on the floor of Lopez Obrador's headquarters, while the chicken and some turkeys pecked aimlessly".

310 'Stumbling and Mumbling', 'Against State Funding of Parties' in Public Choice March 15, 2007,Permalink, http://www.ty pepad.com/services/trackback/6aood83451cbef69e2ood835225d3569e2; See also Michael Pinton Dunschinsky 'Political Funding in Britain: What can we learn from history" Mimeo, History & Policy series, *BBC History Magazine*, May 2008.

311 Ibid

fair elections",[312] is to be taken seriously, did the lack of it for the purposes of the 2011 Jamaican general election, of necessity, call the validity of that election into question at any level of assessment? We are unaware of any such conclusion.

The *quid pro quo*, who pays the piper, relationship that is the essential adhesive, 'the glue' in the proposed ECJ state financing regime, results in indirect *state control* of even such *internal matters* of political parties as "methods of dispute resolution,"[313] and meaninglessly, perhaps, "their aims and objectives."[314]

It can be strenuously argued that as a matter of fundamental democratic principle, *taxpayers* should not be *compelled* to contribute to the support of political parties with whose outlook, image and policies they might well very strongly disagree,[315] and it is obviously not feasible to disaggregate tax revenue into any partisan categorization of taxpayers.

Existing parties could easily become monolithic with generous state support, whereas new parties are almost always at a disadvantage.[316] Any system of financing based largely, or exclusively, on the level of electoral support at a previous election(s) as the ECJ proposes, would tend, inevitably, to have that result.[317]

Since funding, as we have noted, for relatively easy administration reasons, usually goes exclusively to headquarters, this increases the power of

---

312 Richard Crawford, *The Gleaner*, Oct. 9, 2011, p. D12. According to this contributor, who is in favour of full state funding, "... all practical, legal and acceptable measures must, therefore be put in place to guarantee that Jamaica will have *property* [Italics added] funded free and fair elections at all times". His call for 'an official campaign period' of 60 days maximum could be of limited utility only with respect to accounting requirements and free broadcasting concessions, should the latter be adopted. Since it seems to be the bases of much of civil society's thinking that 'who pays the paper calls the tune', it may be expected and is indeed being proposed, without the connection being made explicitly, that the introduction of state provided broadcasting concessions should be accompanied by the monitoring of the use of "lies, exaggerations and excesses [which] have become staple methods of political advertising in Jamaica". See also, 'Regulate election ads', a report by Peyra Williams-Raynor of the position taken by the group Jamaicans United for Sustainable Development (JUSD), *The Gleaner* Aug. 21, 2011, p.21

313 See 'Points of Agreement', Conference on Campaign Financing, mimeo, ECJ, July 10, 2006, p.2

314 Ibid

315 Ronald Mason, in 'Damn dictatorship on campaign financing', supra, argues that, "Those who desire to know will inform themselves and make their free choice [of candidate/party]. ... We do not need to have limits placed on our right to influence the government selection. All influence is not predicted on nefarious expectations. We may have family, partisan and political philosophy preferences".

316 'Election vehicle policy stinks of cronyism', Letter to *The Gleaner*, Tue. Oct 11, 2011, p.A6, by Marlon Johnson, condemning policy in which only the two major parties benefit from substantial import duty concession

317 See "The Gavel", 'Behind the veil of that UNCONSCIONABLE ECJ campaign financing proposal', supra,

party central over regional/ constituency/ grassroots organisation with the known Michelian oligarchical, internal anti-democratic decision-making tendencies. While the need for overall coordination will still, to some degree, be required, the consequential diminishing participation and sharing of responsibility is a huge price to pay at a time of low actual/potential party member/supporter morale and commitment.

State funding, would also tend, in accordance with its degree of sufficiency, to weaken the motivation to engage with the public by way of raffles, fetes, and other, usually *locally* organized, fundraising party/public bonding activities.

In addition, as Sam Younger, then Chairman of the British Electoral Commission, in an interview with *The Guardian* newspaper in February 2004 acknowledged, the regulations on the funding of political parties had:

> caused a number of difficulties for local parties … All the parties are reporting that it is increasingly difficult to get people to act as treasurers of local parties … There are written into the legislation penalties, including criminal penalties. … Not only are the regulations putting people off politics, they have also, apparently, failed to increase trust in politicians. So if the publicity [disclosure requirements] is not helping to restore trust anyway, why bother?[318]

Taken together, these possible/actual party member/supporter developments represent a serious double disincentive which does not bode well for the future of multi-party political democracy as traditionally conceived.

The trend may thus be aggravated where parties tend to become a 'captured' part of the state rather than a vehicle representing citizens' *vis-à-vis* the state apparatus.

One could safely hazard the guess that few, from a demographically representative cross-section of the country, would dispute that "… the needs of political parties are not the greatest priority in terms of public expenditure",[319] particularly given the current parlous state of national finances, almost

---

318 House of Commons Library, 'Funding of Political Parties – A Brief Overview', by Richard Kelly of the Parliament and Constitution Centre, Apr 27, 2006, SN/PC/3138.

319 The British Labour Party in its evidence to the Neill Committee

universally, and certainly in the Jamaican case. In keeping with this position, it has been argued that, in the context of Britain's public finances,

> state political financing is equivalent to paying for the National Trust out of tax. Are parties to be subject to audit and the paraphernalia of Treasury Control? If so, what price [sic] their autonomy from the government machine? 'It is the commitment of the British electorate to parliamentary democracy, and its willingness to work it, which ultimately sustains the system; the parties are part of the expression of that commitment and that willingness'.

That was the *minority* view of the Houghton committee, whose majority said yes to state funding in 1975.[320]

The British Labour Party in its Manifesto for the 2005 General Election proposed to, "... explore how best to support the vital democratic role of political parties, while recognising that campaigning activity *must* [Italics added] always be funded by parties from their own resources".[321]

Even if the Commission's budget is protected from political pressure, it may be inadequate for effective enforcement, given the state's limited resources. In such a situation, any expenditure which is politically linked is unlikely to be a treasury priority.[322] What this will mean is that the political consequences of party and campaign finance regulations are likely to become more sensitive and significant, for the actors in the political process, the greater the gap between perceived need and resources from both the state and the private sector.

And although the intention may partly be to reduce corruption and "level the playing field," it is usually ignored that these methods of regulating state/private political funding are far from neutral in their political effects.

---

320 David Walker, *The Guardian* (UK) 2002, Mar 13, , see http://www.theguardian.com/politics/2002/mar13/constitution.comment

321 The Labour Party manifesto 2005, 'Britain forward not back; Labour, www.labour.org.uk , at p. 111,

322 The somewhat utopian view has been expressed, "So I need people who really have the country at heart and are not looking to the next five years saying, 'What should I do to win the next election?' We've had enough of that". See 'We do not trust them', *The Gleaner*, Dec. 11, 2011, p. D14. Unfortunately for this panellist, we are 'destined' to have more of that in any multi-party electoral system: that, without even the slightest trace of cynicism, is precisely and essentially what politics is about. Can a politician be expected to make decisions which he/she believes will result in the loss of political power, at the next election? 'Unpopular' decisions / policies, ostensibly in the national interest, are taken in the rational expectation on the part of the decision-maker that *ultimately* the results will be to the party's electoral benefit. Internal and indeed public differences of view on this account at times, for leadership changes, if not the emergence of 'splits'.

Of the seven items listed by CAFFE, under the heading, 'The Dangers of unregulated Campaign Financing', the only one we wish to note here is (g), "Unfair advantage to those who by whatever means are able to access great sums of money."[323] The question remains, why should any advantage, in the competitive process that politics, in its very essence, is, be considered 'unfair'.[324] Should all tennis players or other athletes be of the same physical structure/capability and mental toughness and determination and be required to undergo the same amount and type of training so that they can compete 'fairly'? Perhaps, too, they should be 'entitled' to the same kind and value of sponsorship.

For some, who oppose state funding, their position can be simply put: "… the parties have got into trouble by themselves and they should sort themselves out."[325]

While we are not unsympathetic to that view, we wish to take a position based not only on what is, but also what ought to be.

Ideally, from that perspective, the vibrant party never stops campaigning, since, with due regard for the effect of the electoral cycle on the level of intensity of organisational and promotional activity at any given time, "persuading voters is a continuing positive activity". The ongoing nature of political communication and the effort to gain competitive advantage in terms of influence, over even the currently ineligible but prospective voter, on this view, casts serious doubt on the rationale of campaign finance expenditure limits and regulation even during 'official' election campaign periods, however determined. Such attempted restriction might just result in the "front loading of expenditure", as CAFFE seems to have recognised.[326] That the situation depicted in the conduct of politics is not unique is borne out by the unfolding of events in the United Kingdom. Whereas under the *Fixed Term Parliament Act*, Britain will have its next general election some nine months hence, on May 7, 2015, it is reported that, "the campaign has

---

323 Campaign Financing', paper from Citizens' Action for Free and Fair Elections, Presented by Dr. The Hon. Lloyd Barnett, O.J., Chairman, Mimeo, July 10, 2006, p. 4

324 See Ronald Mason 'Damn dictatorship in campaign financing', supra, where the view is expressed that, "I find it even more galling that limits should be placed on the use of one's personal finances to fuel an election win. Yes, this argument will be countered with the statement that we will have only well-healed persons as candidates, So what? … The great masses must be credited with collective wisdom …"

325 David Walker, supra

326 CAFFE, pp. 3, 4, 5 (f).

virtually begun with the UK's political parties seeking to score points well before their manifestos have even been written or a full slate of candidates named".[327]

It seems highly repugnant from such a vantage point for the state, through the ECJ and Parliament, to be given the power to significantly influence the design, and more so, the implementation, of a party's campaign strategy in a supposedly democratic society, ironically, allegedly for the purpose of enhancing democratic values and processes.

Further, as a practical matter, it is not as easy as it may appear to distinguish between core and campaign expenditure, and the Jamaican reality is that party posts such as that of Treasurer and General Secretary, are not full-time and are certainly not salaried, although we happen to strongly believe that the latter ought to be.

Imposing penal provisions of a criminal nature, particularly for breaches which occurred, over say a year, and, worse, several years before, rather than over, perhaps, a stipulated pre- and post- campaign period, might well cause the volunteer pool to dry up, as we have noted has already happened with respect to Britain.

To those who take the 'high ground' on these matters, it may be retorted that any argument that provision of public funds would 'allow' the parties more time to devote to policy development is, at best, spurious: it ignores increased specialization of party functionaries and assumes that political contestation is, or with more time available for contemplation, will necessarily become more policy-driven. [328]

Even if the parties were so inclined, any positive political consequence might still be negated, since it has been argued that, as thinkers like Kierkegraad, Nietzsche and Kaffka realized:

> Like the effect of advertising upon the customer, the methods of political propaganda tend to increase the feeling of insignificance of the individual voter. Repetition of slogans ... numb his critical capacities. The clear and rational appeal to his thinking are rather the exception ... even in

---

327   David Jessop, 'A champion for the Caribbean', *The Gleaner*, Aug. 9, 2014, p. C6.

328   See, 'Issues? What issues? Few J'cans prepared to vote on issues if elections are called now', *The Gleaner*, Thu. July 7, 2011, p. A2: poll results showed little relation between voting intentions and perceived party performance, being 13% support for the JLP and 18% for the PNP, respectively.

democratic countries ... they flatter the individual ... by pretending that they appeal to his critical judgment, to his sense of discrimination ... essentially a method to dull the individual's suspicions and help him fool himself as to the individual character of his [voting] decision.[329]

The inevitability of such a development is in doubt. Instead, parties could become so cocooned by state funds that the alternative survival demands of effective mobilization at the grassroots/fundraising level in confrontation with a public disaffected and suffering from "democratic fatigue", could increasingly appear too daunting a challenge. In that event, what could develop, at the worst, is an insatiable hunger and appetite for taxpayer's money which could obviate the need, and become a ready substitute, for the leg work which is so much more demanding in terms of time, energy and the skills of interpersonal interaction in playing the role not dissimilar to that of one engaged in the 'customer service' function.[330]

One can conceive of the upper representative echelons of the political system becoming increasingly comprised of fame, and, no doubt, in some cases, fortune-seeking members of an emerging political class, progressively insulated, the greater the quantum of state funds supplied, from the demands of a healthy participatory democracy, particularly at the local level.

The organisation of occasional special events such as an all-island bus tour, or other "spectacle", may well become a substitute for the traditional one-on-one interaction expected in a small island geographical space, and thereby provide confirmation that "desperate seekers of power are concerned less with the details of policy and more with political gimmickry."[331] At this level, the parties' political behaviour could then, cynically, be said to be 'bipartisan'.

---

329 Fromm, op. cit. p. 112

330 Indeed the decline of the mass party, almost everywhere, is seen as a "model of organisation (which) is no longer financially sustainable in Western Europe", so the burden of party formation and maintenance rests on the party's office holders and aspirant [public] office holders ... with office seeking rather than policy seeking becoming the dominant rationale of party activity". Hopkin, Jonathan., "The Problem with Party Finance", in Party Politics, *Sage Publications*, Vol. 10 No. 6 p. 631, with references to Mueller, Wolfgang and Kaere Strom (eds) *Policy, Office or Votes? How Political Parties in Western Europe Make Hard Decision'*, Cambridge University Press, (Cambridge, 1999); see also Downs, Anthony, *An Economic Theory of Democracy*, Harper and Row , (New York, 1957) and Kirchheimer, Otto , 'The Transformation of Western European Party Systems' in Joseph Lapalombora and Myron Weiner (eds), *Politicial Parties and Political Development'*, Princeton University Press, (Princeton, New Jersey, 1996).

331 Roger Pride, in Letters to the Editor, "Great Column", the *Jamaica Observer*, Wednesday July 27, 2011, p. 8

Operationally, increased regulation implies increased complexity in substance and procedure and, therefore, difficulty and cost of compliance. Instead of being concerned with 'necessary' systemic changes, party leadership may instead be more preoccupied with managerial administrative issues.

At another level of analysis, state funding represents the further institutionalization of political conflict, broadly perceived, and thereby tends to stultify the emergence of impulses with the potential to be organized into social forces sufficient to be the catalyst for meaningful change. In a political context said to be yearning for a radical shift in the *modus operandi* of the principal actors, state financing tends strongly towards keeping the same players (incumbents at the institutional level) on the same playing field.

It is with merit that the observation has been made that the putative replacement of the mass party model with less mobilisational means of funding "... appears to vindicate the growing 'democratic disaffection' among western electorates",[332] which will most certainly be exacerbated by state funding provided in whatever direct proportion to the level of private funding.

The 'stakeholders' with legislative power, save and except where competitive advantage dictates otherwise, will ensure sufficiency of funds, if genuinely needed, to meet the 'reasonable' needs of their parties. As if in confirmation, incredulously, even before the passage of the legislation and shortly after apparent agreement on contribution limits there is a call for the *doubling* of that limit.[333]

On the other hand, if, as has been concluded, the "Parties confront an existential crisis,"[334] then those who wish to 'cast the first stone' need to bear in mind that while "... the historical evolution of political parties reflect an ongoing adaptation to the contours of civil society,"[335] according to Yishai, the reverse is an equally true representation of the reality of social relations.

---

332 Jonathan Hopkin, 'The Problem with Party Financing: Theoretic Perspectives on the Funding of Party Politics', Department of Government, London School of Economics, J.R.Hopkin@lse.ac.uk, at p.15. Hopkin concludes that as against the 'elite' or the 'cartel' party, the mass party model remains closest to the 'democratic' ideal, whilst the state-financed ('cartel') model is a reasonable pragmatic response to the decline in party membership.
333 Most definitely this does not reflect favourably on the quality of the work done by the Commission.
334 Yishai, Yael, supra, 'p. 669.
335 Ibid

He further observes that "State subventions whetted the appetite of many contenders wishing to share the treasure".[336]

Yishai provides a picture of state funding abuse by party collusion in the Israeli context, where law, "practically eliminates contributions as a source of funding". This, ironically, is an assessment in a nation, as in the case of Jamaica, where parties are "Perceived as archaic and stagnated institutions with low prestige and declining legitimacy".[337]

Cooperation/connivance, depending on one's attitude on these matters, between otherwise rival organisations, on public finance issues in Germany has, in effect, it has been said,

> insulated the party finance arrangements from the effect of scandal, and of resulting public disaffection. Instead of change coming as a result of electoral competition between the big parties, most of the changes in the political finance laws (other than subsidy increases) have come because of appeals by small parties to the un-elected Constitutional Court.[338]

In the Jamaican context, if the JLP and PNP and others lack 'the organisational capacity to generate their own income', it is certainly not, as is the case in some of the Eastern European countries, because they are institutions within a "young democracy", as the island is classified by the ECJ.

Any inability to be currently self-financing, is more likely to be explained by a combination of (a) a lost sense of "mission", sufficient to mobilise support, (b) the increasing centralization and professionalization of political organisation and the practise of politics,[339] (c) the effects, at the institutional and personal level, of the International Financial Institutions' support guidelines, in the context of market capitalism within the so-called global economy, and (d) the society's penchant for indiscriminately copying things

---

336 Ibid p. 670

337 Ibid p. 684

338 Scarrow, supra, p. 666

339 As Blondel has noted, 'The movement towards the middle class which one can trace when one analyses the composition of the parliamentary rank-and-file and leadership benefits social groups which are more exclusive', Blondel, op. cit.. p. 152

foreign in origin, fashion and practice.[340]

PRACTICAL CONSEQUENCES
OF STATE FUNDING

The results of state funding may be summed up as follows:

1. Corruption has not been wholly eliminated, nor has loophole seeking.

2. Parties have naturally received more resources although administrative requirements of a bureaucratic nature (party and state) have increased correspondingly.

3. There has, in consequence, for compliance and other reasons, been a higher degree of bureaucratisation and professionalization in party organisation.

4. The importance of party membership in the forms of voluntary work, dues and other forms of financially related involvement (in fundraising events, for example) has significantly declined.

5. Grassroots party structure and organisation for constant communication and mobilisation purposes (at the cell level) has substantially, as against in keeping with formalistic rituals, when constitutionally necessary, virtually disappeared;

6. Dependence on voluntary donations has also declined, as parties feel less urgently the need to mobilise private funding, especially in difficult national economic circumstances, resulting in the 'average citizen', and certainly the masses, having less disposable income.

---

340 van Biezen reports that the **Portuguese Communist Party** provides an exception to the general pattern of state dependence in that the membership structure still constitutes the most important source of income augmented by contributions by the party's public office holders, and the significant results of its fundraising activities. As Pasquino has pointed out, "a system of public funding may indeed have a supplementary rather than substitutory effect on clientelistic forms of financing", at pp.333, 336 of 'Party Financing in New Democracies, Spain and Portugal,' in Party Politics, *Sage Publications*, Vol. 6 No. 3, (2000), If, as is probable, it is the more established, larger parties which benefit from the public funding formulation (If they did not, they would not approve it in cases such as Jamaica where the ECJ's recommendations require parliamentary approval) the consequence will be that there will be little connection between the rules and practice of party financing and party organisational development. See also Massmacher, Karl-Heinz (1989) "Structure and Impact of Public Subsidies to Political Parties in Europe: the examples of Austria, Italy, Sweden, and West Germany", in Alexander, Herbet E. (ed) *Comparative Political Finance in the 1980s*, Cambridge University Press , (Cambridge, (1989); van Biezen and Kopecky argue that "While parties retain control over candidate recruitment and organisation of parliaments and governments, they are losing relevance as vehicles of representation, instruments of mobilization and channels of interest articulation and aggregation", amounting to the erosion of their social roots, van Biezen and Kopecky, supra, at pp. 236, 240.

ARGUMENTS AGAINST STATE FUNDING   **127**

7. Although, there has been an increase in party political activity (other than in fundraising), especially between elections, this has largely been paid for out of public funds.

Since state financing of politics will always tend to be in 'exchange' for a monitoring/controlling role by an organ of the state, usually some kind of Electoral Commission, over party organisation and activity, one is necessarily called upon to consider the context in which parties operate.

CHAPTER 7
THE POLITICAL CULTURE: CONTEXT FOR LEGAL REFORM

In virtually universal fashion, judging from their critique, the citizenry and 'civil society' groups, including the media, are, by implication, innocent of any share of the blame for what was depicted to have been the miserable performance of the two major parties which had alternated as government since universal adult suffrage in 1944,

> seven decades of their [the parties being editorially described as the 'gangs' in Parliament] combined corruption of the political process and our democracy ... Mr. Golding's declaration, notwithstanding, another general election should not take place without a law that brings transparency to party financing.[341]

In the face of such characterization of a seventy-year period, covering constitutional decolonization and political independence, dating from 1962, only, the indulgent, accommodating, neutral role assigned to the "public", equates to that of the 'disinterested bystander' in the law of tort.[342] If this is indeed the role accepted, that of having observer status, only, in the island's governance then, if not in all cases, it may be arguable that 'people do get the governments they deserve'.

Whatever its popular appeal, we cannot agree, that "(But) as Mr. Golding

---

341 Editorial, 'How the gangs of Gordon House might rescue themselves', *The Gleaner*, Fri. Apr. 8, 2011, p.A6. But for a contrary assessment, see 'Democracy and the State: The case of Jamaica', Carl Stone in *The State in Caribbean Society*, Omar Davies, ed, Department of Economics, University; University of the West Indies, Jamaica, Monograph #2, 1986, pp 106, where it is stated that, "These areas of improvement in the quality of life of the majority of classes represented the commitment of the newly emergent political leaders in the JLP and PNP to use the expanded resources of the state to remove the extreme effects of poverty and inequality in the society ... broad consensus on social democratic goals ..." Note, however, that the very same newspaper in what appears to be a more balanced tone in its Editorial, 'Here's an opportunity, PM', acknowledges: "... This doesn't mean that the PNP is without plenty [sic] history that made Jamaica better, that the party is now without value or merit . . ". *The Gleaner*, Sept. 22, 2013, p. A8.

342 Signifies the role of a witness to an event, who is alert but un-biased/neutral in his observations.

is aware, perception is often more important than the reality it tracks ..."[343] certainly not in a society notorious for rumour-mongering, often from motives less than salutary. If corrective focus is put by ECJ guidelines on cultural idiosyncrasies, public communication weaknesses and the cultivation of a more objective evidence-based orientation in the dialogue on public issues and persons in public office, it might well be a useful preliminary reform exercise.

This naturally takes the discussion to a point where consideration of the defining weaknesses of the island's political culture becomes appropriate. The departure adopted here is to be explained on the basis that law, without the appropriate contextual constraints, in its formulation and administration, will most likely prove to be deficient, and hence ineffective, in the sense of yielding intended consequences.

It is again worthy to note that the ECJ's report does state that, in its view, individuals and organisations will fund political parties on the basis of shared ideology, policy preference or candidate quality.[344]

Except for the turbulent and short-lived PNP flirtation with 'Democratic Socialism' in the 1970's, Jamaica's political discourse cannot be said to have been conducted along doctrinal lines. Most definitely, subsequent to its initial engagement with the International Financial Institutions, and, in particular, the IMF, there has been little scope for ideological posturing or, indeed, significant economic/social policy deviation from program guidelines/conditionalities. Nor have independent candidates in national elections fared well.

With respect to the factor of candidate selection being used as a party

---

343 Editorial, *The Gleaner*, June 27, 2010, p. A8. See, for example, the observations of the then Chairman of the ECJ, Prof. Errol Miller, as reported in the *Jamaica Observer*, Fri. Dec. 9, 2011, p. 4: He was also skeptical, as this writer certainly is, about recent reports on the level of corruption and transparency in Jamaica: "When you look at the number of people reporting that Jamaica is very corrupt you get a figure of more than 80 per cent, which is very high. When you look at the figures in the very same survey for what is your personal experience of corruption it is under 20 per cent. This means there is a perception of distortion in the matter, where we are perceiving the situation to be much worse than it really is. This is something I have always known because we have a tendency in Jamaica to generalize the exception to portray it as a rule, and in that way cast a pall of impropriety and corruption over all of us, and we have to be careful." His advice has certainly not been heeded. Claude Robinson, in "In politics, perception is reality' needs to indulge, as a journalist and tutor, in more rational thinking: that every politician regarded as 'dishonest/corrupt' is to be treated as if, in fact, he is, an outlook to be condemned: see the 'Agenda', the *Jamaica Observer*, Sept. 29, 2013, p.4. This attitude accepts and promotes the anti-rule of law *modus operandi* of some members of the police force in dealing with suspects from the lower orders of society. The difference in the case of politicians is you not only 'shoot first' is figurative, but, similarly, one doesn't bother to ask questions much less seek answers/proof.

344 ECJ Report p.8; See also, Ronald Mason, supra.

---

dollar-magnet, we have seen that it is only very recently that, to its credit, the PNP has established a committee with the mandate of overseeing the process, with the use of universalistic criteria, such as 'personal integrity', etc.[345]

There has, in later years, also been the emergence of the urbanization of the approach to party/politician-elector communication, coincident with the virtual disappearance of the major parties', "group" (PNP) and 'branch' (JLP), grassroots structural link between the division, represented by a Councillor, the constituency represented by an MP, and party head office. This has had an observable impact on, and been reinforced by, the calibre of candidates for political office at both the Local Government and Parliamentary levels, certainly in terms of their greater exposure to secondary/tertiary education. Demographic changes will undoubtedly have consequences for party/supporter relations, financial and otherwise.

Together with the alleged "need" to indulge in massive electioneering circus/celebratory party-style expenditure (expensive sound system, music, free food, liquor and transportation being indispensable components) the above development has worsened the political party finance problem. But the issue assumes the significance of a major 'problem' only if we accept the now established campaign *modus operandi*, and also accept that responsibility for remedial action resides in external sources, to the exclusion of the initiatives available to parties in their own individual survival and competitive advantage interest.

Against this background, it is with some sense of anticipation that one awaits the selection of new candidates by the PNP with the screening mechanism now in place. As for the JLP, the prevailing view, in some quarters at least, seems to be that the viability of a prospective candidate rests significantly on the ability to be self-financing (from personal or personal supporters' resources), at the constituency level. This may, if correct, partly explain the destabilizing effect of the 'coming and going' and the 'crossing of the floor' and change of party allegiance of personnel at the representative

---

345 See Danielle James, 'Over to you Electoral Commission', the *Jamaica Observer*, Wed. June 15, 2011, p. 9 where the letter writer concludes, "*The Electoral Commission* [Italics added] of Jamaica as the overlords of our political system must as a matter of urgency seek to ensure that candidate selections are at all times supported by fair and efficient benchmarks of integrity profiling". The tendency of expecting too much from law, *per se*, and social institutions, without regard for role and mandate, constraints is not an uncommon aspect of the public's expectations of performance.

level witnessed in more recent years.[346] If nothing else, this suggests that even at this rung in the hierarchy of party representation and involvement, any social philosophical/ideological party-connection existing consist apparently, of quite fragile links. If commitment at this activity level is tenuous, at the mass level its replication would seem to warrant no investigation into the 'disconnection' and 'malaise' resulting in the massive decline in membership and, consequently, dues from the most basic party organisational unit/cell members.

Candidate selection procedures official/constitutional as against actual and the resulting consequences for funding at the constituency level would constitute worthwhile subject matter for investigation, taking into consideration such factors as the perceived status/calibre of the candidate, within and external to the party.

With the maturation of political parties, as institutions, and especially in the context of multi-party 'democratic politics', it is increasingly likely that,

> tensions come from social and not ideological causes—the gap between the working class and the top of the intelligentsia is much larger at the parliamentary level than it is at the local level.[347]

In the Jamaican context, such tensions are more likely to increase under the strictures of IMF imposed Government revenue and expenditure targets. This trend will be reinforced by the growing disparity in formal educational standards attained by career political representatives as against the masses.

It needs to be always remembered in the business of the selection of candidates, that, "… even if the raw material of politicians were distributed at random among all social classes, the actual politicians are not likely to be distributed at random".[348]

Bearing in mind the ECJ's observation regarding, "… our recent history of political violence, victimization and the tendency to permanently brand

---

346 The ECJ Report p. 11 is of relevance here. This has been at both the Parliamentary and Local Government level, largely in a one-way direction, with the PNP seeming to have the advantage, as the ideology of the parties converge.

347 Blondel, op. cit. p.143

348 Ibid, p. 132

persons as activists",[349] one of the partial transparency features proposed is that, "The expenditure of political parties shall be summarized and published in the daily newspapers and the Commission's website."[350]

This, one suspects, will generate as much interest to the average voter as published public company financial statements, even to readers who have shares in them. The regulated or unregulated expenditure of parties, and its detailed or summarized components is largely an issue only to the extent that it relates to income. In some quarters, the view is that income should only be a matter of principled concern with regard to the legality of its sources. The 'branding tendency' referred to by the ECJ assumes significance within the context of a relatively immature political system. The negative consequences associated with this 'tendency', serious enough in the Commission's judgment to justify the public non-disclosure of the names of donors, will pass, we feel sure, with the changes already underway in the evolution of the political system and culture, aided by certain forces identified by Marx[351] and noted implicitly by Stone.[352]

Any trends in a positive direction can be buttressed by public education and policy to further undermine the clientilist politician/elector nexus. Otherwise, state funding of partisan political activity could conceivably have the effect of assisting the perpetuation of negatively viewed types of conduct, which might become *more affordable*, perhaps, the greater the extent of state subsidy.

A regulatory regime, over-rigid and detailed, is likely to fail the test of effective implementation/control. On the other hand, the greater the scope for discretion and operational flexibility, the greater, inevitably, the opportunity for non-compliance with any proposed regulation, literally, or its 'spirit', as

---

349 ECJ, p.11.

350 Ibid, p. 12

351 Karl Marx, *A Contribution to the Critique of Political Economy*, Maurice Dobb, ed, (London, 1979).

352 See Carl Stone, supra, at pp. 91, 96, 99, 100, 110 and at p. 34 for Marxian examples of economic circumstances/policy outcomes determining political behaviour. Stone writes: "The attachment of democratization to the political fortunes of socialism as an ideological package meant that the strength of support for democratization disappeared as the socialist management of the economy faltered." Again, at pp. 139-40, he records that, "As the social costs of these [JLP, 1980 IMF] policies have increased pressures on the majority classes, government and politics are seen more as burdens rather than aids to social survival. Political apathy alienation, militancy, anger and feelings of despair and hopelessness have replaced the optimism of the 1990's". Except that crime (non-politically inspired) has replaced militancy, little indeed seemed to have changed, as this depiction virtually mirrors the situation, currently.

the result of favouritism, loophole-seeking behaviour, or outright corruption in its many forms.[353]

EMPIRICISM LACKING

With that in mind, it is to be noted that the potential benefits of comparativism are circumscribed by the fact that while learning from the history of other nations is commendable, the successful adoption of practices reflecting developments taking several decades, and centuries, even, is not always to be realistically expected, however enviable the end result might appear.[354]

The mere adoption of modified or unmodified parts of other electoral systems is easy enough. A profitable starting point with a greater likelihood of achieving paradigmatic systematic behavioural change by the various participants may, however be the design of a well-conceived, widely discussed and agreed multi-media program of political education[355], sustained to the point of saturation. This is with a view to providing the much needed

---

353 See Garth Rattray, "Defining political corruption" *The Gleaner*, Sept. 30, 2013, p. A7, who uses the omnibus term "the misuse of government power". Apparently, without reflection and consequently without refinement/ elaboration, Peter Espeut in 'Ethically challenged', *The Gleaner*, Fri. Sept. 27, 2013, p.A9, lists several forms of behaviour as constituting, for him, corrupt political conduct. It is worthy of note that they can all be the subject of institutional control/oversight: indeed, some have been influence-peddling being at the root of all the issues referred to. He offers not a shred of evidence of any kind to support the contention that, "… all the above is par for the Jamaican political course and now seems so normal … possible that what we think is government policy aimed at national development is actually the private agenda of private special interests … lubricated with huge under the table payments to politicians and political parties. …"Overzealousness - Espeut is a deacon - tends to almost always present hurdles to balance/objectivity, in a display of extreme naivety, surprisingly for a social scientist, states: "… if you don't want people to know you support the party, you must be up to no good. If you are ashamed of the party, don't give money to it". He should certainly know that there was, and indeed currently, are times when certain religious groups/sects face serious persecution, indeed death, by means not entirely humane. They are now regarded as 'martyrs'. We know of no good reason why the national interest and that of private persons and institutions should be presumed to be, inevitably, in conflict.

354 See Franklin Johnston, 'Political party funding. Electoral Commission, transparency', the *Jamaica Observer*, Fri. July 30, 2010, p. 10, where the public display of partisan preference by means of bumper stickers in the USA, and wearing of rosettes by the British, without risk of intimidation, is noted.

355 Without elaboration of his ideas, it would appear that Opposition Leader, Andrew Holness, is in favour of such an approach. In the *Jamaica Observer*, May 5, 2013, p. 26, it is reported that, "He agreed that drafting the actual legislation could take some time and even before that phase of implementation even more consultation and public sensitization may be necessary." Rather belatedly, officials of the ECJ, its Chairman and the Director of Elections, are recognising the importance of this issue as it determines the quality of the political system; see, 'Election Director says educate voters to decrease apathy', *The Gleaner*, Sat. May 30. 2015, p. A4; see also 'Overcoming voter apathy', editorial, *The Gleaner*, June 7, 2015, p. A8, where similar views expressed at a town hall meeting by the ECJ Chairman are endorsed. As with the decriminalization of the possession and use of small amounts of ganja (marijuana) to be *followed* by a campaign of public education, this is another classic case of 'putting the cart before the horse', certainly; see, 'Government plans public education to discourage irresponsible ganja use', the *Jamaica Observer*, Fri. June 19, 2015, p. 18.

palliative to the political/legal problems generated by attitudes/expectations rooted in circumstances of social neglect and decay. This scenario, we well know, but for its divisive tribalistic political aspect, is not unique to Jamaica.[356] The gains from such an initiative could well have profound implications for the financing of political activity and should not be lost to party supporters, regardless of their socio-economic status: compatibility in political terms, should not be allowed to completely outweigh considerations relating to questions of genuine need and merit.

Standing in the way of progress, though, as briefly, if not originally outlined, is an important national characteristic: the penchant to engage in talk rather than action.[357]

There is another cultural hurdle in the way of accurate diagnosis and successful corrective action in the treatment of electoral reform issues as in other areas of national life: a predisposition to prefer rumour, especially if of a scandalous nature, over colourless un-dramatic fact.

It is one thing to say that - "Facts ... are not self-evident. They are selected and interpreted by the mind that surveys them".[358]

It is quite another to concur with the oft-stated misconception that 'In politics perception is reality'.[359]

---

356 See 'The future of market capitalism' a report on the panel discussions at Harvard University on 'Social Entrepreneurship', per Lawrence H. Summers: "It is crucial to provide opportunity to these areas and to do so in intelligent ways, using replicable sustainable and scalable models. ... [since] There is a close correlation between economic prosperity and social cohesion", [one possible initiative being the channelling of unclaimed bank deposits into "an organisation focused on social finance". It is notable that suggestions from the PSOJ/JCC that, for example, "businesses should seek profit opportunities in places that also make a broad societal contribution by employing a lens that focuses on doing well (financially) by doing good" (for society) are not forthcoming. Except for rare examples, such as Douglas Orane, the private sector's tendency is preoccupation with faulting the politician. Its representatives are, therefore, foremost among those to "cast the first stone". See, in this context, the Editorial 'civil society and the gangs of Gordon House', The Gleaner May 15, 2011, p.A8 for an example of such selective blame bestowal.

357 See the report of Prof. Trevor Munroe's contribution at the Editor's Forum on Electoral Reform organized by and reported in The Gleaner, Tue. June 22, 2010, p.A2: "In the eight years there have been throne speeches ... commitments by Prime Ministers and opposition leaders ... consultations and conferences ... but nothing has happened ... this area [party finance and campaign funding legislation] is the one in which, on careful reflection, there has been the greatest gap between words and deeds, between talk and action ..." See also Lipton Matthews, 'Action, not a bag a talk', the Jamaica Observer, Mon. Feb. 24, 2014, p. 13 where the view is expressed that, "... if voters tolerate the complacency of their leaders then they too, like the executives, won't achieve much ... Well-thinking citizens are not suggesting that anyone should dump tones of manure outside Parliament in order to show our disapproval of politicians, like that disturbed French horse breeder, but we insist that Jamaicans should do more than talk for a few seconds.'

358 Downes and Rock, op cit, p. 54.

359 Claude Robinson, 'The Agenda, in politics, perception is reality', the Jamaica Observer, Sept. 29, 2013, p. 4.

As Downes and Rock further note,

> it was alleged that the problem of perception and science are straightened out when looked at from the standpoint of *action*, [Italics added] while they remain obscure and obscuring when we regard them from the standpoint of a knowledge defined in antithesis to action.[360]

And it is from action that evidence is best derived. Compelling inference can, of course, sometimes be drawn from inaction, where such a failure cries out for unprovided explanation.

To regard 'perception' as a substitute for reality is fodder for those who wish to indulge in irrationality and near-absolute subjectivity in 'observation' and analysis.

The persistence and pervasiveness of such a combined 'mindset' does not encourage research as a necessary part of the reform effort: what enough people "think",[361] "believe",[362] "suspect",[363] "argue",[364] "perceive" and what seems "possible"[365], might well become an adequate basis for policy prescription.

The politician's survival instincts, however, directs focus on potential advantages which may accrue from,

> priorities such as politics and policy making ... However, sociological theories differ greatly in their receptivity to the constructs of everyday life and the problems of translating theories ... into social policy terms are not acute in principle, whatever the practical and political obstacles to their effective implementation may be.[366]

What is being implied here, is that the drafting of legal rules in this area of national life would benefit from collaboration between the social scientist the legal academician/ practitioner and the politician.

360　See Downes and Rock, supra, p. 54.

361　See, for example, Peter Espeut, "Shame PSOJ", *The Gleaner* Fri. June 25, 2010. P.A9

362　Ibid

363　See Ian Boyne, *The Gleaner* May 15, 2011, pp. F.5, 8: "... cheap propaganda will definitely resonate on the streets where the trade in ignorance is buoyant. As Golding put it, 'It is not easy for people to understand these complexities, and when they don't understand, they form judgment and get angry'". See, also in relation to the Trafigura affair, the Editorial of the Gleaner Wed. Sept. 1, 2010, p.A6, as it sought, although with an attempt at denial, to link the Coke Extradition 'scandal' to the issue, "as a policy question, to party and campaign financing".

364　See 'Loopholes loom', *The Gleaner* Tue. June 22, 2010, p. A2, first paragraph.

365　ECJ Report, p.9,

366　Downes and Rock, op cit, p. 308

One should not, by implication, fail to acknowledge that,

> the language and emphases of policy documents and political arguments are not constructed as if they were parts of an academic discourse ... shaped by questions of methodology, evidence and intellectual pedigree. On the contrary, their nuances flow from concerns about constituencies.[367]

Nevertheless, the door should not be closed to the potential benefits accruable from consultation with legal and social science experts, as against practitioners of politics, since,

> From time to time. theory and research would have the effect of discouraging officials from supporting recommendations that experts consider to be naïve, discredited or impracticable ... it is always useful to show that proposals are well anchored, even if the demonstration is retroactive.[368]

Downes and Rock, further argue that,

> The epitaph on Marx's tomb rams home the need for theory and practice to be related to each other in an urgent dialectic ... theoretically informed practice feeding back into practically informed theory in a dynamic and self-critical process.[369]

At the same time, one should carefully avoid 'throwing out the baby with the bathwater'. The term is used cautiously since it is agreed that often "... the concepts we talk with are made for purposes of practice and not for purposes of insight".[370] It may therefore be beneficial if would-be reformers are aware 'that data feed theory and theory guides data collection', and that both may thus be useful for policy formation.

That is despite whatever the many unconvinced in societies such as Jamaica may think. This does not mean that one should not, nevertheless,

> continually be aware of the limitations, constraints and distortion of the materials upon which theories [and consequently strategies driven by them] are fabricated ... in such a difficult field of enquiry too rigorous a degree of skepticism night make any analysis impossible.[371]

---

367 Ibid, p.10.
368 Ibid, p. 310.
369 Ibid, p. 320
370 Ibid, p. 54
371 Ibid, p. 48.

These observations apply, we feel, with full relevance to the treatment of our subject matter.

The ECJ reform effort seems to have been untroubled by the implication of the observation that policies based fundamentally on empirical studies rather than assumptions derived from accepted generalizations is the distinguishing features of the scientific approach.[372] One resultant problem to be noted is the possible 'discrepancy between what is scientifically sound and what is constitutionally/ [culturally] possible'. What is adoptable, practically, by those who are practitioners of the 'art of the possible' is often a much more complex issue. This is evident by the apparent miscarriage of the Commission's proposed regime, as it was confronted by the recent expression of hostility to and reservations on even its basic *quid pro quo* grounding principles.

One's problem is not necessarily with functionalism, the approach seemingly taken by the Commission. With respect to its campaign financing proposals, any ensuing misgivings might have been met by the antidote of empirical work, however rudimentary, seeking to test the underlying assumptions. Employing empiricism to chart such a delicate and complicated dynamic process as the politics of electioneering, demands, "... a particularly patient, cautious and attentive methodology ... and it is all too easy prematurely to impose an alien explanatory scheme that obscures vision, ignores problems and pre-empts solution".[373]

We refer to criticisms from 'respected' and 'highly placed' persons, in some cases, disputing the legitimacy of state funding of the parties and campaigns in the press as recently as late 2013. This is *the* essential premise, the *quid pro quo*, without which it is likely that the reform project would not have been contemplated, not even by most non-partisan political commentators. With respect to all the 'stakeholders', the voiceless 'public' excluded, the *September 30, 2008* "*deadline* [Italics added] for both major parties to make submissions to the Electoral Commission ... before a *final* [Italics added] report is submitted to Parliament in November", [2008], [374] makes the time-management handling of the matter unimpressive.

372 Cunningham, Mark D.,: 'Evaluation for Capital Sentencing', Oxford University Press, (Oxford, England, 2010), p. 20

373 Downes an Rock, op cit, p. 175

374 See, 'Last Day for Submission on party campaign Financing', the *Jamaica Observer*, Tue. Sept. 30, 2008, p. 4

In the face of such a timetable fiasco it might have been useful, despite any contemplated difficulty, to have co-opted academicians, some, if not most of whom, one suspects, would not wish to see their active participation in the political process at this level being interpreted as partisan activism: this being a tendency which the ECJ identified as one of the important negative features of the Jamaican political culture.

Such involvement would therefore, entail overcoming the resistance of research-oriented institutions and the scholars and experts who staff them, who may, "... object to the notion that an important aspect of their role is to brief officials and politicians in terms of the offer of distinctive recipes for appropriate responses. ..."[375]

Nevertheless, on balance, it is to be expected that they, "... would claim some ultimate justification for their activities in the realm of the public good. It is somewhat paradoxical, therefore, that so few of their resources are devoted to political activity in general and the making of social policy in particular."[376]

Apart from the problems of role-definition and salience, Downs and Rock make the point, of significance in a research-averse environment, that, "The rigorously academic may simply cancel out the pursuit of competing". And since *competition* is the very essence of democracy, regulations to control/ change political behaviour should be directed by that principle.

Any attempt, therefore, to impose stringent restrictions on campaigning by parties, in the general exercise of the fundamental constitutional rights of freedom of speech and association, will, one expects, be vigilantly tracked and made the target of well-considered challenge. One version of the dilution of democratic competitive party politics takes the form, on this view, of the establishment of a 'national election fund' under the control of the ECJ, whereby contributions from acceptable private sources are put in the fund, "... [which] ... would relieve donors of being labelled as particular party supporters ..." The divergence from 'democratic' principle then becomes exposed: not surprisingly, "private donors would *still be able to ... contribute*

---

375 Downes and Rock, op cit, p. 308
376 Ibid

to a party or candidate of their choice. ..."[377]

The effect on liberal principle of the disclosure lens can be easily misted by the *ethically* questionable practice of some large donors, both individual but especially corporate, of giving to more than one party. This seems, only superficially, to assist in 'levelling the playing field'. It, in fact, strikes a blow at the very essence of what politics is about: competition, choice, commitment.[378]

For Devon Dick, the regular press commentator, "... the excuse that donors will be discriminated against [if disclosed] does not hold water because everybody knows most of the donors and there is no *evidence* [Italics added] of victimization."[379]

CONVENTIONAL WISDOM

It has been propounded that the debate about electoral reforms must be grounded in society's most fundamental ethical principles and values. What one finds, however, is that the ECJ's 'angle of vision' and that of most commentators, most notably that of editors of media houses, represents a predominantly negative portrayal of the disfavoured acts of commission or omission of politicians and their parties, couched in platitudinous pontificatory generalizations about "threats to democracy".

A reform project configured largely by the narrow focus of those with such an orientation to the political process, albeit the predominant one,

---

377 ECJ Report Pt. 1, p. 3. See also 'Campaign finance reform vital to free, fair election', *The Gleaner* Oct. 9, 2011, p. D12.

378 See Ronald Mason, "Damn dictatorship on campaign financing", supra,, "... if state-funded political campaign financing is implemented, you will force us to contribute to both parties equally, much against our choice, just to achieve cosmetic balance [for balance one could substitute 'a accor']. The only disclosure of party contributions I have seen published had major contributors giving equal amounts to both major parties. How sad! Was that truly reflective of their choice? I think not".

379 In *The Gleaner*, Thur, Jan 24, 2013 p. A7, under the heading 'Campaign financing bill doomed'. Dick states that with respect to political parties' operations and/or electioneering, there is "no need for it [state funding] ... with more prudent management ...", claiming further that, "Those four companies which publicly declared their contribution to the political parties are not complaining about ill effects of the declaration: "quite surprisingly, he ignores the most telling aspect of the matter: they contributed equal amounts to both major parties. Be that as it may, he makes the point that this is a subsidy which the taxpayer cannot fund. Support for Dick's argument comes from self-styled libertarian Ronald Mason, supra, "... However the small size of the populace lends itself to greater knowledge of each other ... The ECJ leaves the impression that tainted money is designated according to donor, excessive money designated by whomsoever is perceived to be wealthy and free spending; and money in search of influence as designated by some identification of *quid pro quo* activity", Some may feel compelled to suggest that church goers who put something in the collection plate are not unmindful of the fact that, at its lowest, and, in accordance with their belief and expectations, their after-life destination chances will not be adversely affected, quite apart from not wanting to appear to be less supportive than the 'widow'.

inevitably triggers interventionist impulses with 'control' as their primary motive.

The preferred outlook on our topic does not accord with that which rests on the presumed infallibility of the dictates of 'conventional wisdom' or public opinion, even when scientifically tested. The *possibility* should not be ignored that what passes for 'revealed truth' may indeed, on occasion, reflect "… the sheep like, piggish ways of that tyrant and sycophantic lout, the majority".[380]

As Fromm reminds us:

> We forget that, although freedom of speech constitutes an important victory against the battle against the [old] restraints, modern man is in a position where much of what 'he' thinks and says are things that everybody else thinks and says. … The anonymous authorities like public opinion and 'common-sense' are so powerful because of our profound readiness to conform … and our equally profound fear of being different.[381]

'Best practice' may therefore, for any number of reasons, not be best based on the findings of polls, however venerable the pollster.

In this regard the ECJ could learn from the reform approach adopted in New Zealand,[382] entailing the use of a ten item frame of reference for the evaluation of alternative electoral systems by the Royal Commission on Electoral Reform. With items selected to reflect the concerns to be addressed by way of the objectives to be pursued, this simple yet structured slant to the comparative use of 'precedents' warrants consideration.

TRACING TAINTED MONEY

One of the major concerns of the reform focus is that of 'tainted money' being used to buy political influence, but should tracing of funds tainted in any way be limited, in principle, to the political parties? It does seem that David Smith and/or his Ponzi scheme 'Olint' contributed substantially to both major political parties in the 2007 election. So far, after some seven years, the lens of public morality has been turned onto the political parties only. Were the other

---

380 Pinsky, Robert., 'Local Politics', in *The Figured Wheel New and Collected Poems*, Farrar, Straus & Ginoux, (NY, 1997), p.167

381 Erich Fromm, op. cit. , 1963, pp. 90, 91

382 See Ch. 111 of the Law Commission of Canada Discussion Paper, 'Renewing Democracy: Debating Electoral Reform in Canada", 2002.

recipients of money from Olint, whether in the form of donation or payment, not in the same position as politicians, in terms of knowledge of the nature of the scheme's operations?

Daniel Thwaites adopts what we regard as a balanced, sensible approach to the matter of refund of 'tainted' donations, and the 'selective morality' on which the argument is normally based. The convicted Texan Ponzi scheme operator, Allen Stanford, sentenced to over one hundred years in prison, he notes, contributed to both the Democratic and Republican Party campaigns, in the United States,[383] neither of which, from media reports, plan to make a refund. But then, the Jamaican political parties are presumably expected to adhere to higher moral/ethical standards, to which we make no objection. However, as all cricket-loving people know, he, Stanford, was the sponsor of a major cricket tournament in the Caribbean which had the distinction of bearing his name. One cannot recall any demand ever having been made for what must surely have been very substantial funds to be returned, but, then, sport is not politics.

The 'Ponzi King', Bernie Madoff, Thwaites continues, made substantial donations "… for lymphoma research, hospitals, the Lincoln Centre, the special Olympics, Global Camps Africa, The Metropolitan Museum of Art, City Harvest (to feed the hungry), New York Public Library, universities, too numerous to mention, the Wildlife Conservation Society and many other worthy causes …"[384] The 'class'/category of the recipient can scarcely remove the taint and the moral implications.

Olint, it is pointed out, donated dialysis machines to the St. Joseph Hospital in Kingston and was a major sponsor of the Jamaica Jazz and Blues Festival.[385]

---

383 See Daniel Thwaites, 'The best pay back is reform' *The Gleaner*, June 24, 2012 p.A9. Thwaites and other commentators have not failed to highlight the fact that whereas the operator of Olint has been charged in both the Turks and Caicos Islands and imprisoned in the United States, he has not even been charged in Jamaica. So much for Thwaites 'swift and certain sanctions'. Hugh Wilson, Attorney-at-Law, has put the case for a *legal* obligation to return a 'tainted gift' by the PNP and JLP in Jamaica on his understanding of the Proceeds of Crime Ordinance of the Turks and Caicos Islands. The contorted reasoning indulged in by the Attorney to arrive at what appears to be a pre-determined conclusion is at best unconvincing, quite apart from the unconcern displayed with the issue of the necessary and imperative jurisdictional limits of legislative provisions between states: see 'David Smith's tainted gifts', *The Gleaner*, July 1, 2012, p.A9

384 Thwaites, Ibid. While neither of the parties in the United States have given any indication of an intention to make a refund, nor, to our knowledge, has any of the other beneficiaries mentioned, a newspaper contributor still found it appropriate to say, in relation to the Jamaican parties and the Olint donation received , "… in all this, there was no expression of alarm, no shame, no suggestion of any awareness of the consequences which would flow to persons holding similar positions in any self-respecting organisation", see Olive Nelson , 'Campaign financing from public purse fundamentally flawed', *The Gleaner* , July 8, 2012, p. A9

385 Thwaites, supra.

Enron is noted to have made donations to the University of Missouri, while Jamaican churches invested in and collected interest payments from Olint[386]— all tainted money, it can be argued.

Somewhat ironically, since politicians and their organisations are held in such low esteem, it would appear that nevertheless, the clamour is only for them to feel so 'stained' and 'shamed' as to do the 'honourable' thing and return money received from 'any questionable source'. The reply of Robert Pickersgill, Chairman of the PNP to the effect that there was, 'no moral obligation' to do so,[387] elicited the graphic caustic response, 'wrong jungle, Mr. Pickersgill'![388]

Orville Taylor, a University sociology lecturer, in referring to the David Smith / Olint political contribution put it in these terms: "This classic case of Anancyism[389] has him playing two sides of the fence, with a virtual guarantee that he would be in the bed sheets of both Government and Opposition, whoever wins".[390] One must infer that such a prospect does not exist with respect to large corporations which engage in the identical behaviour, which when indulged in by others is more 'suited for the application of the concept of the self-fulfilling prophecy', and is subject to a convenient highly selective supercilious interpretation. While we would be foolish to trust Anancy, it would seem that it would be quite in order to take the 'noble motives' of large corporations, which give equally to both major parties, for granted.[391] Apparently we should trust them.

THE TRUST FACTOR

Views founded on the notion of trust, to be useful, even for the purposes

---

386 Ibid.

387 See 'No moral obligation to refund Olint money – PNP', *The Gleaner*, Fri. June 15, 2012, p. 1; See also, 'Parties see no reason to return Olint funds', *The Gleaner*, Thu. July 15, 2013, p. A3, which carries the explanatory statement, "you cannot pay back based on a news report, and there have been no court orders".

388 See, Ralston Nembhard, 'Wrong jungle, Mr. Pickersgill' the *Jamaica Observer* on Saturday, June 23, 2012, p. 10.

389 The Jamaican folk character 'Anancy' embodies the essence of slyness and the skills of the supreme 'trickster'.

390 See *The Gleaner*, May 13, 2012, p. G4, where Taylor notes that, "It is bad enough that monied interests bankroll election campaigns and thus, ultimately will want their pound of flesh". Strangely, while he chooses to name David Smith specifically, he avoids any mention of the five published large firms which engaged in the same strategy, if only aimed at influence at a broader and higher level – that of national financial, commercial and economic *policy* and the choice and pursuit of particular underlying and guiding systemic *philosophy*; See also 'The Gleaner*, Thurs. July 18, 2013. P.A3 "Parties see no reason to return Olint Funds".

391 This has in fact been the typical attitude reported in the media, with only rare, negative responses, reflecting a balanced/fulsome interpretation, including self-proclaimed liberal columnist, Ronald Mason, "Damn dictatorship on campaign financing", *The Gleaner*, Oct. 6, 2013, p. A9

of discourse, and more so for policy design, need the benefit of conceptual refinement. Most surveys in this area, one finds, use rather blunt investigative instruments.[392] What we need to know are the features/factors/elements in terms of attitudes and behaviour, commission or omission, as they relate to politicians and their organisations, which when taken together comprise and compromise 'trust', in the respondents' view, in the practice of politics.

To put the matter directly, it would not be surprising if a very large part of the 'malaise', 'despair', 'disillusionment' and consequential 'disconnection' with the political process is found to be very clearly linked, empirically, to its perceived *outcomes*.[393] The rich/poor ('needy/greedy') gap, the existence/adequacy of a social safety net; the rate of unemployment; the level of per capita income; access to quality health and educational services and opportunities for a better quality of life in the foreseeable future with commensurate effort, need, perhaps, to be, explicitly, the litmus test of policy success under IMF program monitoring, or otherwise.

The unconventional position may be taken which, even if shared, would not often be expressed, that citizens, and not only of Jamaica, need to guard against being 'conned', by politicians and others who are, themselves, very often generally 'doing alright', into an acceptance of the recurring exhortation to 'be willing' to make 'necessary sacrifices' for the benefit of an ever receding 'posterity and *future* generations'.

The nature of those outcomes is significantly affected by decisions at the micro level. But which of those private, purportedly patriotic, civil society representative firms, which would lay strong claim to a sense of 'social responsibility', determine

---

392 See Robotham's 'Low party legitimacy: A look at the polls', by Lawrence Powell, *The Gleaner*, Dec. 11, 2011, p. F8. The solution proffered by the two prominent university professors was along the well-worn and somewhat self-interested lines of "... more inclusive involvement of civil society groups in crafting policy ... in the *post* [Italics added] election period." This seems to represent the currently popular 'magic wand' to be waved in this instance, very much after 'the horse has gone through the gate'.

393 See 'Govt's for the few', front page headline in The Gleaner, Fri. July 19, 2013 where the incoming Principal of the University of the West Indies, Mona Campus, is reported as saying "I don't believe they have acted in the interest of the majority of Jamaicans". See also Carl Stone, supra, pp. 139 – 140. What some civil society leaders fail to realize is that perhaps if they had acted under the guidance of a more inclusive interpretation of the 'public interest'. They, the private sector, in particular, would not have done so well, despite how they see and assess their own "performance since the 1970's: record profits are often reported by banks and others while the majority of citizens, including children, "suck salt". See also 'We do not trust them', *The Gleaner*, Dec. 11, 2011, p. D 14 where one panelist said, "... I have an 'iffy' thing about Andrew (Holness) now, *because* [Italics added] he's Prime Minister ... I do believe that sometimes the position and just to please some people, changes them". Another panelist declared "I find it hard to come up with two names" (of trusted politicians): painting with a broad brush perhaps? See then ECJ Chairman, Prof. Errol Miller's views in, 'ECJ Chairman weighs in on vote-buying debate', the *Jamaica Observer*, Fri. Dec. 9, 2011, p. 4.

corporate policy guided by such concerns and indices?[394] Expecting politicians to practise politics as if victory at the polls is unimportant, is not dissimilar to the business class conducting their business operations based on policy decisions ostensibly entirely for the benefit of consumers regardless of the consequences for their organisation's bottom line and their future survival at the personal and institutional levels. In order for national initiatives to be meaningful, in terms of results, must, of necessity, in a free enterprise economy, translate into effective facilitative action by the leadership cadre to enhance, progressively and significantly, the life chances of the majority.

How, from such a perspective, will the Party Registration and financing—party and campaign—promote tangibly the welfare of the average citizen, the 'common'/'little' man?

Using the taxes of such less-than-privileged 'stakeholders' to prop up the multi-party system represents, perhaps, the ultimate betrayal of the essential role of the mass party. 'Physician heal thyself', is an adage not inappropriate to the case, with respect to the political class.[395]

Expecting law, and regulations flowing therefrom, to be a fitting substitute for ameliorating policy results is seemingly delusionary.

Is it likely that unrelieved economic distress, since the mid-1970s in Jamaica, is unrelated to the "low party legitimacy" reflected by a 2010 survey?[396] For present purposes, the poll results of most interest are, (measured in percentages):

Trust and Confidence in Institutions (Reports of a Study)

	Weak Trust	Strong Trust
Government	30.5	14.3
Parliament	30.6	12.4
Political Parties	40.0	6.6
Electoral Commission	19.9	24.8

394 See Carl Stone, op. cit., p. 119, where Stone observes (1986) that "The Jamaican private sector has been militantly opposed to government's regulation of business transactions". In the present context where free market economic principles hold virtually unchallenged sway, one would expect such an attitude to now be even more deeply entrenched.

395 Ibid, pp. 119 et seq. As Stone saw it, "The tendency has been for the state to resort to the 'big stick' of regulation, the provision of more incentives, or the strategy of cooptation, when its policies did not attract popular support [from the private sector].

396 See 'We do not trust them', by Martin Baxter, Gleaner writer, *The Gleaner*, Dec. 11, 2011, p. D 14.

On the question of those interviewed having 'a lot of confidence' in Jamaican Societal Institutions, we find that some major critics, actual or would-be, of the political parties, did not, themselves, fare very well.[397] 'Perception', without actual reported 'foundation' evidence, would seem to have displaced reality in many political issues requiring objective consideration and the exercise of balanced judgment.[398]

Confidence in Institutions

Newspapers	16%
Private Sector	11%
Government	10%
Judiciary	9%
Parliament	8%
Political Parties	6%
Police	7%

These results are indicative of a decay that is clearly more pervasive/inclusive than most commentators acknowledge, since these numbers are out of a possible 100%. If the 'stain' is unsparing in its coverage with respect to public institutions, the diagnostic and remedial effort should probably be more broad-based, institutionally, without regard for popularly accepted views as to the primary locus of corrupt action, and behaviour predisposition, in the conduct of public affairs in the island.

It is suggested, with respect to these 'findings' that the notion of "trust" which overarches so much of the thinking on the state of politics, beyond national boundaries, currently needs to be componentially demystified.

---

397 Ibid.

398 The then Chairman of the ECJ, for example, advised that, "... reports of vote-buying be treated with scepticism, arguing that there was no concrete evidence to suggest that this practice has any real influence on which party wins an election"; "The charge that votes are bought is an impression not necessarily a fact and when we look across the world it's not the person who spends the most money that necessarily wins. ..." As 'it takes two to tango', in almost every conceivable instance of corrupt political behaviour, a transaction requires the participation of more than one person, often not necessarily from the political class. The truth is that many are prepared to 'turn a blind eye'; even when they are not in a matter important to them, as current prospective beneficiaries. Hypocrisy is by no means limited to politicians. Politicians, like the police on this view, are reflective of the dominant values and attitudes of their society, *including* the so-called civil society sector(s). See also 'The evil garrison system', Henley Morgan in the *Jamaica Observer*, Wed. May 4, 2011, p. 11 argues that the level of distrust is a " ... by-product of a process that has conscripted large numbers of Jamaicans to be persons in a political process where the winner takes all ..."

As has been noted, the design of survey instruments is clearly called into question. Whatever the empirically determined constituents of trust in the Jamaican political site, is it reasonable to suggest:

> So next time the celebrated 48% who did not vote seek to blame someone else for the state of the economy, the level of crime, illiteracy, the inability to access health care and all other issues to do with poor governance, just remember blame no one else but yourselves ... Power to the lazy 48 percent: You have successfully hijacked our democratic process and voted into office a new 'independent party', the Voter-less Party of Jamaica.[399]

What is confirmed here is clear: until the real reasons for the 'malaise' and absence of 'trust' are discerned, without the aid of preconceptions, reform efforts like those contained in the ECJ's framework will be like footsteps in quicksand.

POLITICAL PARTY CULTURE

The parties were accused of wrongdoing by commentators in the print media on the basis that they should have known, at the time of the Ponzi scheme's donations, that the money was from a 'questionable' source, putting it at its lowest.

On the other hand, it has been observed by another commentator that "... notwithstanding well-publicized negative news and regulatory warnings to the contrary, the existence of Olint and its ability to give gifts was not illegal."[400]

As the OAS succinctly puts it, in the cover sheet to its 2009 model political finance legislation for the Caribbean, "... many of the 'scandals' ... have not been, strictly speaking, illegal, since the countries of the region have little or no regulation on political contributions or expenditure".[401] There has certainly been no shortage of unsavoury party-financing incidents, a short selection of which we include below, drawn from a mix of counties.

Garth Rattray, the columnist, argues, somewhat platitudinously, that:

---

399   Sophia Matthews, in a letter to the Editor, *The Gleaner*, Fri. Dec. 6, 2012, p. A8; see also the public's commentary on similar and opposed lines at Note 39.

400   Christopher Pryce, 'Smith-Olint intrigue tainted with mischief', *The Gleaner*, Tuesday June 19, 2012, p. A9

401   'Draft Model Law on Registration and Regulation of Political Parties, Paying for Political Parties and Campaigns in the Caribbean', The OAS Secretariat for Political Affairs, 2009, as set out in 'Draft Model Political Parties (Regulation) Bill'.

Whatever else the JLP and PNP choose to do, for the sake of a vibrant democracy and an urgently needed political renaissance, they must ... rise above the accustomed unpleasantness of Jamaican politics. The parties need to eschew the many negatives associated with politicking.[402]

He concurs with the popular view that, "... as far as politicking goes, it's six of one and half a dozen of the other ... [since] The players within both major political parties are similar, and so are their ideologies".[403]

This assessment is partly explicable by the experience of structural and, in the case of many countries, persistently high levels of unemployment arising from features of the capitalist so-called global economy. Clearly, this can only increase the sense of insecurity in a psychological context in which parties and governments will increasingly tend to be viewed through Garth Rattray's unflattering lens.

Noticeably, at the level of analysis at which he engages the issue, there is no nexus established between "the many negatives" and the lack of differentiation of the protagonists on the personal or ideological levels. No causal relationship is discerned. In what respects are the players similar, and what is the explanation for the lack of any significant difference in ideology? Are there seemingly inevitable consequences for the practise of politics which flow from such ideological convergence? Answers to such seemingly simple questions could conceivably have profound implications for more accurate diagnosis and thus more effective electoral reform prescriptions.

Surprisingly, nor does an 'organisation man', like James Moss-Solomon, an experienced senior business executive, reveal any lesser degree of political innocence in his observation:

> The 'political gangs' continue to resist the label that has been quite *rightly* applied with a *broad brush*. It is possible that there are persons in each party who do *not* deserve that description, but they have not sought to distance themselves from those who are really guilty, and so they *probably* [Italics added] deserve the name by not publicly disassociating themselves from the rest.[404]

---

402 Rattray, Garth., 'Political renaissance needed', in *The Gleaner*, Mon. June 6, 2011, p.A9
403 Ibid
404 James Moss-Solomon 'What goes around comes around', in "The Agenda" the *Jamaica Observer* , June 12, 2011, p.4

Despite the apparently fitting application of the phrase "a pox on both their houses" to the two major parties, Moss-Solomon, ends his piece with the ironic admonition, "Please remember to vote".[405] He further observes that,

> their [the parties] very appearance seems to be directed towards discouraging persons of goodwill with trained intellects and honest intentions from serving in any capacity, even as they seem to attract villains [the parties being such that] … an earlier … moment of possible national salvation [was] … lost without much hope of recovery, at least not with the insidious and unhealthy state of the two gangs.[406]

We have noted that *The Gleaner*, editorially, wishes the public to fund 'the gangs' and now Moss-Solomon advises that the public make sure they vote for them. In whose interest then is the preservation of *that* status quo which these civil society business leaders seem so desperate to ensure?

One would wish to ask whether in corporate life it is normal for persons on different hierarchical levels to act as Moss-Solomon and the editor of *The Gleaner* chide politicians for not doing. The essential dynamics of political parties (as voluntary organisations with limited recourse to effective sanctions and, in terms of the variables of structure, purpose, power/authority and the nature of their inherently adversarial competitive environments, internally, and, most certainly externally) is often ignored in their analysis and assessment.

More careful, less stereotypical thinking might suggest important consequential legal and operational implications for discipline in political parties as against business organisations.

In the face of occasionally harsh criticism of the business sector, do we often find its members disassociating themselves publicly from any perceived unbecoming behaviour of superiors? Practitioners in political parties are in a disadvantageous position to seek an opening elsewhere, compared to participants in a business enterprise. The option of finding a comfortable and often a more rewarding place in another organisation is almost non-existent in the context of politics.

At the level of theoretical analysis, if not untrained observation, members

---

405 Ibid
406 Ibid

of different types of organisations will often, for understandable reasons, tend to exhibit different types of behaviour in seemingly similar situations.

STRENGTHENING POLITICAL PARTIES

"Strengthening political parties as primary political organisations", a searchlight of the Canadian regime, cannot be achieved, it is argued here, by doling out very scarce public funds to the parties, with or without a private contribution element.

It is not disputed that, presently, the publicly funded support provided for party representatives and candidates appears to be seriously inadequate: Members of Parliament, Parish Councillors, and Senators need to be provided with the level of remuneration and other support resources which makes it *reasonable* to expect them to effectively function in keeping with the time and energy as well as the reasonable 'official' financial demands of their positions.

Opposition constituency representatives, in particular, many of whom are not MPs, need to engage in policy research and formulation while *in opposition* (promoted and funded possibly, as is the case under the British party financing arrangements, from public revenue). We regard these matters as fundamentally important defining deficiencies of the current Jamaican political system, holding, nevertheless, that except for salaries and the necessary administrative costs associated with the performance of the public *duties* of elected and appointed officials such as Senators, the financing of a party's activities should be the party's supporters' responsibility.

IDEOLOGICAL UNCOMPETITIVENESS

Private sector wimpishness, as represented by the Private Sector Organisation of Jamaica (PSOJ) in its suggestion, referred to above, is, in a back-handed way, indicative of the effect of market capitalism under globalization.[407] In an ideologically uncompetitive world, it may make sense from self-interested unhinged democratic impulses to 'ethically' financially sup-

---

[407] See 'The future of market capitalism', from a panel discussion on social entrepreneurship and the limitation of the capitalist system at Harvard University, reported in the *Jamaica Observer*, Fri. May 6, 2011, p.16. See ALSO John Rapley, 'Inequality and instability' in *The Gleaner*, Mon. June 13, 2011, p. A7 in which he draws from his book 'Globalization and Inequality' (2004) in which it was argued that "growth and development are both necessary features of regime stability"

port both major parties equally: 'six of one, half dozen of the other', as it has been said. Should this become the norm, it would, of necessity, completely destroy any commitment bond between a party's economic and social agenda and a financial supporter. Indeed, not even the calibre of a candidate would be of significance in such a dispensation. The most basic tenets of traditional party/member/supporter relationship would be thereby unceremoniously abandoned in the interest of the private sector's frailty of principle.[408]

When an individual's or organisation's money ends up subsidising a party or parties in relation to which no commitment whatsoever exists, what stage in the evolution of 'party politics' would then have been reached?

---

408   A different focus is adopted by Dwight O. Bernard: 'Politicians are mere pawns', in *The Gleaner*, Sat. June 11, 2011, p. A11. Bernard says "We unfortunately ascribe false power to politicians when real power rests with the special interests in the boardrooms and the criminal underworld ... The privileged sons and daughters ... bank-rolled a Bruce Golding-led JLP to keep their interests alive and well ... many politicians have good intentions when seeking political office ... in advancing the welfare of the poor and destitute by giving voice to the voiceless. ...However, there are forces that are more important than the masses, because these powerbrokers wield unlimited amount of power and profound influence".

CHAPTER 8
THE FUNDING ISSUE

Perhaps it is just as well that the two major parties, at least in their recent public statements, are de-emphasizing the central role of money in successful campaigning. Whereas Peter Phillips of the PNP believes that voters are "focusing more on issues rather than handouts from political parties"[409], Karl Samuda of the JLP does not think that "this extraordinary amount of expenditure is something that any political party should depend on as the means by which they retain power or come to power".

The significance which the views of the parties' two campaign directors will have on the architecture of their electioneering strategies in the future must await the experience of those events, for assessment. Calls for advertising control, for instance, relate, with a few exceptions, to content only and not expenditure limits.[410]

What one wonders, will become of the well-established tradition of a "hyped-up 'rent-a-crowd'" type of organisation and "... paying people to go to the homes of their party sympathizers to encourage them to go to the polling stations to vote."[411] [For 'encourage' in many cases, one can, without trespassing on the truth, substitute the word 'pay'].[412]

In a recent by-election, for example, the public is informed that, "... the JLP deputy leader said unmet demands *from supporters* [Italics added] that they be paid for their votes contributed to the defeat ... It is amazing. Some of them called me indicating what and what they wanted to get people to

---

409 "No more pork barrels? Political parties claim an end to political handouts", the *Jamaica Observer*, Aug.14, 2011, p. 10.

410 Ronald Mason, as one of his suggestion for fixing the electoral system, includes" "Influence the Broadcast (sic) Commission to give parties valuable air time", a matter probably outside its jurisdiction.

411 Michael Burke, 'Organisation, the key to winning elections', the *Jamaica Observer*, Thu. June 2, 2011, p. 11. But see 'Votes for Sale, Some Jamaicans willing to support the party which gives them the most money', The Gleaner, Fri. Nov. 25, 2011, p. A1 by Arthur Hall, Senior staff Reporter; See also 'Not every voter willing to sell vote', the *Jamaica Observer*, Dec. 11, 2011, p. 10, 'Vote-buying intensifies', the Jamaica Observer, Dec. 4, 2011, p. 8 and 'CAFFE shifts focus to campaign funding, vote buying', the *Jamaica Observer*, Fri. Dec. 6, 2012, p. 6.

412 Such legally prohibited and, of course, unreported expenditure can, on a constituency basis on election day only, be (as confided to the writer by a former candidate) anywhere in the region of 3 million dollars, dependent on demographic characteristics and size of the voters list.

come and vote",[413] As the report notes, there are existing penalties for this kind of conduct under s.91 of ROPA. Significantly, it was not denied that this voter behaviour was bipartisan: a price tag for a particular vote was mentioned, as was an approximate number of votes bought by one party. This, in a by-election with little real doubt as to the result.[414] Translated into a general election, financed by some level of state funding, would suggest very forcefully that electoral integrity concerns can scarcely be exaggerated.

This would seem to confirm that the role which legislation plays and can reasonably be expected to automatically play in reform projects in society is strongly situationally determined. What will, not to ask what *should*, electioneering look like as a consequence of the enactment of its reform recommendations? The ECJ leaves its expectations unstated in this respect.

With respect to income from dues, we are aware of the almost universal phenomenon of the loosening of the party/member bond, a matter deserving of local research focus, both at the comparative theoretical and empirical level. It must be noted that this loss of membership has been the experience, too, of the traditional primary workers' representative organisation, the trade union. If free market capitalism and globalization, resulting in less impediment to the movement of jobs and capital across national boundaries, are the explanation for the retreat of labour as 'equals' at the bargaining table, the reasons for party membership decline, may not be entirely unconnected to the prevailing international trade-relations paradigm.

To their credit, the institutional response of Jamaican unions to treat this situation has been joint dialogue, with a view to creative strategizing, geared to counter the emergent trends[415] in the labour force effects of the predominant economic ideology. The 'lesson' of the union movement's response—fierce, in the Jamaican case, as inter-union rivalry has sometimes been, what with the two major unions being directly affiliated to the two major parties—is the recognition that the locus of responsibility for crafting appropriate responsive

---

413 See, Daraine Luton, 'JLP reviews Central Westmoreland [by-election] whipping", *The Gleaner*, Dec 7, 2014, p. A4. See also 'G2K demand sanctions for vote-buying'.

414 'Westmoreland = PNP Country', *The Gleaner*, Dec. 7, 2014, ,

415 See 'Trade Unions seek renewal', the *Jamaica Observer*, Fri. May 27, 2011, p.3, reporting on the two day conference under the theme "A road map for trade unions, relevance and sustainability", organized by the Hugh Lawson Shearer Trade Union Institute of Jamaica, in collaboration with the Friedrich Ebert Stiftung Institute of Germany. With respect to the political party's need to adopt and change, see 'Time to renew JLP, PNP', 'Letter of the Day' by Winnie Anderson-Brown, *The Gleaner*, May 15, 2011, p. D8.

policy action resides in the threatened institution itself.

If political parties are cash strapped, as they seem to be, they can scarcely be expected to have any significant excess/reserve funds available for income-generating activities and projects. Ideology should not feature as a hindrance to investment risk-inherent involvement, since it would appear that 'we are all capitalists now'. Subject to legal requirements, the rich, or better still, the "very rich people", referred to by current British Prime Minister, David Cameron, may, with a little gentle nudging from the treasurers of prospective beneficiary parties, think of creating trusts, endowments or other such funding vehicles, by will, or *inter vivos*. At least in those cases, one would expect control guidelines to be an integral *internal* feature of any such bequest documentation. In this regard, contemplated restrictions on loans for income generating purposes, in particular, warrant review.

The printing/publication area is certainly one that comes to mind as one with income generating promise, as well as for obvious educational, promotional and mobilisational reasons. With the rise in the incidence of the multi-class party phenomenon, indicative of the process of national and institutional ideological maturation,[416] party-financing developments along these lines in Jamaica, and elsewhere, may not be as far-fetched as it may at first appear.

Of significance, in our view, is the fact that the essential character of the political party, that of a private voluntary organisation would not be compromised.

One expects, however, that the remaining funding option, state subsidy, is to be seen as the preferred and chosen one: tax payers, in the aggregate, rarely revolt in any sustained organized fashion, certainly not in 'healthy' multi-party/mature democracies. In the newer democracies one suspects that, within wide limits, legislators, as the targets of policy proposal/ implementation resistance, will benefit from the imperfections associated with information gathering, communication and interpretation existing in such societies, not to mention the instinct to forcefully suppress revolt.

Additionally, in robust and stable multi-party environments, since the

---

416 This is the known tendency under so-called 'healthy' multi-party parliamentary systems of governance, whereby stability, systemically, is facilitated.

shoe can easily be on the other foot, it is only occasionally that established parties will provide the leadership for policy resistance mass mobilization. We have seen that successful new parties do not easily emerge due to financing and other incumbency-related disadvantages. In any event, laws when beneficial to legislators' parties, candidates or personally, can be passed quite expeditiously, and spending tax payers' money seems to present little cause for numerically significant principled concern in such situations.

FULL STATE FUNDING

Full state funding, to be worth serious consideration, would, of course, have to be "adequate", the acceptable quantification of which inevitably presents major problems. But even if consensus could be achieved, the efficacy of such a scheme would require the *effective* prohibition of all forms of financial assistance in cash or kind from all other sources. Monitoring and control under such a regime, given the Jamaican state's meagre resources and the difficulty of tracking money and certain goods and services, would be an unenviable task. This is without taking into account the fact that among themselves, it is acknowledged that Jamaicans are exceptionally gifted when it comes to 'beating virtually any system'.

It has been argued that there are several creative ways to defeat the purpose intended to be served by political financing reform:

(i)   Setting up third party groups such as the PAC's which featured so strongly in the recent United States Presidential election campaign and continue to be a major issue.

(ii) Breaking up large donations, into a number of smaller amounts, ostensibly made by different individuals or groups; and

(iii) Making 'in-kind' contributions which are easily hidden from scrutiny, among numerous other strategies. In the United States, in addition to 'soft money', to be referred to later, there is now renewed concern over what is called 'dark money'.

This is defined as funds raised and spent by groups registered under Section 501 (c) (4) of the Tax Code as ostensibly social welfare organisations, but which, in fact, primarily use their funds for political purposes. Such groups, because they do not have to identify donors, cater primarily to the wealthy. 'Americans for Tax Reform', for example, with the use of such funds, it is reported, extracted pledges on tax and spending policies from Republican politicians.

This method of financing political campaign activity is not easily camouflaged as traditional social welfare charitable work, bearing in mind how the volume of 'dark money' has soared in recent years to coincide with major elections.

As recently as November, 2013, it was reported that actively under consideration in the United States were, "... new rules to curb the political activity of 501(c) (4) 'non-profits ... focus on prohibiting certain political activity explicitly', such as specific support for a candidate in an election.'"[417] Involvement that was formerly regarded as 'non-political democracy-building', such as voter registration and getting voters to the polls, would now be disapproved.

Reflecting the influence on thinking of vested interest representation, the view of conservative Howard Husock, of the think-tank 'Manhattan Institute', is that the 'solution' lies in *reducing* the restrictions on the political role money is permitted to play, since the explanation of the emergence of this source of third party political spending for him is that, "Money denied its traditional voice sought new ways to influence politics."[418]

Since trade unions' very substantial political financial support to the Democratic Party is channelled through 501 (c) (5) groups, it is argued that anonymous wealthy donors may seek to maintain non-disclosure by contributing to 501(c)(6) trade associations such as the United States Chamber of Commerce. Working around the rules can clearly become something of a preoccupation.

Of note, in the opinion of Marc Owens, described as 'a lawyer who works to tackle dark money', the proposed rules are 'sufficiently ambiguous not to shut down the *big* [Italics added] partisan players'. On the other hand, this is while they could restrict non-partisan organisations such as the League of Women Voters which provides information on elections to its members. This could, in other words, be another case of regulation having undesired, unintended consequences.

---

417 *The Economist*, Nov. 30 – Dec. 6, 2013, ' Regulating Political Spending, Lighten our Darkness', p. 43
418 Ibid, p. 44

Significantly, *the Economist* concludes:

> The consultation process is likely to be fierce, but it is still uncertain whether the new rules which emerge will be enforced. Since 2010 only one *small* non-profit has been denied tax-exempt status by the IRS [Internal Revenue Service] on political grounds.

What is perhaps less predictable is whether this move would have been afoot if the ruling Democratic Party was the major beneficiary, rather than their rivals, the Republicans, of the *status quo* situation.

No doubt with knowledge that detection, prosecution and conviction in this area of activity is beset with difficulty, it has been concluded that, "It escapes me how, by publishing the names of contributors of campaign financing, we can hope to correct or prevent these problems".[419] In keeping with this view, since seeking transparency is regarded as a futile search for a palliative to undesirable electoral conduct, it has been proposed that:

> We need to remove the private financing interest from the system and have publicly financed elections and regulation of political parties. There is no room for half-measures. We believe that these extravagant conferences and massive advertising campaigns are unnecessary and a waste of money, but also put us deeper in debt to the special interests. Under public financing these would disappear and candidates would have to debate issues[420] and plans with their constituents".[421]

What is being implied by the letter writer to the press, is that without any private funding at all, there is no transparency issue. This assumes, obviously, that parties would limit their expenditure to or below the amount provided

---

419 Letter of the Day, *The Gleaner*, June 6, 2011, p. A8, 'Reform campaign financing', by Carlton Stewart. *The Gleaner* in its Editorial of Wed. Sept. 1, 2010, at p.A6 argues, somewhat to the contrary, that the PNP's necessary disclosure, by law, of the source of the Trafigura 'donation' "would not have required a leak from a private bank account for the public to know that Trafigura Beheir. ...had made a $31 million 'donation' ... hidden as a payment for services to a supposedly private contractor ... in the absence of reporting requirements, ... finance central and parliamentary parties and their candidates, thereby gaining substantial influence in the formal halls of power". But is not this exactly what the media is trying to do through the influence of 'information'/opinion dissemination, rather than the influence of the dollar? What if the media is representative of a particular class interest? — which might easily be the case in a stratified social system.

420 The response to this assumption, as to the transformation of politics to one of issue confrontation, was delivered by the results of *The Gleaner* Commissioned poll reported in the issue of Thu. July 7, 2011 on p. A2 under the heading, "Issues? What issues?", "Few Jamaicans prepared to vote on issues if elections are called now". The report informed that "The core support of the two major political parties remains strong as the country begins the countdown to the next general elections with issues playing little part in the reasons why persons would vote for either the Peoples National Party (PNP) or the Jamaica Labour Party (JLP) candidate ..."

421 Letter of the Day, *The Gleaner*, June 6, 2011, supra

by the state. Perusal of the literature provides no reason for confidence that this will be the case, especially one would expect, in jurisdictions where the notion of 'the rule of law' is yet to achieve anywhere near sacrosanct status. It would be misleading to suggest that a Jamaican law, by virtue of its presence in the statute books, evokes any mass compliance impulse.

Elaborating on these presumed 'natural' positive consequences of state funding, it may be said that, "A norm is valid *socially* if it is complied with or a sanction is imposed for non-compliance." This definition, as Alexy observes, and contrary to what many in developing legal jurisdictions may think, allows for numerous interpretations, in that,

> the concepts of compliance and the imposition of a sanction for non-compliance are ambiguous. ... One may ask, say, whether it is sufficient for compliance that behaviour conforms externally to the norm or whether compliance ... presupposes certain knowledge and motives on the part of the complying person.[422]

It should be apparent that the latter 'bases' are aspects of the rule-making process, that, against the background of weaknesses in the method and coverage of public communication capability, in Jamaica, is deserving of more than casual consideration.

As against the positivist/functional concept of the validity of law, the ethical concept rests on moral justifiability in accordance with theories of natural law and the law of reason. Efficacy and the procedural legitimacy of law's promulgation give way, here, to 'correctness of content, to be demonstrated by moral justification'.

An advantage of this approach is, apparent: again, the predisposition to critical assessment.

Does the ECJ's regulatory regime reflect processing through any of the possible conceptual screening devices mentioned? Without such scrutiny, legal rules which are taken as having an inherent moral element may well, as Alexy points out, facilitate considerable irrationality and injustice.

The possibility of unsanctioned, non-compliance with regulations such as those of the ECJ's reform project, requires focus on *individual* norms in contrast to norms of the general legal system or subsystem: in any instance

---

422 Alexy, op cit, p. 85

of breach, that is necessarily the level at which enforcement will be applied.

In this respect, it is worth reminding those designing, but particularly those being brought within the ambit of legislative frameworks—despite it being somewhat self-evident, as a matter of practice, that,

> An authoritatively issued norm of a legal system that is by and large socially efficacious does not forfeit its *legal* validity simply because it is frequently not complied with and a sanction is only rarely enforced for non-compliance. Unlike legal systems [or subsystems] individual norms need not be by and large socially efficacious as a condition for legal validity. … One may say of an individual norm, that it is valid because it belongs to a legal system [or subsystem] that is by and large socially efficacious.[423]

The question of perceived moral validity may well, of course, have a strong correlation with the level of compliance.

Much of the existing disagreement/concern which has belatedly erupted among persons long acquainted with the thinking behind and thus the likely 'final' contours of the ECJ's reform mould, reflects little more than the collision between vested-interest perspectives on legal, as against perceptions of political validity.

THE PRIVATE SECTOR ORGANISATION OF JAMAICA'S (PSOJ'S) SOLUTION

Peculiarly, but not altogether surprisingly, the solution proffered by the President of the PSOJ to the possibility of a reduction in contributions as a result of disclosure, is symptomic of the traditional absence of courage which permeates the society from the top. This may be viewed as the inherent reluctance, as Bob Marley would have it, of the unwillingness to, "stand up for you rights" at the aggregated 'national' level, as against in narrow self-interest terms.

It was reported that,

> Concerning the view that disclosing the names of donors would cause a reduction in contributions, Matalon said donors who wished to remain anonymous could donate to the ECJ's election fund since 'there would be

---

423 See also Ronald Mason, 'Damn dictatorship on campaign financing' on the danger that the ECJ "seeks to regulate the freedom out of the electoral process"; The *Gleaner*, Oct. 6, 2013, pA9.

no disclosure requirement for that and the ECJ would be responsible for disclosure [*sic*] [disbursement] of those funds between *both* [Italics added] political parties".[424]

Matalon's suggestion is, of course, not new. It is well known, and he must be privy to this, being a member of one of the most established multifaceted family business conglomerates in the island, that some have sought a risk-free win–win sanctuary by contributing to both major parties only. It follows that third parties with little present prospect of significant electoral success get no support, whatever their democratic role pretensions, declared intentions or potential electoral appeal.

A distributable total in the ECJ's Fund, excluding amounts contributed by such 'public-spirited' sources which sum would depend on a number of factors such as means and generosity, among others, will make any computation of the eventual level of subsidy unpredictable. Relating any such disbursement to what the parties' ideas may be as to 'adequacy' and their 'critical needs', financially, does not make for efficient/effective campaign planning.

In essence, 'big money' ensures its ability to continue to influence, at the very least, the ideological basis, politically and economically, of policy formulation, regardless of which party wins.[425] Now the ECJ is proposed as the conduit. This seems a wholly unacceptable perversion of its mandate and the more worthy sentiments underpinning the notion of public financing, not to mention that its Report states:

> For each financial year the Commission shall recommend to Parliament through the Commission's budget the *total* [Italics added] amount to be allotted for the support of political parties that qualify for funding. The Disclosure Committee of the Commission shall determine the amount to be included in the Commission's budget after consultation with the Nominated Commissioners.[426]

One need only point out, in response to Matalon, that it is the two major political parties which select the Nominated Commissioners and emphasize

---

424 See Ronald Mason's response to this proposal from Matalon in 'Damn dictatorship on campaign financing', supra.

425 See 'Governments for few' front page headline, *The Gleaner* Fri, July 19, 2013, p. 1, with the sub-heading' 'Incoming UWI Principal decries administrations' failure to act in interest of most Jamaicans'

426 ECJ Report, p. 9.

that it is Parliament that will approve the quantum of financial subsidy to be provided through the ECJ.

If the Chairman of the ECJ was accurately quoted, the apparent straightforwardness of the ECJ's proposal becomes more politically and legally complicated than it appears, as demonstrated by the recent case against the former Presidential candidate, John Edwards, in the United States.[427] According to the ECJ's then Chairman, the intention is that all funds donated to political parties will be treated as *trust-funds*, "... and those monies must be lodged in bank accounts of the party. The *Commission* [Italics added] will have access to those funds."[428]

The extent of the bureaucracy that effective monitoring, not only of compliance with parties' internal constitutional arrangements but financial operations, including banking transactions, would require under such regulations, is daunting.

Jamaica's national economic situation is, once again, configured significantly by IMF guidelines, performance stipulations and loan repayment obligations. The extent of the IMF's influence was recently exposed by the extraordinary number of enactments 'rushed' through Parliament involving quite abnormal late sittings so as to satisfy the Fund's expectations. Inevitably, the governing party, in particular, is likely to seek, whatever its true motives, to use this climate of austerity as justification for its inability to be less than

---

427 John Edwards, a highly successful lawyer, is quoted as saying, "there is no question that I have done wrong ... But I did not break the law". The Court prohibited him from making contact "with one of the wealthy benefactors who gave him money that prosecutors say was used to hide the [extra – marital] affair". This use of the funds for personal purposes was allegedly illegal, since 'Edwards should have reported it on public campaign finance returns because it exceeded the $2300 limit per person for campaign contributions'. The charges against him were for receiving illegal campaign contributions and submitting false statements, for keeping and failing to disclose the moneys in public campaign finance reports. Needless to say, Edwards' defense is to the effect, as stated by his lawyer, that 'there's no way that anyone, including Edwards, would have known that the payment [from individuals to Edwards personally] should be treated as campaign contributors: See the *Jamaica Observer*, Sat. June 4, 2011, p5, John Edwards pleads not guilty to finance charges." Edwards was eventually found not guilty. NOTE: The ECJ intends that all constituency expenditure should be recorded and reported on an *annual* basis, as against the present requirement which applies only to the period between nomination and Election Day - a minimum of 16, and maximum of 23 days. See Alicia Dunkley, the *Jamaica Observer* Thursday Sept. 2, 2010, p.3, 'ECJ pushing for changes to political party financing'. The Edwards trial and the more recent case of Jesse Jackson, Jnr, who, between himself and his wife, used donation to finance lavish personal life styles, and, who having pleaded guilty is now awaiting sentence, suggests that where political donations are given to politicians *directly* without specification of use, the issue becomes one of either a presumption that the purpose is political or the equally extreme stricture of banning 'gifts' with the associated legal/moral and individualism/democratic principle implications.

428 Alicia Dunkley, 'ECJ pushes for changes to political party financing'. The *Jamaica Observer*, Thur. Sept. 2, 2010 p.3,

generous in party funding budgetary allocation, whenever such a position is seen as being to its competitive advantage. Instances of such behaviour in Europe and Canada, to which reference will be made, confirms this possibility to be based on more than cynicism.

It is, in this respect, not surprising that, as reported in the press, the then governing party's "... (the) JLP donations dwarf funds collected by the PNP",[429] with the details being, for accounting years ending October 2010 and September 2010, respectively:

	JLP	PNP
Donations (Millions)	52.4	20.0
MPs	1.9	-
Parish Councillors	2.7	-
Membership dues	0.7	8.7
Other	-	1.2
Total Income	57.7	29.9
Expenditure	56.6	29.6

The JLP would be expected, after only three years in office, compared to the PNP's preceding eighteen years, to be in this superior position. Parties operate myopically, not only when they are in opposition, by not utilizing the opportunity for policy formation, but also when in government, by failing to organize and implement viable income-generating arrangements, projects and strategies to see them through the almost inevitable lean years with respect to their own finances. This ignored responsibility is highlighted especially after elections, even for the victorious party, and certainly during years in opposition, especially if this proves to be lengthy.

LIVING WITHIN MEANS

It will be apparent that the position taken is that political parties, whose leadership should be expected to set the tone and standards of conduct and the representational performance required to meet the goals prescribed by the vision pursued, should not be encouraged, much less enabled by the provision

---

429 *The Gleaner*, Tue. Nov. 23, 2010, p. A3

of state funding, to live beyond their means. As governments, interchanging as they have been, in that role since the first election after Universal Adult Suffrage, they seem to similarly lack creativity in achieving optimum results in the management of revenue generating options at the national level

That said, the above figures, as limited as the information is, give no true indication of the real financial standing of either party.[430] The information does not disclose assets, cash reserves, income-generating investments, or liabilities, whether in the form of ordinary bank loans or, as was the case in recent party financing scandals in England,[431] private loans, on whatever terms, perhaps maturing into 'gifts', from supporters, whether individuals or organisations.

One would have expected the ECJ's recommendations to be informed by the British and American[432] experience, at least. That failure may be explained by the lack of any involvement, as far as the writer is aware, of a political scientist or, indeed, even the Parliamentary Counsel in the work of the Commission. These are professionals who, as research-oriented specialists, would be sensitive to the benefit of issue consideration, comparatively.

Membership guidelines for the Commission should certainly have allowed for the co-optation of such expertise and experience. It might also have been conceivable for a person(s) with accounting skills, to have been included, given the substantial financial reporting requirements contemplated by the reform proposals. This last, not with a view to compounding the complexity of reporting detail specified, but the very opposite.

---

430   See Letter of the Day, 'An audit that tells little,' by Glenn Tucker, *The Gleaner* Thu, Sept. 23, 2010, p. A6, the letter writer asks "But how does a report that tells us how the money they have is being spent throws (sic) any light on our main concern, which is where is the money coming from? ... The bulk of these contributions come from moneyed individuals ... with some sturdy strings attached". As is the case under the American system, it is argued that, "Much of this is soft money which does not go into the political structures of the party".

431   See 'Labour treasurer kept party in dark over loan deals', in the Daily Telegraph (London) Mar. 16, 2006; 'Hewitt becomes first Cabinet member questioned over cash for honours', *The Scotsman*, Nov. 23, 2006; Rebecca Smithers, 'City academics advisor resigns after cash for honors accusation', *The Guardian* (London) Jan. 16, 2006; Diane Abbot; "You're right: it's far from alright, Jack', *The Times* (London) Mar. 17, 2006. For a somewhat dated House of Commons Library overview, see 'Loans to political parties', Standard Note: SN/PC/3960, May 2006, by Isobel White and Paul Lester, Parliament and Constitution Centre.

432   *The New York Times*, Thur. May 26, 2011, at p. A34 reports, under the heading, "The Republicans' Chutz PAC" [PAC meaning Political Action Committee], that, "(Now) three members of the Republican National Committee are trying to turn the law on its head with a new Republican Super PAC." The law referred to here is that barring federal office holders and candidates (since Watergate) from soliciting unlimited amounts of money for 'partisan campaign machines'. "The PAC founders", we are told, "blithely and cynically contend that the restriction really only applies to how funds are spent, not how they are solicited". The newspaper further noted that Super PAC, "will compound the damage of the Supreme Court's *Citizens United* decision that overturned restrictions against unlimited corporate donations.

With respect to the verification of financial data provided by parties we refer to the case of **L.G. Callaghan and The Chief Electoral Officer of Canada.**[433] The issue was whether the respondent could legally refuse to certify, for the purposes of reimbursement under section 465 of the *Canada Elections Act*, the claimed advertising expense on the ground that he was not satisfied that these expenses had actually been incurred by the applicants or the candidates for whom they acted as official agents. The applicant argued that the Chief Electoral Officers had no authority under section 465 of the *Act* to review or consider the accuracy of an electoral campaign return filed by or on behalf of a candidate pursuant to section 451. Section 465 provides that where the Chief Electoral Officer is satisfied that the candidate and his or her official agent have complied with their financial reporting obligations, he is required to provide a certificate to the Receiver General for the reimbursement of a portion of the candidate's election and personal expenses. The court concluded that the Chief Electoral Officers had no power under the *Act* to conduct a general investigation into the manner that a registered party spends its funds or helps finance its candidates' campaigns during an election.

The question of the accuracy of "an electoral campaign return", which would involve the issue of whether specified expenses ought to be reimbursed— in this instance, advertising charges under Canada's regulations—is covered in the ECJ Report under the heading, 'Qualification for State Funding'[434] which states that:

> A political party that qualifies for state funding shall be entitled to receive the same, provided that the party, has not provided any false or erroneous information to the Commission in *any* [Italics added] of the documents the party is required to submit annually to the Commission.[435]

The Commission's requirement for the provision of supporting invoices for expenditures does not, without more, address the problem of over or under-invoicing. State subsidy improperly spent could easily be disguised with the cooperation of a supplier whose service qualifies as a legitimate expense under the proposed law.

Scope is provided for engagement in 'mischief' of this kind by the broad

---

433 2010 FC 43 (CanLII)
434 ECJ Report, p. 7
435 Ibid, p. 8

categories of activities for which subsidies for "constituency operations may only be used", which are specified as "(a) Administration", and, "(b) Organisation".

In contrast to the apparent loophole existing in the Canadian regime, as disclosed by *Callaghan*, the contemplated Jamaican situation deals with the issue as follows:

> This Committee (Political Party Finance Disclosure Committee):
>
> 1. shall have the power to investigate the veracity of all applications and returns filed with the ECJ
>
> 2. shall have the power, through its Chairman, to summon before it the officials of any Registered Political Party; and
>
> 3. shall be supported by a staff of forensic auditors for the purposes of carrying out any required investigations.

For the Commission to have the capability to effectively look beyond what appears on the face of reports, especially those of a detailed financial nature, implies the availability of the number and competence of personnel probably far in excess of the financial resources likely to be provided.

This situation becomes more problematic the greater the attempt to control in detail. The ROPA provisions provide an example of this demanding monitoring, and hence largely ignored, approach.

What may seem to be a 'strict' liability formulation is ameliorated by the inclusion of the power to, "suspend the payment of state funding ... if within sixty days of being required by the Commission to correct the particular infraction ... the political party fails to do so".[436]

The contrast in drafting technique of the Australian Commission is significant: the all important criminal law liability *mens rea* element is acknowledged by the inclusion of the word 'knowingly'.[437]

Where the source of party/campaign financial support is private as against state subsidy, as in *Callaghan*, the disclosure concern is of another genre altogether. Here the focus on the party, and, more specifically, its behaviour in government, is to be determined by observed or suspected donor conduct.

---

436 Ibid, p.12
437 Cass and Burrowes op cit, p. 493

With the transparency lens being turned, in the first instance, on the private sector, their temerity was not lost on the Chairman of the ECJ. In defending the partial disclosure option chosen by the ECJ, he challenged proponents of full disclosure[438] to lead by example: "If we are not just seeking to score political points but each [sic] seeking to develop this country, you who believe in full disclosure must practice that."[439]

That parties have failed to make themselves sufficiently attractive to a large enough number of potential dues-paying members, as well as potential supporters of major fundraising events is beyond dispute. In the absence of the touted twin panaceas of public funding and transparency, the result has been a further erosion of a candidate-screening process requiring the demonstration of any degree of political/social philosophical or party ideological/policy commitment being taken seriously into account.[440] What this could mean, procedurally and practically, is that "... political parties move [increasingly] towards those candidates with the ability to raise funding,"[441] which, "... thus opens the gate to persons willing to, and capable of, buying their way, by proxy, to political power."[442] It may be added that such funds may well be 'clean', and such candidate not necessarily of questionable integrity.

---

438   Gary Spaulding, 'ECJ rolls out plans to address campaign financing', in *The Gleaner* Thur. Sept. 2, 2010, p. A4; The Secretary General of the OAS expressed preference for 'complete disclosure [despite] ... the fear factor [political victimization]. legitimate not only in Jamaica", as reported in *The Gleaner*, Fri. Sept. 3, 2010, p. A3; Claude Robinson, in the *Jamaica Observer* June 1, 2008, Sec. 3, p. 6;

439   *The Gleaner*, Thu. Sept. 2, 2010, p. A4, 'ECJ rolls out plans to address campaign financing;" See Peter Espeut, 'Transparency not more secrecy', *The Gleaner*, Fri. July 30, 2010, p.A9; President of the Jamaica Chamber of Commerce, Milton Samuda, argues, "Specifically in relation to party funding, we cannot expect the reform we wish if we ourselves are unwilling to participate in full disclosure, choosing instead to cower in secrecy;" Douglas Orane, CEO of Grace Kennedy Co. Ltd., former Independent Senator, sees the need for full disclosure covering all donations and donors and monitoring pre-campaign expenditure [regardless of size and number, apparently] together with upper limits on donations and maximum campaign expenditure limits, reported in The Gleaner, Thu. July 1, 2010, p. C7

440   "There is a close correlation between economic propriety and social cohesion ... studies show that when less than 5% of the people in an area are positive role models, the area spirals down into crime and violence". The PNP, one letter writer to the press acknowledges, has just [at the time of writing of this article] taken the "very commendable step of establishing an Integrity Commission which vets candidates for the coming election", the *Jamaica Observer*, 'Over to you, Electoral Commission', Wed. June 15, 2011, p.9; See Franklin Johnston, 'Your MP, public servant or recycled rogue?', the *Jamaica Observer*, Fri. May 6, 2011, p. 11; See also Douglas Orane, supra, where "integrity testing" for prospective candidates is proposed, as well as enforcement of the declaration of assets legislation.

441   See Letter of the Day, 'Reform campaign funding', by Carton Stewart, in The Gleaner, June. 6, 2011, p. A8; Michael Williams, General Secretary of the fringe third party, the National Democratic Movement, alleges that "this has caused many who enter representational politics to fall prey to wealthy self-seeking persons", and that "There are well known persons of shady character who by one way or another have found their way into Parliament, See 'Campaign Financing', *The Gleaner*, Mar. 9, 2008. P. A3

442   *The Gleaner*, Editorial, Wed. Sept. 1, 2010, p. A6

At the very heart of these funding issues has been, it can be argued, is the phenomenon of the trend towards the professionalization of politics, in career terms.[443] It can only be this perspective, on the involvement of first time office-seeking candidates and new MPs, which could explain Christopher Tufton's statement that, "... funds spent on campaigning can never be recovered ... If you were to do that [enter politics with the intention of recovering funds spent] it would be unlikely that you would be able to achieve that legitimately ..."[444] The newcomer to politics may be well advised to think long-term about recovering his/her investment in the political process, depending, importantly, on the forms of return/reward expected and most highly valued.

Needless to say, in the prevailing atmosphere where there is considerable tension between the political parties, on the one hand, and the media, the private sector leadership and private citizen commentators, on the other, the prospect is for something of a financial drought from some traditional donors.

With front page banner headlines, such as 'Bruce Fires Back', for example, *The Gleaner* reported the somewhat overdue response of Bruce Golding, the then Prime Minister and leader of the JLP to the description of his party, in several almost-consecutive editorials in that newspaper, as one of the 'gangs' of Gordon House [the name of the Parliament building]. In the capacity of party leader, Golding, it was stated, 'scolded' the editor and the newspaper, saying,

> There is a sustained effort being made by the power brokers of North Street [the location of The Gleaner's head office in Kingston] to harass the government. It is not surprising. It comes from a mentality that ascribes to itself not just a right but a duty to assist parties to form government and to

---

443 See, Garfield Higgins, 'The Agenda', the *Jamaica Observer*, Aug. 17, 2014, p. 9, where the statement is made that "career politician is the scourge of Caribbean party politics. Many of the politicians across the Caribbean have never owned or operated a business, developed a programme from scratch and single-handedly or otherwise burnt the midnight oil to make it succeed, taken calculated risks with their own money."

444 The first-time MP and Cabinet Minister, in an interview reported in *The Gleaner*, Mar. 9, 2008, p.A3, in which no distinction seemed to have been drawn between 'project' funding by donors and friends which would be a version of private political financing, in nature, as against constituency projects, the initiation of which would secure one's political base with constituents, if the support of relevant Ministers could be successfully lobbied. The Constituency Development Fund, for which the JLP had promised in its Manifesto to allocate 2% of the Budget, to be divided between the 60 constituencies, not surprisingly has come under severe criticism from middle class commentators, who enjoy relative job security, if not self-employed status, or being otherwise privileged or of independent means.

take parties out of government. ...We mislead ourselves if we believe the vote is the ultimate lever of political power.[445]

We hold no brief for any individual or group. We nevertheless think it more likely, indeed axiomatic, that casting legislators in the role of profligate villains and traitors,[446] could have serious negative criminological consequences, quite beyond the expectation, and, indeed, could well be very opposed to the intentions of these 'labellers'. If civil society, so-called, and would-be opinion leaders have no respect for Parliamentarians who are, unrelentingly, the targets of furious denigration from these quarters, why should the criminal, confirmed or would-be, display regard for the laws they pass? If Parliamentarians are virtually portrayed as criminals, by virtue of the language used to describe them, why should the criminal, as traditionally defined, feel any unease with such a categorization, personally, or any sense of guilt for anti-social, unlawful conduct?

Indeed, can they be expected to abide by the laws and regulations they pass controlling their own conduct such as the often touted finance campaign legislation?

The newspaper in its editorialized exposé of the parties, consisting of several articles, as "... the gangs of Gordon House, the political parties that have traded state power in Jamaica for more than half a century," seems to be clearly and ill-advisedly overwhelmed by the zeal with which its cause is championed.

The question needs to be put: instead of contributing to the parties in the form of money, only, why not invest their time and energy and competencies? But these are interest group leaders who would almost without exception take the strongest objection to suggestions as to the possible reforming influence

---

445 *The Gleaner*, Mon. May 30, 2010, pp.A1,A3; The leader of the Opposition, then, Portia Simpson-Miller, initially responded to the 'gang' tag by saying that the parties deserved it. Some weeks later she came to their defense by highlighting achievements by way of the "significant gains in tertiary education, health care, telecommunications, labour relations, air and seaport infrastructure, housing, culture and sport". The implication was that, despite the mistakes made by governments of both parties and the lack of significant economic growth, since "the second decade after independence, [1962]. "... many things are taken for granted today which were unattainable for the masses of the people 49 years ago": the *Jamaica Observer*, Fri. June 17, 2011, p.5

446 Since the Gleaner's 'gang' characterization, we have seen prospective Parliamentarians described as 'thugs', by Wayne Campbell, "Save Parliament from the thugs ', Fri. July 15, 2011, p. A8, and more recently , 'criminals', by Thelma Fairweather-Siegel, "Gordon House \criminals must refund me", *The Gleaner*, Fri. Feb. 2, 2008, p. 8; also The Gleaner Editorial, 'The Spectre of Trafigura', Thur. Mar. 13, 2008, p.A6, where the statement is made that "... we may suspect, but cannot know if criminals are attempting to be that way to control the State".

they could bring by direct involvement as participants, rather than abstainers, in representational politics. The typical response one can predict would be some version of, "Do I look crazy to you?"

THE BEHAVIOUR OF THE PARTIES[447]

Bipartisan agreement on campaign financing in Jamaica is not likely to be as easily realized, as was the case in Germany. Over the past four decades, and indeed, until very recently, the island's politics has been characterized by polarization, tribalism and violence. Cartel-like party politics does not emerge or thrive in that environment.

Clear evidence of this, apart from the very long gestation period of the ECJ's proposals, was forthcoming from the substance and tone of comments in the Parliamentary debate on the Report, such as, that, "State financing of political parties is in the interest of protecting the party from becoming vulnerable to funding from questionable sources."[448]

One of the female MPs and Minister in the House of Representatives, Lisa Hanna, has characterized the nature of party political rivalry as being something in the nature of 'bloodsport'. The implication was that one has to expect more than robust criticism, but also that this explains the relatively few women who have taken part in representational politics and thereby the rarity of women in top political positions in the country.

If one were to utilize Hart's theory of rights to analyse the ECJ/political party/Parliament relationship, as MP Warmington trenchantly declared in slightly different terminology, the Commission could be seen as the 'small-scale sovereign' to whom duty is owed: the 'rights' of the ECJ in this formulation would amount to, "... being given by the law exclusive control,[449]

---

447 See Hume Johnson, 'Gender quotas not about preferential treatment', *The Gleaner*, Mar. 16, 2014, p. F6.

448 *The Gleaner*, Thur. Nov. 4, 2010, p. A10. One contributor with a company (project management) background would have, not just donor data correlated with government contract awards [unnecessary if the award process is transparent and guidelines fair], but the parties' accounts should be done by audit firms [at whose expense is not stated, given the rates charged for such work] and, further wants, the Electoral Commission to do "donor trend analyses": see Franklin Johnston, *The Jamaica Observer*, Fri. July 30, 2010, p.10. As Lawyers tend to wear professional blinkers, by virtue of which all problems become amenable to legal solution, so it is with the business manager/consultant, it seems.

449 As the writer sees it, ECJ control extends not only to issues of party funding, with repercussions for the nature of their structure and function and even operational philosophy but also as to matters of constitutional content.

more or less extensive in the area of conduct covered by that duty."[450]

That 'control' may not be easily achieved in the Jamaican party political context where Parliamentarians are, in public view, difficult, if not impossible to be controlled by successive Speakers not lacking sanctions established by convention, standing orders and regulations.

Given the observation above by MP Peter Bunting, then also Opposition (PNP) General Secretary, as to what is but the 'conventional wisdom' in these matters about "questionable sources", this should hardly have been worth the prominent media reportage it received.

In seeking to add specifics to his debate contribution, and in keeping with the traditionalistic small island orientation of personalizing issues and situations, the speaker continued, "The deputy of the JLP should know that when he was fêting certain people who are contributors who are now either charged or convicted, he should [sic] be concerning himself with that source of funding."[451]

According to the press report, "a firestorm then ensued in the House ...", such that, "During the squabble, the microphones on the Opposition benches went dead. A stand-in microphone had to be brought for Bunting. ... However a furious Robertson [MP and also then JLP Minister] unplugged the microphone."[452]

"Meanwhile", the report continued, "Vaz hit back at Bunting when he joined in the debate on the report of the ECJ on party financing", in that,

> He blasted Bunting's People National Party (PNP) for claiming that it backed full disclosure of party funding but had not provided proof that it returned a controversial sum of money to Trafigura Beheer, a Dutch oil-trading company.[453]

---

450 H. L. A. Hart, 'Legal Rights', Stanford Encyclopaedia of Philosophy, Dec. 20, 2001, p. 183.

451 When the then Prime Minister went on a bird –shooting trip to Paraguay with a well-known JLP supporter, which they had been doing for some twenty years, whose engineering firm had obtained large Government contracts, not alleged to have been unfairly obtained, The Jamaica Observer, Thu. June 23, 2011, carried the bold p.3, report headed, 'Vaz [Minister of Information] produces copy of Golding's Paraguay trip cheque'. The paper further stated that, "The provision of the cheque was in response to a newspaper article on Sunday suggesting that the trip was paid for by Seaton "[the contractor]. The report" then triggered calls from the then Opposition for the matter to be thoroughly investigated", the news item concluded.

452 Ibid

453 Ibid. The status of the Trafigura matter at the time of writing (July, 2011), as reported in The Jamaica Observer, Mon. June 20, 2011, pp.1,4, was that "Trafigura court date nears: PNP officials to answer questions by month end", followed on Tue. June 28, 2011, p.4, in the same daily by the report, "Trafigura matter stalls [due to the death of the mother of lead counsel for the PNP officials], "... from whom the Dutch investigators are seeking answers". The Dutch had filed, through the office of the local DPP, a motion in the Supreme Court of Jamaica, under the Mutual Assistance (Criminal Matters) Act.

Whereas the PNP, as we have noted and as confirmed by then Minister Daryl Vaz, came out in support of full disclosure, transparency, as a solution to corrupt political practices, does not seem to have universalistic appeal when either of the party's self-interest is involved.

STATE FUNDING AND DEMOCRACY

The ever-present "belief", feeling", "concern", "worry", "perception" of and about corruption, the possibility of being tempted, and the likelihood of some participants in politics succumbing in Jamaica, and elsewhere, is not a recent development.

The system of public funding and disclosure embraced by the former Canadian Director of Elections, Jean Pierre Kingsley, speaking as the main presenter at a forum on campaign finance reform in Jamaica, was recommended on the premise that without this "democracy would be at stake". Against the experience of numerous Charter-based legal challenges in the Canadian Supreme Court, this view was constrained by the caution that public funding, by itself, would not solve the problems of multi-party representative democracy, although it is predicated by Kingsley, that, "If the political system does not regulate the money, then one may well expect that the money will regulate the system".[454]

Again, entirely without the supply of reasoned explanatory argument, which is certainly required in the Jamaican context, we are informed in strong tones of confirmation of its truth, that a *small majority* of persons interviewed in an ECJ poll were of the view that, "strengthening political parties financially with public funds would help preserve and enhance democracy".[455] To what extent, for example, was the implication of financing from *public funds* made clear, meaning the possibility of additional *taxes*.

Presumptions, such as those inherent in the quote above, implying causal relationships, do not appear to be in order in the absence of sufficient experience with research strategies allowing for the emergence of properly documented, objectively studied, deceptively simple-seeming issues. Phrases such as "help preserve and enhance democracy" are straight-forward,

---

454 Daraine Linton, 'Democracy at stake', reporting in *The Gleaner*, Thu. Dec. 4, 2008, pp. A 1, 3
455 Ibid

uncomplicated enough sounding to the politically sophisticated ear; and they exist certainly in the mature democratic country's populations. Their connotations for purposes of policy design within a *legal* framework, with binding obligations and weighty sanctions, is, on the other hand, a rather highly challenging complex matter.

Despite the fact that "Jamaica ranks second from bottom on the 2007 World Bank Governance Index,[456] being only above Haiti in the Caribbean", this can be no justification for the expectation held by supporters of campaign finance reform that any funding initiatives undertaken would necessarily "enhance the quality of governance". This 'truth' is most definitely not in the 'self–evident' category.

A reconsideration is therefore perhaps not out of order of Professor Trevor Munroe's position, grounded, subjectively perhaps, at the level of the subconscious, supported by the "surprising" purportedly objective poll finding that the "overwhelming number of Jamaicans" embrace the idea that, "We need to structure a system of public funding in keeping with our needs at this time".[457] We put the inevitable question, simply: what in fact, as perceived by that majority; are *our needs*? And, ultimately, from *whose pocket* is that 'public' funding to come? What public goods or services will be sacrificed?

It would not be far short of shocking if an appropriately constructed and explained survey item were to result in a demographically representative majority of respondents in a sample of appropriate size naming the funding of parties, with their taxes, as a current priority. This has, in fact, been confirmed by another poll result, to which reference will be made.

Engrafting a state financed regulatory regime, with the best of intentions, into a hostile financial and politico-cultural host environment, is highly questionable as being the reform exercise most appropriate for implementation at this juncture.

It is arguable, in opposition to the view of the Executive Director of the National Integrity Action (NIA), a former leftist, (and those on the left usually favour state funding,[458] for obvious reasons), that it is the political system and

---

456 The Index uses indicators such as accountability, political stability, level of violence, governmental effectiveness, regulatory quality, compliance with the rule of law and control of corruption.
457 Daraine Linton, supra.
458 *BBC History Magazine*, May 2008, pamphlet, p.3

the very nature of the practise of party politics that is in need of dramatic change, or, to use his word, 'restructuring'.

Given its antecedents, as an entity owned and controlled for a considerable period by members of the omnipotent "21 Families"[459], one would not have expected support for this position to be forthcoming from such a source as the leading daily newspaper.[460]

ORGANISATION VS MONEY

For the columnist, Michael Burke, "Victories in Jamaican elections depend on the ability to get party supporters first to be registered as voters and then, to vote on Election Day".[461] The merit of this assessment may appear dubious in the extreme, as it seems to discount the importance of the swing/uncommitted voter. Its operational validity will nevertheless be confirmed by anyone familiar with the inner workings of political organisations situated within a small island political culture characterized by a dependency predilection and politician/voter patronage relations. And this remains so, even when there is little in the trough: in some situations, 'hope springs eternal'.

If Burke's conclusions seem to unreasonably narrowly circumscribe the essential activities of the 'political cycle', which adequately considered ought not to be the case, the crucial implication is that much of the politicking expenditure seen as necessary may, indeed, be superfluous.

Such a perspective calls into question the issue of the extent of election campaign advertising and attendant costs, which constitute a major item of expenditure. A case which is of some relevance here is that of Germany where under their regulatory regime,

> only a handful of campaign spots are allocated to the major parties, and proportionately less to smaller parties ... [and] the severity of limiting campaign airtime for political parties is enhanced by the consensus of the

---

459 Stanley Reid, in, Essays on Power and Change in Jamaica, Carl Stone and Aggrey Brown, eds, Transaction Publishers, 1977.

460 The Gleaner, Editorial, Tue. Apr. 5, 2011, p.A8 titled 'If the gangs of Gordon House are to change', states under the sub-heading, 'No energy for revolution', that "... what is surprising is that in the face of a need for revolution there is no apparent energy from the [party] leaders ..."

461 The Jamaica Observer, Thu. June 2, 2011, p.11

German states that the political parties may not purchase advertisement time for broadcasts.[462]

Both the United Kingdom and the United States, by their political finance laws, provide subsidies in this regard,[463] with the effect that by being in the income/expenditure equation, the need for private contributions will be 'necessarily' thereby proportionately reduced.

The lack of presentation of detail setting out advertising expense as a percentage of total campaign costs in Jamaica can, one expects, be taken for granted. The consequence is the inability to accurately assess the funding implications which a different policy reform configuration might make. Here again, the lessened usefulness of the ECJ's Report relates directly to its lack of an all-embracing scope. With the money paid for its operations[464], and the length of time taken for the presentation of its Report, with genuine respect, nevertheless, for the *integrity* of the Commission's members, the tax-paying public may feel somewhat shortchanged.

Attorney at law, Jacqueline Samuels-Brown's campaign advertising submissions, entailing control features, might conceivably yield beneficial results for the state of the body politic, if accepted.[465] The odds, we feel certain, are overwhelmingly against it. A paradigmatic shift in the quality of the island's politics could be realized if advertising subsidies were made available and used, as she proposes, to elaborate on the policies, programs and strategic initiatives to be pursued as elements of party platforms which, when aggregated, would accord with, and be reflective of, "… the core values to which we are committed and on which we want to build our society."[466]

---

462 The Law library of Congress, Campaign Finance: Germany, pamphlet, p.2: Jacqueline Samuels-Brown, Attorney-at-Law, and then President of the Jamaica Bar Association, proposes that the reforms should include, "Requirements for free media space/time for political debate", in 'Letter of the Day', 'Trafigura scandal seen as opportunity for change', The Gleaner, Tue. Oct. 12, 2006, p. 8.

463 Parties in the UK do, as Samuels-Brown suggests (note above), receive "handsome subsidies in kind, such as free political and election broadcasts on radio and television": BBC History Magazine, May 2008; The situation in the United States is one in which legitimation may depend on "Increasing the supply of funds (through individual and party contribution limits and tax credits) and subsidies (with free broadcast time and mailings) seems essential, … as does an insistence that federal campaign activity be financed exclusively with regulated , that is 'hard money' funds": Thomas E. Mann in Public Policy Inquiry, 'Deregulating Campaign Finance: Solution or Chimera', Brookings Review, Winter 1998, p.19

464 Dr. Herbert Thompson had not, as most informed persons seem to feel he should do, seen it fit to resign altogether from the ECJ, as not just as the Chairman. His reluctance to yield to public 'pressure', so far (Oct. 2013) may have something to do with the J$8 million per year he would be giving up.

465 See Jacqueline Samuels-Brown, supra.

466 Howard Gregory (Bishop), 'A nation in search of direction', the *Jamaica Observer*, June 5, 2011, p.2

If it is safe to say that some members of the monied class will withhold funding from the parties, given their image, not to mention the state of the economy, what then is the anticipated response of the underclass to the echo-chambered vilification of those who, between them, have promulgated the laws and are certainly to be held responsible, *to some extent*, for the state of law and order, and social well-being in the society? Regardless of the effect that opinion leaders may have, it goes without saying that the 'worse off' will not be able, whatever their inclinations, to make up any resulting substantial funding gap.

It does not, perhaps, need 'expert testimony' to be convinced that in some circumstances of austerity, recession and even depression, some 'rich' will get richer while 'the poor' will get poorer.

Political party effectiveness, as democratic representative organisations, to the extent that this depends on having 'adequate' financing, is, under this dispensation, likely to increasingly depend on the state, where it is an approved provider, for funding.

It is to be noted that the 'threatened' withholding of private funds is being proposed by individuals and institutional leaders most of whom strongly support at least partial funding by the tax payer, regardless apparently, of whether and when "... the gangs ... accept what they have become and set a clear route to recovery which *we* [Italics added] have previously set out. ..."[467] But then, these spokespersons are, it seem, speaking on behalf of a civil society in which the average citizen, as a taxpayer, is not included.

According to one editorial of *The Gleaner,*

> Among the leverage [*sic*] that civil society can exert is the withholding of financial support ... and a lack of cooperation with the parties ... until they return to civilized conduct. The society will tolerate *necessary* [Italics added] delirium tremens while they shed the characteristics of gangs.[468]

---

467 *The Gleaner* Editorial, supra 'Civil Society and the gangs of Gordon House'. The tone here might appear to lend credence to Golding's salvo, reported in *The Gleaner*, Mon. May 30, 2010, pp. A1, A3.

468 'Civil society and the gangs of Gordon House', *The Gleaner*, supra; see also the report of an address to the Rotary Club of St. Andrew by Douglas Orane, CEO of Grace Kennedy, one of the largest regional business conglomerates: 'Orane takes fight to crime', The Gleaner, Thu. July 1, 2010, p.C7, where Orane states: "Certainly, from the perspective of the private sector we ought to take a decision individually not to make donations to political parties until there is demonstrated a tangibly (sic) level of accountability and transparency."

The sociologist might retort that this is easily enough said by members of that class effectively isolated from the consequences of that prescription.

A CASE OF TWO COMPANIES

Apart from the issue of withholding private funding as a means of eliciting compliance with the would-be donor's political reform agenda, we have also witnessed at least two cases where the refund of financial contributions received has been the focus of attention. In one case, that of the 'Trafigura scandal',[469] interest has been widespread and vociferous in its expression, while in the other, the 'Olint affair', concern has been, in contrast, relatively muted, being confined largely to press commentary from persons not from the lower social strata. The lack of widespread negative response in respect to the latter may have a two-fold explanation: those 'victims' from the upper social strata are constrained by embarrassment at their folly in investing in what was a Ponzi scheme, doomed to fail, while the lower orders tend to be media-shy for obvious reasons.

The two situations are distinguishable on the basis of important factors, and their treatment here is limited by that fact. The Trafigura Beheer incident involved a foreign company (Dutch), of that name, which was doing business

---

469 See the following reports: 'Dutch investigators not satisfied with PNP response', where it is stated "Under Dutch law companies are prohibited from making such donations which are considered bribes" in *The Gleaner* Wed. Mar. 12, 2008, p.A2; Editorial, 'The spectre of Trafigura', *The Gleaner*, Thu. Mar. 13, 2008, p.A6; 'Trafigura haunts PNP', the Jamaica Observer, Tue. Aug. 24, 2010, pp.1, 4; 'Campbell bows out', *The Gleaner*, Thu. Aug. 26, 2010, p.A3; 'Dutch want truth', *The Gleaner*, Tue. Nov. 23, 2010, pp. A1,3; 'Online Feedback': 'I am ashamed', 'Passing the Bribery Smell Test', 'International stain', 'Is Jamaica still sovereign?', in *The Gleaner*, Wed. Nov. 24, 2010, p.A9; 'PNP says no documents served in Trafigura probe', the *Jamaica Observer*, Wed. Nov. 24, 2010, p.4; Editorial 'Trafigura: Good the Central Authority found her pen', *The Gleaner*, Wed. Nov. 24, 2010, p.A8, where it was reported that "(Campbell) won out-of-count compensation from the banks whose employees leaked information relevant to his accounts"'; 'PNP peeved at Trafigura revelations', *The Gleaner*, Wed. Nov. 24, 2010, p.A3; 'Vaz [then Information Minister] confident truth on shady Trafigura deal will come out', the *Jamaica Observer*, Thur. Nov. 25, 2010, p.3; 'Talk up: Vaz claims PNP sidestepping Trafigura affair', *The Gleaner*, Thu. Nov. 25, 2010 pp. 1, 3; Editorial, 'Trafigura: Be sure your sins will find you out', the *Jamaica Observer*, Thu. Nov. 25, 2010, p.8; 'JCC [Jamaica Chamber of Commerce] sounds off on Trafigura affair', *The Gleaner*, Fri. Nov. 26, 2010, p.A3; 'On feedback': 'Wrong place', 'What's the fuss?', 'Pot vs. kettle', 'None to lead', 'Deal with it', in The Gleaner, Fri. Nov. 26, 2010, p.A9; 'Portia Simpson-Miller [then leader of the Opposition], Bobby [Pickersgill, PNP General Secretary] served: PNP officials now forced to answer Trafigura questions', the *Jamaica Observer*, Fri. Nov. 26, 2010, pp.1,4; 'KD: [Knight, PNP MP, Attorney and former Minister of the PNP government] Trafigura investigators on fishing trip', the *Jamaica Observer*, Mon. Nov. 29, 2010, p. 4; Franklin Johnston, Dual Citizens, Trafigura, in The Jamaica Observer Fri. Dec. 3, 2010, p. 10: 'Churches call for closure to Trafigura affair' the *Jamaica Observer*, Wed. Dec. 8, 2010, p. 24; 'Trafigura forced election delay, says US Embassy Cable' (WikiLeaks secrets!), *The Gleaner*, Fri. June 3, 2011, p. 1; 'Trafigura court date nears: PNP officials to answer questions by month end': 'Dutch investigators will be in court, says DPP', the *Jamaica Observer*, Mon. June 20, pp. 1,4 where the report advises, "The party has since said the money was returned."

with/for the Government of Jamaica. It made what, at times, was said to be a "gift", at others, "a loan", or even "payment for consultancy services" to the then governing party, the PNP. In the case of 'Olint', its principal and the company are Jamaican and had no contractual relationship with the Government. Only the PNP received money from the Dutch Company, in an amount quite large in Jamaican terms (some thirty plus million dollars), when coming from one benefactor. In the Olint's/David Smith's case, donations were made to both parties, with the amounts as yet definitely undetermined, except that, as the matter was, on one occasion, reported, "The PNP, though, says the JLP received more, as though that gives a moral advantage".[470] Whatever the eventual figures that may be disclosed/confirmed, they will certainly be well in excess of the amount involved in the Trafigura matter, with figures of one, two, and five million United States dollars having been mentioned.

Whereas the Dutch Company was a properly operating legal entity, it is argued that,

> The more profound consideration is that both [PNP and JLP] solicited, and accepted, Smith's money at a time when there were already questions about the legitimacy of Olint. Regulators had been in and out of court with Smith, who was accused of operating an unregistered securities business.[471]

As tends to be the attitude of the regulatory bureaucrats, who always by professionally ingrained instinct, one suspects, take refuge behind rules, *per se*, their interest was engaged largely at the procedural level—that of Olint's registration:[472] the substantive issue, that the business was essentially a Ponzi scheme, even if regulatory hurdles and guidelines were complied with, was de-emphasized in their concerns.

With respect to Trafigura, the then General Secretary of the PNP, was a casualty on two levels,[473] for the issue was further contorted by the fact that

---

470 Editorial, 'Gangs of Gordon House should repay Olint cash', *The Gleaner*, Tue. April 19, 2011, p. A6

471 Ibid

472 It may be true that compliance with registration requirements might well have exposed the business as what it really was. But the absence of compliance should, we argue, have immediately triggered 'shut down' action by the Regulatory Agency.

473 Campbell resigned as General Secretary of the PNP, subsequent to which, leading officers, including the party leader and chairman, were interviewed by Dutch police in the search of evidence of bribery, or a "kick-back". When the Contractor General recommended to the DPP that Campbell be charged with obstructing his investigations, Campbell did what he said was the "right thing to do" and withdrew as a candidate for the North Central Clarendon constituency, "saying as I (Campbell) await the decision of the DPP": *The Gleaner*, Thu. Aug. 26, 2010, p. A3

the company's money was,

> transferred into a bank account under the control of Mr. Campbell ...
> the way, apparently, political contributions are handled to maintain
> donor anonymity. It is urgent [*The Gleaner* editorial argued] that there
> is legislation on the limits ... and transparency ... and perhaps public
> financing of parties.[474]

Indulgence in the "belief", "suspicion", "rumour" syndrome, yields the
conclusion and provides 'revelation' to the effect that,

> In respect to Olint, they [PNP/JLP] could lead the way in helping the
> liquidators recoup as much as possible of the money stolen by David Smith
> by repaying all the funds received for their campaigns. This process should
> be transparent ... It is widely *believed* [Italics added] that several politicians
> who invested in Olint were able to cash out before it collapsed. They too
> should repay any returns beyond their principal.[475]

It should readily be agreed that any weaknesses exposed in the political/
electoral processes should, naturally, be the compass for the direction of
reform.

---

474   Editorial, 'The Spectre of Trafigura', *The Gleaner*, Thu Mar. 13, 2008, p. A6

475   Editorial, 'Gangs of Gordon House should repay Olint cash', supra. Calling on politicians to repay money
"widely *believed*" to have been recouped, represents a continuation of the rumour mongering editorial behaviour
which reflects the societal penchant for hearsay, in the street, as against the juridical sense, over the more
challenging approach of deep, persistent, penetrating, investigation in search of supporting evidence. This is
what Ken Jones refers to as "Bad-mouthing [of politicians] and is what was seen by the United States President,
Theodore Roosevelt, as that which creates, "a morbid and vicious public sentiment and (which) at the same time
acts as a profound deterrent to able men of normal sensitiveness and tend to prevent them from entering the
public service at any price ...", The Gleaner, Tue. June 28, 2011, p. 8. How can a newspaper which passes up no
opportunity to demonize the parties still expect that, nevertheless, "competent experienced managers and persons
with entrepreneur skills" will be attracted to them?: see, *The Gleaner* Editorial, Tue. Apr. 5, 2011, p. A8

CHAPTER 9
REFORM OBJECTIVES

In the interest of convenience and presentation symmetry, an attempt will now be made to extract the goals/issues being targeted by the ECJ as deserving of the, yet to be determined, cost of the proposed regulatory framework.

In its first paragraph, the Report refers to "the vital and important role that political parties play in the life of the country". This is taken to be a sufficient reason to fill the current void with regulations, since "... this [lack of] oversight [sic] is no longer tenable".[476] On the second page, reference is made to a six-item agenda for the continued development and enhancement of the electoral system in Jamaica: "Political party and campaign Financing became the first item on that agenda," we are told.

The first mention of an area of concern, requiring remedial action, is expressed in the negative:

> The danger to be avoided is that no single individual or organisation ... should be able to contribute a sum that give ... sufficient voice and influence to disproportionately influence the decision-making of the party by virtue of the size of that contribution.[477]

Unsurprisingly, this represents one of the oft-expressed fears of commentators at all levels, not only in Jamaica, but internationally.[478] Presumably, though, official 'advisers' and consultants can also 'disproportionately' influence policy, even more significantly with potentially greater national damage,

---

476 ECJ Report, p.1

477 Ibid, p.9

478 See Letter of the Day, 'An audit that tells little' by Glenn Tucker, *The Gleaner*, Thu. Sept. 23, 2010, p. A6: "The bulk of these contributions came from monied individuals with something to gain"; In the United States, the Watergate-inspired electoral reforms of the mid 1970's, "largely failed in their intention to liberalize the nation. Conservatives and business interests were able to bend the new campaign finance rules and Congressional Committee systems to their own ends": The New York Times, Fri. May 27, 2011, p.A27; Professor Trevor Munroe suggests that the existing Jamaican party funding system "is at the heart of endemic and institutionalized corruption in our system of government", The Gleaner, Tue. June 22, 2010, p. A2. It was Senator Munroe, as he then was in *2002,* who moved a resolution "which was agreed to on both sides" for the introduction of a party and campaign funding scheme; Franklyn Johnston in reviewing the MP's role, observes, "(but) he may shake down contractors and dilute the money": The *Jamaica Observer,* Fri. May 6, 2011, p. 11; Jacqueline Samuels-Brown, Attorney-at-Law makes the point that citizens are expected to bear the burden of state funding without the benefit, of or entitlement to, information regarding other sources of funding (being), "... denied the right to make our own assessment regarding which bodies or persons make tainted contributions ... able to disproportionately influence governmental decision-making": The Gleaner, Tue. July 27, 2010. p. A6

and there is not now, nor has there usually been a shortage of those, at quite a hefty cost to the taxpayer. Little, by way of national prosperity, is there to show for their involvement in policy-making/implementation at the micro or macro level.

That, of course, is another issue.

In this connection, it is quite remarkable that the public good that could *possibly* result from party *donor* influence has not been contemplated. This represents yet another instance in which, sadly for analytical insight purposes, arguments appealing largely to sentiment frequently lack intellectual merit.[479] Hence, instinctively, if not as a matter of principle, right of centre parties tend universally to object to trade union financial support of political parties.[480] It would seem that any potential benefit that could flow from such influence relationships hardly matters.

Mention by the ECJ of the role political parties play in "representing general and specific interests" has previously been noted. Again, in a somewhat similar mode, it is said that, "It is *possible* [Italics added] that in their desire to meet representational needs beyond their resources political parties *may* [Italics added] become vulnerable to funding coming from questionable sources".[481]

At page eleven of the Report, we get in explicit language the briefest reference to three of the major negative characteristics of the political system: politically motivated violence, victimization—in the distribution of scarce benefits, whether in the form of jobs, contracts, or appointments—and the tendency to permanently brand strong party supporting persons as 'activists'. The extent to which its reform agenda is expected to prove a palliative to these problems, is not, however, projected. No attempt is made to establish any relationship between the major planks of reform policy initiative—registration, partial state funding, and donation and spending limits—and the mischief(s)

---

479   For an entirely different outlook, see "As Pension Chief Thompson gave work to donors"; *The New York Times*, Sat. Aug. 31, 2013, pp. A1, 15

480   In the UK, from as far back as the Edward Heath Conservative Government, significantly more determined under Thatcher, there has been a running legislative 'battle' in this regard.

481   ECJ Report, p.9. Another perspective is provided by Ronald Mason in 'Damn dictatorship on campaign financing', supra, where he writes, 'The ECJ leaves the impression that tainted money is designated according to donor; excessive money designated by whomever is perceived to be wealthy and free-spending; and money in search of influence, as designated by some identification of *quid pro quo* activity'.

to be addressed. The brevity of the initial Report—after a seven year gestation period—thirteen letter-size pages, simply does not allow for that.

In deference to its apprehension regarding parties' possible vulnerability "… to funds coming from questionable sources", it is proposed that it be, "… an offence for any political party or candidate of a political party [notably, independent candidates were apparently, then, considered of insufficient significance to be included] to knowingly accept or use funds tainted by illegality, or to improperly use funds legally received".[482]

With regard to any set of national values/objectives to be embraced by its recommendations, knowledge of these may only be derived by inference. Mechanistic legalism triumphs in this regard over a multi-disciplinary formulation.

Apart from the three problem areas noted above, the only other express mention of the socio-political factors propelling and directing the reforms effort is the use of the word 'democracy',[483] signifying *a fait accompli*, despite its being qualified by the word 'growing'.

The essential ingredients of a healthy democratic electoral process, to

---

482 ECJ Report, p.12

483 Ibid, p.9; Commentators, at various levels, have enumerated other worthwhile electoral reform objectives usually by focusing on the problem areas or the underlying reasons for the malaise. As a starting point, for example, see Alexis Robinson, 'Our new *Charter of Rights*' in the *Jamaica Observer*, Wed. June 8, 2011, p.17B, where the *Charter*, which guarantees the right to vote in free and fair elections, is held out as a guide that will elicit "respect and uphold the rights of others" and "preserve for [ourselves] and future generations the fundamental rights and freedoms to which they are entitled"; In writing about Canada, John Rapley, saw the recent campaign tempo and tone as going "from prosaic to dramatic", unexpectedly in a society lauded for its "political civility, politeness and, well, predictability": *The Gleaner* on May 2, 2011, p.A7. See Stratmann Howard and Aparicio- Castillo, 'Campaign Finance and electoral competition', in Public Choice (2007) 133, p.107, et seq, where it is noted that Proponents of stricter contribution limits believe it will improve competiveness"; For well-articulated, insightful and inclusive look at the question of proper objectives for a reform effort, adopting a historical approach, see Horace Levy, 'A failure of democracy: the hijacking of a country', in *The Gleaner* May 15, 2011 pp.10,14; see also, Ian Boyne, 'Bruce, gangs and Power Brokers', in *The Gleaner*, June 5, 2011, p. F10; Claude Robinson expects funding reform to "create a level playing field, so that all candidates and parties have equal opportunity to raise and spend money, that is, an *equal* chance of getting elected without being personally wealthy", the *Jamaica Observer*, June 1, 2008, Sec.3, p. 7. To Robinson, as stated in the same article, the purpose of funding laws was to, "prevent money from corrupting the political process", but broadly, solutions would depend on "the philosophy underlying the system and what is (sic) the principle guiding the reform". Put at its worst, reform should seek to get the political parties to "shed the characteristics of gangs", until when, "the society will tolerate necessary delirium tremens …", is the view of the Editorial of *The Gleaner* of May 15, 2011, p. A8; The Secretary General of the OAS, Jose Miguel Insulza, on a visit to Jamaica in 2010, observed: "The limit is important because, even from an ethical point of view, you can't pay your way to Parliament by spending": *The Gleaner*, Fri., Sept. 3, 2010, p. A3; Jacqueline Samuels-Brown, supra, concludes, "Unless this is done [put laws in place to help them to help themselves; to insulate themselves from commercial and criminal influence, local and abroad] we give up our individual liberties in vain and our sacrifices are pointless and to no avail": (*The Gleaner*, Thu. Oct. 12, 2006).

better serve the interests of the majority in the society, are less than adequately treated. In this too-blinkered approach to its task, there is no attempt at a transformational blueprint sufficiently worthy, in terms of prospective societal benefit, to justify the cost to the virtually bare public purse. Put bluntly, this seems to be a case of a 'mission' being pursued without a 'vision'.

This writer trusts that the excursion into what may appear to be more political science than legal issues will be excused by those who might prefer a more narrowly focused approach. One of the fundamental failures evident in the Report is precisely the non-elaboration of the socio-political context in which the proposed legal regulations are supposed to work.[484] This failure amounts virtually to attempting remedial prescription without the benefit of comprehensive diagnosis in the treatment of a patient in need of 'intensive care', which would be the popular, and perhaps agreed, depiction of the state of the island's politics, in medical terminology.

Additionally, the notion that one can realistically expect "... best practices and workable approaches"[485] with regard to regulatory *specifics*, adopted elsewhere to be appropriate in a significantly different socio-political environment is liable at least to be subjected to reasoned challenge.

This is not to question the value of 'learning from history', including other people's history. Favour may be found, for example, with the approach and style of both the Canadian and British electoral reform *studies* which resulted in their relatively comprehensive reports. Insights can, it is well known, often be gained from seemingly quite alien sources. Suggested problem *solutions* are, however, it is well established, best designed with reference to the peculiarities of both place and time. Important elements of the ECJ's regime seem, with respect, to be inspired neither by foreign nor indigenous politico/cultural realities.

THE CANADIAN APPROACH

A glance at Canada's approach to the reform of their electoral system, is beneficial at this juncture. What we find is that there is a deliberate statement

---

484 The importance of cultural context is recognized by Christopher Pryce, in 'Campaign and party financing', the *Jamaica Observer*, Wed. July 21, 2010, p.9.
485 ECJ Report, p.2

of the perceived weaknesses of the regime, as against the objectives to be attained. The *Royal Commission on Electoral Reform and Party Financing (the "Lortie Commission")*,[486] having, in 1989, undertaken 'a comprehensive study of Canada's electoral laws', advocated *explicitly* the following reform objectives:

1. Securing the democratic right of voters

2. Enhancing access to elected office (self-financing candidates)

3. Promoting the equality and efficiency of the vote

4. Strengthening political parties as primary political organisations

5. Promoting fairness in the electoral process

6. Enhancing public confidence in the integrity of the electoral process

Of these, any of which may, or may not, of course, be appropriate for Jamaica, 'promoting fairness' was elevated to the central place, as the overriding value, to direct the formulation of the legal and regulatory scheme which would *guide* the assessment of the complementarity of the development of, and practice in, electoral arrangements. The conclusion was reached by the Commission that in this context, "fairness", a term which resonates throughout the commentary on the Canadian regulations, translated into a requirement for the achievement of "equality of opportunity in electoral processes and institutions".[487] The use of the words "equality of opportunity" repeatedly without elaboration, requires comment. On the personal level, to citizens of an 'enlightened' state it has become acceptable that certain welfare services ought to be provided so as to mitigate the inequality and disadvantages critically consequential for life chances: money, class and colour, differentiations, for example. In the context of multi-party politics, can the use of such an interventionist publicly-financed policy be defended? As targets for the implementation of intended egalitarian strategies, an institution requires quite a different mode of assessment, in the determination of policy efficacy than the individual.

The question may be put: should conferring legal personality on formally registered bodies, whether corporations or political parties, entail any sense of responsibility by the state for their *operational* well-being? The

---

486 Royal Commission on Electoral System Reform and Party Financing, [(The Lortie Commission]1991, Reforming Electoral Democracy: Final Report, Toronto: Dundurn Press

487 Jay Makarenko, supra, p.3

more 'democratic'/ free market oriented the country, the less feeling of any obligation one is inclined to expect in this regard. What justification is there for taxpayers, who are poles apart on many important social/economic factors, bearing the cost of ensuring that parties compete on more *equal* terms, is another way of viewing the the matter. But further, what exactly is meant and contemplated by equality here?

Where are the boundaries to be drawn in assessing the weight to be ascribed to the elements on which any judgment on 'equality' is to be made? Such a concern attaches also to the concept of "fairness", and its promotion by electoral law and derived regulation.

This was a principle which came up for review in **Libman v. Attorney General.**[488] One of the issues dealt with was that of spending restrictions imposed by the Government of Quebec for provincial referendums. The Supreme Court of Canada concluded that governments could constitutionally limit third party spending as a means of promoting equality of participation, as long as the restrictions were not so stringent as to effectively exclude third parties from the political discourse. However, ruling out third party expenditure altogether was too restrictive to be justified as a reasonable limit, "prescribed by law as can be demonstrably justified in a free and democratic society". At paragraph 47, the Court did observe that "spending limits are essential to ensure the primacy of the principle of fairness in democratic elections."

Essentially, the Court in **Libman** seemed to be arguing that 'equality of participation', whatever that means, was a sufficiently worthy political value to justify the seemingly anti-democratic policy of preventing a donor in a free capitalist society from spending his/her money as he/she wished on anything not ostensibly illegal.

It may be obvious that for the purposes of reasoned debate, as against populist exhortation, the concepts referred to by the Court are virtually useless, analytically. There has been no attempt in Canada, or elsewhere, to demonstrate how any assessment of any kind of 'equality' is to be achieved by any particular degree of restriction on third party or other spending. No formula has ever been proposed.

The position is at least arguable that it is sufficiently risky for an Electoral

---

488 [1997] 3 S.C.R., 569

Commission to seem to function as a tool of partisan politicians, since the consequences of policy in this area tend to be discriminatory, even if entirely unintended, in their effects. Parties are never likely to benefit or suffer to an identical extent from political finance regulation.

Courts should perhaps not be called upon to be the arbiters in this area of national life. This may be particularly so when, as in some jurisdictions, the highest ranking Judges are in effect, whatever the form, political appointees.[489]

With respect to item 6 above, the issue of public confidence in the integrity of the electoral process, this has proved particularly problematic in Jamaica, what with frequent allegations of "vote buying", "over-voting/bogus voting"— the latter especially in so-called "garrison" constituencies. Allegations of intimidation, the effect of which is to prevent those who might otherwise support a rival party / candidate from so doing, are not infrequent, although now on a diminishing trend for Marxist dialectical reasons. This public confidence factor, for different reasons, is the subject of similar concerns in Canada, England, the United States,[490] and elsewhere, despite the very marked differences in political culture.

Canada, possessing one of the reputedly less problem-plagued political environments, certainly with respect to the prevalence of party financing corruption scandals, has not proved to be immune to the scourge of disenchantment and discontent. Poll results between 1997 and 2001 disclosed the disquieting data that two-thirds of its citizens had little or no confidence in governments and believed that both federal and provincial political systems were highly or somewhat corrupt.[491]

---

489 With reference to the Caribbean Court of Justice, which is already in some territories, and is supported by many as the final Court of Appeal for Jamaica, in replacement of the UK-based Privy Council, see 'Former CCJ employee [dismissed acting Registrar] says Jamaica should be cautious with court'. The former Acting Registrar, Dr. Leighton Jackson, is reported to be "warning Jamaica against rushing into joining the Court in its appellate jurisdiction as he believes the way in which the institution is being managed is a threat to judicial independence', *The Gleaner* Wed. July 23, 2014, p.A4.

490 While by no means disputing the wisdom reflected by any effort to shorten the time-path to institutional development / maturity, we find it, nevertheless, disappointing that in his reforming zeal, in pointing to the election regulations passed in Canada, 1990, the USA, 1971 and the UK, 2001, Prof. Trevor Munroe, Executive Director of National Integrity Action utterly failed to do so against a consideration of the periods over which those countries have been in existence as 'nations': Even more questionably, is his omission to note that, despite their legislation, the malaise, lack of trust and disenchantment in and with the political systems leaves a very great deal to be desired. See 'On disclosing unknown funders', the *Jamaica Observer*, Wed. July 31, 2013, p. 15. The strongly negative features of the named countries, by their commentators own admissions, will not escape our view. One must, we are reminded, guard vigilantly against the pitfalls of overzealousness and self-righteousness.

491 Centre for Research and Information on Canada, "Voter Participation in Canada: Is Canadian Democracy in Crisis?" Oct. 2001, Montreal, Quebec, p. 16.

A most conspicuous distinguishing feature, as far as Jamaica is concerned, is with regard to actual, sometimes fatal politically-inspired violence, the incidence of which has similarly been diminishing, certainly of an open, robust, widespread nature. Such a policy reform objective would clearly need to be attacked with particularistic strategies, in respect of which the ECJ offers virtually no new initiative. The criminal justice system, from initiation of legislation through investigation, prosecution and sentencing stages, has clearly not been an efficacious solution source.

A recurring theme in the discourse is thus the specifics of the concerns vented, given the experience of the country under consideration.

In given locations, for instance, there may be the need to craft provisions to prevent specific public harm, such as political corruption and bribery, in a variety of forms. The following selection reflects the breadth of the spectrum of perceived problem areas and issues: "... candidate or political party may sell firearms to private individuals in return for a needed financial support for their campaign";[492] "... the concern that wealthy segments ... may be able to perpetually dominate the democratic process ... [by] being able to outspend their competitors during election campaigns";[493] "... require limits on the revenues and expenses of election participants, as well as access to public funding to ensure that all have a fair opportunity to compete for public office";[494] Access to public resources, moreover, helps to ensure that economically disadvantaged individuals and groups are able to have their views and interests heard and taken into account";[495] "... soft money' corrupts for a simple and obvious reason ... donations are given in such huge amounts ... that the donors typically expect to receive something in return for their investment;"[496] "The myth of 'soft money' is that it is contributed and spent for what is euphemistically called" "party building" purposes that are unrelated to influencing federal elections ... But this premise is little more than a widely acknowledged legal fiction ...";[497] "... a fundamental objective

---

492 Jay Makareno, supra, p.12
493 Ibid
494 Ibid
495 Ibid
496 The Hoover Institution, Public Policy Inquiry, 'Campaign Finance: Soft Money: What is it and why is it a problem?' www.campaignfinancesite.org/proposal/soft money1.html, excerpted from www.commoncause.org
497 Ibid

of campaign finance regulation is to ensure that the inequalities generated by the market economy do not undermine the political equality that is a central feature of our democracy";[498] "... regulation must protect voters from their own inadequacies";[499] "... the influence of money of both income and wealth, should be stripped from politics and the underlying principle should be that individuals who earn pay checks that enable them to support candidates and public causes should be as financially limited in their capacity to communicate as those on the public dole;"[500] and, "... why would voters sublimate those forces that now weigh heavily on their vote (party identification, political ideology, positions on key issues, economic performance, and the relative attractiveness of the candidates) in the single-minded pursuit of exercising the moral opprobrium that disciplines the role of money in politics?"[501]

A reform project, one is entitled to expect, should at the national level, certainly, not only be informed, but be focused and structured, by widely discussed and decided objectives. The indigenous characteristics of the institution at the centre of discussion, the political party, should also—to the extent that it would fall pre-eminently into one of the voluntary categories in any typology of organisations—feature prominently in the determination of the reform template. This is without, as the Gavel contends—with some measure of correctness, perhaps—distorting the contours of that design for strictly partisan political advantage/concession, however undeclared/camouflaged. This certainly does not equate to the naïve expectation that their nominated representatives on the Commission would be entirely motivated by non-self-interested party considerations.

There has, unfortunately, been no declaration of intention or acknowledgement that the consequence of the proposals advanced will be to change the attitudes and relations towards and between parties, their leaders, members, supporters and the public.

In the case of Canada, it is also suggested that any regime for party funding must entail the five elements: (i) transparency; (ii) controls on the

---

498 Mann, Thomas E., "Deregulating Campaign Finance: Solution or Chimera?" *Brooking's Review*, Winter 1998 pp. 18-21

499 Ibid; See also Ian Boyne quoting Jamaica's then PM Bruce Golding re the level of the electorate's' political intelligence', in *The Gleaner* May 15, 2011, p. F5.

500 Mann, Ibid

501 Ibid

supply of funding; (iii) controls on the demand for funding; (iv) integrity in the use of the public funding provided; and, (v) ensuring enforcement of the rules in an effective and proportionate manner. It may not be inappropriate to suggest that all these elements are likely to pose serious challenges to the success of the Jamaican reform effort.

QUESTIONS FOR THE ECJ REFORM EFFORT

Will changing the system, in the manner proposed, alleviate the growing public discontent with the political process? Will it be enhanced by internal party democratic practices by, for example, "loosening party discipline so that politicians can act more independently", as has, somewhat unrealistically, in the absence of any such tradition, been suggested, and as some concerned Canadians, in keeping with a higher level of political maturity, also desire?[502] The increasing professionalization of direct political participation, at the elective representational level militates against any such development. Career business managers could scarcely be expected to act contrary to company policy.

Is it likely that the recommendations will assist in deterring corruption and electoral fraud, ensure equity and fairness in the operation of the different elements of the electoral machinery and promote competition[503] on issues *between* candidates and parties, greater internal democracy, where lacking *within* the parties, and more openness and greater sensitivity to the external environment, and, more specifically, the 'ordinary' concerned citizen?

Larger societal goals, distilled from the dominant values embraced by the society, usually include encouraging respect for the electoral process and

---

502   See Democracy Watch (2001), 'Democracy Watch Launches Voter Rights Campaign, calling for Representative, Elected and Honest Government', (Media Release, Tue. Nov. 27, 2001). It must always, however, be remembered that the reality of the political process is not one, conventionally, in which voters choose candidates. See, also, the Report of the Royal Commission on Electoral Reform and Party Financing (The Lortie Commission) February 1992, Canada, as well as responses such as Canadian Study of Parliament Group (1992) "Reforming Electoral Democracy:: Responses to the Lortie Royal Commission", Ottawa, Ontario, May 31, 1992.

503   Jacqueline Samuels-Brown, Letter of the Day, supra, (Oct. 12, 2006), suggests that state subsidies in respect of campaign activities should be linked to total expenditure as well as individual contributions. Without more, this would have the opposite effect of 'leveling the playing field': who spend more would get more. Further, the advantage for incumbents as, against new entrants, individuals or parties, is clear. At the same time, her proposal implies that the state's subsidy would not be available until *after* contributions had been received and expenditures made. If the parties are 'cash strapped', this 'solution' is less than ideal. All of this testifies to the fact that sufficient thought has often not been a feature of reform proposals from even the more public spirited in the population.

---

the political institutions acting within it, thereby fostering public confidence in them.

There is a range of models available, with 'best choice' depending on the particular features exhibited by the political culture, and social and economic circumstances and the identified and agreed specific areas thought to be in need of change. The reform effort would seem to need to focus primarily on seeking out:

- Policies capable of implementation, and
- Effective enforcement mechanisms and arrangements to be carried out by appropriate public agencies.

Problematic in the choice of a funding scheme is the common tendency to take positions with the aim of furthering "a vague and undifferentiated understanding of the concept, democracy"[504], as evidenced by the ECJ's reference to "growing democracy" in its Report to Parliament.[505] The inherent value/policy contradictions which will, of necessity, pose challenges to funding policy formulation, especially for application to multi-class parties, as the PNP and JLP, without doubt, both are, have to some degree been exposed in the parties', including the National Democratic Movement's (NDM), rather limited views and suggestions as to the directions the Commission's recommendations[506] should take.

A simplistic and one-dimensional notion of 'democracy' is inevitably confronted by the antagonism between differentiated socio-economic class interests and reflected by and within the various institutions of society.[507] In

---

504 The concept of 'political equality' is a source of great tension in liberal theories "as recounted by Dahl, in Robert Dahl, *A Preface to Democratic Theory*", University of Chicago Press, (Chicago, Il, 1956), Ch. 1. Tension arises because the classic mass party "represents collective action by the dispossessed, aimed at using government power to bring about major social transformation": see also, Shapiro, Ian, 'Components of the Democratic Ideal', in Albert Breton, et al, (eds), *Understanding Democracy: Economic and Political Perspectives*. Cambridge University Press, (Cambridge, England, 1997), p. 217.

505 436 ECJ Report p.9

506 Whereas the majority of supporters of both parties will have little except the 'widow's mite', to contribute, financially, the relatively wealthy's response to contribution limits might well be that restricting people's freedom to spend their money as they wish is unacceptable state interference.

507 See Pierre, Jon, et al, (2000), State Subsidies to Political Parties: Confronting Rhetoric with Reality, West-European Politics 23: 1-24; In a political context where parties provide no policy choice to electors voters will have no option but to vote for candidates whose ability to represent them has already been mortgaged to narrow wealthy interests (as many argue is now the case in the USA: See Thomas Ferguson, *Golden Rule: The Investment Theory of Party Competition and the Logic of Money Driven Political Systems*, University of Chicago Press, (Chicago, IL, 1995); and West, Darrell *Checkbook Democracy*, Northeastern University Press, (Boston, MA, 2000).

such a situation, it is perhaps unrealistic to expect any attempt, inevitably involving systemic/paradigmatic dislocations, at resolving 'the difficulties of preference aggregation', to be other than unacknowledged or, at the most, glossed over in any exercise seeking to 'please/appease' various 'stakeholders'.

This is not to say that occasionally party representatives will not feel obliged to refer to what, historically, represented the party's *raison d'être* in the attempt to, at least, verbally, appease a declining source of traditional core support.

State funding cannot 'level the playing field' for parties which will always possess unequal organisational ability, and candidate and leadership quality appeal. Put more broadly,

> Competition for political power is at the heart of electoral democracy's claims to approximate popular sovereignty even under the relatively undemanding criteria of polyarchy.[508]

And since, nevertheless, it cannot be denied that funding constitutes one of the determinants of the outcome of competition, "The importance of money for electoral politics in mass society brings market mechanisms straight back into the political arena"[509], despite the urgings of democratic theory, particularly in the more populist incantations.[510]

The Canadian reform focus seems to be exclusively on the voting system and the more general issue of electoral reform.

---

508 Dahl, Robert, *Polyarchy: Participation and Opposition*, Yale University Press, (New Haven, CT, 1991). Dahl argues that the term 'polyarchy' (pluralism) is a more accurate description than 'democracy', when it comes to maximising opportunities for citizens to formulate and express preferences which factor into collective decisions. Such decisions are the results of agreements which treat each centre of interest as well as they can *reasonably* demand. A continuing responsiveness of government to such demands of its citizens is in 'Dahl's formulation to be achieved with the most basic institutional requirements. See for an elaboration of Dahl's concept, Robert Alan Dhal, *Polyarchy: Participation and Opposition*, Yale University Press, (1973).

509 Hopkin, Jonathan, "The Problem with Party Finance, in Party Politics", *Sage Publications*, Vol. 10, No. 6, p. 646, concludes that, "... the least troubling way for parties to finance their activities would be some form of mass-based voluntary subscription on the stylized model of the mass party ... such a solution appears utopian in the current climate", at p. 646.

510 Some commentators' arguments for reform seem to be based not only on a classless version of 'the public', but one in which the public's interest is differentiated into that of 'special interest groups', apart from and also exclusive of the interest of individual citizens/electors. So that whereas mass society's voice may be suspicious of the disproportionate influence of 'big money', big money (from wealthy individuals and corporations) will most likely look askance at trade union financial backing of political parties (a point of contention, certainly in the USA and the UK). For the more 'modern' approach to interest group politics, see, *Voters Parties and Leader* Jean Blondel, Penguin Books, (New York, 1963), Ch. 6.

Given demographic considerations, relevant in Canada's case, such as regional questions and interests, the presence of minorities, aboriginal and gender issues of representation, consideration of 'first past the post', as against some version of the proportional representation option, can, with justification, be given priority.

Their choice of electoral system might give substance to, or detract from, the essential meaning ascribed to the fundamental principle of the "equality of every vote".[511] However, to suggest that changes to the structure and function of the *electoral* system will be sufficient to remedy perceived defects of the *political system*, which, "... fails to represent the broad range of perspectives that characterize our country ..."[512] appears somewhat extravagant. It is the *substance* of political discourse and outcomes[513] which, is the more likely cause of the disenchantment and apathy manifested.

Causes need champions, and procedural refinements which broaden and deepen democratic participation may involve different degrees and types of struggle.

There seems to be no attempted confrontation with the issue of political party renewal in terms of organisation structure, recruitment strategies in keeping with labour market changes, image-makeover or manifesto mission/vision statement re-design, as a possible antidote to the perceived "democratic malaise", which characterizes "the political landscape in Canada and other parts of the world".[514]

Rationality suggests that the institution most directly functionally linked to the electorate, the political party, should itself be the very centre of focus in any properly conceived reform project. What is found in the Canadian case, however, is that there is no reserved place for the reform of party politics. Under the Jamaican ECJ's reform agenda, parties are treated almost entirely in a formalistic administrative-detail-important manner. Such treatment is scarcely commensurate to their societal importance as potential centres of supreme authority, power and responsibility, hence, their intended and

511   Ibid, pp. 3,4,35

512   Ibid, Executive Summary, p. 1.

513   See for example, 'Gov'ts for the few', Incoming UWI principal decries administration's failures to act in interest of most Jamaicans, The Gleaner, Fri. July 19, 2013, p. 1.

514   Ibid. See also 'Time to renew JLP/PNP', Letter of the Day, The Gleaner, May 15, 2011, p. D8, in which the letter writer seems to recognize the 'real' problem for what it is, even though his prescriptions may be contentious.

possible role as major change-agents except when operating under principles emanating from ultra-conservative political thought.

From a research angle we see, for example, no attempt, in either country's case, to correlate levels of voter turnout over different periods/elections as this might have been determined/explained by policy substance differentiation or leader personality or, indeed, particular features prevailing in the national and /or international politico-economic environments.[515]

If voter turnout had always been low, it would not now feature as a 'wake up call' reflective of the less than healthy state of party politics. Since the phenomenon extends across national boundaries, its solution can clearly not be to provide state funding: many of the "malaise-afflicted", "democracy fatigued", countries provide, and have provided, public party and election campaign financing, direct and indirect, coupled with transparency reporting features, and other controls, for several years.

The Law Commission of Canada puts the matter thus:

> Canada prides itself on being a healthy and vibrant democracy. But we cannot be complacent; democracy requires constant tending. Canadians must reflect on the quality of their democratic institutions and ask whether they continue to serve them well. Does it reflect our contemporary needs and values? An important barometer of the health of governance

---

515 Such apparent ignorance of the essential nature and realities of the practice of politics as manifested to an extreme degree by, the Jamaican Attorney and Queen's Counsel, Howard Hamilton, is also evident in the piece 'by medical doctor,: Marvin Williams, ' Politicians stifled the Jamaican Dream', the *Jamaica Observer*, Wed. Jan. 7, 2015 , p. 14. '. . .what Jamaica needs', according to this commentator, ' ... is a new cadre of leaders ... who will put national development above the next election. ..." The conceptualization and implementation of policy involves striving for and gaining political power, a winning of elections in multi-party systems. In the absence of the acknowledgement of such an elementary feature, apparently commendable sentiments amount to little more than populist pontification. See, 'Political parties too caught up with winning elections', in *The Gleaner* Mon. Aug. 15, 2011, p.A7. Hamilton should certainly know better: this is like asking the defence attorney not to be concerned about winning a case. He would benefit from reading Horace Levy's 'A failure of democracy: the hijacking of a country', in *The Gleaner* May 15, 2011, pp. F10, 14, where the pursuit of sound policy is seen as the goal, and election victory the means in political engagement.

The important consequences of the national and international economic context for the nature of the political system is reflected in the report by Conrad Hamilton in the *Jamaica Observer*, Aug. 14, 2011, p.10, "No more pork barrels? Political parties claim an end to political handouts". It is, in our view, an open question as to whether, as Peter Phillips of the PNP claims, the electorate has become more aware and has been focusing on issues, rather than handouts from political parties. The stark reality is that the state of an IMF monitored economy is not likely to be such that handouts can be 'afforded', See also, Jean Lowrie-Chin, "Issues should motivate voters", the *Jamaica Observer*, Mon. June 20, 2011, p.11, where the, as yet approved, ECJ proposed electoral 'system' is seen as "a model for the world". But then, Lowrie-Chin informs us that she has served the ECJ since 1995. Michael Burke, on the other hand, "pray(s) for the day when issues will be primary in Jamaica's elections. But that will only happen when education is about transforming minds from mental slavery to collective maturity"; in 'Organisation, the key to winning elections', the *Jamaica Observer*, Thu, June 2, 2011, p.11.

relationships is the nature and quality of citizens' participation in their democratic institutions."[516]

The National Citizens Coalition Inc. v Canada (Attorney General)[517] case presented the Court with the opportunity to uphold one of the cherished fundamental rights and freedoms. Limits on third party contributions to political parties were struck down on the grounds, somewhat similar to the United States Supreme Court's view in *Citizens United*,[518] that this amounted to an unconstitutional infringement of the Charter-given right to freedom of expression. The restriction was laid down by an amendment to the *Canada Elections Act* which prohibited third parties or individuals from incurring expenses to promote the election of a candidate or to promote or oppose the election of a political party, except when authorized.

Whereas the later case of *Libman,* reviewed above, decided some thirteen years after this, is indicative of the evolving judico/political sentiment in this area, other aspects of the decisions remained unchanged. The most conspicuous was the continued use of undefined popular terms such as 'freedom of expression', in this instance subsumed within broad appeals to fundamental rights, freedoms and values.

What is achieved by this strategy is clear: questions relating to permissible levels of political *contributions* are converted/translated into accepted fundamental rights in democratic society—the right here being that of free *expression*. Such a 'sleight of hand' judicial approach seems fraught with possibly untenable assumptions. It would be rare indeed that a particular contribution can be traced to a specific item of political party/candidate expenditure—somewhat akin to one's taxes being put into the 'Consolidated Fund' or 'Treasury', and an attempt made to trace it into any particular item(s) of public expenditure.

In a most critically insightful commentary, Horace Levy's observation of the Jamaican scenario is less questioning and more assertive than the Canadian attitude, without being vitriolic, in that, on his assessment,

> Their [political parties in the tradition of the American and French revolutions] role ... first and fundamental task ... was that of exercising and

---

516 Law Commission of Canada, Discussion Paper, supra, Preface, iii
517 (1984) 11 D.L.R. (4th) 481, See also Somerville v Canada (Attorney General) (1996) 184 A.R. 241
518 Citizens United v Federal Election Commission, US Supreme Court, 558US No. 8 – 205 (2010)

promoting democracy and people-centred policies ... better participation by populations in political decision-making, manifestly the expansion of democracy as an ongoing assignment ...

The reality though, cloaked by the belief that democracy flourishes because there are regular national elections and a free press, is the substitution of party power for people power ... they have failed to carry out their own historic mission. They have, in effect hijacked the country for their own partisan benefit.[519]

One may be tempted to accept this dismal portrayal, with portions of which we are not necessarily in contention, except on the level of phraseology, involving the substantive and operational meaning of "people power", and "partisan benefit", for example, in the context of a *representative* political 'democracy'. However appealing the notion of 'rule of, by and for the people', in its various incantations may be, we question whether the use of such language by Levy, to characterize the realities of governance by what have tended to become multi-class parties in so-called mature democracies, does not amount to self-deception, whatever its occasionally convenient populist attractiveness.

The implications of the maturation process for political parties and their relations with 'third' parties clearly deserve scholarly attention at the national level.

With the crescendo of recent criticism directed at the parties, sometimes verbalized in contemptuous, scurrilous terms, coinciding in time with the submission of the ECJ's proposal for the introduction of public party funding, it would not be surprising if there is a dampening effect on the donation of private allegedly 'clean' money. To that extent, the 'danger'[520] of "dirty money" contaminating the electoral process may increase and, thereby, facilitate the

---

519 Horace Levy, supra, See also the *Gleaner* editorial, 'Civil society and the gangs of Gordon House', supra, especially the section headed 'colour coded crowds'; Franklyn Johnston, in the *Jamaica Observer*, Fri. July 30, 2010, p.10, argues that "both JLP and PNP are adversaries of the citizen ... the aim [of reform, in Johnston's view] is to be connected within the constituency by small donors, reaching minds and hearts. Many donors mean many votes- true democracy."

520 Claude Robinson refers to, "... the potential danger from criminal or other illicit sources" of political funding, in 'Campaign finance reform and the democratic process', in the *Jamaica Observer*, June 1, 2008, Sec. 3, p.7. He recalls that, "Peter Phillips, PNP Vice-President, first warned of this danger in his 2003 speech in the annual budget debate when he said that he was 'deeply concerned that the drug money connection was also corrupting some individuals in law enforcement and within the political system"

subversion of democracy—the very opposite of the intended effect of the contemplated reforms.

Unless state funding is regarded as 'adequate' by the parties, which is most unlikely to be the case, the scope, provided by any 'gap' for the use of money from 'questionable sources', is likely to continue to be exploited.

Rather than the educational approach, broadly perceived, the chosen route to discouragement of indulgence in this disapproved behaviour, we find, is that of penal sanctions. The Jamaican penchant for 'beating the system'[521] may just be more resistible, if the focus had instead been to get the protagonists to 'take ownership' of the reform project.

It is not enough, in dealing with the Jamaican case to adopt the conclusion, as in Canada, of which Munroe is apparently unaware, that,

> there are more and more signs that many Canadians are disenchanted with traditional political processes; many say that they have lost confidence in their democratic institutions and do not believe that governments adequately reflect their democratic aspirations.[522]

It is clear that, to be meaningful, specifics are required: what essentially constitute those aspirations? As tends to be the case in most such contexts, no answers are provided.

---

521 See, Errol W A Townsend, 'We want a tax we can evade, Peter', the *Jamaica Observer*, Wed. Apr. 30, 2014, p. 13, where the writer says, "Had he done more of the latter [listening more to singer Ernie Smith], he would have better understood that in a society where folks will happily "beat the gate" then buy out the bar, or scale the Stadium wall when the concert is free, to propose a tax that can neither be evaded nor avoided is a non-starter. We just have to mash it down".

522 Law Commission of Canada, Executive summary, supra, p.1

CHAPTER 10
SUBMISSIONS OF THE PARTIES AND THE ELECTION 'WATCHDOG'

We preface our report and commentary with a brief glance at 'alternatives'.

In **Canada,** injunctions are used, but only in election periods, together with *compliance agreements*,[523] and failing resolution, ultimately prosecution: a graduated process which could, with considerable benefit, we feel, be considered for adoption. The *Commissioner* under that regime can initiate prosecutions under the finance laws. The stipulation of sanctions of a criminal nature, only, shifts all enforcement authority, failing settlement by compliance agreement, to the law enforcement agency, which may either be vulnerable to political pressure or may not give priority to political finance violations. This is especially so in a situation, such as Jamaica's, where there is a crisis in the incidence of serious crimes, with the consequential overloading of the justice administration system.

Donations, under the Canadian regime, are, importantly, not subject to a limit. Obtaining a minimum of 15% of votes cast entitles a party to be *reimbursed* 50% of its election expenses.

The **German** regulatory system provides as follows:

(1) where unlawful donations, are accepted, the party pays back three times the amount to the Speaker of the Diet, (Parliament) who is the German equivalent of the Electoral Commissioner.

(2) if any part of a party's assets is not listed in the party's accounts, the fine is two times the amount of the value of the omission.

(3) where a permitted donation is not reported, a penalty of two times the amount is imposed.

(4) concealing the source of a party's means (assets) involves a fine, or a sentence of three years imprisonment.

---

523 This consensual, non-litigious method of breach resolution is, we feel, much to be favoured in the Jamaican context: legislative regulation will be new; the courts are clogged up with cases and issues of these kinds are best resolved quickly and cheaply for obvious reasons. See, 'The ECJ – a rags-to-riches story', by former PM, Edward Seaga, *The Gleaner*, Oct. 20, 2013, p. F9, where he writes "After the 1976 election, although several [election] petitions were filed, only one came to trial within the five-year period. The judicial route was not a practical solution in eliminating electoral fraud".

Notably, nobody has ever been sentenced under the law, as amended to this effect only in 2003: intention is not only difficult to prove, but the provision was passed by a Diet necessarily made up of political parties whose members would be the likely defendants.

With respect to the **British** situation, Professor Bogdanor informs us that from 1981, The Hansard Society's Commission on the funding of political parties, of which he was the Secretary, proposed that state funds be tied to party membership subscriptions, with the expectation that, "… constituency organisations would probably become livelier and more representative organisations than they are today. Moreover, a legal limit could *then* (italic added) be placed on the size of individual donations, thus further limiting the power of big money".[524] Surprisingly, Bogdanor concludes, with apparently complete confidence, that,

> with public funding, the special interests of the wealthy would be weakened while the general interests would be strengthened … compelled to rely upon a large number of small contributions rather than the *tainted generosity* [Italics added] of a few large contributors.[525]

This begs the question, what if the aggregate of small donations, across the parties, proves to be woefully inadequate for campaign 'needs'? Is there no concern at the prospect of the existence of one very large contributor, the state? Why is the 'generosity' of a few large contributors, *ipso facto*, 'tainted'? That is not to suggest that we do not sympathize, in part, with Bogdanor's sentiments, infected as they are with obvious bias.

The experience of several state funded regimes being plagued by a long list of scandals, does not provide affirmation for Bogdanor's assumptions. It is to be borne in mind, also, that the violation of certain democratic and free market principles may be at issue.

This area of finance seems unique, in that the freedom of persons/ institutions to voluntarily negotiate transaction terms is abrogated, in that

---

524 Vernon Bogdanor, Professor of Government at Oxford in 'Millionaires handouts will not sustain a democracy 'The Guardian (UK) Feb 8, 2001. In the New York City's recent Council elections the press reported that: "a group aligned with the City's real estate industry has unleashed a torrent of spending to support pro-business candidates … angering other candidates". "I don't think we've ever seen this kind of big-money outside group trying to hijack local races", said a Democratic candidate …" and one who was therefore unlikely to be regarded as pro-business, The New York Times, Fri. Sept. 6, 2013, p. A20.

525 Bogdanor, supra

loans, or some component part of them, if granted at lower than market rates, are treated as donations in Britain, as is proposed for Jamaica. We regard this as yet another example of the deleterious effects of over-regulation, and can find no justification for the discrimination, based as it is on the nature of the 'business' of the borrower.

The parties' financial reports proposed for submission, in keeping with a common format to be prescribed by law, if not from the aspect of their stipulated number, clearly has definite prospective facilitative review and comparison benefits.

The British Committee on Standards in Public Life was asked by then Prime Minister Tony Blair, to "… review issues in relation to the funding of political parties and to make recommendations …", one of which was for the establishment of an Electoral Commission, "… with widespread executive and investigative powers, and the *right to bring cases* [Italics added] before an election court for judgment".[526]

Any *third party* that has "produced a valid notification to the Commission that it intends to campaign for the electoral success of one or more registered political parties or a particular category of candidates" will, in Britain be 'recognised' as such, and thus bring itself within the ambit of the regulatory framework.

What to the unethical person, complying with the law but not its spirit, could be a loophole is the possible disguise of donations as charges/fees for "admission to any conference, meeting or other event", which are unregulated, since under the *Political Parties Elections and Referendums Act (PPERA)* such charges and other forms of assistance "are not donations".

Donors of sums exceeding the reporting threshold could simply, it seems, be invited, as frequently as financing needs require, to dinners or other events where what is in reality a donation would take the form of a very substantial 'admission fee'. (The American oil company, Enron's, *sponsorship of a Labour Party Conference,* which was not prohibited under British electoral law, was perceived as an attempt to buy influence over government energy policy, especially in relation to gas-fired power stations).

---

526   Fifth Report of the Committee on Standards in Public Life, 'The Funding of Political Parties in the UK', Oct. 1998, Cm, 4057, p3.

The *Companies Act* in Britain, in recognising that directors are really donating company money belonging to the shareholders of 'their' companies, provides controls (S.2.8) requiring shareholders' approval of a resolution for national and European Union political contributions *in excess* of £5000.

In **Germany**, the position with respect to public funding is as follows:

(1) Parties get an amount per vote received *and* money to match dues, subscriptions and donations up to a maximum total. This represents a mix of elements in the party strengthening/public and party member participation in political affairs effort worthy of more than fleeting consideration.

(2) Parliamentary groups get about half of the above.

(3) A further set amount goes to research foundations connected to political parties.

The absence, in Germany, of spending and private donation limits, clearly 'makes for an uncomplicated and easy to administer [political] financial system'.

Since, understandably, the institutional capability of the ECJ does not seem extensive, given economies of scale and the need for restraint in public expenditure, together with the theoretical benefits of functional specialization, insufficient within it, to extend to the drafting of contemplated legislation, where will the responsibility for the initiation of refinement/ amendment of the law reside? Presumably and from the review role proposed for itself, this will rest with the ECJ. Whereas that may seem natural, the fact that after some seven years the Commission is yet to offer a reform framework in its *final* form does not bode well for the handling of such further responsibility.

Given the inherently dynamic nature of politics, in Germany that function, for proposing necessary changes to party and campaign laws and regulations, may be exercised by way of reference of issues by the President of the Federal Diet to an appointed *Commission of Experts* for deliberation.

German experience, and in particular the Christian Democratic Union (CDU) Party scandals between 1999 and 2002, led to proposals for a ban on most donations in the form of cash, making party *leaders*. "... legally responsible for the veracity of party finance reports and making payment of public subsidies contingent on the filing of these reports".[527] This approach is clearly more appropriate where funds are provided on a reimbursement basis, in which case legislative regulation might usefully also seek to establish a link between public subsidies and voter *turnout*, rather than, as at present, exclusively on a party's share of the vote.

As noted, state funding may simply provide the cash to facilitate attempted vote buying in poor and deprived communities,[528] which directly undermines the purpose of manifesto/policy-driven campaigns. The word 'attempted' is used because with secret balloting and even were the electorate possessed of the bare minimum of intelligence, political or otherwise, which is not the case in Jamaica, that is the most that the offer of cash could amount to.[529] The result may well be the consolidation of the notorious Jamaican "freeness mentality syndrome" by virtue of the "success" of populist giveaway tactics.

The German approach is instructive, here, in that, "Members are therefore a financial asset for German parties, the move so since state subventions have been coupled to member fees in [*sic*] 1994".[530]

Their low threshold for state funding qualification, when compared to the ECJ's recommendations, further allows small or fledgling parties access to some level of public financing.

A party Donors Report by way of an official '*DO1* form' is provided in **Britain** for *multiple small donations*, which clearly facilitates compliance. Given the proposed all-inclusiveness of reporting donation and expenditure detail stipulated by the ECJ's currently, consideration of the British practice might well be in order. The **OAS**, in its model legislation, also includes reporting by *donors*, which, fortunately, perhaps, does not seem to have found favour with the ECJ to date.

Non-governmental organisations (NGOs) and private citizens could be given the right to file complaints with the Commission or bring third party actions. This might well amount to a meaningful exercise in the sharing of responsibility for the integrity of the system, which at the same time, it must

---

527 Ansolabehere, Stephen, in *A User's Guide to Campaign Finance Reform*, Gerald C. Lubenow (ed), Rowman, Littlefield Pub, 2001.

528 See, 'Seaga' ECJ – 'rags-to-riches story, Purge elections of vote-buying' supra,

529 See The Jamaica Observer, Fri. Dec. 9, 2011, p. 4

530 Detterbeck Klaus, 'Cartel Parties in Western Europe', Party Politics, Vol. II No 2, p.183.

be acknowledged, opens the door for possibly spiteful, vindictive, mischief-making frivolous behaviour.

What would seem to have been an initial ECJ suggestion for "The establishment of a special Electoral Court with the power to void [a general] election that breach the principles of free and fair elections",[531] as against the voiding of elections in particular constituencies, has apparently for good personal and national security reasons, it seems, not gained much support, not being included in the ECJ Report.[532]

In the reform agenda, we find formal recognition of the need for the creation of the scope and opportunity for civil society monitoring—this is precisely, as we understand it, the essential purpose of CAFFE, especially during elections. Support for this approach is to be found in an ACE Electoral Knowledge Network's publication, which suggests that, "The Political Finance legal system should allow and encourage the participation of civil society and the public in publicizing political finance issues, providing oversight and enforcing the law."[533]

Since the proposals all require party registration as a prerequisite for receipt of state funding, CAFFE seems to be among the few 'stakeholders' which, from the outset formally raised the issue of the treatment of independent candidates,[534] as a substantial, as against a marginal issue of concern.

Interestingly, we note that under CAFFE's papers under the heading 'Disclosure of Donations', without elaboration, the question is posed: "Should there be any disqualifying consequences to the *donors*?"[535] This novel and interesting idea provokes the imagination.

Certainly worthy of emulation is the United Kingdom's Neill Committee's Recommendation to provide funds to "stimulate policy research," implemented under the *Elections (Policy Development Grant Scheme) Order 2002 (S1 2002/224)*, in which a set amount is available each year for distribution by

---

531   Apart from the contents of the Report itself, we are not aware of any other mention of such an idea.

532   See "Meeting with Candidates", undated Mimeo, ECJ, p. 3. It is a matter for speculation whether such a Court, even if a Special Division of the High Court, which only "operates for six months following any election", would find many eager 'volunteer' judges to sit on it.

533   ACE Knowledge Network, Mimeo, July 7, 2006, 'Political Finance Enforcement' p,2

534   CAFFE,'Campaign Financing' paper, undated mimeo, p. 5.

535   Ibid, p. 7

the Electoral Commission to eligible parties "... to assist parties with the development of policies for inclusion in their manifesto".[536]

THE JAMAICA LABOUR PARTY (JLP)

As for the positions of the parties, the JLP[537] supports donation limits (individual/ organisation) over a twelve month period and also election spending limits for parties, constituency organisations and candidates.

Additional donations, not exceeding the *maximum annual totals,* should also be permitted during the *election period.* The good sense thought to be contained in this formulae, is not obvious to us.

The party is also in favour of third party politically related organisations, which spend more money than the contribution limits per annum, being registered. Most such groups tend to spend mostly during elections. How, though, would one know, with certainty, of the true identity of the third party and the amount of money spent, so as to call for its registration?

In the JLP's view, Trusts 'established for charitable or developmental purposes should be exempt from fundraising or expenditure limits', with, however, their annual reports, including financial statements, being submitted to the ECJ (p.7). The recurrent debate in the United States about the unregulated use of vast sums of money during elections, through the medium of the so-called PACs, is highly relevant here. The Trust idea could easily give rise to similar developments and concerns. The party's suggestion that, 'The directorship of such Trusts should be separate from the management of any political party, constituency, organisation or affiliate organisation, is a worthy attempt at non-partisan community development, depending for success, in this respect, on the integrity of the Trustees'. "The party further proposes that state subsidy take the form of, an annual sum payable monthly ... to defray legitimate operational expenses; and a fixed sum after nomination day".

Incumbency advantage is considerable in the proposal, whereby the full amounts at (a) and (b) is payable to parties getting not less than 30% of the popular vote in *three* preceding elections (pp. 7, 8).

---

536 House of Commons, 'State Funding of Political Parties', p.10; A criticism, which is perhaps fair, is that only represented registered parties, i.e. with at least two members in the House of Commons, can be eligible.

537 See The JLP's submission, 'Proposals For Regulating the Financing of Political Parties and Election Campaigns,, Mimeo, 2005', pp. 4, 6, above at pp 77 et seq.

The proposal that a prorated sum to be given to other parties, getting not less than 10% of the vote, implies reimbursement, which is clearly not the ideal funding arrangement for new parties (p.8). (In contrast in Germany, obtaining 0.5% of the vote is sufficient qualification for the receipt of state funding).

Eighty per cent of Government broadcast time, it is proposed, should be surrendered to the ECJ for allocation to the parties during an election period (p.9).

Perhaps, as the Opposition party, at the time of its submission, it is comfortable with a guideline to the effect that Government advertisements during election should be confined to essential public notices only. What is properly to be regarded as 'essential', in a democratic political system, where citizens have a right to public information, and by whom is such a decision to be made, are thorny issues.

Government Agencies should not, it is suggested, be permitted to announce or commence any new project or programme during the prescribed election period (p.9). This would almost, it seems, amount to a partial vacuum in Government and can only make sense, if at all, with a fixed election date, as is suggested, (p.9), unless an earlier election is approved by a two-thirds majority of both Houses.

THE PEOPLE'S NATIONAL PARTY (PNP)[538]

In the PNP's view, "Closed, private, political parties are incompatible with open, publicly accountable democratic government",[539] (p.1). The party, in keeping with this sentiment, fully supports the registration of parties, (p. 2). One wonder if this would be the case if there was no prospect of state funding in contemplation.

If, as the document says, there are "… clear signs that persons with 'big money'—commercial and drug related—are intensifying their efforts to buy

---

538 PNP Policy Commission Document on 'The Regulation of Political Party and Finance in Jamaica' – Mimeo, August 20, 2005.

539 This is a view seemingly shared by Andrew Holness, the present Leader of the Opposition, (2014 as he stated "I take the view that the political party is not a private club and for the enhancement of democracy they should be regulated. We cannot continue to treat political parties as if they are the hidden hand behind the Government and Parliament", the *Jamaica Observer*, May 5, 2013, P. 26.

influence amongst leaders and candidates in political parties ...",[540] then all that any political party has to do is refuse such funds. Further, even if the source is regarded as untainted, one could declare boldly in print (on a receipt, for instance) that the donation is accepted only on *condition* that no benefits should be expected in return—i.e., there are 'no strings attached'! If followed through, in practice, if and when such a party forms the Government, with time, as is the case with almost all significant 'cultural' changes, new attitudinal/expectational norms could emerge.

Subsidy to registered parties is proposed in terms of air time, tax-deductible political contributions, manifesto and policy publication and a stipend for scrutineers and other party election officials. There would seem to be little encouragement for volunteers' involvement at a level of activity where one would expect commitment and dedication to far outweigh a cash reward as the motivation for party-building organisational participation.

In the PNP's view, state subsidy should be based on votes cast and disbursed from a pool "equivalent to a designated per cent of tax revenue", (p 4). There appears to be no attempt to relate this 'solution' to the projected financial 'needs' of the parties. Currently, 2013/2014, the island's fiscal performance is a cause of serious concern, being significantly below budgetary projections and, as expected under the IMF programme guidelines,

An appropriate formula should be found, the party argues, to its credit, for funding newly registered 'first time' election parties, (p 4).

It was its expectation, as the then governing party, that the "Law (Party Registration and Political Financing) [should] be passed before the end of the parliamentary year 2005/2006", (p 4). That law is yet to be placed on the statute books up to mid-2014.

THE NATIONAL DEMOCRATIC MOVEMENT (NDM)[541]

The NDM adopts a view of political parties which is compatible with the perception of them as 'public utilities'. State funding is thus seen as necessary as this,

---

540 Problematically for rule enforcement in Jamaica, such allegations and fears, often repeated in the press, are almost never accomplished by evidence, conspicuously unlike the situation in the United States.
541 'Legislative Framework and State Financing of Political Parties Campaigns and candidates', Mimeo, July, 2006.

will [Italics added] produce a more aware, participating and conscious electorate who (with a special programme of political education *from the political parties*)[Italics added] will better understand their role and responsibilities ... In essence, the taxpayers should pay for the democracy we enjoy, just as they would pay for any social infrastructure and service" (p, 1).

It is not inappropriate to reply that any such programme of education may better, in the national interest, not be entrusted to partisan presenters.

The NDM advocates the setting up of a 'base fund minimum' of $2M to each party, for

> Preserving our democracy through political education. It could be clearly outlined in specific programmes how the funds provided by the state will be used to ensure that the proposal meets the strict guidelines of state funding—including a ceiling on spending in an election year (p. 2).

This appears to involve the sacrifice of that autonomy, and thereby the flexibility to adapt to a dynamic environment which, to a vibrant political organisation, ought to be too heavy a price to pay for state subsidy.

A limit on donations, even from candidates, themselves, the NDM proposes, should be set at One Hundred Thousand Dollars (JMD $100,000.00) This, it could be argued, unless multiple donations are allowed, would probably bring the major parties down to the level of the NDM's fundraising capability. A 'playing field' levelled in this manner could be quite damaging to the political process.

Too little money may be as bad in its effects, for a democratic political process, as 'too much'.

The party's proposal for matching funds from the state, for all political parties, as against campaign funds only, (p.2), would clearly compound the potential problem. [542]

It would seem that whereas the NDM does not wish parties to be 'captured' by 'special interests', it sees no problem with them being in 'state custody'.

---

542 'Campaign Financing', paper from Citizens' Action for Free and Fair Election, presented by Dr. The Hon. Lloyd Barnett, O.J., Chairman, Mimeo, July 10, 2006.

Citizens' Action for Free and Fair Elections (CAFFE)[543]

If, as CAFFE argues, political parties have no visible system of sustainable financing, how, it is legitimate to ask, have they (JLP/PNP) managed to last for 60 plus years?

It is observed that,

> some of these donors [who will always participate in the absence of *full* funding by the state] have been the beneficiaries of government *favours* [Italics added] particularly in relation to the obtaining of government contracts and other official recognition", (p. 2).

The very definite nature of the statement begs, in vain, for documented supporting details, here, or indeed from other civil society groups which, virtually without exception, share this view.

CAFFE's paper, implies the need for expenditure control "… during the long campaigns which *precede* [Italics added] the legal election period", (p. 3). It becomes obvious from that partial quote that controls on expenditure, and state subsidy of the cost of political campaigns, is unlikely to be a neat cut-and-dried, universally satisfying affair, practically.

Unacceptably strict controls on *all* aspects of 'campaigning' would have to be imposed to address this particular perceived mischief. One is left to wonder what the response would be if, say, a Consumer Protection Agency, should seek to regulate the amount of promotional activity in which competing firms might engage in seeking, aggressively, to attract customers.

Conspicuously, all the options reviewed have a common theme, transparency, to which we now turn.

---

543 Ibid, p. 2.

CHAPTER 11
DISCLOSURE / TRANSPARENCY

Of central importance, as an indicator of the Commission's thinking in this regard, is the explanation that,

> The Electoral Commission is not recommending that all disclosure be made public unless after investigation a particular disclosure is found to be false or otherwise in breach of prescribed principles ... based on our recent history of political violence, victimization and the tendency to permanently brand persons as activists, it is our view that full disclosure should [only] be made to a Committee of the Electoral Commission ... to be called the Political Party Finance Disclosure Committee.[544]

The point to be made here is that whereas the public disclosure of *donors* would be dangerous for them in the context of "our recent history ..." it is, strangely, not considered problematic by the ECJ for party *members'* names and other contact details to be published. Be that as it may, one would hope that the terms of reference given, or mandate incidentally assumed, would dictate a more balanced/didactic reform vision. The adoption of a *status quo* preserving perspective stultifies the possible change-agent nature of the Commission's role.

The answer[545] to the several electoral / political issues of concern may not be as simple as Daniel Thwaites envisions: "strict disclosure requirements, spending limits, public financing, swift and certain sanctions for breach".[546] As long as "the perceived or real fear of political victimization by the two political parties" persists, a "shroud of secrecy" will remain, whatever the degree of creativity that is required to 'protect' donors from the negative consequence attendant on transparency in political fundraising.

State funding will never be 'adequate': it will always seem like the practise of good politics to outspend the competition.

---

544   ECJ Report, p. 11

545   Needless to say, each commentator tends to submit somewhat different mix of answers/solutions: see, for example, Carlton Stewart, supra; Daniel Thwaites at Note 582; Franklin Johnson, 'Political party funding, Electoral Commission, transparency', the Jamaica Observer, Fri. July 30, 2010, p.10, also his 'Campaign donations and state funding', the *Jamaica Observer*, Fri. Dec. 2, 2011, p. 10; and Ronald Mason, 'Damn dictatorship on campaign financing', supra.

546   Daniel Twaites, 'The best payback is reform', *The Gleaner*, June 24, 2012, p. A.9

There are those, on the other hand, who take the contrary position: if there is full transparency there is no need for private funding limits.

Free flow of timely accurate information, in a less than fully functionally-literate society is, however, hardly to be expected. Jamaica is indeed a young democracy, being a young nation with an underperforming, if not dysfunctional education system, despite the production of many outstanding students/scholars. The electorate can hardly, as in the case of Canada[547], be taken to be sufficiently mature and intelligent, in political terms, at this stage of the evolution of its political culture, for it to be less than a major challenge to gather the pieces of information, over four to five year periods so as to make 'rational' judgments on candidates, parties and competing policy positions.[548]

The 'full transparency' argument, in terms of donor and contribution disclosure, appealing for its simplicity, assumes the existence of other elements and controls to be effective: a competitive policy-based socio-political environment; a benefits and award system open to public scrutiny;[549] and a vibrant probing/fact-finding, as against sensationalizing, independent media orientation. It may be important enough for it to be noted that by 'independent', here, is meant not only free from *partisan* bias, but also prejudice directed against politicians, as a class and their parties.[550]

Another version of the full transparency view is propounded by the project management consultant, Franklin Johnston, for whom,

> Today, government is the key to growth and the party so pivotal it should be

---

547 This maturity is reflected in the fact that "the Americans put party stickers on their cars and houses ... The British wear their red and blue rosettes proudly", without inciting political violence or even aggression/confrontation by so doing: See Franklin Johnston 'Political party funding, Electoral Commission, Transparency', supra.

548 *The Gleaner* found it conveniently self-serving to justify its continued use of the "gang" label, in reference to politicians, on the basis that the majority of those polled agreed with the appropriateness of the term. Does the Gleaner agree with the majority view that the island would have been better off if it had remained a British Colony?, which Michael Burke calls 'Symptoms of ignorance' in the *Jamaica Observer*, Thu. July 7, 2011, p.11

549 See for example, 'JCC, PSOJ [Jamaica Chamber of Commerce, Private Sector Organisation of Jamaica, respectively] heads lobby for exposure of sub-contractor list, *The Gleaner*, Thu. June 2, 2011, p. A6

550 Wayne Campbell describes "Those in the Parliament" as being "mere puppets on a string who do the bidding of those who fund their political parties". But if it is true, as he continues, that "History has taught us well ... our politicians are not persons of high moral character ... and they will continue to be bought", then they will invariably circumvent, by any creative means necessary, any attempt at regulation, including the solution he proposes: "reform to our electorate/political system [*sic*] which will make it mandatory for all contributions over a certain amount to be made public", see 'Save Parliament from the thugs", *The Gleaner*, Fri. July 15, 2011, p. A8

run as a company[551] as parties cannot be allowed to fail. ...[552] Transparency in public life begins with the party. If the party is tainted what comes from it cannot be clean.[553]

Apart from the fact that transparency can never guarantee the absence of tainted funding, from one who advocates the company/business model as being appropriate for political party operations, it is somewhat surprising that he adopts the anti-free market, anti-traditional capitalist position by extolling the use of public money to shore up failing entities. This can be seen as another instance of shallow thinking, pandering to clichés and buzz phrases, unworthy of their source.

Our observation on the sensitive issues of the literacy, political maturity and intelligence level of the electorate[554] is ignored by the editorial prediction that "Greater transparency will enhance the ability of voters to make judgments about in whose interest policy initiatives may be directed without there first having to be a scandal".[555]

The difficulty of tracking and aggregating multiple-class donors, in possibly significant numbers, over the electoral cycle is clearly under-estimated, in an electorate notoriously short-memoried, aided and abetted by a news media which tends to 'dwell' on what they consider to be commercially newsworthy, normally from a current time-perspective.

Remarkably and ironically, this replicates precisely the much-condemned politicians' behaviour, the difference being that whereas the media sells copies and advertising space, according to perceived reader/viewer/listener

---

551 Equating a political party to a Company is indicative of the naivety of the business 'organisation man' typically incapable of fundamentally distinguishing between organisations on the bases of their nature as determined by membership criteria, purpose, structure (authority/power, sanctions) etc.

552 Objectively, even in a one party dictatorship, if democracy is the goal, as against the preservation of the *status quo*, it is not, in our view, possible to defend this position which, however, is essentially the thinking of the state funding protagonists.

553 Franklin Johnston, 'Political party funding, Electoral Commission, transparency', supra.

554 In 'Issues should motivate voters', Jean Lowrie-Chin, supra, states: "We will never get the representation we deserve [unless we] ... vote for credible constituency representatives rather than simply voting for a party". Unfortunately a mixed bag of MP's are not likely to design a coherent, all-inclusive policy framework with the likely narrow range of interest/expertise they would represent, not to mention lack of research staff and facilities, available to them. The columnist continues: "A conscious electorate and strong voter turnout [in the context of "gangs" and "thugs" probably inherently contradictory] can improve significantly the quality of our leadership", the *Jamaica Observer*, Mon. June 20, 2011, p.11; But see "Issues, what issues? Few Jamaican's prepared to vote on issues if elections are called now", *The Gleaner*, Thu. July 7, 2011. P. A2

555 The Editorial, *The Gleaner*, Wed. Sept. 1, 2010, p. 46

popular preferences, politicians hope to win votes by what *they* must perceive to be rational goal-directed behaviour, in their interpretation of the overall environment in which they function from time to time.

DONATION LIMITS

It is somewhat peculiar that belief in principles of popular political democracy has led to an abandonment of the fundamental principle of seeking to maximize individual choice, as reflected in political or commodity market behaviour, in favour of embracing the notion of a "level playing field."

Some go further, it seems, by equating closer inter-party election results with improved democratic representation and system outcomes. However, the former has been found by Stratmann and Aparicio-Castillo, not entirely without challenge, to be the consequence of stricter funding limits[556]. We find it difficult to comprehend why closer party electoral performance should be the purpose of any kind of policy. This would mean that a party with the most obnoxious platform, however unpopular, while not unlawful, would deserve the 'benefit' of improved electoral performance as a result of state funding/ strict funding limits. The absurdity evident here is explicable very largely by the fact that 'democracy' proponents consistently fail to provide a working definition for the term.

With respect to the assumptions inherent in the ECJ's proposed contribution limits, they seem to have no local or international empirical research foundation. The anticipated response we expect, in what is generally a research-averse environment, will no doubt be: our approach was to find practical solutions to practical problems. But often such "solutions" are found to be practically useless in achieving anything other than cosmetic change.[557]

Low caps on donations, to reduce the role of 'big money' in politics,[558] equates to increasing state funding. There being no past data to provide guidance, and with apparently no study having been undertaken by itself, or

---

556 Thomas Stratmann and Francisco J. Aparicio-Castillo, "Campaign finance reform and electoral competition: Comment, in Public Choice (2007) 133: pp. 107 – 110. John Lott, for example, arrives at opposite results to those of Stratmann and Aparicio-Castillo, in his paper, "Campaign Finance Reform and Electoral Competition"

557 See 'Pass campaign financing laws before increasing donation limits', *The Gleaner*, Wed. July 31, 2013, p. A3

558 See also the examples of Ex-Major, Ray Nagin and Former Governor Bob McDonnell, both of the U.S.A., referred to at Notes 232 and 623, respectively.

commissioned on its behalf, to disclose the difference in the parties' income which would result from caps *at different levels*, the consequence is the arbitrary funding and spending limits formula proposed by the ECJ[559].

The novel point has been made that if limits are necessary because of the danger of corruption in whatever form, then, "By the same reasoning, we should compensate fraudsters for loss of income when we arrest them".[560]

What if individual campaign contributions below the cap, *in total*, far exceed spending limits? What is to be done with the 'excess' cash? Presumably it would have to be used for party administrative or other non-campaign matters. It would be nothing short of heresy for it to be proposed that it should go into any 'Political Fund'. Here again, one encounters the situation where a donor may be prevented from making his contribution for his chosen area of party activity, with its attendant costs, in clear violation of the democratic principle of freedom of choice, not to mention that this is what the current hegemonic politico-economic ideology dictates.

Subsequent to the introduction of spending limits in the United Kingdom, the Fifth Report of the Committee on Standards in Public Life was obliged to comment that,

> the case for national limits was not solely based on the need to ensure a 'level playing field' between the parties at elections and … it was difficult to find firm evidence that differences in spending power had influenced the outcome of several elections.[561]

---

559   See ECJ Report Part 1, p. 9, and ECJ 'Proposed Limits on Contributions/Donations to Candidates and Political Parties', p. 72 above.

560   'Against State Funding', Stumbling and Mumbling in Public Choice', March 15, 2007.
<http://stumblingandmumbling.typepad.com/stumbling_and_mumbling/2007/03/against_state_f.html>

561   Ibid, p. 31; Not surprisingly the new UK Coalition Government is moulding its own reform agenda for this area of political life, including fixed-term Parliaments and "new electoral events", with possibly significant implications for campaigning funding. For the ECJ's repetition of the contrary position, already passed by the House of Representatives and being debated (October, 2013) in the Senate, see 'K.D. Knight knocks ECJ's Campaign funding proposal" *The Gleaner*, Sat. Oct. 26, 2013, p.A3, where their view is reported that "state funding may act as a valuable tool in protecting political equality and electoral competition. …Would create a level playing field by enabling new and small parties and persons of modest means to offer themselves as candidates and compete with parties or candidates who are dominant and, perhaps, are more financially viable". Like the Opposition M.P. Everald Warmington, Government Minister, K.D. Knight argues to the contrary: "When I pay taxes, I want to see certain services provided by Government so that my fellow Jamaicans can drive on good roads, children go to school, hospitals and so on. I am not in favour, whatsoever, of one out of my tax dollar [*sic*] going to anything called campaign finance fund. I am totally against it": a strong view expressed a little late in the day, perhaps. See also, 'Warmington: We can't impose any more burdens on the 'poor', *The Gleaner*, Wed. Sept. 25, 2013, p.A1.

In the United States' case of *McConnell v Federal Election Commission*,[562] it was argued that certain key provisions of the *Bipartisan Campaign Reform Act of 2002*, were an unconstitutional infringement of First Amendment Constitutional rights. The key provisions were: (1) a ban on unrestricted "soft money"[563] donations, made directly to political parties; (2) limits on the advertising that unions, corporations, and non-profit organisations can engage in for up to sixty days prior to an election; and (3) restrictions on political parties' use of their funds for advertising on behalf of candidates. The Court held that the restrictions resulting from these provisions on freedom of speech were minimal, and, further, that the restrictions were justified by the government's legitimate interest in preventing corruption that might result from those contributions/expenditures.

In Jamaica's case, it appears that there are 'legitimate' channels through which 'soft money' could flow. These could, for example, be the sponsorship of mobilisational events such as conferences,[564] at whatever level, dinners at which the charge per plate could be abnormally high and other fundraising events, which would, *prima facie*, not attract limits as donations.

The funding of the cost of the research and the other work involved in the production of a manifesto, together with printing, distribution, and media promotion, outside a campaign period, would represent a considerable contribution. This might conceivably escape any imposed donation restrictions, if creatively handled.

We find that here, again in the instant United States' case, the expenditure of money is perceived as being equivalent, for adjudicatory purposes, to accepted freedoms/rights; in this instance, the 'freedom of speech'. This spurious kind of equation-formulation, displayed in *Buckley,* enables courts to use what appears to be 'short-cut' sentiment-inspired 'logic' to dispose of matters deserving a more direct confrontational attack, without the questionable aid of constitutional camouflage.

One needs to ask, perhaps, in the context of *McConnell*, why shouldn't the institutions concerned be at liberty, in a democracy, to support their

---

562 540 U.S. 93 (2003)

563 'Soft Money', a controversial feature of the United States political system, refers to money donated for so-called party-building purposes, which is not subject to federal campaign finance regulations.

564 See the United States Supreme Court's comment in this regard in *Buckley v Valeo*, 424 U.S., pp. 95-108

chosen political *cause* to their desired extent? The introduction of freedom of *speech* rights seems clearly to cloud the fundamental issue under deliberation. Why should even what the Court viewed as 'minimal' restrictions be acceptable, bearing in mind, in this particular case, the known varying interest represented by at least two of the third party 'lobby' groups involved, unions and corporations.

The right to fully participate in the electoral process in a multi-party political system would seem to render subordinate, any consequential concerns, in this context, about 'speech' rights. These seem only to have a presence as the result of peculiar judicial statutory interpretation, constitutional and electoral.

It may, however, be that ideological issues are more comfortably resolved when clothed in the garb of widely culturally accepted constitutionally-related terminology.

The Court's reasoning can be further faulted: any level of contribution from those sources could be used corruptly if, as alleged, this might be the situation beyond any maximum amount prescribed. Logic and the apparent presumed probability of the corrupt use of funds militate strongly against a favourable view of the decision.

It is at least possible, in this respect, to look kindly on the approach of the American Civil Liberties Union of countering the imposition of *limits* with a requirement for *disclosure* of large donations. Despite the unattractiveness of the 'chilling speech' terminology, contextual imperatives do suggest that disclosure provisions might best be situationally determined and configured.

The United States of America: Donations/Transparency

The rather graphically entitled Bill, "*Democracy is Strengthened by Casting Light on Spending in Elections (Disclosure) Act*", was passed by the United States House of Representatives in June 2010. Its passage was however blocked in the Senate by the procedural strategy of 'failing to invoke closure', which effectively barred the Bill from going to a vote. The American Civil Liberties Union which, while supporting "... the disclosure of large contributions to candidates as long as the disclosure does not have a *chilling effect* [Italics added] on political participation", urged Senators to vote against the Bill, because it would fail to improve the integrity of political campaigns in any substantial way while significantly harming the speech and associational rights of Americans. ... The Constitution guarantees all Americans the right to participate in political debate without risk or harassment or fear of *embarrassment*[Italics added].[565]

Disclosure is regarded as an "Invasion of privacy" by the American Civil Liberties Union, which would, it is claimed, have *'a chilling effect'*, representing a considerable cost, in terms of rights compromised, without a counterbalancing benefit.

Britain: Donations/Transparency

Those who believe—in innocence of the legal standards of proof in criminal law jurisdictions deserving of respect—that disclosure by itself, however full, will necessarily remove doubts as to the propriety of donations need to be instructed by the results of the recent British Labour and Conservative Party 'scandals'.[566] Several of the amounts under scrutiny represented not donations but purported loans from non-commercial sources, even if on purportedly commercial terms. This appears to have been a factor that was apparently initially unconsidered by the ECJ, despite its considerable potential funding significance.

As for the relation between donations and public appointments in Britain, the position seemed to have been viewed by some in terms of corporate behaviour: a company could hardly be expected to appoint as a director one who is a director of the company's main competitor. The equivalent political reality, seems to have found expression in the words of Lord Pym, then Chairman of the Political Honours Scrutiny Committee and former Conservative Cabinet Minister, to a House of Commons Select Committee, to the effect that, "... the committee considered a political donation a point in a nominee's favour as it indicated involvement in public life, and that the nominee had put their [*sic*] money where his mouth is."[567]

---

565 Michael Macleod-Bell, Chief Legislative and Policy Counsel, America Civil Liberties Union,, Press Release – Senate Rejects Disclosure Act, July 27, 2010 (www.aclu.org/free-speech/aclu-letter-senate-urging-no-vote-disclosure-act)

566 See Appendix 1.

567 'Cash for Honours', p. 1

In the case of Dr. Chai Patel, who had donated £10,000 to the British Labour Party, on being rejected by the Honours Appointment Committee, for appointment to the House of Lords, his response was:

> I have never asked for any favour for the money that I have donated. My children suggested that if I had not given this money I would not be seen in this light [involvement in politically immoral/corrupt behaviour] But I happen to support this Government, I gave money to the party because I happen to believe in what it stands for. I can't change what has happened."[568] (The report continued to say that Patel had asked a Queen's Counsel for advice on whether his human rights were being abused by the Commission.)

Patel, having withdrawn his name from the list of peerage nominees, saying that he had not been offered anything in return for his contribution, further stated in a letter to the House of Lords Appointments Commission that,

> I feel that given my accumulated experience and deep sense of public service as well as being able to devote the time to undertake the responsibility effectively, I would be able to make a contribution to the parliamentary process.[569]

Being in no position to vouch for the sincerity of Patel's statements, it nevertheless deserves consideration as to whether it would not be unfortunate, but, indeed nonsensical, if the making of a loan or a substantial contribution to a political party be allowed, because of the near universal culture of suspicion of political corruption, to virtually thereby become a reason, if not the justification, in accordance with popular perception, for disqualification for any appointment, award or honour.

---

568 'Ibid. p. 2, British Conservative Party Chairman, Francis Maude, put it this way: he was not only "very proud" of the people who had loaned money to his party, but insisted that they had not supported the party out of "self-interest", since the Conservatives had not stood much of a chance of gaining power in recent years. The same could be said of the Liberals, and the Lib/Dems over a very considerable period and the Labour party during the Thatcher era. In the Jamaican context, columnist Michael Burke argues that "... most people do not donate without strings attached. They want certain positions and certain favours if their party wins the election": The *Jamaica Observer*, Thu. Dec. 11, 2008, p.10. For Burke, "the only way, however, to stop the need for large contributions from a few people is to have the public pay for the campaigns". Interestingly, Burke continues, "as important as money is ... it is not every problem that can be solved by simply throwing money at it". He does not, however, suggest what else can be thrown at the implied problem(s) caused by large contributions from a wealthy few, except tax-payers' money.

569 Ibid; It is worthy of note that incidents of this nature occurred against the background of the 1997 British Labour Party manifesto promise to "clean up politics", with the pledge to "reform party funding to end sleaze" through the promise commitment to the passage of legislation requiring all parties to declare the source of all donations above a minimum figure, which Labour already did, voluntarily. These commitments were reflected by the *Political Parties, Elections and Referendums Act, 2000*.

It is one thing to decry the failure of the parties to attract bright new talent from the professional and business managerial worlds. It is quite another, as a matter of habit, to cast politicians in the Machiavellian mould, by virtue of which the worthy self-respecting and respectable potential contributor to the political process, whether by election or appointment, is thereby repelled from involvement in partisan politics. To then blame the parties, exclusively, for the failure of a certain category of persons to join them is, perhaps, a peculiar variant of the 'self-fulfilling prophecy'. Such a mindset, as will be apparent, is certainly not indigenous to Jamaica.

British stockbroker, Barry Townsley, withdrew his acceptance of a peerage on the grounds of "press intrusion into his private life", as a result of his having contributed £1.5 million to a City Academy under a Labour government scheme, donated £6,000 and loaned £1 million, on commercial terms,[570] to the party.

The prominent British Labour Party member and Tony Blair critic, Claire Short, who, among others, accused the then Prime Minister, correctly, perhaps, given the party's history, of having abandoned Labour's core principles and grassroots electoral support, summed up the situation, as anyone in Jamaica is yet to depict it,

> What we're getting is a bubble of these clever people who've captured the state, don't need a party, don't need any members, don't have turbulent people having opinions, who then get money from rich people and run our state without consulting anyone else.[571]

As the Labour Party had done in 1997, David Cameron on becoming Conservative Party leader, promised new proposals[572] to "… stop this perception that parties can somehow be bought by big donations either from very

---

570 'Cash for Honours', supra, p. 2

571 Ibid, p.9

572 Ibid p.10; British Prime Minister David Cameron's proposals are:- (1) ban on all loans, unless from financial institutions on fully commercial terms; (2) £50,000.00 cap on donations; (3) tax relief on donations up to £3,000; (4) state funding of £1.20 per vote won at general elections for parties with MPs, plus an annual payment equal to 60p per vote; (5) a new Commission to handle honours; (6) general election party funding limited to £15m; (7) reduction of the number of MPs from 646 to fewer than 600.

rich people or trade unions or business."[573] One will have to wait and see how his premiership fares, in this respect, constrained, as it might be, by the coalition arrangement with the Liberal Democratic Party and the state of the British economy.

Eliminating Cameron's listed sources of funding which are likely to attract suspicion as to the motive of the donor, one is left with membership dues, investments or other earned income and, of course, state subsidy.

In Jamaica, we have noted that the PNP supported full disclosure. Cynicism is not the basis for the view that this was, and is, undoubtedly directly related to its position in favour of public finding.[574] Not only was the party then in opposition, without the benefit of the 'spoils of office', but it is supposed to have repaid the J$ 31million Trafigura money[575] - an amount not insignificant in Jamaican terms, especially soon after facing the considerable expenses incurred in a general election.

According to Attorney Jacqueline Samuels-Brown, in such a context,

> We have the advantage in Jamaica of the realities of what the present system
> of secret donations involves. It is my view that, first of all, the greater good

---

573 Ibid. Perhaps as columnist, Mark Wignall, proclaims "... corruption will always exist as part of the human condition. Governmental corruption will always flourish, especially where it has grown into the culture of our politics. Many Jamaicans are of the view that governance in Jamaica is impossible without a significant dose of corruption". [Especially, one may add, when it works in one's favour]: 'Governance and political intrigue', the *Jamaica Observer*, Thu. June 2, 2011, p. 10. Another letter writer, supportive of "effective disclosure" cites the additional basis for reform in that Jamaica as a signatory to Chapter 11 Article 7(3) of the U.N. Convention against Corruption which requires subscribing states to make good faith efforts to improve transparency in election candidate and political party financing. See also 'ECJ Chairman weighs in on vote-buying debate', the *Jamaica Observer*, Fri. Dec. 9, 2011, p. 4 on the issue of perception versus reality with respect to corruption.

574 Professor Errol Miller, 'Independent commissioners DID NOT CAVE IN', *The Gleaner*, Oct. 3, 2010, p. F5. The 'problem' of dealing with the party-nominated commissioners is perhaps best revealed by Professor Miller's statement in defense of the Commission, accused as, it had been, of 'caving in' to the wishes of the parties and of having 'produced a mouse': "Those who believed in public disclosure (the PNP) could exceed this minimum [threshold, and disclosure only, to the Commission] and act on their conviction. ... Those who disagree with public funding of political parties at this time (the JLP) could refuse to accept the same". This, despite the repeated position that on points of disagreement the independent commissioners made the "final decision" and that the Report was to be tabled "for signing by all commissioners after ruling (sic) by independent commissioners". See Letter of the Day, Jacqueline Samuels-Brown, 'Electoral Commission has produced a mouse ', *The Gleaner*, Tue. July 27, 2010, p. A6, where it asserted that, "It is not easy to make decisions fairly and dispassionately when self-interest is involved". See also Peter Espeut, 'The shame remains', *The Gleaner*, supra. According to Espeut, "what saved the day was the shame of the ruling party, which 'could not agree to further state funding for political parties in circumstances where the Government could not pay civil servants, teachers, nurses and police'. The possible solution to the transparency risk feared by some individuals and organisations is simple: "If your [PSOJ] members don't want anyone to know to whom they gave political donations (their dark secrets), then maybe they shouldn't give any". Peter Espeut, 'Shame PSOJ', *The Gleaner*, Fri. June 25, 2010, p. A9.

575 See 'Trafigura matter stalls', the *Jamaica Observer*, Tue. June 28, 2011, p. 4

requires full disclosure. Second, donations are voluntary, *so* each individual *has* (italic added) to look at the *benefit* and the *cost*.[576]

Although exception can be taken to the Attorney's view, implying the inevitability of motivation by 'self-interest', as determined by a cost/benefit calculation, nevertheless, with Michael Williams, General Secretary of the NDM in concurrence, but without the support of any available evidence, she continued,

> persons sometimes made donations to political parties with amounts that were disproportionate to their income ... they *are* [Italics added] a medium for people who cannot come forward to make the donations, by requiring disclosure and full transparency, we would put a brake on that.[577]

Some commentators have clearly limited their engagement with the island's politics to voting. Were this not so, the certainty of such a conclusion would be mysterious. Lawyers should certainly offer supporting evidence: with that all-exclusive interpretation of the circumstances attending some donations, aspects of the reform agenda proposed are likely to expose *others* to the risk of martyrdom.

As the late former British Labour Party leader and Prime Minister, Harold Wilson, recognised, timing is critical in politics; 'best practice' also has cultural boundaries.

The ECJ's proposal is for the amounts contributed, beyond the threshold, to be made public, while the names of donors are required to be disclosed to a Committee of the Commission. After investigation, it has the duty, "... to report to the DPP cases where suspected tainted money is donated to parties."[578]

---

576 'Loopholes loom, Absence of full disclosure may weaken [ECJ] party-funding proposal', *The Gleaner*, Tue. June 22, 2010, p. A2, reporting the views of participants at a Gleaner Editor's Forum. This view is challenged by that of the British Conservative party: "The identity of 10 backers it had repaid - including a number of foreign nationals - was not revealed ... some of these lenders were concerned not to reveal their identity fearing that it might compromise their existing business arrangements with the government 'Tory lenders feared reprisals', BBC 24 March, 2006 Their details, including one foreign backer, will be provided "in confidence" to the Electoral Commission [as in the Jamaican ECJ proposal]. Initially the party had sought to not disclose to anyone the names of two lenders who requested confidentially [a position one would expect the media, of all critics, to appreciate]. See Cash for Honours supra, p. 5; The robust, if somewhat startling, American response to thinking along such lines might be: "Don't get hung up on purity. In politics purity is a loser": see 'Republicans: We'll not have a perfect challenger for Obama', The *Jamaica Observer* on Saturday, June 18, 2011, p. 12

577 *The Gleaner*, 'Loopholes loom', supra.

578 Ibid, per Dorothy Pine-McLarty, Chairperson of the ECJ's Political Finance Committee.

What of possibly clean money being expended on 'tainted' causes? The Commissioner's manner of treatment is to stipulate that, "It shall be an offence for any political party or candidate of a political party to ... , publicly or improperly use funds legally received".[579]

As a starter, one can ask; would a campaign contribution, privately sourced, that is diverted to cover housekeeping expenses, and vice versa, fall into this category of 'an offence'? The answer, it is suggested, is certainly not as obvious as it may appear.

One *Gleaner* editorial notes that,

> among the more enduring images from the public enquiry into the Christopher Coke extradition scandal was Prime Minister Bruce Golding's gritty insistence on not revealing who paid for the lobbyists who sought to soften America's attitude on the extradition request.[580]

The extradition request referred to was a one-off matter.[581] The financing of anything connected to it at any level could hardly be necessarily connected to party or campaign financing, as normally perceived. Information possessed to the contrary, which might lend credence to the insinuations inherent in the editorial, ought, as a matter of journalistic duty, to have been provided. This becomes even more contentious since the comments were made in the context of discussions of issues of party funding/disclosure/transparency, as revealed by the editorial, in its entirety.

The deliberate and specific identification of, and agreement on, the values to be protected and promoted through the mechanism of the electoral system in Jamaica might require somewhat different prescriptions than have so far been advanced, in order to achieve desired political behaviour/image transformation.

Despite the context of the environment responsible for the emergence of sentiments related above, we note that, "...research indicates that transparency is not sufficient *in itself*, [Italics added] to maintain public confidence in the

---

579 See, ECJ Report, p. 12.

580 Editorial in The Gleaner Fri. Apr.8, 2011, p. A6

581 Our problem with that entire issue was the very troubling failure of those who see themselves as nationalists to pose the question, 'what if the situation was or is reversed in the future?' meaning that the Jamaican Government seeks the extradition of a United States citizen from the U.S. for trial in a Jamaican Court. As is known, the U.S. refuses to submit to the jurisdiction of certain international judicial tribunals of the highest integrity. The protection of *all* citizens should be a matter of governmental instinct.

overall integrity of political funding. It is also important to have effective and independent means of enforcing the rules."[582]

Rules are better enforced when allegations of impropriety, even if not leading to formal charges being laid, are brought to public attention with sufficient specifics to invite meaningful challenge and fact-based defence, where appropriate.

BRING THE ALLEGATIONS TO LIGHT

Smear tactics and/or innuendo, cause individual/collective reputations to face the risk of damage by less than incontrovertible evidence. It is not easy to disprove perceptions or indeed, allegations unaccompanied by specifics.

Given less sustained media treatment, largely due, no doubt, to the firm and reasoned detailed nature of responses challenging the merit of the allegations, have been the reports that persons/companies suspected to have contributed substantially, financially, to the two major parties benefited from "sweetheart deals", as a result.

One such 'case' related to the Dehring Bunting & Golding property acquisition/ investment transaction involving financing by the National Investment Bank of Jamaica, during the PNP's term of office. Two of the firm's principals are prominent members of that party.[583] The other matter was the terms of acquisition and financing of the Sandals Whitehouse hotel property by the hotel's Corporate Group, under the then JLP government, which, *rumour* has it, donated heavily to that party in the 2007 election.[584]

The only observation to be made here, is that support of a political party, by whatever lawful means, should most definitely not be taken to amount to disqualification from engaging in transactions in the 'normal course of business' with the state or its agencies, especially given the island's small size.

The construction of well-considered transaction guidelines, along with a vigilant monitoring agency, is clearly crucial for fact-based corruption prevention purposes. In this respect, Professor Trevor Munroe argues that

---

582 The UK Electoral Commission's submission to the Committee on Standards in Public Life, on Party Funding. Oct. 2010, p. 3.

583 The principals of the Company happened to be well known supporters of the PNP, who would have been expected, personally or otherwise, to have donated generously to that party.

584 *The Gleaner*, May 12, 13, 2011, p.A1;

for information gathering and efficient coordination and cross-referencing proposes, the creation of a single anti-corruption agency,[585] ought to be favourably considered. Operated in accordance with juridical principles, this might well assist in dispelling the often counterproductive, rumour-mongering syndrome.

From the perspective of cost and efficiency, Munroe's proposal does seem to deserve, and, more recently, appears to be getting, serious examination.

Recent international incidents worthy of note, in this context, occurred in,

Trinidad & Tobago:

> In a Jamaican press report headed, "TT Parliament suspends former PM", the story was carried of the former Prime Minister's failure to attend the parliamentary debate, for which he had asked to be excused, relating to his accusation that the present government was "... carrying out the agenda of those who financed them in the election campaign", being, allegedly, those "who were involved in the drug trade".[586] The former Prime Minister, according to the release, had not only failed to attend the Privileges Committee hearing, but to otherwise respond to the other charges against him, despite numerous requests.

Ecuador: It was reported in 2008 that "... documents published yesterday from a slain rebel's computer and confirmed by senior Colombian officials show leftist guerrillas discussing financial contributions to the Ecuadorean president's 2006 campaign".[587]

Puerto Rico: Governor Vila of this United States territory was charged by mainland authorities, along with twelve others, in what the press described, as a "campaign finance probe", in relation to allegations of "illegally raising money to pay off campaign debts". Vila was, we are informed, "elected governor in 2004

---

585 *The Gleaner* Jan. 16, 2011, pp.C1, 3 and C 6, 11; the *Jamaica Observer* Tue. Jan.18, 2011, p.8.

586 The *Jamaica Observer*, Jan.16, 2011, p, 7.

587 The *Jamaica Observer*, Wed. May 18, 2011, p. 16,

on an anti-corruption platform".[588]

In a later Puerto Rican case, an ex-senator was sentenced to five years imprisonment for "... trading political favours for cash and services ... in exchange for promises to block or advance certain Bills as Chairman of the powerful rules committee and to damage the interests of business owners if they refuse to pay".[589]

United States of America:

This is where the federal and state system is so notorious for scandals, and the extent to which 'big money lobby', at both the state and national level for presidential and other public office election campaign financing, features so conspicuously that one specific country representative, and certainly several others, "fear our system" becoming "like the American".[590] Loopholes in the regime, assisted by Court decisions, referred to, may have tempted would-be exploiters to be bolder than was prudent.

There is no shortage of examples in the case of the United States:

A Congressman for New York faced allegations in 2010 that "... he misused his office for fundraising and may have helped with a tax shelter for a company whose chief executive was a major donor".[591]

The photograph of a former United States House Majority Leader was shown in the press as "... he waits for his [three year] sentencing decision ... for his role in a scheme to illegally funnel corporate money to ... candidates in 2002".[592]

The "once ascendant" senator who ran for President on two occasions, John Edwards, was in mid-2011 charged for

---

588   *The Gleaner*, Thur. Nov. 20, 2008 , p. C8; *The Gleaner*, Fri. Mar. 28, 2008, p.13; *The Gleaner*, Tue Feb. 10, 2009, p. A 10.

589   The *Jamaica Observer*, Wed. May 18, 2011, p.25

590   Australia is among the countries which share this dread. See Cass and Burrows, supra.

591   The *Jamaica Observer*, Fri. July 30, 2010, p.27

592   The *Jamaica Observer*, Jan. 16, 2011, p.7

violating campaign finance laws by failing to report campaign donations and diverting the funds to cover private personal expenses. 593 Edwards, an Attorney, summed up his position: 'I have done wrong but I did not break the law'.[594]

Immediately above the Edwards' story, was another report headed "Blagojevich did not Seek Favours, Emmanuel Testifies at Retrial". The former Mayor of Chicago was facing a retrial on accusations of "trying to sell the Senate seat for campaign donations or job offers. ..."[595]

A further recent instance of campaign finance impropriety is that of the ex-mayor who was sued by the State in a claim based on the allegation that "he had illegally used $94,004.00 in campaign money to pay for his criminal defense", in respect of which charges, fraud and tax evasion, he had just finished serving the sentence of imprisonment imposed.[596]

United Kingdom:

If Westminster is rightly called the "mother of Parliaments", it cannot be said to have been an entirely virtuous one. Lloyd George, as the then Prime Minister, has, in virtually all the literature on the subject, been accused, correctly from all accounts, of selling Peerages to the Upper Chamber for party financial contributions.

More recently, both the Conservatives (under John Major) and the Tony Blair led Labour Party have been stained by charges of "sleaze", which have been repeatedly reported internationally.

---

593 *The New York Times*, Thurs. May 26, 2011, pp. A. 16,24.; See also, 'Jesse Jackson, Jnr., facing prison time', *The Gleaner*, Feb., 2013, p. D11 which reports that Jackson who had resigned his seat in the US Congress, and his wife, agreed to plead guilty to charges in an alleged scheme to spend $750,000.00 in campaign funds on personal items which, "... included furs, a gold watch, a football signed by American presidents and even a hat once owned by Michael Jackson".

594 See, 'I have done wrong but I did not break the law', John Edwards pleads not guilty to finance charges', the *Jamaica Observer* on Sat. June 4, 2011, p. 5.

595 *The New York Times*, Thu. May 26, 2011. p, A16

596 *The New York Times*, Fri. May 27, 2011, p. A23.

Lessons in this area of national life appear, however, to be difficult to learn. We thus find that in 2011 a British MP, the first to suffer this fate, was sentenced to eighteen months imprisonment for fraud/forgery connected to political expense claims. The press report states, among other things, "News of David Clayton's sentence reverberated around Westminster days after the *parliamentary standards authority* [Italics added] signalled that it is *set to water down the new rigorous expenses regime after pressure from MP's* [Italics added]. MPs of *all* parties had written to Mr. Justice Saunders, the trial judge, "praising Clayton in the hope that he would be spared a prison term".[597]

One trusts that, with this evidence, of Parliamentarians' behavioural response to enforcement of regulatory sanctions in mind, the requirement in the ECJ's proposals for *Ministerial* approval of electoral regulations will be reviewed.

Under the heading 'UK lawmaker pleads guilty over expenses charges' another case is reported in the following terms:

> His bogus claims were exposed during a scandal over the expense claims of British lawmakers, in which it came to light that legislators had made inappropriate and unlawful use of public money".[598] It was later reported that the MP chose to resign, thereby "avoiding an embarrassing ouster under Parliamentary rules or in a vote of lawmakers.[599]

Finland:

The press report, in this instance, was to the effect that,

> A campaign finance scandal that has dogged Finish Prime Minister ... intensified yesterday as the opposition upped pressure on him to disclose his party's accounts and called for new elections. ... Some 60 members of parliament ... other members of

---

597 *The Times* (London), Sat, Jan, 8, 2011, pp 1, 4 and 6
598 The *Jamaica Observer*, Wed. Jan. 12, 2011, p.20
599 The *Jamaica Observer*, Tue. Jan 13, 2011, p.17.

his Centre Party as well as dozens of other parties' MPs – allegedly accepted US$ 631,000 in campaign funds from an association of Finnish businessmen ... [who] recently claimed they were in return promised support in their bid for permits to build shopping centres across Finland". The allegations were denied, not surprisingly by the PM who was, "ready for an extensive discussion about their own (Opposition parties) campaign finances", as part of a larger debate on election financing.[600]

Germany:

Chancellor Helmut Kohl, then head of the largest conservative party, the CDU, "... accepted large donations without turning them over to the party, thus allowing him to use funds for political purposes but without reflecting their use in the party's accounts".[601] This scandal largely accounted for his political demise.

Bermuda:

In this recent case, the press reported that, "Premier Craig Cannoneir handed in his resignation on Monday night over the so-called Jetgate controversy which has rocked the ruling One Bermuda Alliance (OBA), Governor George Ferguson confirmed ... Jetgate surrounded the use of US tycoon Nathan Landow's private jet to take the premier and two of his cabinet ministers for talks with Landow ... confirmed that he and a group of other US businessmen had donated (US)$300,000.00 to assist the 2012 OBA election campaign, although Landow said cash was wired to a group called The Bermuda Political Action Club and not directly to OBA. Landow insisted that no deal was struck ... and said he received nothing in return for his financial contribution ... denied Cannonier asked him for $2 million in "facilitation money" to help him make casino gambling a reality in Bermuda ... but ... he no longer had any interest in such a project. ... Three months after the 2002 election victory,

---

600   The *Jamaica Observer*, Wed. June 4, 2008, p. 33
601   http://drucksachen.bundestag.de/drucksachen/index.php

Cannonier along with Tourism Minister … and Attorney General … as well as the premier's business manager flew to a meeting in the US with Landow and his associates".[602]

Italy:

This most recent news report, headed 'Corruption scandal rocks Venice', tells of the arrest of "Venice's Mayor and more than 30 other people … in a sweeping corruption scandal in which politicians are accused of financing election campaigns with some €25 million [(US)$34 million] in bribes from the consortium building underwater barriers to protect the lagoon city from flooding. One of a series of bribery probes into major public works projects in Italy, the web of alleged bribery revealed in Venice has many of the same characteristics as Italy's 'Kickback City' scandal of 20 years ago that toppled an entire political class. … The head of the consortium building the so-called Moses barriers was placed under house arrest last year. … He, along with others created a €25 million slush fund abroad that was used to bribe politicians, who then used the money for election campaigns as well as personal gain … The illicit funding was at the city, regional and national levels, prosecutors said".[603]

These 'cases' puts focus on the JLP Treasurer's 'disclosure' that, as is well known, parties tend to experience 'financial hardships' shortly after general elections. However, of much greater significance, for the disclosure/transparency aspect of political party financing reform, is the admission by a 'JLP source' that,

We operate accounts outside of the party accounts so that private sector entities could make donations without drawing cheques directly to the JLP … but it *appears* that this time around the persons who controlled the accounts used the money for their constituency and passed on only a fraction to the JLP".[604]

---

602 'Bermuda premier resigns amid scandal; deputy takes over', The *Jamaica Observer*, Wed. May 21, 2014, p. 11
603 'Corruption scandal rocks Venice', *The Gleaner*, Thu. June 5, 2014, p. C8.
604 See, 'Money woes unsettles JLP', *The Gleaner*, June 24, 2012. p.A6

In less than mature democracies, disclosure under a transparency regime might pose serious personal and enterprise reprisal threats and risks of varying kinds and degrees of seriousness. Consequences, however, can be very dissimilar, comparatively.

It has, for example, been observed that with respect to Britain,

> In the past the (funding) gap was filled by institutional finance ... the major parties have fallen back on rich donors. ... A large donation was a rich man's political levy enabling him to enter, if not the kingdom of heaven, at least the House of Lords. But sunlight, as Mr. Justice Branders once said, is the best disinfectant. Perhaps in the future, a large gift to a party will be seen as a good reason not to give someone an honour rather than grounds to reward them.[605]

Issue has already been strongly taken with this view, which seem to have little to commend it: why should persons deserving the award of a national honour be precluded from making substantial contributions to the political party of their choice?

Some commentators appear to regard disclosure/transparency as something of a panacea for the possible or actual corrupting influence of money in politics. However, even in a country such as the United States of America, with a relatively vigorous investigate press, it is not as easy as some, including Judges in **Buckley v Valeo,**[606] imply to obtain, store and recall information made available as a result of disclosure provisions. Over the election cycle, competition for memory space, in a dynamic society where the average citizen/voter is inundated with 'news', may well result in attrition or what some refer to as 'information fatigue'.

Further, on a practical, in contrast to the ideal/theoretical level, a voter may well have concerns about sizes and sources of political contributions which are substantially outweighed by focus on personal, family, or class-related financial/economic interests.

Neither is it entirely true that disclosure "allows the voter to place each candidate in the political spectrum", as the Court suggests. Candidates or parties, to the extent that they raise substantial amounts in total from

---

605 *Financial Times* (London) Apr. 3, 2002
606 Buckley v Valeo, 424 US.1 (1976), p.67

numerous small donations, will escape that kind of searchlight, especially where reporting thresholds are not very low.

One of the outstanding contradictions inherent in the **Buckley** judgment is revealed in this context. In treating with contribution limits (p. 22), the claim is made that "… the overall effect of the *Federal Election Campaign Act's* contribution ceilings is merely to require candidates and political committees to raise funds from a greater number of persons …", which is in stark contrast to the Court's arguments in relation to Subtitle H, where it was suggested that it was enacted "in furtherance of vital governmental interests in relieving *major* [Italics added] party candidates from the *rigours* [Italics added] of soliciting private contributions. …"

Even if disclosure did provide the alleged benefit identified in the judgment, and it is accepted that some voters do vote sometimes for candidates rather than their parties, the choice of governments in a multi-party system is determined on a party basis. At the aggregated national level the choice is between parties. It is the exception when the candidate who is successful at the polls consistently opposes 'his' party's policies, and yet survives for any significant period.

The Court's arguments, additionally, ignores the reality of the ideological convergence over decades which has resulted ultimately in the emergence of predominant multi-class parties. This development has been aided and abetted by, and is, at the same time, indicative of the increasing professionalization of politics. Without necessarily suggesting that this is an example of 'the means justifying the ends', it is hardly controvertible that career dislocations are not the preferred experience of the members of a 'political class', or any other occupational category.

Increased ideological and, concomitantly, policy flexibility should not be surprising as parties manoeuvre in search of an electoral majority. The need for party discipline simply for survival purposes, particularly in situations of nearly equal parliamentary strength, is likely to prove a serious constraining hurdle to candidate independence. Exceptions might be an issue of importance at the local level, or when so at the national are yet peripheral to those deemed to be 'life threatening' in a partisan political manner.

In summary, the realities of politics do not, with respect, seem to have been adequately taken into account by the Justices of the Supreme Court.

This case does offer one of those opportunities where one can 'learn from history': here the judicial 'history' of the United States. Significant jurisprudence in this case has evolved rather rapidly there, given that country's penchant for defending perceiving breaches of public law provisions as having constitutional implications whenever possible. This is thought to be sufficient justification for the extended reportage and treatment given to this and other cases to which reference is made.

The vigilance with which fundamental rights clauses of their Constitution is guarded, with no imputation with respect to motive, encourages and maximizes the reference of issues concerning political donation and expenditure limits and their disclosure to the Supreme Court for determination as to their legitimacy.

Under the thinking—not always impressive in cogency—which characterizes their approach to these political/electoral issues, they are 'elevated' to fundamental questions of democratic speech and associational individual rights.

The **Buckley** Court, for example, suggests that, "The Act's contribution and expenditure limitations [*sic*] operate in an area of the most fundamental First Amendment activities. …The First Amendment affords the broadest protection to such political expression in order to assure the unfettered interchange of ideas …"

In contrast, Jamaica has, to date, limited political finance regulation under ROPA. This has not resulted in constitutional challenges. The explanation may be two-fold: less creative self-serving behaviour of lawyers, which might well contribute to the lessened public consciousness as to the more active role a now seemingly comatose Independence document might play in politico-cultural matters.

An intriguing aspect of the leading cases, including this, is the quest to seek to achieve a tolerable balance, in the Court's view, between the revered rights sought to be protected and fundamental social/cultural values, often in multi-level conflict.

The Supreme Court, in dealing with the case, in which appellants were various federal officeholders and candidates, supporting political organisations, with the respondents being the Secretary of the Senate, Clerk of the House, the Controller General and the Electoral Commission, noted that, "These appeals present constitutional challenges to the key provisions of the Federal *Election Campaign Act of 1971 (Act)*, and related provisions of the Internal Revenue Code of 1954, all as amended in 1974":

[APPEAL FROM THE UNITED STATES COURT OF APPEALS FOR THE DISTRICT OF COLUMBIA CIRCUIT]

Syllabus

The *Federal Election Campaign Act of 1971 (Act)*, as amended in 1974: (a) limits political contributions to candidates for federal elective office by an individual or a group to $1,000 and by a political committee to $5,000 to any single candidate per election, with an overall annual limitation of $25,000 by an individual contributor; (b) limits expenditures by individuals or groups "relative to a clearly identified candidate" to $1,000 per candidate per election, and by a candidate from his personal or family funds to various specified annual amounts depending upon the federal office sought, and restricts overall general election and primary campaign expenditures by candidates to various specified amounts, again depending upon the federal office sought; (c) requires political committees to keep detailed records of contributions and expenditures, including the name and address of each individual contributing in excess of $10, and his occupation and principal place of business if his contribution exceeds $100, and to file quarterly reports with the Federal Election Commission disclosing the source of every contribution exceeding $100 and the recipient and purpose of every expenditure over $100, and also requires every individual or group, other than a candidate or political committee, making contributions or expenditures exceeding $100 "other than by contribution to a political committee or candidate" to file a statement with the Commission; and (d) creates the eight-member Commission as the administering agency with recordkeeping, disclosure, and investigatory functions and extensive rule-making, adjudicatory, and enforcement powers, and consisting of two members appointed by the President *pro tempore* of the Senate, two by the Speaker of the House, and two by the President (all subject to confirmation by both Houses of Congress), and the Secretary of the Senate and the Clerk of the House as *ex officio* nonvoting members. Subtitle H of the Internal Revenue Code of 1954 (IRC), as amended in 1974, provides for public financing of Presidential nominating conventions and general election and primary campaigns from general revenues and allocates such funding to conventions and general election campaigns by establishing three categories: (1) "major" parties (those whose candidate received 25% or more of the vote in the most recent election), which receive full funding; (2) "minor" parties (those whose candidate received at least 5% but less than 25% of the votes at the last election), which receive only a percentage of the funds to which the major parties are entitled; and (3) "new" parties (all other parties), which are limited to receipt of post-election funds or are not entitled to any funds if their candidate receives less than 5% of the vote. A primary candidate for the Presidential nomination by a political party who receives more than $5,000 from private sources (counting only the first $250 of each contribution) in each of at least 20 States is eligible for matching public funds."

[The above is, obviously, worth review, in some aspects, for comparative system design purposes].

Held: (at p. 3)

1. This litigation presents an Art. III "case or controversy," since the complaint discloses that at least some of the appellants have a sufficient "personal stake" in a determination of the constitutional validity of each of the challenged provisions to present "a real and substantial controversy admitting of specific relief through a decree of a conclusive character, as distinguished from an opinion advising what the law would be upon a hypothetical state of facts," *Aetna Life Ins. Co. v. Haworth,* 300 U. S. 227, 300 U. S. 241. [424 U. S. pp, 11-12]

2. The Act's contribution provisions are constitutional, but the expenditure provisions violate the First Amendment. (pp, 12-59)

(a) The contribution provisions, along with those covering disclosure, are appropriate legislative weapons against the reality or appearance of improper influence stemming from the dependence of candidates on large campaign contributions, and the ceilings imposed accordingly serve the basic governmental interest in safeguarding the integrity of the electoral process without directly impinging upon the rights of individual citizens and candidates to engage in political debate and discussion. (pp. 23-38)

(b) The First Amendment requires the invalidation of the *Act's* independent expenditure ceiling, its limitation on a candidate's expenditures from his own personal funds, and its ceilings on overall campaign expenditures, since those provisions place substantial and direct restrictions on the ability of candidates, citizens, and associations to engage in protected political expression, restrictions that the First Amendment cannot tolerate. (pp. 39-59)

3. The Act's disclosure and recordkeeping provisions are constitutional. (pp. 60-84).

(a) The general disclosure provisions, which serve substantial governmental interests in informing the electorate and preventing the corruption of the political process, are not overbroad insofar as they apply to contributions to minor parties and independent candidates. No blanket exemption for minor parties is warranted, since such parties, in order to prove injury as a result of application to them of the disclosure provisions, need show only a reasonable probability that the compelled disclosure of a party's contributors' names will subject them to threats, harassment, or reprisals in violation of their First Amendment associational rights. (pp. 64-74).

(b) The provision for disclosure by those who make independent contributions and expenditures, as narrowly construed to apply only (1) when they make contributions earmarked for political purposes or authorized or requested by a candidate or his agent to some person other than a candidate or political committee and (2) when they make an expenditure for a communication that expressly advocates the election or defeat of a clearly identified candidate is not unconstitutionally vague and does not constitute a prior restraint, but is a reasonable and minimally restrictive method of furthering First Amendment values by public exposure of the federal election system. (pp. 74-82).

(c) The extension of the recordkeeping provisions to contributions as small as those just above $10 and the disclosure provisions to contributions above $100 is not, on this record, overbroad, since it cannot be said to be unrelated to the informational and enforcement goals of the legislation. (pp. 82-84).

4. Subtitle H of the IRC is constitutional. (pp. 85-109)

(a) Subtitle H is not invalid under the General Welfare Clause but, as a means to reform the electoral process, was clearly a choice within the power granted to Congress by the Clause to decide which expenditures will promote the general welfare." (pp. 90-92)

Here we find explicit consideration being given to what may be conceived in the 'public interest'. In contrast, the ECJ's items of approved expenditure for state provided subsidies are couched in no such appealing nationalistic language.

> (b) Nor does Subtitle H violate the First Amendment. Rather than abridging, restricting, or censoring speech, it represents an effort to use public money to facilitate and enlarge public discussion and participation in the electoral process. (pp. 92-93)

> (c) Subtitle H, being less burdensome than ballot access regulations and having been *enacted in furtherance of vital governmental interests in relieving major party candidates from the rigours of soliciting private contributions, in not funding candidates who lack significant public support,* [Italics added] and in eliminating reliance on large private contributions for funding of conventions and campaigns, does not invidiously discriminate against minor and new parties in violation of the Due Process Clause of the Fifth Amendment."(pp. 93-108)

Given the malaise characterizing the relations between citizens and the political parties and the political process, generally, it is a moot question whether the Court is fulfilling its ideal societal role by limiting itself simply to statutory interpretation. Is the Blairite notion of "relieving *major* party candidates. ... [and]. ... in not funding candidates. ... significant public support, a 'legitimate, vital' governmental interests in a genuinely fully participatory democracy"?

It is an opportunity lost, it could be said, for the Court to point the way towards a more inclusive representation of the society's contending interests, concerns and views.

While most state subsidy arrangements do discriminate against 'fringe' candidate/parties, as reflected in the JLP's submissions to the ECJ, this pernicious dispensation might just conceivably constitute the worthy subject matter for constitutional challenge. Presumably, the members of this 'fringe' category are also contributors to public revenues, in one form or another.

Why should their taxes be disbursed to enable the promotion of others' views and interests but not their own?

The non-neutral political *status quo* preservation effect of the *Act's* effect is not in line with the sentiments below about "[the] unfettered interchange of ideas. ... Political and social change. ..." Today's 'fringe' could well be tomorrow's majority, a possibility inherent in the very essence of 'democracy', it may be argued.

"(d) Invalidation of the spending limit provisions of the *Act* does not render Subtitle H unconstitutional, but the Subtitle is severable from such provisions, and is not dependent upon the existence of a generally applicable expenditure limit. (pp. 108-109)

5. The Commission's composition as to all but its investigative and informative powers violates Art. II, §2, cl.2. With respect to the Commission's powers, all of which are ripe for review, to enforce the *Act*, including primary responsibility for bringing *civil* [Italics added] actions against violators, violate the Appointments Clause. The *Act*'s contribution and expenditure limitations operate in an area of the most fundamental First Amendment activities. Discussion of public issues and debate on the qualifications of candidates are integral to the operation of the system of government established by our Constitution. The First Amendment affords the broadest protection to such political expression in order "to assure [the] unfettered interchange of ideas for the bringing about of political and social changes desired by the people."

"Appellees contend that what the *Act* regulates is conduct, and that its effect on speech and association is incidental, at most. Appellants respond that contributions and expenditures are at the very core of political speech, and that the *Act*'s limitations thus constitute restraints on First Amendment liberty that are both gross and direct."

"*A restriction on the amount of money a person or group can spend on political communication during a campaign necessarily reduces the quantity of expression by restricting the number of issues discussed, the depth of their exploration, and the size of the audience reached.* [Italics added] [footnote 18] This is because virtually every means of communicating ideas in today's mass society requires the expenditure of money. The distribution of the humblest handbill or leaflet entails printing, paper, and circulation costs. Speeches and rallies generally necessitate hiring a hall and publicizing the event. The electorate's increasing dependence on television, radio, and other mass media for news and information has made these expensive modes of communication indispensable instruments of effective political speech."

The italicised quote above seems clearly to be in tension, logically, with the statement below that "The quantity of communication by the contributor does not increase ... size of his contribution. ..." Candidates and parties can only spend what they receive: limiting one (contribution) obviously directly impinges on the other. This may appear to some to be an exercise in single entry/column accounting.

> "The expenditure limitations contained in the *Act* represent substantial, rather than merely theoretical, restraints on the quantity and diversity of political speech. The $1,000 ceiling on spending "relative to a clearly identified candidate," [18 U.S.C. § 608(e)(1) (1970 ed., Supp. IV)], would appear to exclude all citizens and groups except candidates, political parties, and the institutional press [footnote 19] from any significant use of the most effective modes of communication. [footnote 20] Although the *Act's* limitations on expenditures by campaign organisations and political parties provide substantially greater room for discussion and debate, they would have required restrictions in the scope of a number of past congressional and Presidential *campaigns* [Italics added] [footnote 21] and would operate to constrain campaigning by candidates who *raise sums in excess* of the spending ceiling."

The 'problem' represented by total funds contributed exceeding the expenditure limit is left unresolved so far by the ECJ proposals.

> "By contrast with a limitation upon expenditures for political expression, a limitation upon the amount that any one person or group may contribute to a candidate or political committee entails only a *marginal* [Italics added] restriction upon the contributor's ability to engage in free communication." (p.21)

The method by which this conclusion is reached is not obvious, neither is the cogency of supporting arguments advanced to the effect that,

> "A contribution serves as a general expression of support for the candidate and his views, but does not communicate the underlying basis for the support. The quantity of communication by the contributor does not increase perceptibly with the size of his contribution, since the expression rests solely on the undifferentiated, symbolic act of contributing. At most, the size of the contribution provides a very rough index of the intensity of the contributor's support for the candidate. [footnote 22] A limitation on the amount of money a person may give to a candidate or

campaign organisation *thus involves little direct restraint* [Italics added] on his political communication, for it permits the symbolic expression of support evidenced by a contribution but does not in any way infringe the contributor's freedom to discuss candidates and issues. While contributions may result in political expression if spent by a candidate or an association to present views to the voters, the transformation of contributions into political debate involves speech by someone other than the contributor."

Some may think that the larger a donation, the more one would expect the candidate's/party's views to be reflective of those of the supporter.

"Given the important role of contributions in financing political campaigns, contribution restrictions could have a severe impact on political dialogue if the limitations prevented candidates and political committees from amassing the resources necessary for effective advocacy. There is no indication, however, that the contribution limitations imposed by the Act would have any dramatic adverse effect on the funding of campaigns and political associations. [footnote 23] *The overall effect of the Act's contribution ceilings is merely to require candidates and political committees to raise funds from a greater number of persons and to* **compel people** *who would otherwise contribute amounts greater than the statutory limits to expend such funds on direct political expression, rather than to reduce the total amount of money potentially available to promote political expression"..*[Italics added]

This seems to suggest that what is important is not to reduce the potential influence of 'big' money but rather to maximize its *sources*: hence the opening of the door to 'political expression' through the much maligned Political Action Committee (PAC). The merits to be derived from this contribution, limit/source distinction is elusive. (p. 22)

The *Act's* contribution and expenditure limitations also impinge on protected associational freedoms. Making a contribution, like joining a political party, serves to affiliate a person with a candidate. In addition, it enables like-minded persons to pool their resources in furtherance of common political goals. The *Act's* contribution ceilings thus limit one important means of associating with a candidate or committee, but leave the contributor free to become a member of any political association and to assist personally in the association's efforts on behalf of candidates. *And the Act's contribution limitations permit associations and candidates to aggregate large sums of money to promote effective advocacy.* [Italics added].

By contrast, the *Act*'s $1,000 limitation on independent expenditures "relative to a clearly identified candidate" precludes most associations from effectively amplifying the voice of their adherents, the original basis for the recognition of First Amendment protection of the freedom of association. See *NAACP v. Alabama*, 357 U.S. at 357 U. S. 460. The *Act*'s constraints on the ability of independent associations and candidate campaign organisations to expend resources on political expression "is simultaneously an interference with the freedom of [their] adherents," *Sweezy v. New Hampshire*, 354 U. S. 234, 354 U. S. 250 (1957) (plurality opinion). See *Cousins v. Wigoda*, 419 U.S. at 419 U. S. 487-488; *NAACP v. Button*, 371 U. S. 415, 371 U. S. 431 (1963).

In sum, although the *Act*'s contribution and expenditure limitations both implicate fundamental First Amendment interests, its expenditure ceilings impose significantly more severe restrictions on protected freedoms of political expression and association than do its limitations on financial contributions."

On the issue of choosing to keep in place restrictions on big money donations, the Court reasoned that,

"The *Act*'s $1,000 contribution limitation focuses precisely on the problem of large campaign contributions—the narrow aspect of political association where the actuality and potential for corruption have been identified—while leaving persons free to engage in independent political expression, to associate actively through volunteering their services, and to assist to a limited but nonetheless substantial extent in supporting candidates and committees with financial resources. [footnote 31] Significantly, the *Act*'s contribution limitations in themselves do not undermine to any material degree the potential for robust and effective discussion of candidates and campaign issues by individual citizens, associations, the institutional press, candidates, and political parties.

We find that, under the rigorous standard of review established by our prior decisions, the weighty interests served by restricting the size of financial contributions to political candidates are sufficient to justify the limited effect upon First Amendment freedoms caused by the $1,000 contribution ceiling."

According to judicial opinion in this leading United States Supreme Court case,

'Disclosure provides the electorate with information as to where political campaign money comes from and how it is spent by the candidate in order to aid the voters in evaluating those who seek federal office. It allows the voters to place each candidate in the political spectrum more precisely than is often possible, solely on the basis of party labels and campaign speeches. The sources of a candidate's financial support also alert the voter to the interest to which a candidate is more likely to be responsive and thus facilitate predictions of future performances in office.'[607]

Research conclusions which have been referred to, do not seem to support this conclusion in **Buckley**, but then Judges, even at the highest level are drawn from the society and are, one may with some hesitation suggest, not entirely immune from the influence of the prevailing orthodoxy in terms of the thinking and expectations in this or any other area of national life due for adjudication.

Additionally, access to reformation over the electoral cycle, even with the existence of a vigilant investigative media, must overcome, as has been suggested, several hurdles.

As against the prospective benefits contemplated in **Buckley**, we set a somewhat different experience:

"We" [the United Kingdom] Hayden Phillips continues in his Report, … currently have a funding system with a large degree of transparency, and yet trust in how parties are funded has not increased even though more information than ever before is in the public domain,[608]

Donor contributions and identities, for example, are posted on the Electoral Commission's website, unlike the ECJ's proposal for disclosure, on this level, to be, normally, only to itself.

The lesson here is that transparency, to be effective, is not only an expensive exercise but can have a negative effect in creating more suspicion, "on account of more and newly available information", causing donors to be more reluctant to contribute, quite regardless of whether suspicions harboured by the public, or contributors themselves, have any basis in fact.

---

607   Buckley v Valeo, 424 US.1 (1976), p.67
608   Hayden Phillips, op. cit. p. 33

CHAPTER 12

IMPLEMENTATION / ENFORCEMENT

Even if, as Jean Lowrie-Chin claims, the system proposed by the ECJ is a "model for the world"[609]—never mind the fact that the OAS,[610] only recently, in seminar discussions on the Jamaican situation, saw it useful to design a model system for the Caribbean—what of its effective enforcement prospects?

It is instructive here to note *The Gleaner's* concern as to whether another state institution, constitutionally established, in an era when the incidence of murder and other serious crime has assumed crisis proportions, "... has the capacity and resources to robustly pursue the cases brought before it."[611] If the Office of the DPP, cannot be provided with the level of resources necessary for its efficient operation, it would not be surprising if the Electoral Commission fares even worse.

Most commentators who see the need for party finance regulation want, like Franklin Johnston, the international project manager, "tight controls".[612] The monitoring regime contemplated by Johnston seems quite burdensome, given its likely bureaucratic complexity, cost and hence difficulty of administration for the ECJ and the parties, alike. The premature adoption of sophisticated procedures within a low administrative capability host environment, is perhaps an example of the penchant to indiscriminately copy that which is foreign.

Political parties in Jamaica, whether on the level of administration or financing, cannot be treated in a manner appropriate for multi-national, or even national corporations, in terms of the degree of elaboration built into their control mechanisms.

---

609 Jean Lowrie-Chin, "Issues should motivate voters", supra.

610 See 'The imperative of political financing reform' by Jose Miguel Insulza, Secretary General of the OAS, in *The Gleaner*, Tue. Aug. 31, 2010. p.A7.

611 Editorial, "The DPP and fighting corruption", The Gleaner, Wed, June 15, 2011, p. A8. See also 'Tough going at under-resourced DPP', the *Jamaica Observer*, Mon. Dec. 16, 2013, p.18.

612 See Franklin Johnston, 'Political party funding, Electoral Commission, Transparency', supra.

The ECJ's approach—against the background of the massive backlog of cases in the court system, at all levels, and the very long time it often takes for many serious matters, such as murder cases, to be tried —is, nevertheless, for breaches, seeming to justify prosecution, to be referred to the state prosecutorial agency, the DPP.[613]

If the Commission has to depend on another agency, such as the DPP or the legislature, bearing in mind that the ECJ has nominated political representatives among its membership, for action or resources, vigorous enforcement could be at risk. Institution of *civil* action for some breaches would have the advantage of not having to rely altogether on the DPP for a case to go forward to the courts, the DPP's Office being reportedly overwhelmed with a backlog of cases, as it has, indeed, been for years.

It is not altogether unthinkable that negative publicity may be a more potent deterrent than an imposed penalty, and may be an option worth considering, especially in cultural environments, unlike Jamaica's, currently, where the electorate does not suffer from short-term memory, or where the popular perception is not that "they are all the same".

Further, compliance may be promoted by the creation of a schedule of *well*-publicized *offences and penalties*, the latter graduated according to the seriousness of the violation. The failures in state / citizen communication ought not to be allowed to continue with respect to new legislation, especially when the essential objective is to bring about socially significant behaviour change on different levels. The necessary legal fiction of the presumption of knowledge of law, by virtue of which, "ignorance of law is no defence" is a curtain behind which states should be afforded only limited escape from their 'disclosure' duty to citizens.

With acknowledgement of economies of scale, which necessarily limit the scope in Jamaica for specialized institutional oversight of regulatory

---

613 'Government Workers still not filing statutory declarations'. The *Jamaica Observer*, Oct. 16, 2011, p.20, where it is reported that the Commission for the Prevention of Corruption has, it is reported, failed in its nine-year quest to get Parliament to enable it, rather than the case-overloaded, bogged-down DPP's Office to institute action for non-compliance. See 'K.D. Knight knocks ECJ's campaign funding proposal', in which the former Minister, now Senator and QC, is reported as also taking 'issue with a proposal that an imposition of a sanction or penalty by the commission shall not preclude institution of criminal proceedings [by the DPP] for contravening the campaign financing provisions', The *Gleaner*, Sat. Oct. 26, 2013, p.A3.

legal mechanisms, it may be contended, nevertheless, that if the functioning and funding of political parties is as crucial for the system of representative democracy as is believed, then the question of the body to be given the role of formal arbiter becomes all-important. The powers[614] which will inhere in the occupant of that role will prove to be decisive of the value of *any* reform effort.

Rachael Maddow of the United States television station, MSNBC, commenting on the election financing regulation enforcement performance of the Federal Electoral Commission, rated it as, "the worst sheriff in the world".[615] This assessment related specifically to the apparently improper use of some US$90,000.00 by an elected official in breach of campaign finance laws. Despite the concerns expressed as to the impropriety of the transaction, there was no investigation, the Commission preferring to accept the suspected wrongdoer's clearly self-serving explanation. The lesson learnt by the Commission from the incident was summed up with its words: "Maybe we should not be so trusting".[616]

Enforcement of, and changes to, regulatory provisions in Germany rests with the *Constitutional Court* which in 1992, on appeal by the Green Party challenging the new funding formula and disclosure thresholds, ruled as follows,[617] based on the observed growth of anti-party public sentiment:

(a) The Court overturned some of its earlier decisions.

(b) It 'dictated' an inflation related absolute limit on the total amount of public funds paid to parties.

(c) It restated prohibitions against a party receiving more than 50% of its income from public funds.

(d) It removed tax concessions for donations from corporations and associations and severely reduced the threshold for tax-deductibility for individuals.

(e) It lowered the disclosure threshold for donors, rejecting the 'complicated formulas devised in the 1980's'.

---

614 The CDU Party, after attempting to evade income disclosure requirements (involving large cash donations and transfers from secret bank accounts,), underwent leadership changes, as a direct result, and was forced to pay back millions in subsidies and penalties.

615 *MSNBC*, 'The Place for Politics', Mon. May 16, 2011

616 Ibid

617 Party Finance Case VII,85BVerfGE264(1992), pp. 299 - 306

(f) It rejected the principle that had been at the heart of the system since its own 1966 ruling, namely: 'that public funds must be used exclusively to subsidise election campaigns', and which could now, therefore, be used for all types of party work and activity.

Jamaica's predilection for non-enforcement particularly, *when not inconvenient* to members of the police force, Members of Parliament or indeed, individuals and organisations at all levels of society, is highlighted by regular press columnist, Peter Espeut,

> This [non-disclosure to the public of the names of party donors] is similar to anti-corruption legislation where each MP is required to declare their personal assets in secret to an entity set up by Parliament, so that an unknown watchdog can compare their assets over time to detect any unusual increase in wealth which might be due to corruption. The fact is that no one has ever been prosecuted under this ineffective legislation".[618] [There has been finger pointing by the then JLP Prime Minister aimed at delinquent Opposition MP's, as a negative counter-attack for the then PNP Opposition's declared preference for full public disclosure of party donations, as against the JLP's favoured partial disclosure position].[619]

---

618 Peter Espeut, "Shame, PSOJ", *The Gleaner*, Fri. June 25, 2010, p. A9. Espeut continues: "The only information made public is whether a parliamentarian has made a declaration or not. I do not believe any serious effort is made to cross-check whether the secret declarations are correct or whether the assets of family members of public officials have made any sudden, unexplained jump". Non-enforcement, in this case, is not difficult to explain, if not excused Jacqueline Samuels-Brown puts it, "It is not easy to make decisions fairly and dispassionately when self-interest is involved", Letter of the Day, 'Electoral Commission has produced a mouse', supra. In an evenly-matched two-party context, as in Jamaica, "the shoe can be on the other foot", after any election: hence, interest here is joint. Espeut should know that regulations enacted by Parliamentarians to govern the behaviour/ activities of politicians are not likely to be vigorously enforced, in a cultural context with a pronounced feature of non-compliance and non-enforcement. Perhaps this might have urged "The Gavel", The Gleaner's Parliamentary reporter to call for the removal of the four politically nominated persons (two by the Prime Minister and two by the Leader of the Opposition) from the Electoral Commission, arguing that "We do not share [MP] Warmington's view that Parliament should be the body that determines how the ECJ functions ... We believe the current set-up serves only to reinforce the two-party [JLP/PNP] system and could also undermine the stated objectives of the ECJ", The Gleaner, June 13, 2011, p.B12. This is a view directly opposed to that of Jean Lowrie-Chin (who has served on the Commission since 1995) who extolls the substantial benefits derived from the presence of the political appointees, in that, "without the knowledgeable and vigorous participation of politicians we would not have had such a thorough and effective reformation (*sic*) of the Representation of the People Act. The meticulous attention to detail ... has given Jamaican an electoral system that is a model for the world." Peter Espeut goes even further than "The Gavel" and questions the independence of the "so-called independent members" saying that "their names have been agreed upon by both parties, not that they necessarily have any thoughts independent of the political parties ... [and] should be ashamed to put their names to such useless recommendations ..." *in The Gleaner* Fri., July 30, 2010, p. A9. Silburn Clarke, in a full-page ad in *The Gleaner* of Oct. 3, 2010, p. F.14 wants an expanded ECJ to include "more civil society representation". Notably in the composition of the Commission is the absence of anyone from academia, in particular the Department of Government of the University of the West Indies.

619 See "Golding tackles PNP on party financing issues", the *Jamaica Observer*, Mon. Nov. 20, 2010, p. 4.

Quite apart from the question of enforcement, there is, of course, the matter of implementation of proposals in the first place.

Stringent laws are only as effective as a means of behaviour change and thereby social control, to the extent of the legal system's administrative, investigation and enforcement capability. Without normative cultural traditions of self-discipline, and compliance impulses in relation to legal rules and regulations, *per se*, the more ambitious the new electoral regime, in terms of the degree of divergence from the traditional, the more problematic one would expect implementation and enforcement to prove.

This situation can only be made more challenging by the scheme's complexity and sophistication, which seeking to close all the conceivable loopholes would inevitably entail. This is perhaps the reason causing a self-styled 'realist' to conclude that, "The funding of political parties is being proposed by some well-known idealists who have both feet planted in mid-air".[620]

A heavy-handed/club-fisted approach to the issue of anonymous donations is reflected in the ECJ's unqualified statement that "sanctions will be enforced for donations from anonymous sources"[621], yet no prohibition beyond a *maximum*, nor any consequential limit-circumventing strategy regulations are contemplated. This is despite the fact that the JLP argued for this in its written proposals in 2005, as did the PNP, although without any allowable maximum being suggested.[622]

Nassmacher's comment is not irrelevant at this juncture, that, "In short, where disrespect for law and institutions are the prevailing attitudes, enforcing a party finance regime is almost impossible".[623]

Even in respect of the very Constitution itself, the island's legislative implementation record is far from impressive. Horace Levy reminds us, for example, that,

---

620 Glen Tucker 'An audit that tells little', supra.

621 'Points of Agreement', Conference on Campaign Financing, ECJ, July 10, 2006, p.3. Under the UK regulations, anonymous contributions of less than £200 are allowed.

622 Jamaica Labour Party, "Proposals for Regulating the Financing of Political Parties and Election Campaigns", *Mimeo*, 2005, p.5; PNP Policy Commission Document on, 'Regulation of Political Parties and Finance' [*sic*] in Jamaica,' 2005, p.3.

623 Nassmacher, Karl-Heinz (2003) 'Monitoring Control and Enforcement of Political Finance Regulation' in IDEA Handbook on Funding of Parties and Election Campaigns.

The 1974-75 throne speech in Parliament promising comprehensive reform of the 1962 [Constitution] document was followed by bipartisan discussions in the 1980's and two Parliamentary Commissions in the early 1990's. Out of these came a Charter of Rights which took Parliament 17 years to finally ratify in March 2011 ... It matters little that Parliament meets weekly only one afternoon into the evening, or that local government elections are postponed three times in three and a half years.[624]

Political party and campaign financing deliberations, we are reminded by Professor Trevor Munroe, commenced in *2002* when, as a then PNP government Senator, he moved a resolution on the matter.[625]

The ECJ has missed deadlines for the submission of its recommendations. Despite the closeness of the general elections, held in December of 2010, and the reportedly unhealthy state of the parties' finances, Part 2 of the Commission's Report dealing with Campaign Financing had not yet been made public at the time of writing of the first draft in April of that very year.

SANCTIONS

On the question of sanctions, there seems to be limited regard for culpability in keeping with the fundamental requirement of the criminal justice system. The falsity of information provided, for example, could be entirely unintentional, being due to inadvertence, mistaken belief or error of fact. No doubt the likely response will be that the ECJ must be trusted to act sensibly, according to the merits of each situation, and to exercise discretion as dictated by the circumstances. However, it is precisely because of the ECJ's portrayal of "our recent history ...", why this is an approach to be avoided.

---

624 Horace Levy, "A failure of democracy: the hijacking of a country", supra.

625 See "Munroe urges action on talked-to-death legislation", *The Gleaner*, Tue. June 22, 2010. p. A2; In the PNPs submission to the ECJ outlining views on reform in 2005, as the governing party, then, it anticipated passage of the regulatory law by 2005/2006, 'PNP Policy Commission Document on Regulation of Political Party and Finance in Jamaica'.

The Report, after six years' preparation, allows no room for the discretionary, *non-penalizing*, treatment of infringements.[626] Such a situation represents nothing less than a "field day" for lawyers, a plentiful supply of which is enjoyed by both major parties. Additionally, a broad scope for partisan political 'mischief-making' and finger pointing is thereby provided, a feature of the island's politics definitely in no need of further promotion.

When we look at the enforcement provisions of the ECJ's proposals, one finds that to "knowingly accept or use funds tainted by illegality or to improperly use funds legally received",[627] will result in the candidate or party facing legal liability of some kind. Officers of the party will not be liable, even if they are the actual recipients of the funds, it seems, contrary to the position with respect to liability for financial reporting breaches.

After investigation by the Political Party Finance Disclosure Committee, the Chairman of the ECJ may take, "… such action as is permitted by this law", or report the matter to the DPP together with its findings, "… for further investigations to be undertaken in the matter: if it shall appear that a criminal offence may have been committed."[628]

The sanctions mentioned in the report are limited firstly, to specific breaches relating to qualifying conditions for the receipt of state funding, including the provision of, "… false and erroneous information in documents submitted to the Commission."[629] For such offences the prescribed penalty is the suspension of the payment of state funds, if the "… infraction is not corrected within sixty days of being required to do so by the Commission".[630] It is noteworthy that 'knowledge', here, does not seem to be a requisite element, nor is the seriousness of the error of significance.

---

626 With respect to breaches resulting in persons being 'debarred from participating in elections, whether temporarily, for a period of time or permanently, being disqualified from being a candidate, forfeiting contributions or donations, including donations to the National Election Campaign Fund, being suspended as a registered political party, and being struck off the list of registered political parties' in addition to public apologies, return of contributions, fines, Government Senator and QC, K.D. Knight has 'pledged to lead a fight', saying "I think they have gone too far. … That can have a serious effect on how Government operates in democracy": see, 'K. D. Knight knocks ECJ: campaign-funding proposal', *The Gleaner*, Sat. Oct. 36, 2013,p, A3. The ECJ would of course respond that their objective is precisely the preservation and enhancement of 'our democracy', as argued by Knight's past colleague, Senator Wentforth Skeffery, in that '"while it was desirable to do everything to preserve the country's democracy, a national campaign fund may be unpalatable!", *The Gleaner*, Sat. Oct 26, 2013, p. A3.

627 ECJ Report, p. 12

628 Ibid

629 Ibid

630 Ibid

Further in the Report, we are told that for fines imposed, in relation to the "Financial Reporting Requirements", it is the "officers" who shall be personally and jointly liable for fines, "... levied against the party. ..."[631] Personal liability seems to attach here to *officers*, regardless of their *bona fides*, the exercise of reasonable care and diligence and the absence of any fraudulent/wrongful intention.

The Political Party Registration regime, one would expect would confer on the *party* the necessary element of legal personality to attract legal liability, as is in fact the case in the proposals where the improper acceptance and/or use of funds is engaged in.

While we are sure that there needs to be no fear that any punitive aspect of the legislation will have retroactive effect, many prospective, if not present, office holders may well be quite wary of retaining or seeking those voluntary party posts. Company directors tend to be paid, which is a difference of some significance. And 'best practice' does suggest that political parties do need to recruit, train and engage in planning for officer succession. Prolonged potential liability uncertainty is most definitely not facilitative of such an exercise.

The very cautious, hedging language of the "offence" paragraph readily discloses the temerity with which the issue of sanctions has been approached. But although the British legal regulatory regime had been abandoned as a model, "because it was found to be a bad fit for Jamaica",[632] did their experience of a long, tortuous, multi-layered course of detailed investigations, without charges being laid, in relation to several allegations of fundraising impropriety,[633] explain the less-than-robust ECJ sanctions proposals?

One final direct comment on the ECJ Report is warranted. It is a *Minister of Government* who is required to approve any regulations made,

> for the better carrying out of these provisions [everything in the Report] and, *in particular*, but without prejudice to the generality of the foregoing, for establishing procedures and *prescribing fines* and *other sanctions* for a

---

631 Ibid, p. 11

632 Janet Morrison, head of the PSOJ's Justice Reform Committee, speaking at the Gleaner Editor's Forum, reported in *The Gleaner*, Tue. June 22, 2010, p. A2. She continued, quite significantly, "I think even the September deadline ... is not enough time for us to put together legislation *that would suit everyone* and meet all the *urgent* issues we are here discussing" [Italics added].

633 See Appendix I.

breach of any of the provisions set out herein or for prescribing anything required or permitted by these provisions to be prescribed.[634]

This being the case, can one expect the reform effort to be sufficiently robust to withstand the attrition of self-interest, whoever the Minister happens to be, from time to time?[635] There is, as far as we know, no country precedent which suggests an affirmative answer.

The whole notion of independence, autonomy, freedom from political interference/ influence, together with any possible substantive benefit to be derived from clothing the ECJ with Constitutional status and authority, is thereby substantially negated.

Despite this, if not because of it, it is even more critically important that the Commission seeks to use the powers given to it to ensure compliance without seeming to be an 'unwitting political tool' by changing the nature of the political process, unless absolutely unavoidable, by party de-registration or the voiding of an election, for example. As we are reminded, the ECJ functions within environmental constraints partly forged by,

> the existence of a relatively open, partial rank order and the accompanying disintegration of a self-legitimating consensus increases the difficulty of its rule-making function. Acting on the mandate from the state, which is a supposedly neutral overseer of social conflict [a role some will find quite objectionable], it is forever caught up in antagonism of private interests [not necessarily patently material] and made the tool of one faction or the other.[636]

---

634 ECJ Report, p. 12

635 If the position of the Chairman of the Integrity Commission is anything to go by, the prospects are not favourable, see The Gleaner, Wed. Dec. 18, 2013, 'Integrity Chairman calls for amendment to Act'. In China, an official known for expensive watches, so much so that he became known as 'Mr. Watch' was in August 2013 sentenced to fourteen years imprisonment for graft "… a year after he became a symbol of a callous and corrupt bureaucracy when Chinese internet users circulated photographs suggesting that he had been living beyond his means". Apart from being accused of taking bribes, he was also charged with "processing assets of unclear origin": The New York Times, Friday September 6, 2013, p. A10. The Jamaica Observer, Mon. Sept. 23, 2013, p. 28, also reported the case of Bo Xilra, one of China's, reportedly most up-and-coming politicians. This is perhaps a current example of what, in China, is considered 'tough sanctions', 'harsh punishment' 'strict enforcement of laws with teeth'. He was deprived of political rights for life and all his personal assets were confiscated after conviction for corruption bribery, embezzlement, and abuse of power. It seemed that Bo's conspicuously luxurious lifestyle, which included the gift of a French Villa, led to his downfall, as this did not go unnoticed by the public.

636 J. W. Harris, op. cit., p. 153. See also Professor Archibald McDonald, 'Governments for the few', supra, 'Damn dictatorship on campaign financing', Ronald Mason, supra, 'Behind the veil of that UNCONSCIONABLE ECJ CAMPAIGN-FINANCING proposal, "The Gavel", supra. 'Transparency, not more secrecy', Peter Espeut, supra; 'Shame, PSOJ', Peter Espeut, supra; 'Expect resistance to anti-corruption measures, says Munroe' Luke Douglas, the Jamaica Observer, Wed. June 1, 2011, p.3.

For what it is worth, the British Electoral Commission does at least set out its enforcement goals, explicitly, as follows to:[637]

a) ensure the transparency and integrity of party and election finance that voters expect.

b) eliminate any benefit that those we regulate may obtain by failing to comply with the law.

c) bring those failing to meet their regulatory obligations into compliance; and

d) deter non-compliance.

This is within a context with a predisposition to seek to gain compliance by providing *advice* and *guidance*, with emphasis on rule clarity and impartial application.

If 'the proof of the pudding is in the eating', then the prospects of effective ECJ oversight and monitoring of the parties' finances is rather bleak. The Auditor General's Office was not complimentary in its report on the ECJ compliance with its own reporting obligations under S. 16 of the *Electoral Commission (Interim) Act*. One major daily newspaper reported that, "The auditor general had rapped the electoral body last year [2012] for not submitting audited financial reports to *Parliament from its inception in 2006*". As a result of the fact that the ECJ "... ignored a directive of the Ministry of Finance ... [the press report informed] ..." this resulted in an excess salary payment of $4.66 million. ..."[638]

With no intention to antagonize the proponents of abolition, those who clamour for stiffer/harsher penalties for defaulting public figures might wish to consider the imposition by the Chinese judiciary of the *death penalty* on a former vice-mayor for corruption, "... involving bribery, embezzlement and abuse of power".[639]

---

637 'Party Funding', The (UK) Electoral Commission's submission to the Committee on Standards in Public Life, Oct, 2010, p. 39. In similar fashion to the ECJ's recommendations, the British arrangement mandates a monitoring function to ensure compliance. The UK Commission is armed with no mechanism to sanction breaches, except "referring suspected criminal offences to the police (the DPP in the case of Jamaica) as *any other interested party can*," (p, 41 of the UK Commission's Report).

638 *The Gleaner*, Tues, Feb 5, 2013, p. A2, 'ECJ moves to set house in order'.

639 *The Gleaner*, Fri. May 13, 2011, p. A4.

CHAPTER 13
OPTION OUTLINES

We now turn to look, selectively, at legislative options in this area of the political life of selected countries, only to the extent not already considered.[640]

EUROPE, GENERALLY

In Europe, van Biezen has noted what she calls, "… the exceptional relevance of the state in party finance", to the extent that it shapes, if not determines, not only how parties organize but, "… has a bearing on the normative connotations associated with the place of political parties in modern democracy". The increasingly prominent role of the state in the funding of parties, a process to be followed in Jamaica if the ECJ's proposals are accepted and implemented,[641] should, according to van Biezen,

> be understood in the context of, and has been legitimized by, an ideational transformation by which parties have gradually come to be seen as necessary and desirable institutions for democracy. Moreover, the direct involvement of the state in internal party affairs [as would be the case in Jamaica under the ECJ's registration and state funding qualification requirements] has contributed to a transformation of parties from the traditionally voluntary private associations towards parties as public utilities.[642]

---

640 See, for example, partial references to other countries' approaches at pp. 157, 165 – 169.

641 At least two Senators have, more recently, joined the MP who has consistently opposed state funding. See 'K.D. Knight Knocks ECJ's campaign – funding proposal', *The Gleaner*, Sat. Oct. 26, 2013, p.A3. Senator Wentworth Skeffery in the same report, while in support of state funding as "it was desirable to do everything to preserve the country's democracy, a national campaign fund may be unpalatable ", as, "we will have to have the correct answers to sell to the people of Jamaica". If state funding is promised largely on the basis of 'big money influencing the outcome of elections, Senator Lambert Brown would, on that premise alone, be against. According to him, "This view belittles the wisdom and prudence of our people, of the voters, of the choices they have made over and over, where incompetent parties and Ministers with access to comparatively more resources have lost elections time and again". In Senator Brown's view, the focus of the ECJ should be to ensure that the spending limits and other provisions of the Representation of the People's Act are adhered to: The Gleaner, Sat. Nov. 2, 2013 pp. A1, 3., Government Senator says there's no evidence for Big-Money fears'. See, however, with respect to the JLP's leadership election, 'Big money seeking to influence JLP election – Derrick Smith', *The Gleaner*, Sept. 22, 2013, p. A3.

642 van Biezen, Ingrid, "Political Parties as Public Utilities", in Party Politics, *Sage Publications*, Vol.10 No.6, (2004), p. 701.

The expenditure of taxpayers' money is usually accompanied by calls for "monitoring", "control", and "accountability".[643] The *quid pro quo* is therefore apparent: state subsidy requires and involves state regulation.

Historically, commercial enterprises and those involved in them as shareholders, were invested with legal personality and clothed with the protection of limited liability by direct state legislative action.

At the political level, as against the industrial and commercial, it seemed, however, that "... the legal codification of parties would develop only long after parties first emerged as political actors,"[644] compared to the joint-stock/limited liability company. Noticeably, whereas one of the planks of the electoral reform platform is to safeguard the public's interest, which includes prosecution fines, bans and possible imprisonment, in the interest of democratic governance, little has been done to effectively protect that interest in relation to the operations of commercial/industrial enterprises—so-called consumer *protection* legislation/institutions being virtually 'paper tigers'.

In the Jamaican context, it is safe to say that, "the juridification of parties" will only occur in conjunction with the availability and distribution of significant levels of state funding.[645]

The tendency to informal relations within a traditionalistic culture can be expected to place not inconsiderable hurdles on the path to universalistic electoral jurisprudential development. The 'peculiarity' of judicial reasoning on occasions, in case law, and which may become increasingly apparent as operational experience with reform recommendations accumulate, will also pose conceptual challenges: the efficacy of law only becomes revealed

---

643 As most recently reported, before state funds are disbursed to a candidate or party, in addition to satisfying the ECJ's criteria, compliance with ROPA's and certification by the Political Ombudsman that there was no existing breach of the Political Code of Conduct, will be required: See 'Senate approves campaign financing recommendations', *The Gleaner*, Nov. 3, 2013, p.30. The enforcement, as currently proposed, will be the responsibility of non-politically appointed Commissioners together with the Director of Elections.

644 Van Biezen, supra, p, 712.

645 As in Britain, Jamaican parties were socialized into an adversarial political culture (both main parties having emerged with umbilical links to the two main rival trade unions. For the foreseeable future it is most unlikely that the perception and reality of electoral vulnerability will be mitigated by any consensual yearnings evolving into a mutually beneficial accommodation leading to a cartelization approach on the state funding issue.
One does not expect such a catalyst to come from the trend of professionalization among "Full time politicians planning a long-term career [who] come to regard their political opponents as fellow professionals, who are driven by the same desire for job security", [Katz and Mair (1995) supra, p,23] Minister of Justice, Mark Golding, despite the very prolonged period of discussion of electoral reform, is reported as saying that there is no immediacy in terms of implementing the (ECJ) recommendations, as they will be subject to Government's ability to finance the proposed campaign finance system'; The *Jamaica Observer*, Nov. 3, 2013, p.20

on authoritative interpretation and enforcement.[646] Statutory interpretation can, in an area as sensitive as this, clearly pose considerable adjudicatory challenges.

Within the context of what the ECJ calls 'a growing democracy', one might not have expected its proposals to be in accord with, "... the overall picture that emerges ... of party finance legislation being much more rigorous, less permissive and less liberal [as] in the newer democracies [of eastern Europe] than in the long established ones."[647]

One might also have expected that the young democracy label would have precluded premature absolutisation of prescriptions, given a political system still at the incipient stage of its evolutionary development.

We say this, despite the fact that, comparatively, van Biezen and Kopecky include Jamaica in their list of 'Established democracies', in their article, *"Exploring the possibility of regional variation in the types of party-state linkages"*, on the basis of the following criteria:

(a) Availability of public funding for parties

(b) System of regulation of party finances

(c) Constitutional recognition of political parties

(d) Corruption of political parties.

Jamaica, then, 2007, had a showing of (a) No (b) No (c) No and (d) - , with a mean score of 3.7, where N = 17 of a total of twenty-two countries. The authors concluded that, "... the combination 'no state subventions' and 'no regulation of party finances' occurs most often in Africa, such as in the cases of Botswana, Mauritius and Senegal (three such cases also exist among the established democracies, namely, India, Jamaica and Switzerland)".[648] At least

---

646 An example of an enforcement culture based on the presentation of evidence in situations of corruption which would escape the ECJ 'net' and may not, to the average Jamaican, be regarded as serious, is provided by 'Former United States Governor, Bob McDonnell and his wife who were indicted for corruption: The Gleaner's, January 23, 2014, p. C6, report refers to donation of a private jet, a dress for the mayoral inauguration, and "allegedly the start of a four-year pattern of ... squeezing gifts and loans out of a benefactor who expected them to promote his company's products in return". In 'Integrity chairman calls for amendment of act', [*Integrity in Public Life Act* of Trinidad and Tobago] the reason given was that the amendment of the legislation would allow it [the Commission] to act rather than be almost entirely dependent upon the cooperation of those being investigated", *The Gleaner*, Wed. Dec. 18, 2013, p. D11.

647 van Biezen 2004 supra,, p. 715

648 Van Biezen, Ingrid and Kopecky, Peter, 'The State and Parties, Public Funding, Public Regulation and Rent-seeking in Contemporary Democracies' in Party Politics, *Sage Publications*, Vol. 13., No. 2, (2007), p.242.

in the case of Jamaica that seems to be about to change with respect to (a), (b) and (c). Contemplated reform might be premised on the basis that this will guarantee a negative with respect to (d).

GERMANY

Despite where Germany may rank in terms of the maturity of their system of governance, given its 'recent' political experience, we take the view that German arrangements might have been worth greater attention by the ECJ. At the national level, membership fees and dues still constitute 20 – 25% of the two main parties' budget. Even more significantly, at the regional and local party levels, state subsidies are in relation to membership fees paid, since 1994. Poguntke sums up the situation as being one in which, "… German parties have moved closer to the sphere of the state but, like amphibians, however, not lost their ability to 'swim in society'".[649]

As against the complexity of the Canadian funding regime, which has resulted in several lengthy judicial reviews and analyses at the highest level, the German legal provisions on public financing are notable for their simplicity.

For cultural and compliance facilitating reasons alone, this should commend itself for adoption with appropriate adaptation. There, the focus is almost entirely on the parties,[650] in contrast to the Jamaican position where existing legislative campaign expenditure regulations under *ROPA* apply only to candidates; political parties are yet to be constitutionally recognised, although the Commission now, however, proposes that they be accorded legal status and their operations directly monitored.

The question calling for attention in Germany, has often been, it is said, "… the *fair* [Italics added] distribution of government funds to the parties and on the tax treatment[651] of private donations, thus causing frequent changes

---

649 Poguntke, Thomas, 'Parties in a Legalistic Culture: the case of Germany', in Katz and Mair (eds), How Parties Organize, Change and Adapt in Western Democracies, *Sage*, (London, 1995), pp 185-215.

650 The German Basic Law (Constitution) guarantees the role of parties in the political process: "Political parties shall participate in the formation of the political will of the people". No doubt against the background of the Hitlerite experience, it is further provided in Article 21 paragraph 1, that "Their internal organisation must conform to democratic principles. They must publicly account for their assets and for the sources of their funds".

651 The ECJ proposes, at page 11 of its Report, that "all contributions to political parties shall be tax deductible". This incentive is obviously diluted by any final contribution limit imposed. On the other hand, to benefit from the concession necessarily involves some level of exposure.

in legislation".[652] This is largely because parties in Germany receive funds "... in proportion to the latest election results *plus* [Italics added] a partial matching of €0.38 per donated Euro for private contributions up to €3,300".[653] It is obvious that since electoral support can, and does occasionally, change radically before elections, aspects of this formula certainly do not represent an ideal 'one-size-fits-all' solution. One-term governments in multi-party parliamentary systems reveal the dynamic nature of the practise of politics. The question therefore becomes, can and should state funding arrangements take this aspect of reality into account?

As with the ECJ's proposals, German parties are required to submit annual financial statements to the Diet [Parliament] which need to disclose only contributions of *more than* €10,000 per year. Tax credit of €825 (€1650 for joint returns) may be claimed, or private individuals may choose to deduct fifty per cent of their donations, limited to €3,000, from taxable income. However, the most striking feature of the regime, given the prevailing orthodoxy, is that "... there are no limits on private or corporate contributions" and "there are no limits on campaign spending."[654]

BRITAIN

Under the British system, state-provided in-kind benefits to parties and their representatives have included free mailing, free broadcast time at elections, as well as funds for representational activity and policy development, for those parties *represented in Parliament*.

Notably, despite its long parliamentary history, the parties received statutory recognition and regulation only in 1998 under the *Registration of Political Parties Act* and the *Political Parties Elections and Referendum Act of 2000*. A perusal of those enactments will disclose that, despite a claim to

---

652 Not only did the ECJ's disappointingly flimsy Report have a six year gestation period, but despite the fact that it claims that the second Report on 'Campaign Financing' will only require amendment to existing legislation, (*The Representation of the People Act*), that is yet to be submitted to Parliament, (ECJ Report, p2); although for the second Report, "a firm timetable to complete the process" in THREE months was announced by the ECJ's Chairman as reported in *The Gleaner*, Thu. Sept 2, 2010, p A4, that was some nine months ago. If the two major parties disagree on essential elements, it could conceivably be overtaken by the next general election. The prospect of "frequent changes in legislation" being made, as experience with the law's administration warrants, is decidedly dim in Jamaica's case.

653 Law Library of Congress, 'Campaign Finance: Germany', pamphlet, undated, p.1

654 Ibid, p.5

the contrary, the basic elements of that regime are very much reflected in the ECJ's proposals.

In a comprehensive review of the British model, Hayden Phillips[655] incorporates the design of different scenarios, together comprising an interesting and useful mix of possibilities, from which to choose. The following broad headings deserve mention here:

1. Further limits on *spending* by candidate and parties, as is now done for campaigning,[656] so as to *close the gap* between income and expenditure. This might encourage more local campaigning and therefore greater voter engagement in their communities, with less emphasis on catering to the expensive 'high-tech' communication expectations which is now a feature of modern campaigning.

2. Closing disguised "third party" donation loopholes, bearing in mind the cost of compliance and monitoring of elaborate regulations.

3. Public funding might be provided to (a) encourage voter turnout by linking funds to votes received and (b) stimulating increased party membership by linking some part of funding to verified party membership dues collected ("matched funding").

4. Link provided state funds to defined party political activities: training, policy research, public education programs. This might promote competition, based more on policy expertise and competence, and less on the glitz/communications skill of a campaign public relations consultant.

---

655 Hayden Phillips, supra, scenarios presented are: (1) Minimal Change: is there a need for change; (2) Donations controlled through increased transparency and public scrutiny with no cap on donations; (3) Reduce the amount parties can spend on campaigning at elections; (4) Cap on donations in addition to greater transparency and greater expenditure control; (5) Greater levels of public funding through a general subsidy, or publicly funded incentives to increase donations in addition to a cap on donations, increased transparency and greater expenditure control. A subsidy might take any of the following forms, (a) general (b) targeted or (c) voter – led incentive scheme.
The merit of Phillips' review is that all options proposed have their perceived advantages and disadvantages comprehensively considered and attached, calling clearly for compromise in the choice of any scheme or mix of schemes; See also, "Transparency, The current system [UK] the legal framework", in 'Party funding', the Electoral Commission's submission to the Committee on Standards in Public Life', Oct. 2010, pp. 6 – 15. In Hayden Phillips' view, people ought to be allowed to spend their money as they choose and one should avoid using a financial mechanism to change the behaviour of political parties, which is also more in keeping with the traditional concept of them as voluntary organisations.

656 Note that spending only counts against the national spending limits if it is incurred to "promote electoral success" and relates to the cost of party broadcasts, advertising, leaflets to voters, cost of manifestos and policy documents, market research, media events, transportation and the cost of rallies and public meetings as set out in the Political Party Election and Referendums Act.

5. Up to 2006, with 50 – 80% of the three main parties' income represented by donations, there was still no cap in place for corporate or private funds, although amounts and the identity of donors had to be reported to the Electoral Commission.

6. Loans, since the *Electoral Administration Act of 2006*, are now covered by the same transparency regulations as donations (a loophole that would clearly have been provided by the initial omission of any treatment of loans in the ECJ's Report available for perusal at the time of writing of the first draft).

7. To be effective, spending limits [especially, as in Jamaica, where there is no fixed election date] must apply all the time and not just during an 'election period', as, otherwise, the Prime Minister's party would have a considerable strategic advantage, at least theoretically.

8. Regulations specifically provide the sanction of 'forfeiture' of funds tainted in any way. [In contrast the ECJ's recommendation, not without stout objection, is that it may forfeit funds in *addition* to a Court's penalty for certain breaches. Possible action by the DPP scarcely falls into the category of high drama and sometimes it is the effect on the national psyche which is the decisive measure of the efficacy of corrective action. One would hope that with respect to this issue of forfeiture and other sanctions, the ECJ is not intimidated by its surrogate status vis-à-vis Parliament: the ECJ is to be dependent on Parliament for funding for its own operations, as well as the necessary approval of its recommendations, including penalties for breaches and enforcement administration oversight.][657]

In *R v City of Westminster Magistrate's Court*[658] sections 54(1) (a) and 58(2) of the *British Elections and Referendum Act, 2000*, were considered. Under section 54(1) (a) donations to political parties over a specified amount may come from a donor on the electoral roll, whereas under s.58, a breach can lead to an Order by the Magistrate's Court of forfeiture of an amount

---

657 Public confidence once lost is not easily regained, especially in an area of national life so prone to suspicion and rumour where 'facts', viewed from the vantage point of 'consequence', often rest solely on a foundation of belief or perception. The British experience has been that, despite vigilance under the provisions of the *Political Parties Elections and Referendum Act*, to ensure that parties only retain permissible donations as defined, ". . .tracker survey shows a recent decline in the proportion of the public confident that the authorities would take appropriate action if someone was caught breaking party finance rules, from 41% at the end of 2008 to 31% in 2009: The [UK] Electoral Commission supra, p.18

658 [2010] 1 All ER 1167

equal to the donation. It was held that once it is shown that a donation had been accepted from an impermissible donor and had not been returned, a magistrates' court should, if asked to do so, in almost every case exercise its power under s.58(2) by ordering forfeiture. The donor involved in this case had been entitled to registration, but had not been so registered. The court determined that the test of acceptability of a donation, as laid down by Parliament, was whether the donor was registered in an electoral register and not whether they could be.

AUSTRALIA

Cass and Burrowes' review of the legislative evolution of the Australian regulatory framework provides useful insights for the reform project in Jamaica. This is so, despite their starting point where it is stated that, "… as a subset of a discussion about public trust and accountability, it has a long pedigree in Australia [although] … legal literature on campaign finance is relatively sparse".[659]

In sum, the authors find that, "The *complex relationship* between providing public support for elections, encouraging private *participation* in public political activity, regulating that activity and public controls on political party conduct is a constant theme of the current regulatory context."[660]

By a process of distillation, the following can be said to be the noteworthy features of this Commonwealth member's electoral system: control of advertising content and expense, and the role of the media; transparency,[661] with the expectation that parties will be discouraged from providing favours to donors and so enhance the 'legitimacy of legislative proposals' by identifying 'the avenues of influence'—this is despite the conclusion that empirical research on whether campaign donations influence policy decisions is equivocal, "… and is really unanswerable,"[662] given the range of

---

659 Deborah Z, Cass and Sonia Burrows, Commonwealth [of Australia] Regulation of Campaign Finance – Public Funding, Disclosure and Expenditure Limits, *Sydney Law Review*, Vol. 22, pp. 476 – 526,

660 Ibid, p. 478

661 This is not to say that there was party unanimity on the issue. To the Liberal Party, then, disclosure constituted a grave infringement of civil liberties, a violation of privacy and posed a threat of victimization, particularly by certain trade unions. It is to be noted that disclosure requirements do not extend to donations for party maintenance or administrative expenses, so long as such funds were not used for election purposes, a categorization that is decidedly problematic, so, "This loophole continues to the present day".

662 Cass and Burrows, supra, p. 479

variables which influence political decision-making (further complicated by the fact that some private sources of funding donate to more than one party); preoccupation with the issue of the control of third party political expenditure such as "laundering" through devices like trusts and foundations, formerly not subject to legislative reporting requirements by way of returns to the Electoral Commission; the history of legislative regulation has proved to be one in which, "As soon as one loophole is closed, another will open"; spending limits were repealed in 1980 after subsisting for some eighty years, on the basis of unconstitutionality, in that limits, by a somewhat similar argument as in *Buckley v. Valeo*[663], in the Supreme Court of the United States, amounted to unreasonable restraint on freedom of communication, on the proportionality principle of statutory interpretation; public funding was introduced by way of amendments to the *Commonwealth Electoral Legislation Amendment Act*, only in 1983; indirect state subsidy of political activity exists by virtue of the *compulsory voting* [Italics added] legal provision, as well as tax-deductibility of candidate's election expenses and the costs for provision of staff, telephone service, offices, postage and research; despite such direct and indirect financial support it is reported that this, "... has not diminished political participants' enthusiasm for seeking donations from large or specialized interest groups ... Nor ... had it led to a much greater degree of transparency generally in the system".[664]

Importantly, it was the Australian Commission that proposed penalties for breaches in respect of which, to knowingly submit false returns could attract monetary penalties (up to a fine of A$10,000.00); annual *subscriptions*, as in the Jamaican case, is unregulated, which seems to clearly provide a loophole through which large contributions can flow, disguised as dues; candidates' contributions to their own campaigns were not disclosable, a feature which is likely to find favour with Jamaican politicians; expenditure disclosure, without any limits in place, reflects the preference of a limited number of Jamaican press correspondents; with the introduction of a ban on paid political advertising, struck down as unconstitutional by the High Court, in

---

663   (1976) 424 US Supreme Court; Contra, Libman v. A.G for Quebec (Canada); See also Nationwide News Pty Ltd. v. Wills (1992) 177 CLR 1. For Australian funding and disclosure regulations, see Denny Meadows, "Open election funding or hide and seek?", (1988) Legal Services Bulletin, 13(2)65

664   Cass and Burrows , supra, p. 493

the *Australian Capital Television* case,[665] of necessity, came the introduction of free promotional time to be allocated along the lines of the United Kingdom's model, conditional on the parties' disclosure of donation income and expenditures; in 1992, under the *Commonwealth Electoral Amendment Act*, parties and their state branches were obliged to submit annual returns of all receipts, payments and debts, required later to be audited, in place of returns only for election donations and expenditure, later, in 1997, simplified to require the listing of *total* amounts of expenditure only, rather than every transaction, so as "to alleviate the worst of the bureaucratic requirements associated with annual returns". [The ECJ proposals (Report, p. 11) require the reporting of "all receipts and expenditures" with no threshold]; annual reporting by *donors* was introduced to facilitate cross-checking [Under the ECJ's proposed regime (p,11) donors are required to report contributions over (J)$100,000.00, with the matter of 'associated entities' dealt with as under the *Companies Act* and the *Banking Act* definitions]; entities associated with the political parties also became subject to disclosure regulations; interestingly, it was considered necessary to increase public funding, justified, on the ground that since donor disclosure had been introduced, as some clamour for in Jamaica, donors had become more reluctant to contribute; the experience was that compliance with new regulatory initiatives was "variable", due, instructively, to a lack of preparation and planning for disclosure and the inadequacy of accounting systems; loans, unsecured or at less than market rates of interest, which, conceivably, might be converted into "investments" or "gifts", remain an area of concern; generally speaking, the system is 'haunted and inspired' by the persistent fear of, "... heading down the American road for funding" involving, as it does, "... the exclusivity of the political race in the United States".[666]

The Australian scheme outlined above has provoked mixed responses: the system has been regarded by some as "money gathering exercised through public funding"; funding, it has been argued, should, as in the Canadian case, be by way of reimbursement, so as to "prevent" profiteering out of federal elections; there should, some urge, be a cap on public funding, with a restriction on the amount expendable on campaigns; and the conclusion

---

665 Australian Capital Television Pty v Commonwealth (1992) 177 CLR 106
666 Cass and Burrows, supra, p. 523

has been reached that "… all that has happened is a blowout in both public (doubled since 1993) and private funding as parties engage in an increasingly expensive bidding war at elections."[667] The cumulative effect, then, has not resulted in decreasing the parties' heavy reliance on private sources of financing, which was the primary objective of the provision of state funding.

The explanation may be but little and rarely acknowledged: the financing of politics necessarily involves compounding ideals with imperatives of expediency, power and self-interest. That being the case, no system will be immune from corrupting influences. And judicial determination of the degree and effect of that influence is not always predictable.

United States of America

The experience of the United States with donation caps, and the consequences for "influence peddling", has been documented by Drazen, Limão and Stratman who have found that, in what they call their 'bargaining model',

> the effect of a cap that is not too stringent on the amount a lobby can contribute *improves* [Italics added] its bargaining position relative to the politician … increase the payoff from lobbying which will therefore increase the equilibrium number of lobbies where lobby formation is endogenous. Caps may then also *increase* [Italics added] aggregate contributions from lobbies and *increase* [Italics added] politically motivated government spending.[668]

As to the 'debate' whether contributions buy policy favour, a result seemingly taken as given by most commentators in Jamaica, Ansolabehere

667 Carmen Lawrence's speech on "Renewing Democracy: Can Women Make a Difference?" August 17, 2000, quoted in Cass and Burrows p, 526. In conjunction with this, the results of the 2006 MORI public opinion poll found that it was thought that "Capping donations at a level that would limit the influence of wealthy donors over political parties and *ensure* [Italics added] that small, individual donors became more important to the parties", see Party Funding the (UK) Electoral Commission, supra, p.24; the inclusion of the critically important word "ensure" would seem, to taint the project with researcher bias. The inference has to be that the wealthier contributing more would still, on this formulation, have more influence than poorer persons making smaller contributions.

668 Political Contribution, Caps and Lobby Formation: Theory and Evidence, by Allan Drazen, Nuno Limão and Thomas Stratman, *Mimeo*, Oct 22, 2006, abstract This seems to confirm the common concern of Espeut and others in Jamaica, and elsewhere, who see the splitting up of contributions as an easy way of evading such restrictions, especially in enforcement delinquent environments.

et al, in a review of several studies, found little or no impact of PACs[669] contributions on roll-call votes in the United States, although, "... they do suggest that a subset of donors, mainly corporate and industry PACs, behave as if they *expected* favours in return and *may* in fact receive a reasonable rate of return on their contributions".[670]

On the general issue of emphasis on private, as against state funding, Pippen, Bowler and Donovan found confirmation for the hypothesis that a state's make-up (in terms of party representation) and ideology is an important determinant of whether it adopts, and, if it does, the strictness of campaign finance laws.[671] For obvious reasons, it is left-of-centre parties and states at the regional and national levels which tend to more strongly favour public funding. We note that ideological convergence, if not disappearance in confrontational terms, has meant that those traditionally classified as capitalists no longer seem to find it repugnant to substantially support ostensible left-of-centre parties.

For Epstein, with respect to the United States, given state, party and society linkages, the party might best be seen as, "an agency performing a service in which the public has a special interest".[672]

Of direct relevance to our discussion, he suggests, for the reason advanced by Franklin Johnston above, that so important is that interest, that it is, "... sufficient to justify governmental regulatory control, along with the extension of legal privileges but not governmental ownership or management of all the agency's activities".[673]

The manner in which the Supreme Court of the United States has dealt with the notion of privileges in this context may usefully be prefaced

---

669 PAC represents groups which under the American electoral system are not regulated and are used as the medium to contribute by wealthy, often undisclosed 'principals', acting as third party groups or individuals, on behalf of highly partisan political activists, supporting, but not sponsored by a candidate or party. They are the machinery used to escape the regulatory restrictions in the United States. Wealthy individuals and corporations can, without declaring their identity use these third party groups to channel money into political campaigns at different levels. The massive sums at the disposal of these unregulated groups is, of course, also spent on activities such as advertising, and otherwise, detracting from a rival candidate and party.

670 Ansolabehere, Stephen, and de Figueiredo, John M., and Snyder, Jr., James M., 'Why is there so Little Money in U. S. Politics?' *Journal of Economic Perspectives*, Volume 17, Number 1, (Winter 2003), p. 126.

671 Pippen Johnson, Bowler Shawn, and Donovan Todd, 'Election Reform and Direct Democracy: The case of Campaign Finance Regulation in the American States', *American Politics Research*, 30: 559-82.

672 Epstein, Leon: *Political Parties in the American Mould*, University of Wisconsin Press, (Wisconin,1986), p. 157

673 Ibid.

---

with remarks on the quite controversial, relatively recent decision in the Supreme Court case of *Citizens United* v *Federal Election Commission*[674] with commentary on limited aspects of *Austin v Michigan Chamber of Commerce.*[675] The furore generated by the former is largely limited to those regarding themselves as "liberals" / "progressives", who tend to be supporters of the Democratic Party of the United States, as against the "conservatives" / "establishment" / "Wall Street crowd", who generally support the Republican Party. This is of significance only from a self-interest political perspective as affected by the composition of the Supreme Court bench.

In essence, the matter to be determined was whether the argument by the Michigan Chamber of Commerce that the restriction in the *Michigan Campaign Finance Act (MCFA)* preventing it from using *general* treasury funds (instead of funds specifically allocated for political purposes) to place a newspaper advertisement in favour of a particular candidate was constitutionally unenforceable. As is usual in these circumstances, the allegation was that the prohibition amounted to a breach of rights enshrined in the First and Fourteenth Amendments.

Rights referable to fundamental law, in this instance the Constitution of the United States, tend to give rise to frequent actions, seeking to protect them from infringement, which end up in the higher courts, as reflected in the number of challenges to electoral law provisions. The same is true of Canada under its *Charter of Rights.*

In the case of Jamaica, proposed electoral law provisions under the auspices of the Electoral Commission are not likely to have the benefit of the culturally / psychologically important sacrosanct cloak of the Constitution, if and when challenges are made to the ECJ's regulatory regime. Perhaps its judges may manage to avoid any allegation of indulgence in perfidious judicial interpretation, however noble the motives: assessing 'rights' in terms of 'money'.

It is, nevertheless from a somewhat similar 'angle of vision' that the motivating force behind the ECJ's reform effort is seen in the most unappealing light – the pervasive assumption of the existence/probability / appearance

---

674 United States Supreme Court 558US No 08 – 205(2010).
675 Austin v Michigan Chamber of Commerce, 494 U.S. 652 (1990).

of corruption associated with financial support of partisan political activity. Instead of focus on negative behaviour, enacted basic national law tends to establish rights. Without compromising the application of logical reasoning, a fault which seems to find occasional accommodation in Court decisions at the highest level, it may be a considerable challenge for Jamaican judges to depart from the thought process of their brothers elsewhere. Should they manage to do so, it would represent a considerable advance in judicial analysis, being not bound by United States legal precedent at any court level.

Such an effort would undoubtedly be aided by a reform rubric guided by expressly stated values and would, arguably, add 'stature' to the details subsumed within them.

Whereas the court at first instance found the restriction in *Austin* to be lawful, the Appeal Court agreed with the Chamber and, accordingly, reversed the decision.

It would seem that the purpose of the *Act* was to facilitate the relatively easy *tracking* of funds used for political purposes, in the interest of transparency. That objective is obviously facilitated by the use of funds specifically earmarked for, placed in and disbursed only from such an account.

The Appeal Court in *Austin v Michigan Chamber of Commerce* found as follows:

> 1. Section 54 (1) does not violate the First Amendment. pp. 657-666. Although 54(1)'s requirements burden the Chamber's exercise of political expression, see *FEC v. Massachusetts Citizens for Life, Inc. (MCFL)*, 479 U.S. 238, 252, they are justified by a compelling state interest: preventing corruption or the appearance of corruption in the political arena by reducing the threat that huge corporate treasuries, which are amassed with the aid of favourable state laws and have little or no correlation to the public's support for the corporation's political ideas, will be used to influence unfairly election outcomes. (pp. 657.660).
>
> 2. Section 54 (1) is sufficiently narrowly tailored to achieve its goal, because it is precisely targeted to eliminate the distortion caused by corporate spending while also allowing corporations to express their political views by making expenditures through *separate segregated* [Italics added] funds.
>
> 3. There is no merit to the Chamber's argument that even if 54(1) is constitutional with respect to for-profit corporations, it cannot be applied

to a non-profit ideological corporation such as itself. The Chamber does not exhibit the crucial features identified in MCFL, supra, that would require the state to exempt it from independent spending burdens as a non-profit corporation more akin to a voluntary political association than a business firm. MCFL's narrow focus on the promotion of political ideas ensured that its resources reflected political support, while the Chamber's more varied by-laws do not.

Also in contrast to *MCFL*, which took no contributions from business corporations, more than three –quarters of the Chamber's members are business corporations, whose political contributions and expenditures can constitutionally be regulated by the State, and who thus could circumvent 54(1)'s restriction by funnelling money through the Chamber's general treasury (pp. 661-665).

4. Section 54(1) is not rendered under inclusive by its failure to regulate the independent expenditures of unincorporated labour unions that also have the capacity to accumulate wealth, because the exclusion does not undermine the State's compelling interest in regulating corporations whose unique form enhances such capacity. Moreover, because members who disagree with a union's political activities can decline to contribute to them without giving up other membership benefits, a union's political funds more accurately reflect members' support for the organisation's political views than does a corporation's general treasury. (pp. 665-666).

5. Similarly, the exemption of media corporations does not render the section unconstitutional. Restrictions on the expenditure of corporations whose resources are devoted to the collection and dissemination of information to the public might discourage news [494 U.S. 652, 654] broadcasters or publishers from serving their crucial societal role of reporting on and publishing editorials about newsworthy events; thus, their exemption from the section's restrictions is justified." (pp. 666-668).

According to the head note in the report of the case, the arguments surrounded the *"Bipartisan Campaign Reform Act of 2002,* as amended. Under the *Act,* federal law prohibits corporations and unions from using their general treasury funds to make *independent expenditures* for speech that is an "electioneering communication" or for speech that expressly advocates the election or defeat of a candidate". An electioneering communication is said to be "any broadcast, cable or satellite communication" that refers to a clearly identified candidate for federal office, and is made within 30 days of a primary election. Corporations and unions may establish a PACs for express advocacy or electioneering communication purposes.

The facts were that when Hillary Clinton ran in the Democratic Party primary elections seeking nomination as candidate for President, the appellant, *Citizens United*, a non-profit corporation released a documentary critical of her. *Citizens United*, on the basis of the 30 day period referred to above, produced television ads to run on TV and cable networks. The action brought was to seek a declaration and injunction, in anticipation of possible civil and criminal litigation, for breach of the prohibition contained in Ch. 441b of the *Bipartisan Campaign Reform Act*. Relief was sought on the grounds that the *Acts'* disclaimer, disclosure and finance reporting requirements were unconstitutional.

Whereas the District Court found, by summary judgment, for the Federal Election Commission, the Supreme Court held that:

> 1. The question whether Ch. 441b applied in the Hillary Clinton case could not be decided on narrower grounds which would not have the effect of "chilling political speech", "speech that is central to the First Amendment's meaning and purpose".

> 2. The Court overruled *Austin v Michigan Chamber of Commerce*, stating, in doing so, that that case "thus provides no basis for allowing the Government to limit corporate *independent* [Italics added] expenditures". And since the First Amendment bars Congress from making any law "abridging freedom of speech", the prohibition was found to be "an outright ban on speech, backed by criminal sanctions", [since "although the PAC created by a corporation can still speak, it is a separate association from the corporation"]. In reply it might be said that the Court of Appeals did provide a basis for the limitation, namely, that "they are justified by a compelling state interest ... influence unfairly election outcome.[676]

> 3. "The Court noted that in addressing challenges to the *Federal Elections Act*, the Court in *Buckley v Valeo* had upheld limits on *direct contributions to candidates*, [Italics added] 18 USC Ch. 609(b), recognising a governmental interest in preventing *quid pro quo* corruption". As will be seen, this is the basis used also to justify the expenditure restriction in *Austin.*

---

676 Court of Appeal at pp. 657, 660.

---

4. The protection of free speech, even from a corporation, was held to be inconsistent with the rationale of the **Austin** decision, which had been to prevent corporations from obtaining "an unfair advantage in the political market place", given "the corrosive and distorting effects of immense aggregations of [corporate] wealth", then recognised in that judgment.

5. The Court then stated in contrast to the thinking in **Austin,** but reflected in **Buckley** that, it "concludes that *independent expenditures* [Italics added] by such third party groups such as **Citizens United,** do *not* [Italics added] give rise to corruption or the appearance of corruption. *That speakers may have influence over or access to elected officials does not mean that those officials are corrupt* [Italics added]. And the appearance of influence[677] or access will *not* [Italics added] cause the electorate to lose faith in this democracy". It is here apparent that the basis of the difference in the approaches of the courts (Appeals in **Austin** and Supreme Court in **Citizens United)** is political rather than legal. Needless to say the influence of contrasting political attitudes by judges will have important legal consequences.

6. In line with the conventional wisdom, in reference to what the Court chose to term, *"Political Speech",* it observed that, "political speech is so ingrained in this country's culture *that speakers find ways around campaign finance laws".* [Italics added]

7. [On the quite centrally relevant Jamaican issue of "disclosure"], it was conceded by the Court that "… challenges would be available if a group could show a *'reasonable probability'* [Italics added] that disclosing its contributors' names would subject them to threats, harassment, or reprisals from either Government official or private parties". In the context of the political culture of the United States, it was held that Citizens United's argument that "disclosure requirements can chill donations by exposing donors to retaliation, was rejected, since it offers no evidence that its

---

677 See Claude Robinson, 'In Politics Perception is reality', for a contrasting view in the *Jamaica Observer,* "The Agenda", Sept. 29, 2013. p.4

members face the type of threats, harassment, or reprisals[678] that might make Ch. 201 unconstitutional".

Arguments advanced by the Court in following *Buckley*, with respect to the unconstitutionality of limits on independent expenditure, are in a very literal sense instructive as to the manner of judicial reasoning. Among the more important propositions, the following have been singled out for mention:

1. (b) Because *Citizen United's* narrower arguments are not sustainable, this Court must, in an exercise of its judicial responsibility, consider §441b's facial validity. Any other course would prolong the substantial, nationwide chilling effect caused by §441b's corporate expenditure ban.

In overruling *Austin, and McConnell v Federal Election Commission* in, and on, a similar respect and ground, the Court continued at,

2. (a) political speech must prevail against laws that would suppress it by design of inadvertence. ... There is no basis for the proposition that, in the political speech context, the Government may impose restrictions on certain disfavoured speakers." It was also the Courts view that, "*Austin* interferes with the open marketplace of ideas protected by the First Amendment. (*New York State Board of Elections v. Lopez Torres*, (552 U.S. 196)). Its censorship is vast in its reach, suppressing the speech of both for-profit and non-profit, both small and large, corporations. (pp. 32-40)".

(b) The *Buckley* Court did not invoke the overbreadth doctrine to suggest that §608e's expenditure ban would have been constitutional had it applied to corporations and unions but not individuals. ... Less than two years after *Buckley*, *Bellotti* [First Nat. bank of Boston v. Bellotti], reaffirmed the principle that the Government lacks the power to restrict political speech based on the speaker's corporate identity, 435 U.S., at 784-785. Thus the law

---

678 The Court's attitude, here is virtually the opposite of what prevails in the Jamaican political culture: see, for example, Claude Robinson, 'Campaign Finance reform and the democratic process', the *Jamaica Observer*, "The Agenda", June 1, 2008, pp.6, 7, where he writes, " ... It must be recognized that in our small society some potential donors may have a well-founded fear of victimization and may want to keep their contributions secret". The ECJ itself, in fact, premised its state-funding stance on a likely fall-off in support from larger donors who prefer anonymity for reasons directly attributable to the nature of the island's politics, hence the 'need' for the state to fill the financing gap. The few exceptions to this line of thought include columnist Devon Dick, who claims that, "The excuse that donors will be discriminated against does not hold water because everybody knows most of the donors and there is no evidence of victimization"; *The Gleaner*, 'ECJ Report', Jan. 24, 2013, p. A7, The solution to any donor identity dilemma for Peter Espeut is simple: "If your members (The Private Sector Organisation of Jamaica) don't want anyone to know to whom they give political donations, then maybe they shouldn't give any", see, 'Shame, PSOJ', *The Gleaner*, Fri. June 25, 2010, p.A9.

stood until *Austin* upheld a corporate independent expenditure restriction, bypassing *Buckley* and *Bellotti* by recognising a new governmental interest in preventing "the corrosive and distorting effects of immense aggregations of [corporate wealth ... that have little or no correlation to the public's support for the corporations political ideas". 494 U.S., at 660, (pp. 25-32).

(4) Because §441b is not limited to corporations or associations created in foreign countries or funded predominantly by foreign shareholders, it would be overbroad even if the Court were to recognise a compelling governmental interests in limiting foreign influence over the nation's political process. (pp. 46-47)."

The ECJ's impermissible donor provisions does take the issue raised here of foreign electoral influence into account. This, to some, was one of the troubling aspects of the 'Trafigura scandal'; also directly connected to this concern is the *British Elections and Referendum Act, 2000,* as considered in *R v City of Westminster Magistrate's Court,* specifically §54(1) and 58(2).

(d) The relevant factors in deciding whether to adhere to *stare decisis,* beyond workability –the precedent's antiquity, the reliance interests at stake, and whether the decision was well reasoned - counsel in favour of abandoning *Austin*, which itself contravened the precedents of *Buckley* and *Bellotti.* As already explained, *Austin* was not well reasoned. It is also undermined by experience since its announcement. ... The Court returns to the principle established in *Buckley* and *Bellotti* that the government may not suppress political speech based on the speaker's corporate identity. No sufficient government interest justifies limits on the political speech of non-profit or for-profit corporations." (pp. 47-50).

In this respect, at least, there is common ground between the highest Courts of Canada and of the United States as to the approach to be adopted on these issues.

The Supreme Court in **Buckley** used the term, "the transformation of contributions into political debate",[679] which it sees occurring when donations are given directly to candidate or parties, and which thus "involves *speech*, [Italics added] by someone other than the contributor". Rather than heightening conviction in the logical soundness of the Court's decisions, repetitive appeals to these popular sentiments, prove, if anything, to have an attenuating effect. Specious contrived propositions are not strengthened by adorning them with the veneer of constitutionality.

Whereas decisions at this level (Courts of Appeal, United Kingdom Privy Council, etc.) are often by a majority, the notation indicating the extent to which the Supreme Court Judges differed in **Citizens,** is interesting enough to be set out here:

> Kennedy, J., delivered the opinion of the Court, in which Roberts, C. J., and Scalia and Alito, JJ., joined, in which Thomas, J., joined as to all but Part IV, and in which Stevens, Ginsburg, Breyer, and Sotomayor, JJ., joined as to Part IV. Roberts, C. J., filed a concurring opinion, in which Alito, J., joined. Scalia, J., filed a concurring opinion, in which Alito, J., joined, and in which Thomas J., joined in part. Stevens, J., filed an opinion concurring in part and dissenting in part, in which Ginsburg, Breyer, and Sotomayor, JJ., joined. Thomas, J., filed an opinion concurring in part and dissenting in part".

---

679 *The Economist*, Aug. 18, 2001, p.3, reported that, "a United States Federal Judge ruled that controversial *snapshots* [Italics added] of **Barbie,** an iconic plastic doll, were protected by the photographer's *free-speech rights*, [Italics added] Mattel, which makes the dolls - plans to appeal," see **Mattel Inc. v Walking Mountain Production**, 353 F. 3d 792 (9th Cir. 2003). It may, with some justification, be said, without approving the N. Korean Government's depiction of the United States, "as the graveyard of human rights", (The Gleaner, Thu. Aug. 28, 2014, p.C7) that the United States' positions on certain human rights and the international institutions protective systems established, is at the very least ambivalent. It has not seen it appropriate to recognise the International Criminal Court's jurisdiction over its citizens nor its citizens should not be subject to any adjudicatory process, but ones with national jurisdiction nor has it ratified the International Covenant on Economic, Social and Cultural Rights, since according to the then American Ambassador to the UN Human Rights Commission, "that would mean citizens could sue their government for enforcement of rights", (*The Economist*, Ibid, p.20). The impulse to resort to the U.S. Constitution as *the source* of rights which are seemingly challenged thus becomes perhaps more readily understandable, as does the somewhat peculiar judicial language used to discuss them. Further, whereas " certain human rights in the civil and political realm have attained the status of moral absolutes", it is nevertheless, a "new idea for Americans to think of themselves as having human rights as well as constitutional or statutory rights", according to Kenneth Roth of Human Rights Watch, as reported in *The Economist*, supra, pp. 19, 20. This seems to suggest that the United States, often described as a country instinctively pragmatic, is yet to work out the 'philosophical grounding' on which different, yet not dissimilar, rights are predicated.

CHAPTER 14
SILLY SEASON EXPECTATIONS

Those who are innocent of activist political involvement at the internal organisational level can be forgiven for not comprehending the intention-deficit seemingly reflected in political finance legislative inaction.[680] Wanting the money does not necessarily translate into wanting the legal regulatory regime on which it is pre-conditioned. And the more 'teeth' there are in stringent reform proposals, the less eager potential beneficiaries are likely to be to take the money or insert the teeth.[681]

This is because any major political party, even when relatively unpopular, is usually able to muster sufficient financial support, come election time, to put up a decent show: if it didn't, it wouldn't have remained a major player in the political arena for very long.

Needless to say, it is the larger parties which—but for a coalition arrangement, which is foreign to Jamaica's experience and an unrealistic prospect—tend to control the legislative agenda.

The period leading up to the expected announcement of the last general election in Jamaica, the campaign and the general parliamentary election, held on December 29, 2011, having come and long gone, it may still be worth reviewing some of the then relevant accompanying commentary.

---

680   It will be recalled that at both the individual and civil society group level there was the call, some two years ago, for electoral reform legislation to be in place *before* the December 2011 general election. The position to date, November 2013, is that while the Senate has approved the ECJ's recommendations, this is against the background of such strong objections/concerns, regarding even the fundamental factor of state funding, that the next step will be: submission to Cabinet for approval, then to the Parliamentary Draftsman for Cabinet's approved provisions to be incorporated into a Bill which will then be tabled in the House of Representatives for discussion. The Leader of the House has given a commitment for the Bill to then go before a Joint Select Committee of both the House and the Senate for deliberation: see the *Jamaica Observer*, Nov. 3, 2013, p.30. It is only after the report of the Joint Select Committee's review of the Bill is presented that a vote is to be expected.

681   See Olive Nelson, 'Campaign financing from public purse fundamentally flawed', *The Gleaner*, July 8, 2012, p.A9. Nelson observes that whereas "The need for urgent change is, indeed, impatient of debate ... there is no appetite for change among the legislator". She further notes that "In no other organisation is the customer expected to pay for the advertising campaign of which he is the target ..." Indeed some, such as Senator K.D. Knight, to his credit, while being against the provision of state financing, are also more likely therefore on the basis of principle, against giving the legislation sharp teeth: see 'Senate approves campaign financing recommendations' (In Senator Knight's absence). The *Jamaica Observer*, Nov. 3, 2013, p.30. One is not being cynical in saying that this 'approval' was more a PR gesture to the civil society lobby, impatient as it has been for implementation.

Without the benefit of the essential *quid pro quo* of state funding,[682] some were apparently sufficiently politically naïve to expect *voluntary* declaration of funding sources by the parties.[683] It seemed to have entirely escaped their awareness that the parties' agreement to limited disclosure, as finally proposed by the ECJ, was predicated on monetary consideration, in keeping with the Law of Contract, and not political morality. This is yet another variation on the theme—'he who pays the piper'[684]—in this instance, it may be said, with the state doing the paying and the ECJ attempting to call the tune.

The charge can be laid that state funding on such a basis puts the state in no superior ethical position than the large private donor, the 'possibility' of whose disproportionate decision-making influence is said to be such a matter of concern. What is 'bought' here, in a state finance grounded regulatory scheme, is not 'favours' of whatever nature, but something even more fundamental:

---

682   Arthur Hall, Snr. Reporter, 'Tell us who pays', The Gleaner, Thur. November 24, 2011 pp. A1, 2 where reference is made to poll results showing that 7 out of 10 Jamaicans "agree with the call for political candidates to publicly state the source of the money used to finance their campaign". According to Professor Trevor Munroe of the National Integrity Action Forum "the poll result shows the mature thinking of Jamaicans and the recognition that the people need to know who pays the piper so they can look out for who is calling the tune. What the poll result means is that there should be voluntary compliance for this election". Not having had to deal, perhaps, with private sector donors during his days as President/Chairman of the Communist Workers' Party of Jamaica, Munroe is still unaware of the typical *modus operandi* of that sector in such matters. See also 'Parties still won't reveal donors', The Gleaner, Fri. Nov. 25, 2011, p. A3, An instructive exchange of views is reported in 'Donors Stay Silent', Jamaica Observer, Nov. 27, 2011, p. 4, where the JLP's representative on the ECJ, Tom Tavares-Finson, termed the call for disclosure "disingenuous", since it was only part of a wider framework, "which is predicated on state funding", while the PNP's representative raised several areas of concern/ reservation on political/legal grounds; 'End secret campaign financing now', full page advertisement by National Integrity Action Limited, The Gleaner, Wed., Dec. 7, 2011, p. C12; 'We won't tell' sub-titled 'Parties reluctant to expose financial backers', The Gleaner, Dec. 11, 2011, p. A11 by Tyrone Reid, Senior Staff Reporter; 'In taking the soul out of elections', James Sinclair in The Gleaner, Wed. Mar. 14, 2012, p.9; notes that Jamaican elections used to be fun-filled occasions … tantamount to the arrival of Santa Claus. Alas, no more … , In the "Return of Electoral Expenses" to the Electoral Commission, as if to provide comic relief, we find candidates declaring total campaign expense of J$75,000.00 (US$882.00); J$82,000.00 (US$953.00); J$230,000.00 (US$2,674.00); J$27000.00 (US$313.00). Two of the six listed candidates submitted amounts of J$2.796 million (US$32,511) and J$6.222M (US$72,348.00): See the Jamaica Observer Mon., Apr. 2, 2012, p.15

683   See Edmond Campbell, Senior Staff Reporter, 'Parties agree to regulate campaign financing', The Gleaner, Thur. Dec. 8, 2011p. A 4; Tyrone Reid, supra.

684   In a discordant variation on this theme, we are told of Donald Trump's filing of two ethics complaints against a Democratic state Attorney General accusing him of misconduct. The facts as reported are that the Attorney General "solicited donations from Trump's *daughter*, even as Schneiderman's (the A.G.) office was investigating the real estate mogul's 'Trump University' .allegedly for "persistent fraud and illegal and deceptive conduct and violated federal consumer protection law". The Financial Gleaner, Fri. Dec. 27, 2013, p.7.

See also, 'Think Tank Lists Donors, Playing Down Their Role', The New York Times, Sat. Dec. 14, 2013, p. A. 13: "Senator Elizabeth Warren reportedly ignited a debate in Washington over whether such corporate donations to prominent research organisations result in academic-styled policy papers and newspaper opinion pieces, that are designed to move corporate agendas"; with respect to Democratic support from the health care sector, the article continued; "The donations have come at a time when the organisation (sic) has been a strong advocate of President Obama's health insurance programme.

legislative agreement motivated by the expedient, opportunistic, self-serving search for 'rents'.

But if the views of the so-called 'civil society' spokespersons and 'stakeholders' are not to be given precedence over the voice of the multitude, party and campaign financing by the state should not even be on the national agenda at this time, despite contrary claims by Professor Munroe[685]. Poll results, published just before the last general election, showed some 72% of the sample declaring that, "No, it'll be a burden on the country", against 18.8% in favour of state funding.[686]

The ECJ's proposals, not having received the necessary approval of both the House of Representatives and the Senate and Cabinet to reach the Office of the Parliamentary Draughtsman in time for the passage of legislation, being very likely to be rightly stuck at the Parliamentary *debate* stage for some time, the call in some quarters was for limited voluntary compliance.[687]

'Voluntary', in this regard, did not simply mean in the absence of a mandate by law, but also, for the then governing party, the JLP, that "... designated persons *within the party* [Italics added] would carry out the necessary oversight (although) the JLP was not averse to the identification of an independent person to help oversee the process",[688] in relation to monitoring sources of funding and spending limits. The context, of necessity, would presumably be as set out in

685 Trevor Monroe, Executive Director of the National Integrity Action, in 'Where is the campaign finance bill?' referred the Minister with responsibility for Electoral matters to his promise to the effect that "the public can expect a campaign finance bill to be before Parliament in the first quarter of the financial year beginning April 1, 2013". *The Gleaner*, Wed. Feb 20, 2013, pA8. See also 'NIA banking on Paulwell's Campaign Finance Bill Commitment', the *Jamaica Observer*, Tue, Mar. 5, 2013, p.8, where Minister Paulwell is reported as explaining that politicians were to be blamed for the delayed drafting of legislation, as, whereas it was understood that "... both political parties would address their concerns [with the ECJ's recommendations] to the ECJ. ... Different members of the same party submitted conflicting comments to the ECJ. Consequently, the ECJ wrote back to the parties to request that the concerns be clarified and streamlined". A serious flaw in the thinking of both the Minister and the Commission becomes exposed: even at this late stage of the exchange of views, the forthright expression of genuinely held opinion, no matter how 'conflicting' is, we believe, to be welcomed. There is little to be gained in arriving at what is, in reality, a false consensus. See also, 'Campaign-financing reform delayed again', *The Gleaner* Fri. July 12, 2013, where Munroe asks for Minister Paulwell's "new deadline", in circumstances where the Minister in the same publication (p.4) is reported as stating that he "has no control over the pace at which the campaign finance bill is brought to Parliament", explaining that he "spoke out of turn" in, earlier, having set a deadline.

686 Sunday Finance, the *Jamaica Observer*, Nov. 27, 2011 p.3. The sample size of 649 is obviously a matter to be borne in mind in arriving at definitive conclusions, in the absence of relevant demographic data, in what was an internet poll. Despite the long standing sense of urgency in having legislation passed, it is not 'public' expectation/ demand that has triumphed: the acting Leader of Government Business in the House, Senator Mark Golding, has seen it appropriate to observe that "... they, (the regulations) will be subject to Government's ability to finance the ... system", the *Jamaica Observer*, Nov. 3, 2013, p.30.

687 Edmund Campbell, 'Parties agree to regulate campaign financing', *The Gleaner*, Dec. 8, 2011 p. A4

688 Ibid

the, yet to be politically agreed and officially approved, ECJ proposals.

Serious objections and at least 'concerns' which continue to confront the Commission's recommendations from loud-voiced and influential senior 'fearless' party members and media commentators, made any such voluntary regulation entirely unlikely. So it proved.[689]

In this context, Donald Reece reminds us that one of the points articulated by the 'Occupy Wall Street' protestors was the question of the "honesty, of *government* [italics added] institutions".[690] It can be argued that a proposal for party officers to monitor the integrity of their own party's funding (source and quantum) is not likely to find favour with a public heavily pregnant with suspicions and rumours relative to issues of honesty, trustworthiness and transparency in and of the parties and the political process, generally.

Parliamentarians have, in fact, been ineffectively supervised by the parties with respect to their statutorily required personal declaration of assets.[691] But even if there was one hundred per cent compliance, how would that, together with "... the revelation of major donors ... help to raise the level of trust at least among the independent voters?"[692]

Some major donors have declared themselves[693], perhaps in response to the then ECJ Chairman's appeal.[694] The "breaking of the ice", as the former

---

689 See 'Tell us who pays', The Gleaner, Thur. Nov. 24, 2011, pp. A1,2; '/Parties won't reveal donors', The Gleaner, Fri. Nov. 25, 2011, p. A3; 'Donors Stay Secret', Jamaica Observer, Nov. 27, 2011, pp. 1.4; 'We Won't Tell', The Gleaner, Dec. 11, 2011, p. A11; 'Who paid the Piper?', The Gleaner, Jan. 8, 2012, p. A5; 'We Fund Them', The Gleaner, Dec. 25, 2011, p. A3.

690 Guest Columnist, Donald Reece, 'A matter of trust', The Gleaner, Fri., Dec. 2, 2011, p. A9

691 While members on both sides of the House have been delinquent, without the imposition of any sanction to speak of over the years, then Prime Minister, Bruce Golding, called the PNP 'hypocrites' for supporting the disclosure of party donors while some of its MPs had failed to make their declaration of assets under the Parliamentary Integrity of Members Act; the Jamaica Observer, Mon. Nov. 20, 2010. See also, Alicia Dunkley, 'MPs evade Integrity Committee' in, Inside Parliament, the Jamaica Observer, Oct. 16, 2011, p. 18. In 'New bill too kind to parliamentarians', "The Gavel", in The Gleaner, Mon. Mar. 17, 2014, p.B7, argues that whereas the fine for failing to make required statutory declarations is a move in the right direction, nevertheless, the Bill 'is proposing a major let-off for parliamentarians. No longer is the jail time two years, as is the case under the soon-to-be-repealed law, but it will be six months'.

692 Donald Reece, The Gleaner, Dec. 25, 2011 p.A3

693 See, 'We Fund them', The Gleaner, Dec. 25, 2011, p. A3.

694 Edmond Campbell, Senior Staff Reporter, The Gleaner, Thurs., December 15, 2011 p.A3.
See also, 'We Fund Them', The Gleaner, Dec. 25, 2011, p.A3 where the provision of equal amounts to the two major parties was variously described by the corporate representatives of the five firms as, "... part of our corporate responsibility"; "... guarding against the real danger of state capture by special interests or worse, by criminal elements ..."; "... a demonstration of ... commitment to transparency, a signal to the political parties that we expect them to do the same in the governance of the country ..."; "fully supportive of the democratic process ...", and indicating a belief in "democratic representation which reflects the desires of the majority and not a few. ..."

Chairman puts it, by donors declaring the giving of equal sums to both major political parties, will be seen by some, as a betrayal of the very essence and core value of democratic politics, competition and choice. This is nothing less than the proverbial 'throwing out the baby with the bath water'. In this instance it may be said that the bath tub is also being thrown away.

It is worthy of note that the ECJ's invitation to corporate contributors to make public their donations was not extended to all donors. It was limited to those 'who believed in full transparency'. In effect, the glorification of 'playing two sides of the fence' and/or 'hedging of bets' by these financiers of both *major* parties, is instead seen as "a fine stand for transparency",[695] and is taken, apparently, not to represent an instance of one of the alleged major funding concerns, relating to the effect of big money in politics: the buying of policy favours,[696] among other 'returns'.

It is here worthy of note that benefits/favours need not be specific/ immediate on the personal/individual or institutional level. Economic philosophy preservation cannot be regarded as being without value.

In Jamaica, as against the case in the 2012 United States Presidential election campaigning, the recurring concern is not specifically with PAC's, 'super' or ordinary, but, rather,

> Did some candidate have massive personal wealth that the country was not aware of. ... Was there financing by sources which must remain a deep dark secret? Were there any inflows to the election coffers from Government contracts and leaks in the public purse? ... We [The Gleaner's Council, which included two professors among its members] ... would not be surprised *if* the two parties accepted money from people or entities of questionable character and sinister motives.[697]

---

695 Editorial, *The Gleaner*, Wed. Dec 28, 2011, p. A8; See also Tyrone Reid, Senior Staff Reporter, 'OAS lauds disclosure of campaign funds', *The Gleaner*, Jan. 1, 2012, p.A3, where the rationale for equal donations to the PNP and JLP is explained; "... we feel that they each possess the diversity of talent and *resources* capable of taking Jamaica forward ...".

696 Editorial, *The Gleaner*, Wed. Jan. 18, 2012, p. A8.

697 The *Jamaica Observer*, Thu. Dec. 22, 2011, p. 32; See also Nicholas Confessore, 'Outside Groups Eclipsing G.O.P AS Hub of Campaigns Next Year', *The New York Times*, Sun. Oct. 30, 2011, pp. 1, 20. The Supreme Courts *Citizens United* (2010) decision is here referred to as the facilitator of the continuing influence of "big money" in the United States politics, by legitimizing "the role of outside groups, which operate free of many of the legal restrictions that govern the official parties", in nor for example, having to disclose names of donors. Such groups, Political Action Committees, (PACs), are said to "answer only to a few dozen deep-pocketed donors, rather than the elected officials who oversee traditional party efforts": This in a situation where the amounts likely to be raised by such groups rival what the *formal* Republican Committees will spend, with the Democrats being somewhat behind, in what has been perceived as an unprincipled case of, "if you can't beat them, then join them".

Commentators from academia, at least, should display appreciation of the need for objectivity in making assertions, which might easily be misconstrued as having a factual basis. One is entitled to expect conclusions from such a source, even if tentatively stated, to reflect rigorous scholarly unbiased enquiry.

At another level, the 'confusion' in the thinking surrounding these issues is well exemplified by one letter writer to the press who, in support of disclosure, proposes state funding of a "modest total" for specified purposes, and at the same time suggests that contributions to the parties be taxed to finance the state's subsidy.[698]

Any argument that, "... the political parties are unwilling to lessen the potential for threats to our democracy brought about by secret campaign financing",[699] is clearly limited in its value by its politico-cultural contextual irrelevance. At a much more fundamental level, that there has been no social / political upheaval, despite sustained severe hardship for decades, should be sufficient proof of this. Could it be that any such violent urgings have been 'transferred' to the personal relations level where mobilisational leadership is uncalled for together with the absence of other protest management skills, such as strategic planning and coordination?

In somewhat similar vein, is President Obama's dubious conclusion that "... if people cannot trust their government to do the job for which it exists— to protect them and to promote their common welfare—all else is lost."[700]

---

698 See 'Who paid the Piper ?', *The Gleaner* , Jan. 8, 2012, p. A5 where, without any attempt to validate their estimate, it is declared that two billion dollars is a conservative estimate of the money spent by the two major political parties in the lead-up to the December 29, 2011, general election. Franklin Johnston in the *Jamaica Observer*, Fri. Dec. 2, 2011, p. 10 calls for "war for disclosure so as to avoid some of the 'skim' of contracts becoming donations".

699 Letter of the Day, by Robert Logan, *The Gleaner*, Tue. Jan. 17, 2012, p. A 6. While Mr Logan suggests that the parties should be persuaded to accept funds only from tax compliant companies or individuals, this 'stipulation' would not appear to be appropriate for other private organisational types: the perceptual discrimination persists, even into the realm of tax policy. No computational effort was made to provide even rudimentary figures with which the viability of the "Letter of the Day" proposal could be assessed. See, also, Franklin Johnston. The *Jamaica Observer*, Fri. Dec. 2, 2011, p. 10 where he argues for state funding to 'modernise political parties', but yet, " our taxes should not fund campaigns or politics (sic) work."

700 The Gleaner, Dec. 11, 2011, p. D14

With regard to the second aspect of a government's job, and the need for appropriate action, he ignores the important element of 'time'; with respect to the first, even more dangerously, the question of the *modus operandi*, the 'how'.

For some in Jamaica, the 'how', with respect to the vastly important task of promoting 'their common welfare', seems to rest largely on the passage of electoral reform finance regulation.

So what should one make of the Executive Director of the National Integrity Action's demand of the new government—with the last election having been held on December 29, 2011—for the introduction of 'Campaign finance reform in the first 100 days'?[701] Firstly, as a former Senator, and from his doctoral thesis,[702] he should be familiar with the pace of the legislative machinery, even in matters purported to be of urgency and in the national interest, and, allegedly, eliciting bipartisan support. He certainly ought to have known how unrealistic such an expectation was. Alacrity in the pursuit of reform, it is claimed, should be assisted by the fact that,

> the recent decision by both the JLP and the PNP to agree to a system of campaign finance reform would not have happened without the growth of public demand for probity and more effective combat of corruption.[703]

Such a version of the situation, institutionally self-serving,[704] uncomplicated by reality, and effectively disproved by the parties' disclosure positions in the election held just over three weeks later, reflects a worrying disregard for the inter and intra-interest-group dynamics of party politics in

---

701 *The Jamaica Observer,* Dec. 11, 2011, p. 6

702 Ph.D. Thesis : 'The Politics of Constitutional Decolonization: Jamaica, 1944 – 62', Institute of Social and Economic Research, UWI, (Kingston, Jamaica, 1972)

703 The *Jamaica Observer,* supra. The truth is that while there has been no conspiracy of silence on these matters, the outcry has been more like the melodic incomprehensibility of the language of the deep American South to the uninitiated ear, aggravated by the competing babble of cell-phones in a confined space, such as a coach on a noisy old railway train. Rationality, objectivity and logical coherence have been missing from much of the commentary.

704 Munroe is Executive Director of the National Integrity Action Forum, an anti-corruption lobby organisation. Credit is often taken whether due or not, especially if possible without committing trespass on any one's turf.

a less than mature environment.[705] The matter was, however, put into proper perspective, if not in particularly elegant language, by the then Prime Minister, in that office for only a few weeks, following his predecessor's resignation, in announcing that, "I am in favour of disclosure, and I am in favour of limits, *but* in accepting those two I am also in favour of state funding."[706]

COMMUNICATION FAILURE

The perceptual and expectational conflicts and divergences inherent in the positions of various 'stakeholders' was only revealed in late 2013 in Parliamentary deliberations on the ECJ's recommendations. The claimed bipartisan 'acceptance' of the Report seems to have rapidly evaporated.[707] Within days of voicing 'acceptance', with reservations, fundamental planks of the ECJ framework were being challenged by leading party spokesmen.[708] This after a considerable period of study, consideration and consultations by the Commission at different levels, international, regional (internally) and

---

705 In 'Hurt by the gangs of Gordon House', Daraine Luton, Senior Staff Reporter, reports that, "Finance Minister, Dr. Peter Phillips, has argued that Jamaica's politics has not yet matured to the state where practitioners of the craft can be entrusted with the responsibility of using the floor of Parliament to decide on the appointment of key technical officers within government Appointments referred to include that of the Governor of the central bank. Ironically, the new procedure is supposed to be appointment by the Governor General on the recommendation of the Cabinet, comprising as it does a number of the same insufficiently mature members of the same body. Phillips sees such a role for the 'floor' of Parliament, "Further down the road as we build (sic) greater maturity" ... (as he too longs for the day when Parliament would have a greater say, but cautioned that unless the approach to politics changes, that day may not come any time soon).Continuing, he noted that, "Ironically, when we had to deal with electoral reform, the only way we could have got a modicum of stability in those arrangements was to take critical decisions out of the ambit of the Parliament". "The Gavel" and others would point to the neutralization of that intended effect by the very deliberate inclusion of two representatives from the two major parties on the ECJ, to which Phillips must be taken to have been referring.

... "the suspension of the quest for partisan advantage in relation to some critical issues that must be discussed", in the interest of "... the ... survival of the State and its good governance, called for by the Minister of Finance might have been more convincing as a matter of principle, were it not obviously so self-serving coming from a leading *Government* representative.

706 The *Jamaica Observer*, Dec. 11, 2011, p. 6.

707 See, 'ECJ wrong this time', by 'The Gavel', The Gleaner's Parliamentary Reporter. *The Gleaner*, Mon. Apr, 16, 2012, p.A6. At this late stage, that such strongly negative views have been expressed, calls into question the wisdom of the convention that the ECJs proposals are accepted by Parliament without amendment: see the reported views of Opposition MP, Everald Warmington, Government Senator AJ Nicholson and MP Raymond Pryce, above.

708 As against the ECJ's approach of limited disclosure, The Attorney-General's call is for full disclosure. Apart from burdensome recording / accounting implications, such a basic objection, at this time, makes nonsense of Professor Munroe's demand for legislation to be passed within the new Government's first 100 days in office: See, 'All campaign donations should be made public – AJ Nicholson', the *Jamaica Observer*, Apr. 15, 2012, p. 22. As to the Legislative Agenda, see, 'Not a single' Bill taken to Parliament by Gov't in first 100 days – Chuck', the *Jamaica Observer*, Wed. Apr. 18, 2012, p. 3; the *Jamaica Observer*, Dec. 11, 2011, p. 6, reports Peter Phillips, M.P. and Minister of Finance, as saying that he expected that the legislation "will be passed as soon as it is drafted and taken before Parliament".

national, with submissions from civil society groups and national political party organisations, involving two nominated representatives of each of the two major parties in its membership.

In this communications fiasco,[709] it is not merely recommendations, *per se,* which were the target of objection. Indeed, the perception of a claim by the ECJ to having a *multi-pronged role,* giving rise, it is implied, to certain offensive Report provisions, has also come under severe attack.[710]

This 'situation' makes questionable, as MP Everald Warmington[711] and the Gavel[712] have argued, the wisdom of having political party representatives on the Commission at all, especially under the current remuneration arrangement. The first issue is that, as the MP has stated, the public should not be required to pay salaries, of whatever amount, to persons whose membership is justified on the basis of protecting the interest of the political parties. Secondly, despite the tradition now apparently being departed from, of Parliament accepting ECJ proposals without comment or amendment what has amply been demonstrated by the apparent breach of that convention is that, in fact, the inclusion of the political representatives may represent duplication of participation and consultation with that particular interest group.

State funding, in the JLP leader's view, would fill the gap created "… as donors, craving anonymity, withhold support."[713] It is not to be presumed that, such donors would be cash rich individuals and larger well known national institutions, driven more by sensitivity to the uprightness of their public image, than the possibility of getting their 'snouts into the trough'. Some, as we have seen, evaded the difficulty of disclosure of political choice by what some may see as 'getting the best of both worlds'.

---

709 It seems obvious that it is either that the ECJ's politically nominated members were deaf to the voices of their party members, or that there was a failure in the transmission of those views, or that it is only now when there is fuller Parliamentary debate, including in the Upper House (Senate) that views reflecting independent thinking are being aired. If the ECJ had been made aware of such dissenting views, it might have been useful for their non-acceptance to have been recorded in the Report.

710 For Government Senator KD Knight's comments suggesting that "… the ECJ was setting itself up to be judge, legislator, police and Cabinet combined". 'KD backs Warmington', in *The Gleaner,* Mon. Apr. 16, 2012, p. A6. The views of Peter Phillips, M.P. and Minister of Finance, are reported in 'House accepts ECJ report on campaign financing but … ' the *Jamaica Observer,* Thu. Apr. 12, 2012, p. 4.

711 See Daraine Luton, 'Taxpayer shouldn't foot election bill', *The Gleaner,* Wed. Nov. 3, 2010, p. A3, Gary Spaulding, 'We can't impose any more burdens on the poor', The Gleaner, Wed. Sept. 25, 2013, p. 1., also Professor Errol Miller, 'Electoral Commission is not bleeding taxpayers', *The Gleaner,* Wed. Jan. 12, 2011, p. 8.

712 "Remove politicians from ECJ", *The Gleaner,* Mon. June 13, 2011, p. B 12

713 The *Jamaica Observer,* Dec. 11, 2011, p. 6.

It is on this level that policy-influence becomes most readily observable: the maintenance of the *status quo*, systemically, under which donors are not merely more likely to benefit, but without any conspicuous significant contribution to society's well-being, their very survival is indeed guaranteed.

The supreme irony here is that with respect to 'benefits/ spoils', in the form of certain jobs at least, "Poor Jamaicans feel that only supporters of (the) winning party should get public sector jobs."[714] These are, of course, those positions in respect of which it is, by virtue of the political culture, assumed that recruitment can be most directly clientistically influenced.

So, perhaps, instead of the National Integrity Action focusing on, "partnering with the Office of the Political Ombudsman in launching a public education programme to enhance citizens' engagement in detecting, deterring and facilitating punishment for breaches of the Political Code of Conduct,"[715] it might consider engagement in the more fundamental task of greater urgency: that of ascribing a unifying operational/functional meaning to the island's ostensibly appealing motto, 'Out of Many One People'. This is a motto which is in conspicuous collision with the tribalistic nature[716] of the country's politics, effectively perpetuated largely by less than satisfactory system outcomes, especially for the deprived masses. If those outcomes were perceived as fair and equitable, much of the mischief associated with the political/electoral systems, one suspects, strongly, might gradually recede. This, we hold to be indicated by one possible reasonable interpretation of their above-quoted survey response.

Biased policy outcomes is 'matched' by bias of another kind. In the same Gleaner editorial, lavishing praise on the five declarant firms for what was seen as a "... profoundly historic development, for which their leadership deserves high commendation", which some would see as an example of corporate cowardice, the nakedly skeptical observation is also made that, even when the parties volunteer information on a *supposedly* [Italics added] high-minded commitment to transparency such as in the publication in

---

714 Janice Budd, Associate Editor, 'Food for the Winners, Starvation for the Losers', *The Gleaner*, Mar. 4, 2012 p, 14
715 The *Jamaica Observer*, Dec. 11, 2011, p.24
716 See the reported views of new/young 2011 general election candidates, in the *Jamaica Observer*, Tue. Nov. 22, 2011, p. 4 and Janice Budd, supra

recent times of their operational accounts, these *appear* [Italics added] to understate normal operational expenditure and income.[717]

The built-in institutional prejudice is evident in the disparate treatment given to political parties, as against private sector entities which, at best, can be accused of fence-straddling and, at worst, of playing the game of 'heads, we win, tails, we win'.

The ambivalence frequently displayed in the discussion of the political process is betrayed by the manner in which a basic principle of democratic society is acknowledged by the editor,

> it is a right of the individuals and corporations to make financial donations ... to the party whose policies they find will best advance the interest of the country. Given the opaque environment within which these contributions are now made, *the public has no way of determining* whether these are on the basis of *quid pro quo* and, therefore, whether the policies and actions of a government are disproportionately skewed to a favoured donor.[718]

This perverse pathology of politics persists, despite the absence of any attempt at offering supporting evidence. The 'self-fulfilling prophecy' attitude to politics seems to be, when in doubt assume the worst, and then behave as if that assumption is the truth.

But then, the uncertainty which is the defining characteristic inherent in the choice of the words, "opaque", "no way of determining", "whether [or not]" makes attention to finding and publishing evidence unnecessary. This would seem to be a classic example, unfortunately, of the media norm with respect to the treatment of issues of a party political nature.[719] The aggressive *investigative* role of a mature, responsible press is seemingly being abdicated.

---

717 Editorial, *The Gleaner*, Wed., Dec. 28, 2011, p. A8. As David Walker has put it, "The guango comes from the same neck of the woods as the (Nigel) Wicks Committee on standards with a mission to crimp and control politicians and their parties, in case they get up to mischief".

718 Ibid; see the almost identical language used to discuss the matter in 'Ethically challenged', Peter Espeut, *The Gleaner*, Fri. Sept. 29, 2013, p.A.9.

719 See David Walker, *The Guardian* (UK) Mar 13, 2002, op. cit., where the admission is boldly made: "We, the press, love to despise parties ... we treat Mittal as if it were evidence of moral turpitude rather than system failure ... Partisanship is the state's dirty little secret ..." ['Mittal' refers to the UK Company controlled by the Indian-born billionaire, Laksmi Mittal, reported to be one of, if not the richest man in Britain, who owns steel Companies and who has contributed to the Labour Party over the years. In 2002 a scandal erupted because it was said that he influenced government policy – having donated £125,000.00 the previous year. More specifically, he is said to have benefited significantly, financially, by then PM Tony Blair playing a part in having applicable tariffs reduced in Romania. For details, see http://www.economist.com/node/998906]

For clarification, in principle, we see absolutely nothing wrong with those in glass houses throwing stones, where warranted. In this respect, at least, there is a lot to be learnt from the American media.

At the level of policy, to fit this mould, party politics would have to be class-based for there to be any semblance of policy-framework coherence: either that, or politicians would have to be moronic, and the electorate grossly unintelligent.

But then, as James Delingpole has said,

> We seem to have reached a state of intellectual decline where virtually the whole of western culture has forgotten to think and argue from first principles. Instead ... we're all handed this starter pack of the various right-on notions we're now supposed to believe in and if we dare to question them, we're written off as pariahs, freaks, dangerous troublemakers.[720]

Further, as it has been noted by Mark Forsythe,

> But in the age of the soundbite, its [persuasion by rhetoric] a much simpler business. Gone are the logical *proofs* [Italics added] and the structure of an argument. What's left are the rhetorical tricks that can be applied to one sentence, the pull-quote.[721]

It is still to be widely acknowledged that there is no clearly demarcated, much less fixed, intersection at which the pursuit of policy and the practise of politics meet. And in the country case under investigation, politics is the business of catering to significantly demographically differentiated groups and their members, based on economic interest, subcultural values and other important factors. Delineating the boundaries of 'legitimacy' is, as a result, not always convenient for the theoretician or the practitioner, especially in a multi-class party context; this applies not only to policy *action*, but public relations posturing.

If the practice of politics may correctly be analogously described as being like 'a bed of nails', certain environments may well give rise to a sharpening of those nails. It has been said by David Walker:

---

720 James Delingpole, 'Is even Radley not safe from lentil-eating progressives?' The Spectator, Nov. 23, 2013, p. 31.
721 Mark Forsythe, 'Save the Soundbite', *The Spectator*, Nov. 23, 2013, p. 16. See, however, the views of David Walker who argues that, the costs of democratic politicking could be cut. Future electioneering could revert to shabby amateurism - the sort that individual [small] donations could pay for', David Walker, 'Party Poopers', *The Guardian*, op. cit.

Democratic romantics fantasise about populist-regeneration; mass parties reborn, The Institute for Public Policy Research has lately been agonising, the [British] Labour Party much in mind, about how far some loosening of control freakery [the opposite of what the ECJ seeks to achieve] would encourage local party activity. But why should hedonistic people join parties that will only rarely be fun? One good reason might be if parties were a portal to jobs, paid or unpaid, or some preferred status in the community ... for which membership of a party might be a recommendation. Shock, horror: it is a mark of our contempt for parties that the suggestion is so counter-cultural.[722]

Timid firms seeking not to appear politically-partisan cannot help to dispel "... the fear of stigmatisation and victimization of donors,"[723] whether overstated or not: what some would-be reformers perhaps quite innocently achieve, it has been argued, amounts to "... taking the soul out of elections."[724] The exhortation is not superfluous that "in our quest to root out corruption we

---

722 David Walker, Party Poopers', *The Guardian* (UK) Mar. 13, 2002, op. cit.

723 ECJ Report, p. 11.
And since there will be no such fear by donating to very peripheral third parties with no chance of success, no donation whatsoever was made by any of these "principled" firms to any but the two major parties with almost equal popular support, historically 'See Peter Townsend, of the National Democratic Movement (NDM), 'Fund third parties too', *The Gleaner*, Fri. Dec. 6, 2012 p. A8, who alleges that "the message of systemic changes and positive reforms being offered by the NDM did not reach the people because of the paucity of funding for its campaign." See also the views of Colin Virgo, PNP representative (new and young) as reported in, "Young candidates differ on campaign financing', the *Jamaica Observer*, Tue. Nov. 22, 2011, p.4. Contribution limited to the two major parties did not prevent Bruce Bowen, then President and CEO of one of the island's two largest banks declaring that his bank is "... fully supportive of the democratic process ... equal contributions to the main political parties in order to help facilitate their campaign activities and allow for presentation to the public on their goals, plans and priorities for the economy and overall [sic] country."

724 James Sinclair, in what appears to be a 'tongue in cheek' letter to the Editor, the *Jamaica Observer*, Wed., Mar. 14, 2012 p.9 argues that recent electoral developments, "... illustrates how far the Government of Jamaica is moving away from the [political] culture and traditions that gave individuality to the country", by having, for example, "... eliminated the offering of any type of material reward to would-be voters" and, pointedly, "political parties take money from individuals and swear that they are not influenced by the gift. It is a form of snobbery to assume that accepting a would-be politician's generosity influences decisions in the [secrecy] of the voting booth". Interestingly, *The Gleaner* of Fri., Mar. 9, 2012, on p.1, reports the filing of an Election Petition seeking to have the Supreme Court declare an MP's election declared null and void in that "... (though) several of his agents corruptly gave monies to persons. "... as payment to vote for him ..." and for "giving foodstuff to persons on the voter's list for the constituency ... for the purpose of procuring (sic) the persons to vote for him ..." Once monies from state funding can be mixed with contributions from other sources, it would not be easy to prevent its use for such purposes, this is without prejudice to the truth, or otherwise, of the allegations against the MP.
One of the new candidates entering the 2011 election was of the view that the increased spending cap of $10 million per constituency would suffice, "if it is that we are only covering the cost of paraphernalia and PR and if it is not going into buying elections.", The Jamaica Observer, Wed. Nov. 30, 2011, p.6 For a candid expression of differing views on state funding and disclosure of sources of funding across party lines, see, the *Jamaica Observer*, Tues. Nov. 22, 2011, p. 4, 'Young Candidates differ on campaign financing', by HG Helps, Editor-at-Large.

must seek to avoid distorting the political process."[725] While some might see the creation of an electoral commission as reflecting a commitment to multi-party parliamentary government, in the case of Britain this was regarded as,

> the latest expression of … deep ambiguity about democratic politics. The commission recently plastered the country with posters urging people to register to vote. Who for? It does not seem interested in the obvious answer.[726]

MP's Independence

With the ECJ's primary funding focus being on registered parties, rather than candidates, the independence on the part of the individual party-affiliated politicians, which some wish to see, will not materialize until the multi-party system and concomitantly the electorate within it, 'matures' significantly. Should this happen, it will inevitably be an evolutionary process,[727] even if shortened by persuasion through an educational campaign perhaps under official state auspices, with or without sanctions/incentives, or otherwise 'learning from history'. As against the result of any such process must be set the recognition that, "… without messy, compromised political parties, how do individual choices [of electors/elected representations] ever agglomerate into a rational basis for government?"[728]

The notorious instability of coalitions, universally, is indicative of the need for a certain minimum level of procedural and substantive ideational compatibility for effective organisational functioning.

---

725 Vernon Daley, 'Avoid error in campaign reform', *The Gleaner,* Apr 29, 2008, p.A7. See also Ronald Mason, 'Damn dictatorship on campaign financing' on the danger that the ECJ "seeks to regulate the freedom out of the electoral process"; *The Gleaner,* Oct. 6, 2013, pA9.

726 David Walker, *The Guardian,* op. cit.

727 Nassmacher, Karl-Heinz, 'Comparing Party and Campaign Financing in the Western Democracies'; in Arthur B. Gurlicks (ed) Campaign and Party Finance in North America and Western Europe, Boulder Co. Westview, 1993, p. 262; See also Macleod-Ball, Michael, ACLU Chief Legislative and Policy Counsel's letter to the U.S. Senate on the *Disclose Act,* <www.aclu.org/free-speech/aclu-letter-senate-urging-no-vote-disclose-act>: "The *Disclose Act* would inflict unnecessary damage to both privacy and First Amendment rights. Small donors to small organisations risk losing anonymity while the bill allows larger, mainstream organisations to be exempt from donor disclosure. Imposing these kinds of imbalanced disclosure obligations on certain kinds of organisations would only serve to further distort the fairness of our current campaign finance laws. The Constitution guarantees all Americans the right to participate in political debate without risk or harassment or fear of embarrassment. The Senate has done the right thing by blocking the *Disclose Act*."

728 David Walker, op. cit.

REFORM OVERZEALOUSNESS

Political finance reforming zeal seems to have now reached the stage where no matter how remote the connection between incidents involving money, on the one hand, and politics or politicians, on the other, this is somehow seen as having party and campaign financing implications. It is as if state funding will rid the persons participating in the political process of just about all of their unsavoury personal or corrupt political tendencies.

When local government councillors were arrested and charged for alleged lottery-scam involvement, the presumption,[729] immediately, was that the proceeds of such activity were directed, in whole or part, to cover personal, or party, *political* expenses. The episode, we were told, emphasized, yet again, the urgent need for legislative political financing reform.[730] The fact that scores of other non-political individuals had also been and continue to be arrested, on the basis of similar allegations, did not militate against that self-fulfilling prophecy conclusion in any way.

THE LEGISLATIVE REALITY

The General election held in December 2011 should not have been called in the opinion of the Jamaica Council of Churches (JCC), "... without the issue of campaign financing being passed through Parliament. ..."[731]

That exhortation was made, despite the fact that no *draft* legislation had yet been prepared. Such a proposal, which was the popular civil society stance, was clearly reflective of how out-of-step good intentions can be with reality. Such a divergence was evident then, even before the lingering attempt by the new Government to arrive at an agreement with the IMF had achieved

---

729 In 'Electile dysfunction', Ronald Mason, for reasons of topicality, perhaps, asks, somewhat out of the context of his piece, "Would the state funding of political parties lead to a decrease in the number of political dynasties? ... would be difficult to legislate ... rejecting the dynasty members at the polls," *The Gleaner,* Jan. 19, 2014, p. A. 9.

730 See 'MoBay reacts to shock 'scam' arrests', *The Gleaner,* July 20, 2012, p. A3; See also 'PNP under fire – JLP insists arrested councillors resign', the *Jamaica Observer,* July 20, 2012. The Trafigura saga and subsequently that of Olint also was seen as confirmation of the urgent need for state funding. Disclosure requirements would most likely have been the answer to Trafigura and greater vigilance by the financial institutions' regulatory and monitoring agencies would have contained the mischief in the case of Olint.

731 See 'Wait for the Law, JCC urges Government to stay put until [ECJ] recommendations are legal', *The Gleaner,* Fri. Oct. 7, 2011, p. D8; 'Campaign finance reforms unlikely before next poll', the *Jamaica Observer,* Oct 16, 2011, p. 12, reports the JCC as "calling on the political parties to adopt the ECJ's recommendations for the current election campaign even though the related legislation is not in place", without the "price" of the parties' cooperation and agreement (state funding) being paid or even being payable, given the state of the country's finances.

tangible results. And it is known that, agreements with the IMF usually involve 'belt tightening', resulting from inevitable cuts in public expenditure. Pronouncements at the Ministerial level[732] were ignored by many in positions of leadership in the society, who preferred to engage in wishful thinking, without any regard for the stages involved in the legislative process, and the pace at which it traditionally functions.

Additionally, it would seem that the basic point was missed by the JCC leadership and others, that legislation involving imminent expenditure has immediate budgetary consequences. National Budgets are normally a once per year exercise and, given the very substantial cost involved in public political financing, that could hardly be handled as an off-budget item.

After all the dramatic sense of urgency aroused, and displayed in favour of party registration and state financing measures being immediately put in place, the resulting deep sense of disappointment seems clearly unjustified, objectively.

According to the Minister responsible, while it is intended that a Bill for registration of parties will be tabled in the current [2013] parliamentary year, "Campaign Financing will come in the next legislative year."[733] We have recently, however been informed, apologetically, that he spoke out of turn as, "… it is entirely outside of my control …"[734]

---

732 "… let us not panic. The funds have to be found …" stated the Minister with portfolio responsibility, Daryl Vaz, referring not to party and campaign financing by the state, but the money needed for election machinery expenses, required by the ECJ for itself and its operations. See also, 'Jamaica has worst debt-to-revenue ratio in Moody's rating universe', by Steven Jackson, Business Reporter, The Gleaner, Wed. July 27, 2011, p. C 6. While waiting for its own funding, the EOJ stated that it "was ready as it can be" for its required activities during the then imminent general election, the Jamaica Observer, Oct 9, 2011, p. 17, and see also, 'EOJ wants funding in time for general election', The Gleaner, Sat. Oct 8, 2011, p A3.

733 See 'No campaign financing bill this year', The Gleaner, Mon Jan 14, 2013, p A8. At least one M.P. is reported as insisting that the Report should go back to the ECJ for further consideration before re-submission to Parliament for further debate since, rightly, in our view, he does not wish to be bound by a convention by which Parliament normally 'rubber-stamps' reports from the ECJ. Consequently, he argues, "It can't be sent to parties [sic] and then from parties it goes to being a bill."

734 See 'Paulwell: It is out of my control', The Gleaner, Fri. July 12, 2013, p. A 4. Parliamentarians have broadened the scope of their scrutiny of the ECJ beyond its reform recommendations to include its [ECJ] cost, see 'ECJ being dragged before Parliament to defend [its members'] salaries'. The Gleaner, Mar. 13, 2014, p. A 3. Whereas MP, Everald Warmington wants state payment to the ECJ political representatives to cease, MP Raymond Pryce, in objecting to the Commission's reluctance to appear before Parliament's Public Administration and Accountability Committee, was "… baffled as to why a public body would think it is above the process which good governance demands": an example of selective commitment to 'transparency', usually the norm, perhaps?

CONCLUSION

Manifestation of the withering of the 'social roots' of parties takes several forms:

> the weakening of party identifications, the erosion of traditional cleavages, increasing party dealignment, rising levels of electoral volatility, rapidly declining numbers of party members, and the deterioration of the relationships between parties and collateral organisations.[735]

David Walker puts it in a data-supported manner as follows:

> If they lack people, parties certainly lack money. In 1997, Labour's [British Labour Party] membership subs paid for 8%. Affiliation fees from the unions contributed 27%, but those suspicious donations made up nearly two-thirds of revenue. For the Tories, gifts paid for £9 out of every £10 spent and even for the Lib Demo donations outweighed subs by two to one. Individual members are not, in other words, going to make parties honest. Only the state can.[736]

Walker, earlier in his piece, referred to the fact that, "Labour is back to its early 1990's level, (membership) after the blip around 1997". That there was a 'blip' is of supreme interest to us, in that significant changes in party membership level or level of voting, especially at general elections, are precisely the kind of phenomena which deserve research attention. It would be quite interesting to discern the reasons for that 'blip'.

Where failure of party management has contributed to such a generalized consequence, the existence of a regulatory system of party finances might well be, "... the first empirical indicator of the management of parties by the state",[737] a relationship which seems decidedly incestuous.

The globalization of political and economic ideology, together with technological innovation, inevitably lays tracks for the direction of electoral mechanisms and legal systems. Large parties which spend very substantial sums of money, may still experience financial difficulties under a system of public

---

735 See Dalton, Russell J. and Martin, P. Wattenberg (eds), 'Parties without Partisans: Political Change in Advanced Industrial Democracies', Oxford University Press, (Oxford, 2007).

736 David Walker, 'Party Poopers', *The Guardian*, op. cit.

737 van Biezen and Kopecky, supra, p 239

funding, depending on factors such as the efficiency of intra-organisational transactions, campaigning strategy choice and financial management skills.

Further, the attractive assumption that state funding promotes democratization of the electoral and political processes is challenged by the conclusion that,

> No empirical studies appear to have been done to test the hypothesis that the greater the source of public funding available to support new participants into an increasingly expensive[738] political process the more likely a wider range of people who will be able to participate.[739]

Some, it is worth repeating, individually and institutionally, will always use money to much better effect than others. Additionally, if apathy is rampant, with respect to citizens' participation in the political process, money is unlikely to significantly alter that orientation. In this regard, it would be interesting if even rudimentary data was provided relating party expenditure to electoral results, over time,[740] taking into account the changing value of money. It is admitted that the essentially unofficial/informal nature of many political party relationships and, thereby, transactions, in a small island in the developing category, presents a major hurdle.

In some mature European democracies, Whiteley's summation of the reasons for the "decline of party activism and membership" is no doubt relevant: 'state capture', or excessive state regulation resulting in the "stifling (of) voluntary activity at the grassroots level". The second explanation offered is that the robustness of parties is being undermined by "the growth of relatively more remote new forms of participation", such as chequebook and internet transactions and interest group and third party organisational involvement, including the donation of money which, taken together, provide

---

738 According to a dated (2002) view on this issue, while, as "the speaker of the California Assembly once quipped, 'Money is the mother's milk of politics (he was later indicted) ... what parties do costs money but can hardly be called expensive, compared, say, with voluntary organisations for the birds or the blind. Total spending on last year's election would not have powered a single campaign by Ford. Costs were low, it is true, because we still have oddly restrictive rules on media use", David Walker, 'Party Poopers', *The Guardian*, op. cit.

739 Cass and Burrows, supra, p. 495.

740 On the danger of policy choice, without an evidential basis, see Senator Lambert Brown's views in, 'Government Senator says there's no evidence for BIG-MONEY FEARS', *The Gleaner*, Sat. Nov. 2, 2013, pp. A1, 3.

allegedly "alternative outlets for political action outside traditional forms of participation such as [direct] party involvement."[741]

The data analysed by Whiteley suggests that, "... there is a generational dimension to these trends [disengagement, etc.] with the recruitment of new age cohorts being problematic everywhere but particularly so in high-regulation countries ... more generally",[742] and since, parties "... greatly assist the process of aggregating diverse political interests and also in getting losers in the political process to accept democratic decisions", a weakening of parties in terms of their representational function is "... likely to make government in general more difficult (arising from policy gridlock and institutional sclerosis) as parties are diverted from a concentration on policy-making to a preoccupation with rent-seeking options".[743]

In the present state of party / public disengagement, and given the effects on potential donors in the worsening economic climate, rather than emphasis on fundraising, what we witness is the convenient "marriage of the Honourables" (Government members in the governing party) and the Opposition (the Honourables in waiting); the exchange, the *quid pro quo*, is state financing for regulation. Within the parties, the voices against this bargain have been few. Mutual interest has, in this instance, at least, almost completely triumphed over the usual perceptual "demonizing of the opposition ... mudslinging, vindictiveness".[744]

Despite this, so negative is the general mood that a press guest columnist poses questions that, although of fundamental importance, are no doubt

---

741   Paul F. Whiteley, University of Essex, UK, 'Is the party over? The decline of party activism across the democratic world', Party Politics, 17(1) p. 21; See also Dalton, R.J. (2005) Citizen Politics, Washington, D.C.: Congressional Quarterly Press; Scarrow, S. E. (2000), 'Parties without Members? Party Organisation in a Changing Electoral Environment' in Dalton, R.J., and Wattenburg M.P., 'Parties Without Partisans: Political Change in Advanced Industrial Countries', Oxford University Press; (Oxford, 2000) and Webb, P.D., Farrell, D.M. and Holliday (eds) (2002), 'Political Parties in Advanced Industrial Democracies', Oxford, OUP. The argument that the state, through funding and other transactional relationships with parties, apart from undermining the incentive for parties to sustain "key relationships between citizens and the state" turns on another factor: if parties can rely on the state for significant funding, to that extent are they less compelled to seek and retain members and supporters from civil society.

742   David Walker writes that, "The Tories are gerontocratic; the nationalists and the Liberal Democrats have not found youth's elixir either ..." and, earlier, that, "Parties are weak unmodernised still in many ways. Yet Britain has a formidable apparatus to screen, check and invigilate them", David Walker, 'Party Poopers', The Guardian, op. cit.

743   See Olson, M., The Rise and Decline of Nations: Economic Growth, Stagflation and Social Rigidities, Yale University Press, (New Haven, CT, 1982)

744   Hylton, Stanley G., Senator for Sale: Ann Unauthorized Biography of Senator Bob Dole, St. Martin's Press, (New York, 1995), p. 166.

well outside the scope of the terms of reference of the ECJ reform project. Nevertheless, the very critical issues adverted to, especially the latter question, suggest that prospective gain from any recommendations forthcoming might just be negatived by their irrelevance ": ... can", she asks, "the current crop of politicians make it happen for Jamaica?; Does the current political system even make it possible?"[745]

If political parties, well established and functioning within the contours of traditional moulds, are facing a decline in strength and resources, and, as a result, are less able to mediate between the citizen and the state, what this would rationally seem to demand is their renewal or replacement. We find it difficult to support the position that state subsidy would now appear to be the natural and appropriate stage in their historical development. Impulses toward institutional perpetuation, need to be inherent, or internally generated in keeping with a sense of mission and the inculcation and preservation of a commitment to institutional integrity in behaviour and practice.

Not only are the standard explanations of the party/citizen disconnection incomplete, but they fail to account for the pervasiveness of the malaise across national boundaries, significantly differentiated by the level of national prosperity, state/party integration, data collection, sophistication and *mass use* of currently available first-world facilities and transaction methods.

A reliance on, and hunger for, public funds could reach a point, as in Germany, where "... even where scandals lend salience to the issue of party finance reform, parties will not necessarily sacrifice assured economic gains for possible political pay offs". The ECJ must therefore use the powers given to it to ensure compliance 'without becoming an unwitting political tool' by changing the nature of the political process unless absolutely unavoidable, by party deregistration or the voiding of an election, for example.[746]

In the United States and Britain which have had "over a century's worth of experience with finance campaign laws", scandals are certainly, as is well known, not rare.

---

745 'Bad politics breeds bad government,' by Suzanne Leslie Bailey, Guest Columnist, *The Gleaner,* Fri. Mar. 22, 2013, pA9

746 Susan E. Scarrow "Explaining Political Finance Reforms, Competition and Contest", in Party Politics; *Sage Publications,* Vol. 10. No. 6, p.653

As Hayden Phillips puts it in his review of the British situation, then current and in prospect,

> A healthy democracy needs healthy political parties ... , Tackling party funding alone will not resolve the problem of cynicism ... , The central challenge is for the politicians themselves across a much wider front ... any changed system of party funding should try to bolster public confidence and help recapture the true vision of party politics as serving the public.[747]

Although some seem to see it as the sole area deserving of reform focus, party finance is clearly but one of several critical areas of 'perfectibility' in transformational and representative government.

If inter-party competition is to be policy-driven, then any state funding provided should, one would be entitled to expect, be so directed.[748] This is especially important for opposition parties, otherwise state funding could simply contribute to a culture somewhat graphically described as "politics of the belly", in which promises, however sincere, of the beneficial results of proposed policy implementation, seem too remote to be sufficiently satisfying to an electorate, suffering from policy-results myopia.

Having said that, we are not inclined to the seemingly attractive simplistic solution advanced that,

> Given the *will of both donor and party*, [Italics added] the management of the *existing* [Italics added] arrangements [under *ROPA*] can be significantly improved without a cent from the Treasury and the already overburdened tax payer.[749]

No amount of 'will', should it unexpectedly become manifest, is likely to prevail over the many obstacles in the way, the most substantial, perhaps, being the absence of any attempt at a sustained non-partisan campaign of values-based political education in all its contextually important aspects. Such an initiative might best be attempted, perhaps, by a committee under

---

747 Hayden Phillips, supra. This conclusion is to be seen against a background where, as elsewhere, trust in politicians and political parties "... been subject to a long term decline ... people feel distant from parties (which) are only interested in them at election times. (Trust in MPs was at 29%, and whereas in the 1950s 1 in 11 persons was a party member, in 2006 it was 1 in 88).

748 As against Jean Lowrie-Chin's expectation with respect to the 2011 general election, that "Issues should motivate voters", the *Jamaica Observer*, Mon. June 20, 2011, p. 11, see 'Issues? What Issues? Few Jamaicans prepared to vote on issues if elections are called now', *The Gleaner*, Thu. July 7, 2011, p.A2.

749 *The Gleaner*, Ibid.

the auspices of a suitably constituted Electoral Commission,[750] with power to co-opt, and with any necessary expansion of its terms of reference/mandate.

As has been evident throughout our treatment of the issues covered, this is an area of national life in which virtually almost all evidence tends to be anecdotal, and where *a priori* 'reasoning' is generally considered acceptable. Further, the preferred presumption in relation to politicians and political parties, once any issue touching them can be viewed from a negative angle, is one of guilt.[751]

Despite this stereotype, honest, intelligent, educated young persons are expected to be recruited by the parties in an environment in which positive media images do not make for sensationalism.

As Jean Blondel has put it,

> "It is easy to poke fun at politicians" ... They must also have a strong will-power and a rather thick skin. They must be able to sustain public criticism without being plunged into defeatism or anger or both. These abilities may not amount to a readily definable technique; they are nonetheless abilities which a random selection of citizens, or of party members is not likely to possess.[752]

---

750 See 'Remove politicians from ECJ', "The Gavel" supra (The Gleaner's Parliamentary reporter), *The Gleaner,* Mon. June 13, 2011, p.B12, where it is argued that "... the time has come to remove the politicians from the centre of the Commission's operations. ... Our discomfort though is with the four nominated members ... two nominated by the Prime Minister and two nominated by the Leader of the Opposition ... believes it is unhealthy for democracy for the PNP and the JLP, which have monopolized the political process to be given such free rein over the political process ... serves only to reinforce the two-party system and could also undermine the stated objectives of the ECJ ... to protect the electoral process from the immediate direction, influence and control of the Government which may influence a(sic) its functioning to the detriment of persons with opposing views who may wish to participate in the process". Examples of political self-serving influence exerted by the two parties provided are, firstly, their agreement on the boundaries of new constituencies created with the result that, "... independent commissioners only get involved if the parties cannot agree what portion of their stronghold to give up". Secondly, "We can see no justification for the suggestion "that state funding should not apply to any five or more members of parliament who contested as independent members at a general election but subsequently formed a political party ... it gives a feel (sic) of the political parties using their muscle to keep out possible real competition. ...The job of the ECJ Commissioner should be reserved for independent, technically competent people with integrity and testicular fortitude and not self-serving politicians". For The Gavel's consistency of position, see 'Behind the veil of that UNCONCIONABLE ECJ campaign financing proposal', *Gleaner,* Mon. Nov. 4, 2013, pp. A 6, 7.

751 An example of this is provided with the recent suggestion by the Commissioner of Police in, 'Ellington wants accused to prove legal fees untainted, *The Gleaner,* Wed. Oct. 23, 2013, p. A3, to the effect that "the force (police) recommends that persons *charged* [Italics added] for gun crimes and drug-trafficking crimes prove to the satisfaction of the courts that their legal fees are not tainted money". Logistically, if they are presumed to be innocent, until trial and conviction, [unless such an accused has previous conviction(s) of such a nature] this requirement is unacceptable, unless, perhaps, the accused do in fact have such previous convictions.

752 Blondel, Jean, *Voters, Parties, and Leaders: The Social Fabric of British Politics",* Penguin Books Ltd, (New York, 1963), pp. 131, 132.

Nobody would deny that there are conditions under which these abilities are more likely to develop, which points, also, to the potential multi-directional gains to be derived from a well-considered campaign of political education.

The implication is that the ECJ may be accused of engaging in a less than fulsome consideration of factors, relating to *the modus operandi* of the parties, the nature of the competition between them and the extent to which obedience to their survival instincts has disfigured the island's political culture. Such an exercise, focused on establishing causal relationships, would largely determine the scope and direction of a worthwhile reform effort.

A discourse centred around the values agreed and declared as constituting the reform motif might, with merit, have then assumed a pre-eminent place in the Commission's undertaking. As it is, it would seem to have been cerebrally un-excited by the scale of the demands and opportunities presented by its task, ambitiously perceived.

An interesting conclusion on the British situation may not be entirely inappropriate here, in spite of oft repeated widespread declarations of opposite sentiments,

> It (state funding) holds as a statement of principle, but these days has a Nietzschean, end of history ring to it. In their contempt for partisan identification in politics, maybe the British electorate, and the media
>
> which purports to speak for it, are indeed expressing their lack of commitment to parliamentary democracy.[753]

Reform, adequately considered, should not exclude the obligation of assessing what the impact of proposed changes might be on all the actors in the political system. Apart from the necessity of making sense of the reform effort, "… [it] is important that voters [who, as tax payers, will be subsidising the parties] have confidence that any changes to the regime will be effective,"[754] which obviously presupposes their workability to achieve reform objectives.

---

753 David Walker, 'Party Poopers', *The Guardian*, op. cit.

754 'Party Funding', The [UK] Electoral Commission's submission to the Committee on Standards in Public Life, Oct. 2010; See also, Committee on Standards in Public Life, 'Review of Party Funding: Issues and Questions', London, Sept., 2010.

It is anticipated that many of the views expressed will be controversial, and thus challenged, resisted and opposed, whether on the theoretical, practical or 'factual' level. This would mean that our purpose has been achieved. Even at this stage, the debate needs, we feel, to proceed along paths less conventionally taken.

APPENDIX I[755]

CRIMINAL INVESTIGATION – UNITED KINGDOM

Corrupt procurement and award of honours is legislated against by the Honours (Prevention of Abuses) Act, 1925, and the Public Bodies Corrupt Practices Act, 1889. The Metropolitan Police investigated three complaints they received under these Acts. The police also carried out investigations into whether false declarations were made to the Electoral Commission, which is an offence under the Political Parties, Elections and Referendums Act, 2000. On 27 March 2006 it gave MPs more details of its inquiry into the complaints and the Public Administration Select Committee agreed to postpone its hearing in order not to prejudice possible police action. The criminal inquiry and the Electoral Commission investigation both stretch back to 2001.

6 April, 2006 – The Electoral Commission announced that its own investigation was to be suspended until the police completed their inquiries. The Commission was not satisfied that election funding laws had not been breached.

METROPOLITAN POLICE INVESTIGATION

13 April 2006 – The Metropolitan Police arrested former government adviser, Desmond Smith, under the *Honours (Prevention of Abuses) Act*. Smith, head teacher of All Saints Catholic School and Technology College, was a council member of the Specialist Schools and Academies Trust, which helped the government recruit sponsors for the City Academy programme. Lord Levy was the President of the Council for the Trust.

12 July, 2006 – Lord Levy was arrested by the Metropolitan Police in connection with the enquiry.

20 September, 2006 – Businessman Christopher Evans was also arrested by the police in connection with the enquiry.

---

755 Wikipedia, 'Cash for Honours', <https://en.wikipedia.org/wiki/Cash_for_Honours> accessed 03 December, 2008

22 November, 2006 – The police questioned Secretary of State for Health, Patricia Hewitt a serving cabinet Minister, for the first time, as a witness in the investigation,

14 December, 2006 – The police questioned Prime Minister, Tony Blair, at Downing Street, as a witness; he was not arrested or interviewed under caution.

15 December, 2006 – The police questioned Jack McConnell, the First Minister of Scotland.

January, 2007 – The police questioned, under caution, John McTernan, the Director of Political Operations at 10 Downing Street, who was seconded to the Scottish Labour Party to run its campaign for the Scottish Parliament general election of 3 May, 2007.

19 January, 2007 – Ruth Turner, Director of Government Relations at 10 Downing Street, was arrested by the police, under the *Honours (Prevention of Abuses) Act* and also on suspicion of perverting the course of justice. She was later released on bail. She was the first salaried Government official to be arrested in the inquiry, which followed a search of 10 Downing Street's computer systems by an independent IT expert.

26 January 2007 – Prime Minister, Tony Blair, was questioned in Downing Street for a second time – once again, as a witness and not under caution. At the request of the police, the 45 minute interview was not publicly revealed until 1 February 2007, for what they described as "operational reasons". A Metropolitan Police spokesperson stated that Blair was only being "interviewed as a witness" but declined to state whether the interview related to alleged breaches of the *Honours (Prevention of Abuses) Act* or alleged perversion of the course of justice. However, on June 25, 2007, Channel 4 News reported that the police had originally asked for an interview under caution, and that Blair had said that this would require him to resign as Prime Minister. The police had then re-considered and interviewed him as a witness, rather than a suspect.

30 January, 2007 – Lord Levy was arrested again on suspicion of conspiracy to pervert the course of justice, while still on bail from the previous arrest. He was subsequently bailed.

7 February, 2007 – The Crown Prosecution Service confirmed that head teacher Desmond Smith would not face any charges.

20 February 2007 – On reporting to a police station under her bail terms, Ruth Turner was interviewed for a second time and re-bailed.

2 March 2007 – The Attorney General, Lord Goldsmith, obtained an injunction to prevent the BBC from broadcasting a story about the investigations relating to an email that the BBC had seen.

5 March 2007 – After a request to the Attorney General, the BBC was allowed to reveal that the email was sent by Number 10 Downing Street's aide, Ruth Turner, to Tony Blair's chief of staff, Jonathan Powell, and concerned Labour's chief fundraiser, Lord Levy. The BBC was still not allowed to reveal the contents of the email.

6 March, 2007 – After both the police and the Attorney General failed to obtain an injunction, *The Guardian* newspaper revealed that the police had shifted their focus from whether there was an effort to sell peerages to whether there had been a conspiracy to pervert the course of justice. It emerged that Turner and Levy had held a meeting in 2006, an account of which was passed by Turner's lawyers to the police, and the police were seeking clarification as to whether Levy had asked Turner to "shape" the evidence she gave to Scotland Yard. On the same day, *The Daily Telegraph* newspaper revealed that Ruth Turner had not actually sent the email, because she feared it would be damaging if it fell into the 'wrong hands'. Later in the day, the BBC got the injunction against them lifted, and confirmed that their story was similar, in substance, to that published in *The Guardian*.

20 April, 2007 - The police sent their file on the investigations to the Crown Prosecution Service.

5 June, 2007 - Lord Levy and Ruth Turner were re-bailed in connection with the inquiry.

26 June, 2007 - On the day before Tony Blair left office, The Telegraph reported that American actress, Courtney Coventry, was flown into the UK, at taxpayers' expense, to give evidence in the Cash for Honours investigation.

28 June, 2007 - The day after Tony Blair left office as Prime Minister, it

was reported that the police had interviewed him a third time, sometime in early June, and, again, not under caution.

Crown Prosecution Service Assessment

The Metropolitan Police team investigating the affair, led by Assistant Commissioner John Yates, handed its main file on the Cash for Peerages inquiry to the Crown Prosecution Service (CPS) on Friday, 20 April. Under English law, it was up to the CPS to decide whether to bring charges against any of the 136 people interviewed.

On 4 June, 2007, the CPS asked the police to undertake further enquiries, following reports that the police were pressing for Tony Blair to be called as a prosecution witness in any trial.

On 7 July, 2007, the CPS confirmed that they had all the information they needed from the police, to decide whether to bring any charges, and it was confirmed that the new Attorney General, Baroness Scotland, would take no role in the case, to avoid the appearance of political influence.

On 20 July, 2007, the BBC reported that the CPS would bring no charges. The CPS stated, in its reasoning for this decision, that "If one person makes an offer. ... etc., in the hope or expectation of being granted an honour, or in the belief that it might put him/her in a more favourable position when nominations are subsequently being considered, that does not of itself constitute an offence. Conversely, if one person grants ... , etc., an honour to another in recognition of (in effect, as a reward for) the fact that that other has made a gift ... , etc., that does not of itself constitute an offence. For a case to proceed, the prosecution must have a *realistic* [Italics added] prospect of being able to *prove* [Italics added] that the two people *agreed* [Italics added] that the gift ... , etc., *was in exchange* [Italics added] for an honour", and that on its assessment, "There is no direct evidence of any such agreement between any two people, the subject of this investigation".

APPENDIX II

OAS SECRETARIAT OF POLITICAL AFFAIRS "MODEL LAW ON REGISTRATION AND REGULATION OF POLITICAL PARTIES"

The OAS Secretariat for Political Affairs presented model legislation, "as a starting point for continued discussion", and not as a 'one-size-fits-all' solution. Of particular interest are the following clauses:

> 4(3) In the exercise and discharge of its functions, the Commission [equivalent to the ECJ] shall not be subject to the direction or control of any other person or authority.

We find, nevertheless, that cl. 75 (1) and (2) give the relevant Minister regulation-making powers, similar to those proposed by the ECJ, including regulations "(d) for securing the submission to the Commission of accounts relating to the assets and liabilities, income and expenditure of political parties; (e) prescribing the form and manner in which records of donations shall be kept ... ; (f) the keeping by political parties of proper books of accounts ... form content ... of accounts by political parties; (h) prescribing the manner in which moneys allocated to a party [state funds] under this *Act* may be accounted for; and (i) penalties not exceeding ... [for] the contraventions of any provision of this Act for which no penalty is provided."

6(1) is to the effect that only candidates of a registered political party, or independent non-party affiliated candidates, will be eligible for election at the polls.

Since 60(8) seems to make regulations, after registration, the *quid pro quo* for public financing, as under the ECJ's proposal, one may ask why shouldn't a party which does not accept state funding be allowed to contest an election without being registered, rather than suffer the all-inclusive ban under 30(4)(a)?

> 12(5) importantly provides that, on registration, "... a political party shall be a body corporate with perpetual succession and may sue and be sued in its corporate name. ... and enter into any contract or other transaction as any legal person". This is a provision worth considering in the case of Jamaica.

Immediately, the question becomes, are political parties, under this clause, subject to the provisions of the *Companies Act*, in the absence of any legislative specification to that effect, such as the proposal at 12(6) that a party shall not, by virtue of 12(5), be "liable to pay taxes as a body corporate"? Clause 72(2) treats unincorporated associations, similarly for the purpose of proceedings for breaches of the *Act*.

The OAS' draft stipulates, for different breaches, the cancellation of the Certificate of Registration, in 16(1), 26(4), 27(5), 28(4) (b), and 30(3). A party may also be barred from registering for a prescribed period, 28(4) (b).

25(2) (a), requiring accounts to reflect "all sums of money received and expended ..." is sensibly modified by 39(2) (a) and (b) which seek to establish the possibility of recording/reporting thresholds. This does not, however, seem to be a concession accompanying

26(1) which relates to the first submission of party accounts after the coming into force of the legislation or the registration of a party.

With respect to sanctions, these range from the imposition of a fine, as in 27(2), to a fine or imprisonment—by far the most common punishment, as in 32(4). Where the offence is a continuing one, the punishment also carries a *per diem* fine until the breach is corrected as in 27(7). Second or subsequent offences may also carry greater punishment, as is contemplated, for example, by 43(1) and (2).

Failure to submit election expense returns within the specified period after an election, carries the risks of the *forfeiture of one or more seats*, and also the money from the Political Party Fund (30(2)) to which it is entitled for ... consecutive parliamentary years. The forfeited seat is, under this Model Draft, to be "awarded" by the Electoral Commission to some other party on the "basis of a formula set out in guidelines for that purpose", (30(5)).

We cannot conceive any such proposal having the remotest chance of eliciting, in Jamaica, the support necessary from the politically appointed representatives on the Commission and MPs, or Senators, even, for its passage into law. Quite apart from its grossly anti-representative-democracy nature, the "guidelines" mentioned would presumably require to be ministerially established, which, one expects, would never materialize.

The Draft covers loans (31(1) (d)), as is now the case in the United Kingdom, and more recently under ECJ recommendations, and thereby closes a ready loophole which was previously scandalously exploited in England.

Important definitions are set out under Clause.31, the more crucial being "donation", "permissible donor" and "election advertisement".

The expenditure loophole provided by the use of third party groups (the much discussed PACs issue in the United States) is treated by 31 (8). As set out, in broad general terms, this will clearly be more effective in controlling expenditure by third party supporters of a candidate or party than the ECJ's "connected/affiliated person" provision.

The regulation-evading tactic of 'anonymous' donations, which has also been considered by the ECJ, is dealt with in the Draft Model by seeking to set one limit for a financial year and another for the 'campaign period', thus anticipating the multiple-donations-just-below-the- limit ploy, (33(2)).

35(1) is the clause which deals explicitly with contribution limits both, as with anonymous donations, on an annual basis and over the 'campaign period'. The clause is two-edged, in that it not only applies the limits to the parties, 35(2), but also to donors, 35(1). We find the notion of a 'campaign period' for these purposes ill-conceived: the pro-active, communicative, vibrant party is, ideally, perpetually campaigning.

Receipts are to be issued for donations, 34(3), regardless, it seems, of the sum involved, which seems to rule out otherwise legal contributions at mass events such as conferences and rallies.

Generally, improperly received or impermissible donations must either be returned , sent to the Commission, for payment into the Political Parties' Fund, or forfeited to the state by a Court on application by the Commission or the DPP. Interestingly, although these breaches relate to matters of public law, where sanctions are normally of a criminal nature, involving a fine, fine or imprisonment, or both, in most instances, the burden of proof is set at the civil standard, 35(4), which is a matter of legal principle of considerable concern.

On moral grounds, it could be said that no "tainted", "illegally" obtained money should be utilized in the electoral process. Such funds paid over to the Commission, as stipulated, however, will eventually be disbursed to the parties, no doubt: dirty money entering the system through the front door, it seems.

Due respect is paid to the traditional criminal requirement for 'mens rea' in determining guilt by the introduction of mitigating phrases, such as, taking all "reasonable steps", "exercised all due diligence", "did not know and could not reasonably have known", etc.

Clauses 43 and 44 seek to prevent the evasion of the limits on donations, identification of the source of contributions and the breach of the "permissible donor" restriction. The operative words here are "concealment or disguise", "purpose of circumventing", "knowingly gives any information ... identity of the donor or the amount ... which is false", "or with intent to deceive withholds material information ... identity ... or the amounts ..." All such breaches attract the sanction of a fine or a term of imprisonment.

The fear expressed by donors, even in mature democracies with experience of political finance regulation, about the possibility of reprisal/victimization is ignored. Indeed, what is likely to prove a deterrent of some effect to prospective donors, certainly in Jamaica, is the stipulation that further to disclosure of identity, those donors who contribute above a given annual amount, and also during the campaign period, must submit a report.

The important feature of a limit on campaign expenditure is contained in Clause 45, which at sub clauses (4) and (5), seek to monitor and control preferential media coverage charges above a minimum figure. Campaign expenses, surprisingly, does not include "travel", among other items. Strange, in the context of Jamaican political practice, is the naming of the "promoter" as the person/entity responsible for campaign expense control, with the description of this role being peculiarly, and perhaps typographically erroneously provided, in the margin heading, "Eligible *promoters*" [Italics added], by the words: "Election advertisements shall not be published by any person who is not a permissible *donor*" [Italics added], (Clause 48).

Ethical considerations are brought into tension with the present financial and economic environment faced by most political parties, internationally, not to mention the difficulty of monitoring the application of "... political or *any other pressure* [Italics added] on a person ... to receive donations ...". When does friendly/aggressive persuasion become pressure? It is not difficult for those with a 'regulate in detail' orientation to become over ambitious in seeking to control behaviour.

Part VI carries the heading, "State Financing of Political Parties". Of note is the fact that the status of new parties is not explicitly treated, although the term "qualifying political parties" is used in some of the funding schemes/options offered.

Clause 60(7) is certainly problematic, in that it requires repayment by a party of unspent balances, "within 21 days after the date on which it ceases to qualify for allocation of moneys from the Fund. ..." This approach is as beset with difficulties of implementation as the other option of a reimbursement by the Commission of monies *properly* spent by a party. In both cases, neither of which is particularly attractive for adoption, the processing time factor needs to be recognised as being critically important for the production of accurate figures.

Suspension of payments from the Fund, 63(7), for non-compliance with any of the regime's provisions is bolstered by the possibility of forfeiture of the right to funding for the remainder of the electoral term, together with the Commission's right to deduct any funds not satisfactorily accounted for from a future disbursement. This does have merit.

Again, one finds the proposal at 66(4) to be a cause of some concern, stating as it does, that:

> Not later than the day immediately *before* [Italics added] the date set for the election a political party shall repay to the Commission the unspent balances, as at the date when its books and records of account are closed, of all the moneys that had been allocated to it pursuant to this Part".

In real political life terms, it seems incredible that this obligation is expected to be regarded as a priority, taking the timing into account. Parties' books and records of accounts will be closed at different times, if what is referred to here is their financial year, the normal 'end' of which may be a matter of days before Election Day. The extent of the input of current or former practising politicians and accountants in the drafting process seems to be clearly called into question.

Falsification, suppression, concealment or destruction of documents relating to a party or candidate and the supply of false or misleading information to the Commission, "knowingly or recklessly", with the intention of enabling the evasion of the provisions carries a fine or imprisonment or both, 71(3).

APPENDIX III[756]

THE [NETHERLANDS]
POLITICAL PARTIES SUBSIDIES ACT

Section 2

1. The Minister [of the Interior and Kingdom Relations] shall grant a subsidy to a political party that has taken part in the last elections held for the Upper or Lower House of Parliament with its name *(aanduiding)* above the list of its candidates and to whose list one or more seats have been assigned as a result.

2. The subsidy shall be granted per calendar year.

3. No subsidy shall be granted to a political party which, [on the first day of the calendar year], does not have at least 1,000 members.

Section 3

1. For the purpose of the application of this Act, a political party can designate one political youth organisation and enter into a written subsidy agreement with it. A political youth organisation can be designed by no more than one political party.

2. For the purpose of the application of this *Act*, a political party can designate one political science institute and enter into a written subsidy agreement with it. A political science institute can be designed by no more than one political party.

Section 5

1. The subsidy shall be granted for expenses directly connected with the following activities:

    a. Political training and education activities *(politiek e vormings- en scholingsactiviteiten)*

    b. Providing information

    c. Maintaining contacts with sister parties outside the Netherlands

---

756 The European Court of Human Rights, Application No.58369/10: 'Staatkundig Gereforeerde Partij v. The Netherlands'.

d. Supporting training and education activities for the cadre of sister parties outside the Netherlands

e. Political science activities

f. Activities aimed at promoting political participation by young people

g. Recruiting members

h. Involving non-members in subsidisable activities of the political party

i. Recruiting, selecting and supporting political office holders

j. Activities within the framework of election campaigns.

Section 16

1. If a political *party* [Italics added] has been sentenced to a non-suspended fine for contravening one of the Articles 137c, d, e, f or g or Article 429 *quater* of the Criminal Code *(Wetboek van Strafrecht)*, its entitlement to subsidy shall lapse automatically for a period beginning on the day on which the *conviction* [Italics added] becomes final. This period shall be:

a. One year if the fine is 1,125 euros (EUR) or less

b. Two years if the fine is more than EUR 1,125 but less than EUR 2,250

c. Three years if the fine is more than EUR 2,250 but less than EUR 3,375

d. Four years if the fine is more than EUR 3,375...."

The provisions of the Criminal Code referred to in section 16(1) prohibit insult of groups on the ground of race, religion or philosophical conviction, heterosexual orientation, or physical, mental or intellectual handicap, (Article 137c); public incitement to hatred, discrimination or violence against others on the same grounds (Article 137d: this Article also mentions discrimination on the ground of gender); public expressions, other than in the context of factual reporting, containing such insult or incitement (Article 137d: this Article also mentions discrimination on the ground of gender); participating in, or supporting, activities aimed at discriminating on the above grounds, and on gender, (Article 137f); and discrimination on the ground of race, committed professionally or in office, (Article 137g).

APPENDIX IV

SECTIONS REFERRED TO IN THE REPRESENTATION OF THE PEOPLE ACT (ROPA)

6.—(1) Subject to the provisions of subsection (2), every person employed by any person for pay or reward in reference to an election in the constituency in which such person would otherwise be entitled to vote shall be disqualified from voting and incompetent to vote in such constituency at such election.

(2) A person shall not be disqualified from voting at an election of a member to serve in the House of Representatives by reason that he is employed for pay or reward in reference to an election in the constituency in which such person would otherwise be entitled to vote, so long as the employment is legal.

(3) Persons who may be legally employed are:

(a) returning officers, election clerks, presiding officers, poll clerks, enumerators, scrutineers, messengers, constables and persons otherwise necessarily and properly employed by an election officer for the conduct of the election;

(b) official agents or sub-agents of candidates;

(c) persons engaged in printing election material on behalf of a candidate;

(d) persons employed, whether casually or for the period of the election or part thereof, in advertising of any kind, or as clerks or stenographers or as messengers on behalf of a candidate or prospective candidate, so, however, that the total number of persons so employed does not exceed one for each three hundred electors in the constituency, and that the name, address and occupation of every person so employed is communicated, in writing, to the returning officer.

PART VI. Financial Provisions

53.—(1) On or before nomination day each candidate or prospective candidate shall give notice in writing to the returning officer appointing either himself or some other person as his election agent and specifying an address within the constituency to which all claims, notices, writs, summonses and documents may be sent, addressed to the candidate or to his agent.

(2) Every candidate may at any time give notice in writing to the returning officer revoking the appointment of his agent and in the event of such revocation, or of the death of the agent, whether such event is before, during or after the election, then forthwith another election agent shall be appointed and his name and address declared in writing to the returning officer.

(3) Every election agent appointed under sub-section (1) may act in relation to any matter required to be done in any polling division by a sub-agent, and anything done for the purposes of this Act by or to a sub-agent in his polling division shall be deemed to be done by or to the election agent and any act or default of a sub-agent, which, if he were the election agent, would be an illegal practice or other offence against this Act, shall be an illegal practice and offence against this Act committed by the sub-agent, and the sub-agent shall be liable to punishment accordingly; and the candidate shall suffer the like incapacity as if the said act or default had been the act or default of the election agent.

(4) Not later than one clear day before the poll the election agent shall declare in writing the name and address of every sub-agent to the returning officer.

(5) The appointment of a sub-agent shall not be vacated by the election agent who appointed him ceasing to be election agent, but may be revoked by the election agent for the time being of the candidate, and in the event of such revocation or of the death of a sub-agent another sub-agent may be appointed, and his name and address shall be forthwith declared in writing to the 'returning officer, who shall forthwith give public notice of the same.

(6) Every document delivered to the address referred to in the notice under subsection (1) shall be deemed to have been duly served upon the election agent and every selection agent may, in respect of any matter

connected with the election for which he is acting, be sued in any court having jurisdiction over the place where such address is situated.

54.—(1) The election agent of a candidate himself or by his sub-agent shall appoint every sub-agent, and messenger employed for payment on behalf of the candidate at an election, and hire every committee room hired on behalf of the candidate.

(2) A contract whereby any expenses are incurred on account of or in respect of the conduct or management' of an election shall not be enforceable against a candidate at such election unless made by the candidate himself or by his election agent, either by himself or by his sub-agent:

Provided that the inability under this section to enforce such contract against the candidate shall not relieve the candidate from the consequences of any illegal practice having been committed by his agent.

(3) Except as permitted by or in pursuance of this Act, no payment and no advance or deposit shall be made by a candidate at an election or by any agent on behalf of the candidate or by any other person at any time, whether before, during, or after such election, in respect of any expenses incurred on account of or in respect of the conduct or management of such election, otherwise than by or through the election agent of the candidate, whether acting in person or by a sub-agent; and all money provided by any person other than the candidate for any expenses incurred on account of or in respect of the conduct or management of the election, whether as gift, loan, advance, or deposit, shall be paid to the catndidate or his election agent and not otherwise:

Provided that this section shall not be deemed to apply to a tender of security or any payment by the returning officer or to any sum disbursed by any person out of his own money for any small expense legally incurred by himself, if such 'sum is not repaid to him.

55.—(1) Subject to the provisions of subsection (2), no expenditure shall be incurred in relation to the candidature of any person at any election in excess of ten million dollars.

(2) In determining the total expenditure incurred in relation to. the candidature of any person at any election regard shall not be had—

(a) to the deposit required to be made by the candidate under paragraph (b) of V subsection (5) of section 23; or

(b) to any expenditure incurred before the issue of the writ for the election in respect of services rendered or materials supplied before the issue of such writ.

56.—(l) No expenditure shall be incurred in respect of the candidature of any person at any election except by the candidate, or his agent, or some person authorized in writing by the agent.

(2) Every person who contravenes subsection (1) shall be guilty of an offence and, upon summary conviction thereof before a Resident Magistrate, shall be liable to a fine not exceeding one hundred dollars or to be imprisoned for any term not exceeding six months.

57. No payments shall be made by any candidate to any person other than his agent in connection with his candidature at any election except—

(a) expenditure for his personal living expenses during the period of the election to an amount not exceeding ten thousand dollars; and

(b) petty expenditure to an amount not exceeding two thousand dollars: Provided that this section shall not apply to any candidate who is his own official agent.

58.—(l) No expenditure shall be incurred in respect of the candidature of any candidate at any election, by any person authorized in writing by the agent of such candidate, in excess of the amount specified in the authorization.

(2) Every person who contravenes subsection (1) shall be guilty of an offence and, upon summary conviction thereof before a Resident Magistrate, shall be liable to a fine not exceeding one hundred dollars or to be imprisoned for any term not exceeding six months.

59.—(l) Subject to the provisions of subsection (2), where any expenditure is incurred in contravention of the provisions of section 55, 56, 57 or 58, the person by whom such expenditure was incurred and the candidate in connection with whose candidature it was incurred shall, in addition to any other penalty to which either of them may be liable, be deemed to be guilty of an illegal practice.

(2) No candidate shall be deemed to be guilty of an illegal practice by reason of any other person having incurred any expenditure in connection with the candidature of the candidate in contravention of any of the provisions of section 55, 56 or 58 if the candidate proves affirmatively that such expenditure was incurred without his knowledge or consent and that he took all reasonable steps to prevent the incurrence of such expenditure.

60.—(1) Within six weeks after election day every election agent shall make an election return to the returning officer for the constituency in which he acted as an election agent.

(2) Every return made under this section shall contain a full statement under the appropriate head specified in the return of all expenditure incurred in connection with the election by or on behalf of the candidate by whose election agent the return is made and shall be supported by vouchers for all payments in excess of four dollars.

(3) Every return made under this section shall contain a full statement of all moneys, securities, or the equivalent of money, received by the election agent from the candidate or from any other source in connection with the election.

(4) Every return under subsection (1) shall be in the prescribed form and shall be sworn to before a Justice by the agent by whom it is made.

(5) Every return under this section shall be supported by a declaration sworn to before a Justice by the candidate stating-

(a) that the return fully and accurately sets out all payments made by the candidate himself; and that to the best of his knowledge, information and belief the return is a full and accurate return of all expenditure incurred by any person and of all moneys, securities or the equivalent of money received by the election agent from any source in connection with the election:

Provided that where a candidate acts as his own agent this subsection shall not apply.

(6) [Deleted by Act 1 of 1989.]

(7) The returning officer, within ten days after he receives any return

under this section, shall publish a summary thereof in a daily newspaper accompanied by a notice of the time and place at which the return and the documents in support thereof can be inspected.

61.—(1) Every claim against a candidate at an election or his election agent in respect of any expenses incurred on account of or in respect of the conduct or management of such election which is not sent in to the election agent within twenty-one days of the date upon which the expenses were incurred shall be barred and shall not be paid; and an election agent who pays a claim which is barred under this section shall be guilty of an illegal practice.

(2) All expenses incurred by or on behalf of a candidate at an election, which are incurred on account of or in respect of the conduct or management of such election, shall be paid within six weeks next after election day and not otherwise; and an election agent who makes a payment in contravention of this provision shall be guilty of an illegal practice.

85.—(l) A person guilty of an offence of illegal hiring or illegal payment shall, on summary conviction before a Resident Magistrate, be liable to a fine not less than ten thousand dollars nor more than forty thousand dollars and in default of payment to imprisonment with or without hard labour for a term not exceeding twelve months.

(2) A candidate or an election agent of a candidate who is personally guilty of an offence of illegal hiring contrary to the provisions of section 83 or of illegal payment shall be guilty of an illegal practice.

91.—(1) The following persons shall be deemed guilty of bribery within the meaning of this Act:

(a) every person who directly or indirectly, by himself or by any other person on his behalf, gives, lends, or agrees to give or lend, or offers, promises, or promises to procure or endeavour to procure, any money or valuable consideration to or for any voter or to or for any person on behalf of any voter, or to or for any person in order to induce any voter to vote or refrain from voting, or corruptly does any such act as aforesaid on account of such voter having voted or refrained from voting at any election;

(b) every person who directly or indirectly, by himself or by any other person on his behalf, gives or procures, or agrees to give or procure, or offers, promises, or promises to procure or to endeavour to procure any office, place or employment, to or for any voter, or to or for any person on behalf of any voter, or to or for any other person in order to induce such voter to vote or refrain from voting, or corruptly does any such act as afore-said on account of any voter having voted or refrained from voting at any election;

(c) every person who directly or indirectly, by himself or by any other person on his behalf makes any such gift, loan, offer, promise, procurement or agreement as aforesaid, to or for any person, in order to induce such person to procure or endeavour to procure the return of any person as an elected member of the House of Representatives, or the vote of any voter at an election;

(d) every person who, upon or in consequence of any such gift, loan, offer, promise, procurement or agreement, procures or engages, promises or endeavours to procure the return of any person as an elected member of the House of Representatives, or the vote of any voter at any election;

(e) every person who advances or pays, or causes to be paid, any money to or to the use of another person with the intent that such money or any part thereof, shall be expended in bribery at any election, or who knowingly pays or causes to be paid any money to any person in discharge or repayment of any money wholly or in part expended in bribery at any election;

(f) every voter who, before or during any election, directly or indirectly, by himself or by any other person in his behalf, receives, agrees or contracts for, any money, gift, loan or valuable consideration, office, place or employment, for himself or for any person for voting or agreeing to vote or for refraining or agreeing to refrain from voting, at any election;

(g) every person who, after any election, directly or indirectly, by himself or by any other person on his behalf, receives any money or valuable consideration on account of any person having voted or refrained from voting, or having induced any other person to vote or refrain from voting at any election.

(2) The following persons shall be deemed guilty of treating within the meaning of this Act—

(a) every person who corruptly, by himself or by any other person, either before, during or after an election, directly or indirectly gives or provides, or pays wholly or in part the expenses of giving or providing any food, drink, entertainment or provision, to or for any person for the purpose of corruptly influencing that person or any other person to vote or refrain from voting or at such election, or on account of such person or any other person having voted or refrained from voting at such election;

(b) every elector who corruptly accepts or takes any such food, drink, entertainment or provision.

101.—(1) Every election agent who—

(a) contravenes or fails to comply with the provisions of section 60:

(b) in any return made under section 60 makes an entry which he knows to be false or does not believe to be true, commits an offence.

(2) Every candidate who—

(a) at an election contravenes or fails to comply with the provisions of subsection (5) of section 60;

(b) in any declaration made under subsection (5) of section 60 makes any statement which he knows to be false or does not believe to be true, commits an offence.

(3) Every election agent who commits an offence under subsection (1) or candidate who commits an offence under subsection (2) shall be guilty of an offence and on conviction before a Circuit Court be liable to a fine not less than twenty thousand dollars nor more than eighty

thousand dollars or to imprisonment for such term as the Court may impose being a term not less than three years; and the Court may, in addition to such fine or imprisonment, order that the election agent or candidate be disqualified from holding any post of election officer for a period not less than seven years from the date of conviction.

103. Any person who is convicted of any offence declared to be an illegal practice under this Act shall, in addition to any other penalty for such offence be incapable during a period of ten years from the date of his conviction-

    (a) of being registered as an elector or voting at any election of a member of the House of Representatives or of any Parish Council or of a Councillor of the Kingston and Saint Andrew Corporation; and of being elected a member of the House of Representatives or of any Parish Council or a Councillor of the Kingston and Saint Andrew Corporation, or, if elected before his conviction, of retaining his seat as such member or Councillor:

    Provided that where the person convicted is a candidate-

    (a) the reference to ten years shall be a reference to fifteen years; and

    (b) he shall be disqualified from holding any post of election officer for a period of fifteen years:

    Provided further that in the event of any appeal the incapacity shall continue until the appeal is determined and thereafter unless the conviction is quashed, remain in force for a period of ten years or fifteen years, as the case may be, from the determination of the appeal except the court hearing the appeal shall direct that the period of ten years or fifteen years, as the case may he, shall run from the date of conviction.

AUTHOR BIOGRAPHY

Leon HoSang, a Jamaican Attorney at Law, is a graduate of London and City Universities where he studied Law and Management, respectively. He was called to the English bar at Lincoln's Inn. In returning to Jamaica he taught full-time in the Department of Management Studies, University of the West Indies, Mona Campus, and subsequently completed a doctoral thesis: *Wage Policy, Life and Labour Under the IMF; Jamaica 1977-1994.*

A member of the Senate in the 1970's, the author contested the general parliamentary election in 1976. Having lost, he decided that once was enough.

Since then he has practiced law full-time, taught law courses and Industrial Relations, occasionally, and provided consultancy services in the latter. He has also contributed articles to newspapers, regional labour and law magazines and journals (including a critique of The 'Jamaican Bail Act of 2000', published in the *West Indian Law Journal*). The author has made presentations at several seminars, sponsored by his law firm and in the past for the trade union movement and business organisations.

Dr. HoSang has also made submissions containing suggested changes of a radical nature to Parliamentary Committees established to consider the amendment of labour legislation. His major writings to date have involved engagement in empirical research.

ACKNOWLEDGEMENTS

Invaluable assistance with typing, and commendably efficient organisation of the material, from disorderly notes was provided by Kerine Dobson, then law student, now Attorney at Law. Thanks to Hyacinth Dobson, Legal Secretary, par excellence as well as Landa Shereves, Secretarial Assistant. Symone Lawrence, then law student, now Attorney at Law, was also called upon to assist with a critical review of some of the cases cited, during her internship, and did so quite impressively.

Gratitude must be extended to Dahlia Bateman, a Jamaican attorney in Canada for extensive material on that country's regulatory regime and to my son, Anton, who provided magazine and journal articles which might not otherwise have been accessed.

Finding an editor who could bridge the legal/political arenas, particularly given the contentious nature of the latter, was solved when my editor/publisher, Lena Joy Rose, assumed the task. I wish to thank her for her sensitive guidance and warm encouragement.

www.ingramcontent.com/pod-product-compliance
Lightning Source LLC
Chambersburg PA
CBHW071732270326
41928CB00013B/2642